THE
EVOLUTION
OF POPULATION THEORY

Contributions in Sociology
Series Editor: Don Martindale

Black Belonging: A Study of the Social Correlates of Work Relations Among Negroes
Jack C. Ross and Raymond H. Wheeler

The School Managers: Power and Conflict in American Public Education
Donald J. McCarty and Charles E. Ramsey

The Social Dimensions of Mental Illness, Alcoholism, and Drug Dependence
Don Martindale and Edith Martindale

Those People: The Subculture of a Housing Project
Colette Pétonnet. Rita Smidt, Translator

Sociology in Israel
Leonard Weller

The Revolutionary Party: Essays in the Sociology of Politics
Feliks Gross

Group Interaction as Therapy: The Use of the Small Group in Corrections
Richard M. Stephenson and Frank R. Scarpitti

Sociology of the Black Experience
Daniel C. Thompson

The Incomplete Adult: Social Class Constraints on Personality Development
Margaret J. Lundberg

Handbook of Contemporary Developments in World Sociology
Raj Mohan and Don Martindale, Editors

The New Social Sciences
Baidya Nath Varma, Editor

The Population Challenge: A Handbook for Nonspecialists
Johannes Overbeek

Victims of Change: Juvenile Delinquents in American Society
Harold Finestone

The Fence: A New Look at the World of Property Theft
Marilyn E. Walsh

The Taming of the Troops: Social Control in the United States Army
Lawrence B. Radine

A DOCUMENTARY SOURCEBOOK

THE
EVOLUTION
OF POPULATION THEORY

EDITED BY

JOHANNES OVERBEEK

CONTRIBUTIONS IN SOCIOLOGY, NUMBER 23

GREENWOOD PRESS
Westport, Connecticut
London, England

To my son, Bertrand

The Evolution of population theory.

    (Contributions in sociology; no. 23)
    1. Population—Addresses, essays, lectures.
I. Overbeek, Johannes.
HB851.E8 301.32'01 76-43138
ISBN 0-8371-9313-3

Library of Congress Catalog Card Number: 76-43138
ISBN 0-8371-9313-3

First published in 1977

Greenwood Press, Inc.
51 Riverside Avenue, Westport, Connecticut 06880

Printed in the United States of America

ACKNOWLEDGMENTS

"Population, Production and Income Distribution" by E. R. A. Seligman: from Principles of Economics (8th ed. New York: Longmans Green, 1919). Reprinted by permission of the publishers.

"An Economist's View of Population" by J. M. Keynes: from Manchester Guardian Commercial (August, 1922). Reprinted by permission of The Guardian.

"Food and Population" by E. M. East: from Mankind at the Crossroads (New York: Scribner's, 1924). Reprinted by permission of the publishers.

"The Optimum Size of Population" by A. B. Wolfe: from Population Problems in the United States and Canada ed. L. J. Dublin (Boston: Houghton, Mifflin, 1926). Reprinted by permission of R. T. Foster.

"Considerations on the Optimum Density of a Population" by C. Gini: from World Population Conference, Proceedings (London: Arnold, 1927). Reprinted by permission of the publishers.

"Modern Population Trends" by R. F. Harrod: from The Manchester School (April, 1939). Reprinted by permission of the publishers and the author.

"The Population Scare" by J. J. Jewkes: from The Manchester School (April, 1939). Reprinted by permission of the publishers and the author.

"Economic Problems of Population Change" by F. W. Notenstein: from Proceedings of the Eighth International Conference of Agricultural Economists (London: Oxford University Press, 1953). Reprinted by permission of the International Association of Agricultural Economists.

"The Economic Theory of Fertility" by H. Leibenstein: from Economic Backwardness and Economic Growth (New York: Wiley and Sons, 1957). Reprinted by permission of the author.

"An Economic Analysis of Fertility" by G. S. Becker: from Demographic and Economic Change in Developed Countries ed. National Bureau of Economic Research (Princeton: Princeton University Press, 1960). Reprinted by permission of the National Bureau of Economic Research Inc.

"World Population" by C. Clark: from Nature (May, 1958). Reprinted by permission of the author and MacMillan Journals Ltd.

"Population, Economics of" by W. B. Reddaway: from Chamber's Encyclopedia (Vol. XI, 1966). Reprinted by permission of the publisher.

"The Future Numbers of Mankind" by C. Darwin: from Humanity and Subsistence. (Lausanne: Librairie Payot, 1961). Reprinted by permission of Nestle.

"The Economic Effects of Fertility Control in Underdeveloped Areas" by A. J. Coale: from Human Fertility and Population Problems (Cambridge: Schenkman, 1963). Reprinted by permission of the publishers.

"Population Problems in Developing Countries" by Y. Guzevatyi: from International Affairs (September, 1966). Reprinted by permission of the author.

"A Summary of Limits to Growth - its Critics and its Challenge" by D. H. and D. L. Meadows: from Paper Presented at Yale University (September, 1972). Reprinted by permission of the authors.

"Economic Policy and the Threat of Doom" by J. E. Meade: from Resources and Population eds. B. Benjamin et al. (New York: Academic Press, 1973). Reprinted by permission of the Eugenics Society.

"World Population and Food Supplies: Looking Ahead" by L. R. Brown: U.N. World Population Conference 1974 Conference Background Paper (March, 1974). Reprinted by permission of the author.

"Economic Growth in a Stationary Population" by J. J. Spengler: Unpublished paper presented at the Annual Meeting of the Population Association of America (April, 1971). Reprinted with permission of the author.

CONTENTS

PREFACE

The problem of excessive population growth is increasingly recognized as one of the most difficult issues of our era. More and more universities are now setting up courses containing population materials. There is also a growing number of population institutes, some of which organize special short courses and workshops on demographic questions.

Although the population crisis is progressively taking on new dimensions, it would be a mistake to believe that population problems have been entirely neglected in the past. In fact, one finds discussions of population questions in the literature of the 16th century. Since the beginnings of the 19th century economists and other social scientists have increasingly devoted attention to population problems.

The aim of this selection of readings is to provide teachers, students, and others interested in population theory with a volume of readings that will familiarize them with some aspects of the great debates in population theory from Malthus to present times. This volume is largely restricted to the ideas of thinkers -- mainly economists -- who inquired about the relationship between population and resources.

The book confronts authors who express concern about the negative implications of population growth with social scientists who are more optimistic about the socioeconomic consequences of population growth. Some of them are openly natalistic. This reader also covers a controversy that received wide attention in the 1930's, i.e., that of economic maturity and the negative effects of a declining rate of population growth on investment opportunities.

No book can be all-inclusive. The topic of the economic analysis of fertility, for instance, has reluctantly been given little attention. We fully recognize the importance of this subject but considerations of space prevented extensive coverage.

This reader not only contains articles which are not easily available but also includes two translations of papers written by European authors. This book could well be used in undergraduate and graduate courses in "population economics" and "population studies" as taught by sociologists and economists who specialized in demography. The articles will familiarize the student with many of the great names in past and present population theory, and it is hoped that this volume will add life and color to population courses. In selecting the materials I have tried to keep the needs and capabilities of the average reader in mind although it has been assumed that he knows some basic economics.

Since none of the footnotes contained vital information, they have been omitted. An exception has been made for reading 25 which text includes a number of quotations.

The editor is grateful to the East-West Population Institute of the East-West Center, which gave the financial support needed to complete this work.

THE
EVOLUTION
OF POPULATION THEORY

INTRODUCTION

The first economic population theories appeared during the Mercantilist period in Europe (1450-1750). These mercantilist proposals were definitely pronatalist, possibly for the following reasons:

(a) Europe had been ravaged by the plague from 1347 onwards. In a number of areas half or one-third of the population had been carried off by the Black Death.

(b) Mercantilists found the ultimate sources of wealth in foreign trade and the accumulation of gold and silver. It was thought that a large population would lead to a large national output. More output meant more exports, and if imports could be kept low the surplus on the balance of trade would become larger; this in turn would cause the inflow of gold and silver to expand.

(c) Conscription did not exist and armies consisted of mercenaries. A large and expanding population would guarantee an ample supply of soldiers and sailors at low cost.

(d) According to mercantilist wage theory, leisure preference among the working classes ran high. Wages had to be kept low; otherwise idling and loafing would be promoted. Population growth and concomitant increases in the labor force would keep wages down.

In the last half of the 18th century, many writers no longer endorsed population growth as enthusiastically as the Mercantilist pamphleteers had done. The negative effects of population growth were beginning to be noticed. Moreover, it was recognized that food supplies often tended to regulate population upwards as well as downwards, so that increases or decreases in agricultural output were followed by expansion or contraction in numbers of people. Thus, at least in Europe, population was to a large extent conditioned by output. From this it followed that increases in fertility might merely result in an increase in the death rate, and therefore in more distress and misery, unless demographic expansion were accompanied by agricultural growth. For that reason, many writers of the 18th century rejected the simple Mercantilist teachings, which nearly always contained proposals encouraging marriage and childbearing.

Many contributions of 18th century writers are of interest. The writings of Richard Cantillon (1680-1734) are an example. His Essay on the Nature of Commerce in General (1755) is perhaps the most systematic treatment of economic principles before the publication of Adam Smith's Wealth of Nations. The Essay helped to shape subsequent economic thought and Cantillon manifestly anticipated Malthus. Cantillon believed that the number of inhabitants of a nation is conditioned by the means of subsistence, and that an increase of food will not only facilitate but also prompt an expansion of the population. In such countries as China, said

Cantillon, agricultural output and therefore population had reached their
extreme limit. Birth and death rates were high and approximately in equilibrium. Mortality was the main regulator of the population, which would
expand after good harvests and contract after bad ones.

In such European countries as England and France, said Cantillon, food
production and population had not reached maximum levels. The customary
living standard of Northwestern Europe included relatively decent clothes
and dwellings and even some luxuries such as wine and beer. The land
areas allocated to the production of these commodities had been withdrawn
from the production of agricultural products. The higher the customary
living standard, Cantillon contended, the lower the population density.
People in Europe apparently felt that if they could not guarantee to their
descendants the customary living standard, deferment of marriage or celibacy were the proper response. Consequently, population had remained at
a respectable distance from its maximum level and both birth and death
rates were much lower than in a country like China. Marriage patterns
and not mortality functioned as the crucial factor in the regulation of
numbers.

It was, however, the Italian economist Giammaria Ortes who, in his basic
text Riflessioni Sulla Populazione Delle Nazione per Rapporto All Economia
Nazionale (1775), comes closest to Malthus. Population, if not checked,
tends to increase geometrically at intervals of thirty years, he argued.
But of course checks come into play; otherwise we would be living "like
dried herrings in a barrel". Among the checks he mentioned were the
irrational size of most nations (too big or too small), unevenness of
income distribution, and excessive taxes. Ortes further advocated the
need for an "ideal" nation with an adequate land area, neither too big
nor too small, in which a stationary population would live in ease and
comfort. He suggested that zero growth of population would be achieved
by the "virtuous celibacy" of half the population.

Malthus himself cannot be understood unless it is realized that he was at
the outset a utilitarian. For our purpose it is enough to recognize that
the social philosophy of the utilitarians aimed at the greatest happiness
for the community as a whole. The minimization of misery and the maximization of welfare were their supreme goals. To demonstrate the bearing
of theory on currently significant questions was also typically utilitarian, as was the desire to alter people's opinions by explaining to them
where their real interest lie. Malthus is usually described as a rather
conservative member of the utilitarian circle, in the sense that he was
less critical of the established church and the existing class structure
of English society than were other members of the group.

In the absence of obstructing checks, said Malthus, any population can
easily double itself in a twenty-five year period. But, because of the
limited amount of arable land available and the fact that successive
applications of labor and capital to a given area of land eventually
result in diminishing increments in output, food production will normally
increase at a much slower pace. As a result, said Malthus, there exists
in every old established country a pressure of numbers on the available
food supplies. Positive checks, or those that increase the death rate
such as famine, and preventive checks, or those that reduce the birth
rate such as postponement of marriage, keep population in balance with
food production. According to Malthus, in order to avoid harsh positive
checks, man should given additional consideration to the more humane

preventive checks. As a matter of practical policy -- and here he was a
true utilitarian -- Malthus urged the practice of "moral restraint",
meaning postponement of marriage until one could afford to rear children.
Although in his day, as is still true today, too many people rushed into
marriage without due regard for the future, Malthus hoped that with improved education people would gain a better understanding of their true
interests and learn to act according to them. This would imply that people
would limit the size of their families so that population would expand at
a lower rate than agricultural production, thus increasing man's material
well-being.

The utilitarian tradition reached perhaps its highest development in John
Stuart Mill (1806-1873). His father, James Mill, was the most faithful
disciple of Jeremy Bentham, the founding father of utilitarianism, and
throughout his entire life the younger Mill embraced the idea that the
greatest happiness of everyone was the supreme consideration. In application of this principle Mill gave Malthus's teachings on population a
more positive twist. A voluntary restriction of family size by the
laboring classes would benefit society and the working classes themselves
immensely if only because it would facilitate full employment at rising
wages. As Mill revised utilitarianism and broke down its intellectual
isolation, he also infused more humanism into it. As a well-defined
school of thought, utilitarianism has now ceased to exist; but as a viewpoint it is still very much alive, though its dogmatism has been toned
down. To the extent that social scientists have a deep interest in the
well-being of mankind, they are utilitarian. Mill's version of utilitarianism is known to have greatly influenced such writers as the Swedish
economist Knut Wicksell (1858-1926). Because the utilitarian viewpoint
underlies the reasonings of the classical economists and their followers,
its world-wide influence has been incalculable.

After Malthus, the negative effects of population increase were expressed
in clearer and more forceful terms, and so was the need for population
control by means of artifical contraception. From Mill onwards the population question was clearly subordinated to the law of diminishing returns
which was thought to prevail in 19th and early 20th century Europe. The
density of Europe, he said, was more than sufficient to enjoy all the
advantages of an elaborate division of labor. Any further increase in
population and labor force would decrease per capita output because of
the prevalence of diminishing returns, especially in agriculture.

Wicksell refined these ideas. He framed an entirely new concept -- that
of an optimum population -- and also pointed to the growing economic
vulnerability of many Western European countries. Because of population
growth, he said, they had to expand the volume of international trade,
and thus their economies had become dangerously dependent on outside
supplies of food, raw materials, and fuels. This meant that living
standards in these areas had become mortgaged to all sorts of circumstances
over which these countries had little or no control. Growth of numbers
could only increase this dependence.

In the second half of the nineteenth century the teachings of the classical economists and liberalism in general began to encounter opposition.
Some of the cautious and somewhat uncheerful conclusions of Malthus and
other classical economists seemed to be belied by rising living standards
which were due to agricultural development in North America (which was
producing wheat supplies beyond previous imagination), rapid capital

accumulation in the Western world, and a high rate of technical and organizational progress. It also came to be increasingly argued that a decline in fertility was the inevitable byproduct of social and economic improvement.

At the same time the theories of the classical school were increasingly opposed by protectionists such as Carey, socialists of all colors, nationalists, and imperialists. In 1864 the Roman Catholic Church rejected economic liberalism in a document entitled "Syllabus Errorum" (catalogue of errors). It is very difficult, however, to find comprehensive statements on these subjects because the population aspect received only scant attention, especially in Anglo-Saxon literature. The critical statements of Carey and Marx, however, are perhaps the most explicit and have therefore been included in this reader.

The classical school ended in 1871 when the first works of marginalist writers such as W. S. Jevons and C. Menger appeared. Whereas the classical writers had placed special emphasis on the costs of production (supply) as the main determinant of value, the marginalists explained value by emphasizing demand (the utility received by the consumer). They also recognized the principle of diminishing utility, i.e., the fact that successive portions of a good yield declining satisfaction.

Although the rise of the marginalist school marked a major transformation of current economic thinking, the teachings of the classical writers were not lost. Second and later generations of the marginalists built upon the bases laid by the classicals, as well as the founders of the marginal-utility school and Western economic thought, remained flexible enough to assimilate new developments as they arose.

As noted before, the Swedish economist K. Wicksell had pointed to the growing frailty and dependence of the Old World on North American food supplies as a result of population expansion. After World War I, John Maynard Keynes developed this argument in his essay The Economic Consequences of the Peace. The interruption of communication lines during the war had made the inhabitants of Europe more aware of their extreme dependence on foreign supplies. Keynes also pointed to the investments that population increase necessitated to maintain the existing capital-labor ratio and thus output per capita.

At the League of Nations World Population Conference, held in Geneva in 1927, Professor E. M. East, a geneticist and agricultural economist who joined Harvard in 1909, presented the first calculation of the earth's "maximum" population. The idea of a maximum population first received attention in his work Mankind at the Crossroads published in 1924. Estimating that 2.5 acres would be needed to feed one person, he set the world's maximum population at 5.2 billion people because only 13 billion acres could possibly be cropped.

Participation of non-Western scientists in the population debate increased during the period between the First and Second World Wars. The Indian scholar R. Mukerjee wrote many articles and papers that dealt with population theory in general and India's population problems in particular. This reader contains a paper which, although dated, has lost none of its relevance so far.

Between the two world wars nationalism was once more on the rise in Europe. However nationalism may be defined, reduced to its barest essence it amounts often to collective vanity and selfishness. In Italy and Germany a new ideology called fascism sprang up. It contained elements of the older nationalism, along with imperialism, socialism, and racism. Its emergence was due perhaps to such factors as economic distress, mutilated national pride, and the demoralization that occurred in postwar Germany and to a lesser extent in Italy. With fascism came demographic nationalism. Empire-building required manpower, and the fascist regimes encouraged an increase in population by prohibiting emigration, suppressing the advocacy and practice of birth control, imposing taxes on bachelors, and subsidizing marriages and large families. Some of these measures had already been part of the mercantile system of politico-economics.

During the Great Depression, which began in the United States in 1929, the entire Western World was plagued by heavy unemployment. In 1933, 25 percent of the British labor force was unemployed. Between 1935 and 1937 Britain's national income grew, but at a very slow rate. In 1937 the unemployment rate was still 20 percent. Only in 1940 did a new period of brisk economic expansion begin, but this was due mainly to sharply increased defense spending.

It seemed to such economists as John Maynard Keynes (U.K.) and Alvin Hansen (U.S.A.) that the economy of their respective countries had entered into a stage of somnolence, and that time would bring no improvement. In their writings we find the essence of the "economic maturity thesis" and the concept of "secular stagnation". A satisfactory level of production and employment, these national income theorists reasoned, depended on the level of aggregate demand, of which investment demand (by private-sector firms) was a major component. The three generators of private investment, population growth, the economic development of new areas, and technological innovation which had proved to be so potent in the 19th century were now weakening.

By the 1930's the rate of population growth in the Western World had visibly declined, opportunities for settlement and exploitation of new areas were shrinking, and the rate of technological change was declining. Consequently, Keynes argued, the demand for capital investment was declining with insufficient outlets for available savings. Since the absorption of savings by investment activity was a main prerequisite for satisfactory maintenance of employment and output, the economies of such countries as the United Kingdom and the U.S.A. were now threatened by a permanent underemployment of such available productive resources as labor and capital assets.

Keynes and Hansen did not advocate an increase in the rate of demographic expansion, but recommended instead that their government discourage over-saving and encourage investment spending. Sir Roy Harrod (U.K.), however, went further and proposed a scheme of family allowances to stimulate population growth. The theory of secular stagnation came under heavy attack and some writers argued that in spite of periodic disturbances the long-term trend of output and income was upwards. Jewkes gave a direct answer to Harrod, whereas other writers such as G. Terborgh and H. Staudinger theorized in more general terms. The maturity thesis dispute no longer seems to be a major issue among economists in the 1970's, but since in most countries of the Western World the rate of population growth is falling again, some of the assertions often made in the 1930's may find new expression.

The period after World War II was characterized by an alarming increase in the rate of the world's population growth, especially in the less affluent countries. As a result numerous studies appeared concerning the problems associated with these increasing numbers. In the Western nations the growth was due to rising fertility, which was the outcome of such factors as earlier marriage, lower celibacy rates, and an increase in the desired family size. In the low-income countries of Asia, Africa, and South America the high rates of demographic increase were attributable rather to a combination of traditionally high birth rates and sharply declining death rates, the latter due to improved public health measures and the introduction of medical knowledge and skills developed in the West.

Interest in the "population explosion" and economic development has led to a great number of studies emphasizing the detrimental effects of rapid population growth on living standards. New developments in economic thinking such as growth theory helped to clarify the problems created by rapid demographic expansion. Yet the argument that growing numbers did not matter or were actually beneficial did not die and has found defenders in such writers as Colin Clark. Postwar economic theory relied heavily on the concept of continued economic growth.

A research question which received increased attention after the second world war was the relationship between fertility and income. Professor Harvey Leibenstein made a pioneering effort in his attempt to find out to what extent the benefits of an added child are weighed against the costs. After a challenging attempt to conceptualize the benefits and costs attributable to an additional child, he proceeds to a description of the nature of the shifts in satisfactions and costs as socio-economic development proceeds. His conclusion is that in the development process the economic utility of children drops while the costs of rearing children rise sharply.

Using the neoclassical model of consumer behavior Gary Becker treats procreation as a choice among alternative courses of action with particular reference to price and income variables. Considering only the short run in which preferences and values can be assumed to remain constant, Becker concludes that the impact of rising incomes on fertility may well be positive. If, however, income changes are viewed longitudinally, modifications in taste and values can no longer be ignored. As opposed to Becker, Leibenstein does in fact take the long term view.

The unprecedented expansion of the 1950's and the 1960's, however, made people increasingly aware of the problems associated with such economic growth. In the late 1960's a change in attitudes took place and a growing number of voices called for a curbing of economic and demographic expansion. The biggest push to no-growth arguments came from a study published by the Club of Rome entitled The Limits to Growth, which argued that exponential growth of such variables as population, consumption of nonrenewable materials, and industrial pollution cannot go on for much longer in our finite world. Unless we deliberately halt economic and demographic growth, the report asserted, the environment will suffer irremediable deterioration leading to ecological disaster, industrial collapse, and mass famine.

The 1960's also saw some change in Soviet thinking on population problems.
From the end of World War II to the mid-sixties, demographic thinking
in the Soviet Union was rigidly marxist and violently anti-Western. The
idea that demographic expansion might have some adverse effects on
economic development was strongly rejected. The past decades, however,
witnessed the rise of more flexible attitudes. Several Soviet authors
such as the economists B. Z. Urlanis and Y. N. Guzevaty expressed their
concern over runaway population growth in a number of low-income countries.

Continuing population growth and rising affluence have spurred a soaring
demand for food which has resulted in a number of studies of the world
food situation. Lester Brown's paper written for the United Nations
World Population Conference in Bucharest (1974) introduces the reader
to this subject.

The last reading relates to the economic implications of a stationary population. The decline of birth rates in the U.S.A. after 1957 seemed to
suggest that the baby boom following World War II was drawing to a close.
The fall in fertility since 1957 has been continuous, and there is now
substantial probability that in the United States and a number of other
industrialized countries fertility is coming closer to replacement levels.
In fact West Germany, East Germany, and Luxembourg have already achieved
a balance between birth and death rates. A better understanding of what
exactly low or zero population growth involves is clearly in order, and
Professor J. J. Spengler's paper seems a proper introduction to the
debate.

PART ONE

THE POPULATION CONTROVERSY FROM MALTHUS TO WORLD WAR ONE

READING 1

The following reading contains Malthus's own forceful statement of his principle of population. Thomas Robert Malthus (1766-1834) studied at Cambridge University, took orders in the Church of England, and taught at a college in Haileybury, England.

The following two chapters are taken from the third edition of <u>An Essay on the Principle of Population</u>.[1] Here Malthus argues that population, unless checked, constantly tends to increase and even outstrip the production of food supplies. Because of the strong attraction between the two sexes, population can easily double every 25 years if nothing stops it. Food supplies, however, cannot be produced that fast. Due to the law of diminishing returns in agriculture (which says that successive applications of equal quantities of labour to a given area of land will, beyond some point, result in less than proportionate increases in output), the speed at which food production can be made to increase is much lower. At best it will increase in an arithmetic ratio (1.2.3.4. etc.). In each 25-year period, therefore, one can expect a uniform increase of output equal to the amount produced at the starting point.

That population does not exceed food supply is due to the operation of checks or obstacles to population growth, of which Malthus distinguishes two kinds. The preventive checks such as birth control or delayed marriage reduce birth rates. The repressive or positive checks such as famine or environmental decay increase death rates. The two checks, says Malthus, are inversely related: an increase in one leads to a decrease in the other. Obviously, the preventive checks are to be preferred to the repressive ones. Malthus had his reservations about birth control and recommended instead the postponement of marriage.

The later editions of Malthus's Essay differ from the first in that they are more elaborate and emphasize the desirability of delayed marriage, which Malthus terms "moral restrainty".

---

1 Source: T. R. Malthus, <u>An Essay on the Principle of Population</u>, (3rd ed., London: Johnson, 1803), pp. 1-16.

THE PRINCIPLE OF POPULATION
Thomas Robert Malthus

CHAPTER I

STATEMENT OF THE SUBJECT. RATIOS OF THE INCREASE OF POPULATION AND FOOD.

In an inquiry concerning the future improvement of society, the mode of conducting the subject which naturally presents itself, is

    1. An investigation of the causes that have hitherto impeded the progress of mankind towards happiness; and

    2. An examination into the probability of the total or partial removal of these causes in the future.

To enter fully into this question, and to enumerate all the causes that have hitherto influenced human improvement, would be much beyond the power of an individual. The principal object of the present essay is to examine the effects of one great cause intimately united with the very nature of man, which, though it has been constantly and powerfully operating since the commencement of society, has been little noticed by the writers who have treated this subject. The facts which establish the existence of this cause have, indeed, been repeatedly stated and acknowledged; but its natural and necessary effects have been almost totally overlooked; though probably among these effects may be reckoned a very considerable portion of that vice and misery, and of that unequal distributions of the bounties of nature, which it has been the unceasing object of the enlightened philanthropist in all ages to correct.

The cause to which I allude, is the constant tendency in all animated life to increase beyond the nourishment prepared for it.

It is observed by Dr. Franklin, that there is no bound to the prolific nature of plants or animals, but what is made by their crowding and interfering with each others means of subsistence. Were the face of the earth, he says, vacant of other plants, it might be gradually sowed and overspread with one kind only; as, for instance, with fennel: and were it empty of other inhabitants, it might in a few ages be replenished from one nation only, as, for instance, with Englishmen.

This is incontrovertibly true. Through the animal and vegetable kingdoms Nature has scattered the seeds of life abroad with the most profuse and liberal hand; but has been comparatively sparing in the room and the nourishment necessary to rear them. The germs of existence contained in this spot of earth, with ample food, and ample room to expand in, would fill millions of worlds in the course of a few thousand years. Necessity, that imperious all-pervading law of nature, restrains them within the prescribed bounds. The race of plants and the race of animals shrink under this great restrictive law; and the race of man cannot by any efforts of reason escape from it.

In plants and animals the view of the subject is simple. They are all
impelled by a powerful instinct to the increase of their species; and
this instinct is interrupted by no reasoning or doubts about providing
for their offspring. Whereever, therefore, there is liberty, the power
of increase is exerted; and the superabundant effects are repressed
afterwards by want of room and nourishment, which is common to plants
and animals; and among animals, by their becoming the prey of each other.

The effects of this check on man are more complicated. Impelled to the
increase of his species by an equally powerful instinct, reason interrupts
his career, and asks him whether he may not bring beings into the world,
for whom he cannot provide the means of support. If he attend to this
natural suggestion, the restriction too frequently produces vice. If he
hear it not, the human race will be constantly endeavouring to increase
beyond the means of subsistence. But as by that law of our nature which
makes food necessary to the life of man, population can never actually
increase beyond the lowest nourishment capable of supporting it; a strong
check on population, from the difficulty of acquiring food, must be constantly in operation. This difficulty must fall somewhere; and must
necessarily be severely felt in some or other of the various forms of
misery, or the fear of misery, by a large portion of mankind.

That population has this constant tendency to increase beyond the means
of subsistence, and that it is kept to its necessary level by these
causes, will sufficiently appear from a review of the different states
of society in which man has existed. But before we proceed to this review, the subject will perhaps be seen in a clearer light, if we endeavour to ascertain, what would be the natural increase of population
if left to exert itself with perfect freedom; and what might be expected
to be the rate of increase in the productions of the earth, under the
most favourable circumstances of human industry. A comparison of these
two rates of increase will enable us to judge of the force of that tendency in population to increase beyond the means of subsistence, which
has been stated to exist.

It will be allowed, that no country has hitherto been known, there the
manners were so pure and simple, and the means of subsistence so abundant, that no check whatever has existed to early marriages from the
difficulty of providing for a family; and no waste of the human species
has been occasioned afterwards by vicious customs, by towns, by unhealthy
occupations, or too severe labour. Consequently in no state that we
have yet known, has the power of population been left to exert itself
with perfect freedom.

Whether the law of marriage be instituted, or not, the dictate of nature
and virtue seems to be an early attachment to one woman; and where there
were no impediments of any kind in the way of an union to which such an
attachment would lead, and no causes of depopulation afterwards, the
increase of the human species would be evidently much greater than any
increase which has been hitherto known.

In the northern states of America, where the means of subsistence have
been more ample, the manners of the people more pure, and the checks to
early marriages fewer, than in any of the modern states of Europe, the
population was found to double itself for some successive periods every
twenty-five years. Yet even during these periods, in some of the towns,

the deaths exceeded the births; and they consequently required a continued supply from the country to support their population.

In the back settlements, where the sole employment was agriculture, and
vicious customs and unwholesome occupations were unknown, the population
was found to double itself in fifteen years. Even this extraordinary
rate of increase is probably short of the utmost power of population.
Very severe labour is requisite to clear a fresh country; such situations are not in general considered as particularly healthy; and the
inhabitants were probably occasionally subject to the incursions of the
Indians, which might destroy some lives, or at any rate diminish the
fruits of their industry.

According to a table of Euler, calculated on a mortality of 1 in 36, if
the births be to the deaths in the proportion of 3 to 1, the period of
doubling will be only 12 4/5 years. And these proportions are not only
possible suppositions, but have actually occurred for short periods in
more countries than one.

Sir William Petty supposes a doubling possible in so short a time as
ten years.

But to be perfectly sure that we are far within the truth, we will take
the slowest of these rates of increase; a rate, in which all concurring
testimonies agree, and which has been repeatedly ascertained to be
from procreation only.

It may safely be pronounced therefore, that population when unchecked
goes on doubling itself every twenty-five years, or increases in a
geometrical ratio.

The rate according to which the productions of the earth may be supposed
to increase, it will not be so easy to determine. Of this, however, we
may be perfectly certain, that the ratio of their increase must be
totally of a different nature from the ratio of the increase of population. A thousand millions are just as easily doubled every twenty-five
years by the power of population as a thousand. But the food to support
the increase from the greater number will by no means be obtained with
the same facility. Man is necessarily confined in room. When acre has
been added to acre till all the fertile land is occupied, the yearly
increase of food must depend upon the amelioration of the land already
in possession. This is a stream, which, from the nature of all soils,
instead of increasing, must be gradually diminishing. But population,
could it be supplied with food, would go on with unexhausted vigour;
and the increase of one period would furnish the power of a greater
increase the next, and this, without any limit.

From the accounts we have of China and Japan, it may be fairly doubted,
whether the best directed efforts of human industry could double the
produce of these countries even once in any number of years. There are
many parts of the globe, indeed, hitherto uncultivated, and almost un-
occupied; but the right of exterminating, or driving into a corner where
they must starve, even the inhabitants of these thinly peopled regions,
will be questioned in a moral view. The process of improving their
minds and directing their industry, would necessarily be slow; and
during this time, as population would regularly keep pace with the

increasing produce, it would rarely happen that a great degree of knowledge and industry would have to operate at once upon rich unappropriated
soil. Even where this might take place, as it does sometimes in new
colonies, a geometrical ratio increases with such extraordinary rapidity,
that the advantage could not last long. If America continue increasing,
which she certainly will do, though not with the same rapidity as formerly,
the Indians will be driven further and further back into the country, till
the whole race is ultimately exterminated.

These observations are, in a degree, applicable to all the parts of the
earth, where the soil is imperfectly cultivated. To exterminate the
inhabitants of the greatest part of Asia and Africa, is a thought that
could not be admitted for a moment. To civilize and direct the industry
of the various tribes of Tartars, and Negroes, would certainly be a work
of considerable time, and of variable and uncertain success.

Europe is by no means so fully peopled as it might be. In Europe, there
is the fairest chance that human industry may receive its best direction.
The science of agriculture has been much studied in England and Scotland;
and there is still a great portion of uncultivated land in these countries.
Let us consider, at what rate the produce of this island might be supposed to increase under circumstances the most favourable to improvement.

If it be allowed, that by the best possible policy, and great encourage-
ments to agriculture, the average produce of the island could be doubled
in the first twenty-five years, it will be allowing probably a greater
increase than could with reason be expected.

In the next twenty-five years, it is impossible to suppose that the produce could be quadrupled. It would be contrary to all our knowledge of
the properties of land. The improvement of the barren parts would be a
work of time and labour; and it must be evident to those who have the
slightest acquaintance with agricultural subjects, that in proportion
as cultivation extended, the additions that could yearly be made to the
former average produce, must be gradually and regularly diminishing.
That we may be the better able to compare the increase of population and
food, let us make a supposition, which, without pretending to accuracy,
is clearly more favourable to the power of production in the earth, than
any experience that we have had of its qualities will warrant.

Let us suppose that the yearly additions which might be made to the
former average produce, instead of decreasing, which they certainly would
do, were to remain the same; and that the produce of this island might
be increased every twenty-five years, by a quantity equal to what it at
present produces: the most enthusiastic speculator cannot suppose a
greater increase than this. In a few centuries it would make every acre
of land in the island like a garden.

If this supposition be applied to the whole earth, and if it be allowed
that the subsistence for man which the earth affords, might be increased
every twenty-five years by a quantity equal to what it at present produces, this will be supposing a rate of increase much greater than we
can imagine that any possible exertions of mankind could make it.

It may be fairly pronounced therefore, that, considering the present
average state of the earth, the means of subsistence, under circumstances

the most favourable to human industry, could not possibly be made to increase faster than in an arithmetical ratio.

The necessary effects of these two different rates of increase, when
brought together, will be very striking. Let us call the population of
this island eleven millions; and suppose the present produce equal to
the easy support of such a number. In the first twenty-five years the
population would be twenty-two millions, and the food being also doubled,
the means of subsistence would be equal to this increase. In the next
twenty-five years, the population would be forty-four millions, and the
means of subsistence only equal to the support of thirty-three millions.
In the next period the population would be eighty-eight millions, and
the means of subsistence just equal to the support of half of that number.
And at the conclusion of the first century, the population would be a
hundred and seventy-six millions, and the means of subsistence only equal
to the support of fifty-five millions; leaving a population of a hundred
and twenty-one millions totally unprovided for.

Taking the whole earth instead of this island, emigration would of course
be excluded; and supposing the present population equal to a thousand
millions, the human species would increase as the numbers 1, 2, 4, 8, 16,
32, 64, 128, 256, and subsistence as 256 to 9; in three centuries as
4096 to 13, and in two thousand years the difference would be almost
incalculable.

In this supposition no limits whatever are placed to the produce of the
earth. It may increase for ever, and be greater than any assignable
quantity; yet still the power of population being in every period so
much superior, the increase of the human species can only be kept down to
the level of the means of subsistence by the constant operation of the
strong law of necessity acting as a check upon the greater power.

CHAPTER II

OF THE GENERAL CHECKS TO POPULATION, AND THE MODE OF THEIR OPERATION.

The checks to population, which are constantly operating with more or
less force in every society, and keep down the number to the level of the
means of subsistence, may be classed under two general heads; the preventive, and the positive checks.

The preventive check, is peculiar to man, and arises from that distinctive
superiority in his reasoning faculties, which enables him to calculate
distant consequences. Plants and animals have apparently no doubts about
the future support of their offspring. The checks to their indefinite
increase, therefore, are all positive. But man cannot look around him,
and see the distress which frequently presses upon those who have large
families; he cannot contemplate his present possessions or earnings,
which he now nearly consumes himself, and calculate the amount of each
share, when with very little addition they must be divided, perhaps,
among seven or eight, without feeling a doubt, whether if he follow the
bent of his inclinations, he may be able to support the offspring which
he will probably bring into the world. In a state of equality, if such
can exist, this would be the simple question. In the present state of
society other considerations occur. Will he not lower his rank in life,
and be obliged to give up in great measure his former society? Does any
mode of employment present itself by which he may reasonably hope to
maintain a family? Will he not at any rate subject himself to greater
difficulties, and more severe labour than in his single state? Will he
not be unable to transmit to his children the same advantages of education and improvement that he had himself possessed? Does he even feel
secure that, should he have a large family, his utmost exertions can save
them from rags, and squalid poverty, and their consequent degradation in
the community? Any may he not be reduced to the grating necessity of
forfeiting his independence, and of being obliged to the sparing hand of
charity for support?

These considerations are calculated to prevent, and certainly do prevent,
a great number of persons in all civilized nations from pursuing the
dictate of nature in an early attachment to one woman.

If this restraint do not produce vice, as in many instances is the case,
and very generally so among the middle and higher classes of women, it is
undoubtedly the least evil that can arise from the principle of population.
Considered as a restraint on an inclination, otherwise innocent, and
always natural, it must be allowed to produce a certain degree of temporary unhappiness; but evidently slight, compared with the evils which
result from any of the other checks to population.

When this restraint produces vice, as it does most frequently among men,

and among a numerous class of females, the evils which follow are but too
conspicuous. A promiscuous intercourse to such a degree as to prevent
the birth of children, seems to lower in the most marked manner the
dignity of human nature. It cannot be without its effect on men, and
nothing can be more obvious than its tendency to degrade the female
character, and to destroy all its most amiable and distinguishing characteristics. Add to which, that among those unfortunate females with which
all great towns abound, more real distress and aggravated misery are
perhaps to be found, than in any other department of human life.

When a general corruption of morals, with regard to the sex, pervades all
the classes of society, its effects must necessarily be, to poison the
springs of domestic happiness, to weaken conjugal and parental affection,
and to lessen the united exertions and ardour of parents in the care and
education of their children; effects, which cannot take place without a
decided diminution of the general happiness and virtue of the society;
particularly, as the necessity of art in the accomplishment and conduct
of intrigues, and in the concealment of their consequences, necessarily
leads to many other vices.

The positive checks to population are extremely various, and include
every cause, whether arising from vice or misery, which in any degree
contributes to shorten the natural duration of human life. Under this
head therefore may be enumerated, all unwholesome occupations, severe
labour and exposure to the seasons, extreme poverty, bad nursing of
children, great towns, excesses of all kinds, the whole train of common
diseases and epidemics, wars, pestilence, plague, and famine.

On examining these obstacles to the increase of population which I have
classed under the heads of preventive, and positive checks, it will appear
that they are all resolvable into moral restraint, vice, and misery.

Of the preventive checks, that which is not followed by irregular
gratifications, may properly be termed moral restraint.

Promiscuous intercourse, unnatural passions, violations of the marriage
bed, and improper arts to conceal the consequences of irregular connexions,
clearly come under the head of vice.

Of the positive checks, those which appear to arise unavoidably from the
laws of nature may be called exclusively misery; and those which we
obviously bring upon ourselves, such as wars, excesses, and many others
which it would be in our power to avoid, are of a mixed nature. They
are brought upon us by vice, and their consequences are misery.

In every country, some of these checks are, with more or less force, in
constant operation; yet notwithstanding their general prevalence, there
are few states in which there is not a constant effort in the population
to increase beyond the means of subsistence. This constant effort as
constantly tends to subject the lower classes of society to distress, and
to prevent any great permanent amelioration of their condition.

These effects, in the present state of society, seem to be produced in
the following manner. We will suppose the means of subsistence in any
country just equal to the easy support of its inhabitants. The constant
effort towards population, which is found to act even in the most vicious

societies, increases the number of people before the means of subsistence
are increased. The food therefore which before supported eleven millions,
must now be divided among eleven millions and a half. The poor consequently must live much worse, and many of them be reduced to severe distress. The number of labourers also being above the proportion of work
in the market, the price of labour must tend to fall; while the price of
provisions would at the same time tend to rise. The labourer therefore
must do more work, to earn the same as he did before. During this season
of distress, the discouragements to marriage, and the difficulty of
rearing a family are so great, that population is nearly at a stand. In
the mean time, the cheapness of labour, the plenty of labourers, and the
necessity of an increased industry among them, encourage cultivators to
employ more labour upon their land; to turn up fresh soil, and to manure
and improve more completely what is already in tillage; till ultimately
the means of subsistence may become in the same proportion to the population, as at the period from which we set out. The situation of the
labourer being then again tolerably comfortable, the restraints to population are in some degree loosened; and, after a short period, the same
retrograde and progressive movements, with respect to happiness, are
repeated.

This sort of oscillation will not probably be obvious to common view;
and it may be difficult even for the most attentive observer to calculate
its periods. Yet that, in the generality of old states, some such
vibration does exist, though in a much less marked, and in a much more
irregular manner, than I have described it, no reflecting man who considers the subject deeply can well doubt.

One principal reason why this oscillation has been less remarked, and
less decidedly confirmed by experience than might naturally be expected,
is, that the histories of mankind which we possess, are in general,
histories only of the higher classes. We have not many accounts, that
can be depended upon, of the manners and customs of that part of mankind
where these retrograde and progressive movements chiefly take place. A
satisfactory history of this kind, of one people and of one period, would
require the constant and minute attention of many observing minds in
local and general remarks on the state of the lower classes of society,
and the causes that influenced it; and to draw accurate inferences upon
this subject, a succession of such historians for some centuries would
be necessary. This branch of statistical knowledge has of late years
been attended to in some countries, and we may promise ourselves a
clearer insight into the internal structure of human society from the
progress of these inquiries. But the science may be said yet to be in its
infancy, and many of the objects, on which it would be desirable to have
information, have been either omitted or not stated with sufficient
accuracy. Among these perhaps may be reckoned, the proportion of the
number of adults to the number of marriages; the extent to which
vicious customs have prevailed in consequence of the restraints upon
matrimony; the comparative mortality among the children of the most
distressed part of the community, and of those who live rather more at
their ease; the variations in the real price of labour; the observable
differences in the state of the lower classes of society with respect to
ease and happiness, at different times during a certain period; and very
accurate registers of births, deaths, and marriages, which are of the
utmost importance in this subject.

A faithful history, including such particulars, would tend greatly to elucidate the manner in which the constant check upon population acts; and would probably prove the existence of the retrograde and progressive movements that have been mentioned; though the times of their vibration must necessarily be rendered irregular from the operation of many interrupting causes; such as, the introduction of or failure of certain manufactures, a greater or less prevalent spirit of agricultural enterprize; years of plenty, or years of scarcity; wars, sickly seasons, poor laws, emigration, and other causes of a similar nature.

A circumstance which has perhaps more than any other contributed to conceal this oscillation from common view, is, the difference between the nominal and real price of labour. It very rarely happens that the nominal price of labour universally falls; but we well know that it frequently remains the same, while the nominal price of provisions has been gradually rising. This is, in effect, a real fall in the price of labour; and, during this period, the condition of the lower classes of the community must be gradually growing worse. But the farmers and capitalists are growing rich from the real cheapness of labour. Their increasing capitals enable them to employ a greater number of men; and, as the population had probably suffered some check from the greater difficulty of supporting a family, the demand for labour, after a certain period, would be great in proportion to the supply, and its price would of course rise, if left to find its natural level; and thus the wages of labour, and consequently the condition of the lower classes of society, might have progressive and retrograde movements, though the price of labour might never nominally fall.

In savage life, where there is no regular price of labour, it is little to be doubted that similar oscillations take place. When population has increased nearly to the utmost limits of the food, all the preventive and the positive checks will naturally operate with increased force. Vicious habits with respect to the sex will be more general, the exposing of children more frequent, and both the probability, and fatality, of wars and epidemicks, will be considerably greater; and these causes will probably continue their operation till the population is sunk below the level of the food; and then the return to comparative plenty will again produce an increase, and, after a certain period, its further progress will again be checked by the same causes.

But without attempting to establish in all cases these progressive and retrograde movements in different countries, which would evidently require more minute histories than we possess, the following propositions are proposed to be proved:
1.   Population is necessarily limited by the means of subsistence.
2.   Population invariably increases, where the means of subsistence increase, unless prevented by some very powerful and obvious checks.
3.   These checks, and the checks which repress the superior power of population, and keep its effects on a level with the means of subsistence, are all resolvable into moral restraint, vice, and misery.

The first of these propositions scarcely needs illustration. The second and third will be sufficiently established by a review of the past and present state of society.

This review will be the subject of the following chapters.

READING 2

Nassau William Senior (1790-1864) studied and taught at Oxford University. With John Stuart Mill, he belongs to the second generation of classical economists.

He firmly held the view that, in a progressive society such as England in his time, man's desire to better his position in the world and to prevent his position from deteriorating would induce him to limit his procreativity to the extent that numbers would no longer tend to increase beyond food production. Delayed marriage ("prudence", in Senior's words) guaranteed the maintenance and even the improvement of customary living standards. Senior's optimism was reinforced by his belief that in agriculture diminishing returns were often counterbalanced by technological progress, whereas in industry returns were always increasing.

Later in the 19th century the French writer Arsene Dumont (1841-1902) propounded a theory reminiscent of Senior's. It was that man's ambition to improve his relative position is strong enough to bring about a significant decline in fertility. A small family facilitates a man's ascent, and in a situation of increasing social mobility (such as Western Europe in the 19th century) ambitions are fostered and family size decreases.

Senior and Dumont provide us with the first clues as to why, in the late expanding phase of the demographic transition birth rates begin to decline. It is now a well-established phenomenon that at a certain stage of socio-economic development fertility drops. There is still no absolute certainty about the reasons for this fall, but Senior was among the first to have a theory.

Senior stated his view in his Political Economy (1850) and his Two Lectures on Population (1829). The following reading consists of a letter Senior wrote to Malthus in which he stated his case very succinctly. The letter was first published as an appendix to the Lectures.[2]

---

[2] Source: N. W. Senior, Two Lectures on Population, (London: Saunders, Otley, 1829), pp. 73-82.

A LETTER TO MALTHUS

Nassau William Senior

Lincoln's Inn,
March 26, 1829.

My Dear Sir,

Pray accept my sincerest thanks for the reply with which you have honoured
my letter, and for the instruction which it has afforded me.

I find, however, that the differences between us, though still I hope not
great, are rather greater than I had imagined. I will venture again to
intrude on your attention, in the hope of making them still smaller.

First, as to the facts.

I must have expressed myself ill, if I have led you to suppose that I
assert any thing like an universal increase of the proportion of subsistence to population. When I say that subsistence has generally increased
in a greater ratio than population, I mean, that if we look back through
the history of the whole world, and compare the state of each country at
distinct periods of two hundred or three hundred years, the cases in which
food has increased during the preceding period of two hundred or three
hundred years, in a greater ratio than population, will be found to be
more numerous than those in which population has increased during the preceding period in a greater ratio than food. I admit that this increase
has not been steady; it has been subject to the oscillations which you
have so well described. The cessation of a civil war, the acquisition of
a new and abundant material of food, mechanical inventions, enabling the
importation of a considerable supply of food at a less expense of labour
than must have been employed to produce it at home, improved modes of
cultivation and transport, and the change from a restricted to a free
internal corn trade -- each of these causes would be sufficient to occasion an immediate increase of food. In this country every one of them has
been experienced. As each has begun to act, it has, no doubt, been followed by an increase of population; an increase which, in many cases,
cannot have fully shown itself until some time after the cause increasing
the supply of food had been in full operation. Under such circumstances
a retrograde movement must have taken place. Still I apprehend that, in
the absence of disturbing causes, the retrogression would not be to the
point at which food and population relatively stood, before the first improvement took place. I conceive the progress of human society to resem-
ble the children's puzzle of a snail, which we are told every day crawled
up the wall four feet and fell back three. If we had always fallen back
the whole four, we should still be ill-fed savages, earning a scanty subsistence by the chase. And yet in England we have many disturbing causes.
We have the poor laws to increase our numbers, the corn laws to prohibit,
under ordinary circumstances, the importation of subsistence, and a com-

mercial code by which the perverse ingenuity of centuries has laboured to
fetter and misdirect our industry.

Secondly. As to the accuracy of our respective forms of expression.

I fully admit, that in all old countries, perhaps in all countries whatever, population is always pressing against food; and that the pressure
not only prevents the increase which would take place, if it could be removed, but occasions premature mortality. But as society advances in
what appears to me to be our natural course, for it is the course for
which nature has fitted us, this pressure generally, though not universally, diminishes. The proportion of those who now die in England from
want, is probably less than it was two hundred years ago; it certainly
is less than it was six hundred years ago. I still think myself, therefore, justified in saying, that there is a tendency in the pressure to
diminish. I admit that human nature tends to marriage directly, and to
the increase of subsistence only indirectly, and through the intervention
of forethought. It may be said that, strictly speaking, man has no natural tendency to produce food, or to better his condition, but to consume
food, and to have his condition bettered, and, through the intervention
of reason, to the accomplishment of these results. But reason, in some
degree or other, is as natural to man as passion. On this ground I speak
of man as a rational animal, as having a tendency towards the ends, which
he pursues through the intervention of forethought, as well as towards
those which he pursues at the dictates of passion. In this sense I speak
of any people as having a desire to increase their subsistence, (for that
is what I mean when I speak of the tendency of subsistence to increase),
stronger than the desire which leads them to increase their numbers.

The third, and by far the most important question, is the effect which
your mode, or my mode, of stating the law of population, is likely to
produce on the reader's mind.

I fully agree with you, that a statement which should imply that the increase of food can, in the absence of constant vigilance, restraint, and
self-denial, exceed or even keep pace with that of population, would lead
to the most mischievous error. I am grateful to you for having drawn my
attention to the possibility of such a consequence being inferred from my
expressions, and I certainly shall take care to prevent it for the future.
I do not think that any thing which I have said would lead an attentive
reader to such a conclusion; but after all the number of attentive
readers is so small, that no writer is justified in neglecting the idle
and the careless.

But while I admit that false and dangerous inferences may be drawn from
the naked and unexplained proposition that food has a tendency to increase
faster than population, I must add that inferences as false and as dangerous may be drawn, and in fact have been drawn, from the proposition that
population has a tendency to increase faster than food. Nothing can be
more accurate than your statement, "that population is always ready and
inclined to increase faster than food, if the checks which repress it
are removed." But many, perhaps the majority of your readers, adopt the
proposition without the qualification. They seem to believe that the
expansive power of population is a source of evil incapable not only of
being subdued, but even of being mitigated. They consider man not as he
is, but as he would be if he had neither forethought nor ambition;

neither the wish to rise, nor the fear to sink, in society. They deny the
possibility of permanent improvement, and regard every partial amelioration as a mere Sisyphaean labour.

"Were the whole mass of human sustenance," observes a distinguished writer,
"produced by the soil now under cultivation to be increased twofold by the
"efforts of human ingenuity and industry, we may assert, as an undoubted
"truth, that the only effect, after the lapse of a few years, would be
"found to have been the multiplication in a like proportion of the number
"of its occupants, with, probably at the same time, a far increased pro-
"portion of misery and crime."

No one can doubt the anxiety of the eminent person whom I have quoted, to
promote the welfare of mankind; but the tendency of this passage is to
damp every attempt to make labour more productive.

Unhappily there are many whom indolence or selfishness, or a turn to des-
pondency, make ready recipients of such a doctrine. It furnishes an easy
escape from the trouble or expense implied by every project of improvement.
"What use would it be," they ask, "to promote an extensive emigration?
"the whole vacuum would be immediately filled up by the necessary increase
"of population. Why should we alter the corn laws? If food were for a
"time more abundant, there would be a proportionate increase of population,
"and we should be just as ill off as before."

There are many also, particularly among those who reason rather with their
hearts than their heads, who are unable to assent to these doctrines, and
yet believe them to be among the admitted results of political economy.
Such persons apply to the whole science the argumentum ab absurdo; and
instead of enquiring into the accuracy of the reasoning, refuse to examine the premises from which such objectionable conclusions are inferred.

Undoubtedly these opinions are not fair inferences from your work; they
are, indeed, directly opposed to the spirit of the greater part of it;
but I think they must be considered as having been occasioned by a mis-
conception of your reasonings. They are prevalent now: before the
appearance of your writings they were never hinted at. I trust, however,
that, unsupported as they are by your authority, they will gradually wear
away; and I anticipate from their disappearance not merely the extin-
guishment of an error, but the removal of an obstacle to the diffusion of
political knowledge.

                    Believe me,
                        My dear Sir,
                            Yours, very sincerely,
                                N. W. SENIOR

READING 3

In the following reading, also a letter, Malthus replies to Senior
(reading 2). Technological advances and the importation of cheap foreign
cereals (corn) will certainly help to improve real living standards,
Malthus states, but such improvements will be lasting only if the preventive check, moral restraint, is widely adopted.[3]

[3] Source: Ibid., pp. 82-86.

A REPLY FROM MALTHUS
Thomas Robert Malthus

East India College,
March 31, 1829.

My Dear Sir,

We do not essentially differ as to facts, when they are explained as you
have explained them in your last letter. We are also quite agreed that
in the capacity of reason and forethought, man is endowed with a power
naturally calculated to mitigate the evils occasioned by the pressure of
population against food. We are further agreed that, in the progress of
society, as education and knowledge are extended, the probability is,
that these evils will practically be mitigated, and the condition of the
labouring classes be improved.

But is the passage which you have quoted in your last letter, when taken
with the context, essentially inconsistent with these our opinions? It
must be allowed, that it is not expressed with sufficient caution. In
pronouncing as an undoubted truth, that the only effect of doubling the
quantity of food in a country, would, after the lapse of a few years, be
found to have been the multiplication in a like proportion of the number
of its occupants, with probably a far increased proportion of misery and
crime, the author has evidently gone too far; but in what appears to me
to be the intended conclusion of the passage, I am disposed to agree with
him.

The two main propositions which I have endeavoured to prove from history
and experience, are, "That population invariably increases when the means
"of subsistence increase, unless prevented by powerful and obvious checks;
and, "That these checks, and the checks which keep the population down to
"the level of the means of subsistence, are, moral restraint, vice, and
"misery."

Now I cannot but allow that it is a fair inference from these propositions
that, if in any country means of doubling the quantity of food were
suddenly discovered, population would increase with extraordinary rapidity, so as to overtake, or nearly to overtake, the food; and that the
permanent condition of the labouring classes would not depend upon such
discovery, but exclusively on the question of the final increase of moral
restraint, or the moral condition of the population; which I think is
nearly the substance of the passage which you have quoted, when taken with
the context.

In the same manner I must allow that it follows from my principles, that
if by a free trade, corn were obtained much cheaper, and a labouring
family could really command a much larger quantity of it, population
would unquestionably increase with greater rapidity than before, so as to

reduce the increased corn wages; and that the final condition of the
labouring classes would not depend on this change which had taken place
in the law, but upon the greater or less prevalence of the moral checks
to population after the peculiar stimulus to its increase had subsided;
and repeated experience has shown that the facility of obtaining food
at one period is not necessarily connected with the formation of more
general habits of prudence subsequently.

It does not by any means follow from these principles, that we should not
use our utmost endeavours to make two ears of wheat grow where one grew
before, or to improve our commercial code by freeing it from restraints.
An increase of population is in itself a very decided advantage, if it be
not accompanied by an increased proportion of vice and misery. And the
period during which the pressure of population is lightened, though it may
not be of long duration, is a period of comparative ease, and ought by no
means to be thrown out of our consideration. It is further to be observed,
that the experience of such a period may sometimes operate in giving to
the labouring classes a taste for such a mode of living as will tend to
increase their prudential habits. But it is obvious, that without this
latter effect, the pressure of poverty cannot be permanently lessened.
And when the principal question is distinctly respecting the permanent
condition of the great mass of the labouring classes, as in the latter
part of my Essay, the interests of that body, which ought to be considered as the main interests of society, imperiously require that we should
not call off their attention to the chances of a great increase of food,
but endeavour by every proper means to direct their view to the important
and unquestionable truth, that they can do much more for themselves than
others can do for them, and that the only source of an essential and
permanent improvement of their condition, is the improvement and right
direction of their moral and religious habits.

> I am, my dear Sir,
>   Very truly yours,
>   T. ROBT. MALTHUS.

READING 4

John Stuart Mill (1806-1873) came from the very heart of the utilitarian movement. His father, James Mill, was a confirmed Benthamite and he gave his gifted son an extraordinary education. At age 13 John embarked upon the study of political economy; before he was twenty he had assimilated all there was to be known in this field.

In 1825, when Mill was 19, he took part in a debate on population at the "Cooperative Society", an association devoted to public debates and the spread of the teachings of Robert Owen. Mill gives a short account of the debate in his Autobiography (chapter 4). When Mill wrote his Principles of Political Economy in the 1840's he apparently used the materials contained in these addresses. The speeches, however, have a greater freshness than the relevant chapters in Principles.

Mill makes the law of diminishing returns the basis of the Malthusian population principle. This law explains why food cannot increase faster than at an arithmetical ratio. A certain population density, says Mill, is necessary for the enjoyment of the benefits of the division of labor and specialization. Hence, up to a certain threshold, population increase is advantageous, but beyond that point it is detrimental. Mill firmly believed that in almost all European countries this threshold had already been reached or overstepped.

The reading that follows consists of Mill's first speech before the Cooperative Society. The second one is of lesser interest and has been omitted. The manuscript of these addresses has been preserved by Professor H. J. Laski and was published on his advice in the Journal of Adult Education.[4]

---

[4] J. S. Mill, "Two Speeches on Population", The Journal of Adult Education, Vol. IV (October, 1929), pp. 38-61.

TWO SPEECHES ON POPULATION
John Stuart Mill

The charge which was brought against my honourable friend, of not understanding Mr. Owen's system, was in the first place untrue, and if true,
it was irrelevant. Untrue, because notwithstanding the vehemence with
which Mr. Owen's friends have reiterated the charge, they have as yet
failed of showing any one instance in which he has misrepresented the
system. Irrelevant, because if it were ever so true that my honourable
friend does not understand Mr. Owen's system, we are not now discussing
Mr. Owen's system, but the principle of population; and in any other
assembly than this, the principle of population might have been discussed
without adverting to Mr. Owen's system at all. It is true that if we
should come to the conclusion that no system which does not provide a
check to population can possibly be of any permanent utility, and if Mr.
Owen's system does not provide a check to population, Mr. Owen's system
must be as inefficient as the rest. But this proposition, however closely it may follow as a corollary from the principle of population, surely
is not a part of the principle; still less is the truth of the principle
of population itself in any degree dependent upon the goodness or badness
of Mr. Owen's system. The principle of population would have been just
the same, though Mr. Owen and his system had never been heard of. First
settle the general principle, and then there can be no difficulty in
applying it to the particular case. If the principle of population can
be shown to be a necessary consequence of the immutable laws of nature,
it follows, of course, that neither Mr. Owen nor any other person, not
commissioned to work miracles, can have it in his power to set these laws
aside.

I wish, sir, to make this subject as clear as possible: and when the
clearness of the subject has been impaired, and the difficulty of coming
to an agreement, a difficulty already so great, has been still further
enhanced by the different meanings which different speakers have chosen
to attach to a word, I am willing to give up that word, and to sacrifice
whatever advantage my case might have derived from its employment, rather
than that any unnecessary obstacle should stand in the way of a clear
understanding of the subject. In the present discussion, it appears to
me that some such confusion as I have described has arisen from the application of the word "capital" -- a word which almost all the speakers have
employed, and which scarcely any two of them seem to have understood in
the same sense. One gentleman has confounded capital with money, and
insisted that production could go on without capital, because it would
go on if we had leather money instead of gold and silver, which is certainly true, but nothing at all to the purpose. Another gentleman understands capital to mean nothing more than the materials and the instruments
of production; another extends it a little wider, and includes under it
the whole of the surplus which remains after the immediate wants of the
labourer have been supplied; and others, of whom I am one, include under
the word capital all that portion of the produce which is in any shape

whatever applied to the purpose of reproduction, whether as buildings, implements, materials, or in paying or feeding the labourers. A word which has so many significations is unfit for philosophical discussion, and I shall discard, not only the name, but the very idea which it implies. In doing this, I wish it to be understood how great is the concession which I make. The whole of the arguments of Mr. Owen's friends are founded upon the assertion that subsistence will follow mouths. Now, granting this, I might fairly reply that subsistence must precede mouths. Obvious and important as this proposition is, I will consent to waive it. I will consent to argue as if, in order to set the labourers to work, it were not necessary to have accumulated a previous supply of implements, buildings, seed and material together with food sufficient to maintain the labourers, at least till the first year's harvest could be gathered in. I will consent to let the controversy rest upon this single question, whether subsistence would follow mouths.

Now, sir, I admit that subsistence would follow mouths; that every addition to the mouths would occasion an addition to the subsistence, but I maintain that the addition to the subsistence would be not by any means proportional to the addition to the mouths; I maintain that there would be a much greater addition to the mouths than there would be to the subsistence, and consequently that the condition of the whole would be deteriorated. I rest this assertion upon the immutable laws prescribed by nature with regard to the productive powers of the soil.

It is a well-known fact that after a piece of land has been cultivated up to a certain point, any further increase of cultivation must be attended with a considerable diminution of return. If the labour of ten men on the soil produce a return of ten bushels, the labour of a second ten men, superadded to the former ten, will not produce so much as ten bushels, and the twenty together will not be able to produce so much as twenty bushels, probably not more than seventeen or eighteen. By increasing the labour you increase the return, but not in the same proportion. By doubling the labour, you do not double the return. It is perfectly clear, therefore, that if the first ten labourers had not more than enough to eat, when they had ten bushels to themselves, the twenty will not have a sufficiency, when they have only seventeen or eighteen bushels among them. If another ten labourers be added to the population, the return to their labour will be still less -- probably not more than five or six bushels. An addition of ten to the population causes an addition of five or six only to the production; there will now be thirty labourers and they will only have twenty-four bushels among them; they will therefore be still worse off than before.

This is the death blow to the gainsayers of the principle of population. They all say, as so many persons said in this room, that subsistence would follow population. I answer -- so it would; but as soon as that point of cultivation was attained at which any further application of labour to the soil is attended with a diminution of return, subsistence would follow population, it is true, but it would follow at a rate which is much slower, and which is every day growing still slower than before; it would follow at a limping, halting pace, and would be continually falling more and more behind.

What that point is it is impossible exactly to say, but that there is proof positive that not in this country alone, but in almost all the

countries of the old Continent, it has been long since attained. The
proof is that in all these countries it has been found necessary to cultivate the barren soils. Land, as is well known, is of various degrees of
fertility. In this country land, even of the ninth and tenth degree of
fertility, has long since been taken into cultivation. But it is demonstratively certain not only that we should never have cultivated the ninth
and tenth, but that we should not even have cultivated the second quality
of land, if we could have gone on applying our labour to the land of the
highest quality, without any diminution of return as at first. If the
labour of ten men on the best land produces ten bushels, and the labour
of ten men on the second best can produce only nine, so long as every
additional ten men could continue on the best land to produce ten additional bushels it could never be the interest of anybody to employ them upon
the second best, and produce no more than nine. The farmer who had, as
almost all farmers have, land of all degrees of fertility on his farm
would employ all his labourers in adding to the productiveness of the best
land and would leave all the other land untouched. But does this happen?
We find, on the contrary, that the inferior lands are cultivated; and
some lands are in cultivation which, with a given quantity of labour, do
not yield probably one-tenth part as much as the best land of all. And
how, I once more ask -- how can this be accounted for? Why should the
farmer employ any of his labourers on the inferior lands, if he could
employ them to greater advantage on the better qualities? He can have no
reason but one: and that one is satisfactory. The better sort of lands
are now cultivated up to so high a point that any additional labour employed upon them would not now yield a greater return than it does upon
the very worst lands which are at present in cultivation.

This great truth -- the limited fertility of the soil -- was the grand
proposition of my honourable friend's speech: it was the basis on which
his whole argument was founded. Most extraordinary it is, that not one
of those who answered him condescended to notice this fundamental principle, but went on assuming that every addition to population would occasion
an equal addition to the produce, just as if the contrary had never been
demonstrated. Even now, when the proposition has been separated from the
various other propositions which my honourable friend was under the necessity of mixing up with it, and held up naked to the view of this assembly
-- I cannot expect that a truth so new to most of those who are present
should be acceded to at once. It will doubtless be objected that a very
small proportion of the population can, and does, produce food for the
whole; and that the period when there shall be any danger of a deficiency of subsistence, if indeed it can arrive at all, is at any rate far
distant.

Let us give to this objection as much as it is worth. Let us suppose that
a community is established on the principles of Mr. Owen. A gentleman on
the other side has affirmed that in his native county one man can produce
food sufficient for the support of five. Let us suppose, then, that in
this community one-fifth of the population is employed in the production
of food, and the remaining four-fifths in the production of clothing, of
lodging, and the other necessaries and conveniences of life, in the practice of medicine, in the cultivation of knowledge, and in the government
of the community, for some sort of government, I presume, would be needed
even under Mr. Owen's system. I shall suppose also that food sufficient
for the whole community could at first be raised, without having recourse
to any but the very best quality of land, and without being reduced to

the necessity of applying labour even to the best land with a diminution
of return. This, it is to be observed, is granting much more to the
system than the warmest of the panegyrizers have as yet ventured to claim.
No one has as yet affirmed that under Mr. Owen's system food for the whole
community could be raised on the very best land. When we consider how
very limited in extent in this and most other countries land of the highest
quality is, and how small a proportion it bears in this country, not only
to the whole land of the country, but even to the whole of the land which
is in cultivation, it is obvious that I am granting infinitely more than
the boldest of my antagonists would dare to ask. Yet I do grant it,
because I have no occasion to deny it; false though it be, my argument
would be equally good if it were true. Let us see, then, what would be
the consequence.

Population would increase, additional mouths and additional hands would
be brought into play; these additional hands, if applied to the best
soils, would not produce a proportional increase of return. They must
either be applied to inferior soils, or to a higher cultivation of the
best; in either case they would be attended with an additional, but not
proportionate, addition to the return. If one man could previously raise
food for five, one man, probably, could now raise food for no more than
four. As it is one of Mr. Owen's rules that no other article shall be
produced until the community is supplied with all the food which it requires, a greater proportion than before must betake themselves to the
production of food. One-fifth of the population was formerly sufficient
to produce subsistence for the whole. One-fourth would now be requisite.
Three-fourths only, instead of four-fifths, would remain to supply the
other wants of the community. These wants, therefore, could not be so
well supplied as before. If the community was not previously better
clothed, better lodged, better attended when sick, and better governed
than enough, they could not now be well enough clothed, well enough lodged,
well enough attended nor well enough governed.

If population went on, the time would speedily come when one man would be
unable to produce more food than enough for three. One-third of the population must now be employed in raising food; and two-thirds only would
remain for other purposes. With every increase of population, the proportion employed in raising food must be increased; it would rise from
one-third to half, from half to two-thirds, three-quarters, five-sixths;
and from the properties of the soil the progression would be very rapid;
until at length the labour of each man applied to the soil would not be
able to produce more than enough for the subsistence of one. Then must
the whole of the population apply themselves to the production of food.
There would be no clothes, no houses, no furniture. There would be no
physicians nor legislators. There would be nothing for elegance, nothing
for ease, and nothing for pleasure; mankind would be reduced to the level
of a very low kind of animal, having just two functions -- that of raising
and that of consuming food. After population had reached this point, if
it were still to increase, the surplus, it is evident, could not be supported. There would then not even be enough food. Starvation must overspread the community, until the destruction of the surplus population had
reduced it again to that number for which food can be provided, and food
alone.

Let it not be objected that this period is far distant. The consummation,
indeed, it is to be hoped, is far distant. The dreadful end of the series

might be long delayed, though not so long as may be supposed. But though
the end of the series may be distant, the series itself has long since
commenced. That progressive deterioration which if not checked must end
in destruction, commenced from the moment when it became necessary to
cultivate any but the finest soils. The cultivation even of the second-
best land demonstratively proved that additional labour could not be
applied to the best land without a diminution of return. From that moment, every extension of cultivation drew, and must draw, a greater and
greater proportion of the labourers to the production of food, and must
leave a smaller proportion to the production of everything else. Let Mr.
Owen's system be ever so admirable; let his arrangements for the employment of labour be ever so efficacious: it would nevertheless be true
that unless the whole of the food requisite for the nourishment of the
community could be raised, not only without cultivating any but the very
best soil, but without expending more than a very small quantity of labour
even upon the best soil itself, every increase of population must continually draw a greater and greater proportion of the labourers to agriculture, leaving a less and less proportion for all other pursuits, and consequently deteriorating the condition of all. With every extension of
cultivation, after the inferior lands come under tillage, all most have
less food, or less something else.

There is only one case in which this would not be strictly true. Although
there would every day be a less and less proportion of the population to
be spared for the production of the comforts and conveniences of life, it
is possible that by improvements in machinery and more extended applications of the principle of the division of labour, this smaller proportion
might be able to produce enough for all. That this principle has been
powerfully called into action in this country there can be no doubt; and
it is the only cause why the increase of our population was not stopped
centuries ago by starvation and misery. But as the increase of population
is constantly going on; as the proportion of labourers which can be
spared from the production of food is constantly diminishing; there must
likewise be a constant succession of improvements in production, and we
shall be as ill off as before. But a constant succession of improvements
in production is what we cannot look for under any circumstances, and
least of all under Mr. Owen's system, where the benefits of the invention
are to be shared with a hundred or a thousand others, and the labour is
for the inventor alone. That constant succession of improvements which
would be improbable even when the inventor is permitted for a time to
enjoy the entire fruits of his invention may be pronounced impossible
where he can have but a hundredth or thousandth part.

From the moment, then, when additional labour can no longer be applied to
the best land with the same return as at first -- a moment indicated by
the commencement of tillage on the inferior lands, the further increase
of population must deteriorate the condition of all, unless accompanied
by a constant succession of improvements in production. And even if it
be so accompanied: if for every man who comes into the world a new invention be made, which enables that man to add as much to the produce as
he does to the mouths which are to consume it, no one, to be sure, is
worse off; but give us the invention without the additional man, and all
will be better off. In every case, therefore, after inferior land begins
to be tilled, for every increase of population a portion of the physical
comfort of the people is sacrificed; or, at any rate, postponed to something else. Up to a certain point it is desirable that it should be post-

poned to something else. A certain density of population is absolutely
necessary for the complete enjoyment of the benefits of the social union.
Up to that point it is desirable that population should increase, even
though it did take something from the physical comfort of each. But
beyond that point every increase of population has the effect of rendering
the condition of each less favourable than it would otherwise be; beyond
that point, therefore, whether under Mr. Owen's system or any other system,
an increase of population is not desirable.

I should like to know, sir, what the gentlemen on the other side will say
in answer to this. One thing I hope will not be very clearly understood.
That unless they deny that original property of the soil, by which an
increased application of labour is attended with a diminished rate of
return, all that they can say is nothing to the purpose. They may endeavour, indeed, to evade this principle -- they may say that by the application of labour the most barren land may be made equal to the most
fertile, and this I know they will say, for this reason, because they can
say nothing else; but I have to request that when they do say it, all who
hear me will have the answer ready. It is this: You may fertilize the
most barren land -- you may increase its produce tenfold; but it must be
increasing the number of your labourers a hundredfold. A gentleman de-
clared on the former evening that if you had not twenty times the produce
it is only because you have not twenty times the population. The incor-
rectness of this assertion I hope is now evident. For my part, I am per-
suaded that not with a thousand times our present population -- indeed,
with no amount of population -- and with our present means of production,
could we raise twenty times our present produce. Without some gigantic
invention, some machine, or other mode of increasing the productive power
of labour, all the men in the universe, concentrated on to this island,
could not, I am satisfied, raise more than three or four times our present
produce.

After what I have said, it is scarcely necessary to state how cordially I
agree in the resolution which was moved on the preceding evening, "That,
etc."

There were two objections brought against the principle which still remain
to be answered, and on which it may not be useless to add a few words
more.

A gentleman affirmed on the former evening that the principle of population is unnatural; that it is contrary to nature and therefore cannot be
true. What he meant by nature and unnatural, he did not tell us; indeed,
he did not seem to know; nor did he offer any proof that the principle
of population is unnatural. What he meant by nature I cannot tell. I
will tell him what I mean by nature. I mean all the things which we see
and feel: the sun, moon, and stars, men and animals, trees, plants, and
shrubs, the earth with all its productions and these various phenomena.
If all this be not nature, I should like to know what is. Now then, to
what part of all this does the gentleman consider the principle of population to be contrary? Is it contrary to the sun and moon? contrary to
the stars? contrary to the trees and shrubs? to the sea? to the wind?
to an earthquake or a volcano? If, sir, as is abundantly manifest, a
man would make himself ridiculous by saying that the principle of population is contrary to any of these, I should like to know how that which is
not contrary to any part can be said to be contrary to the whole.

But the gentleman may reply that it is contrary to some supposed law of nature. If he can prove this, I have done. But to what law of nature is it contrary? It is a law of nature that fire burns; is it contrary to that? It is a law of nature that water freezes; is it contrary to that? No, but it is a law of nature that to every application of additional labour, the soil yields a diminishing return; and to this law of nature it is so far from being contrary, that, as I have shown, it is a necessary consequence of it.

If the word unnatural has any meaning at all, I suppose it has some indistinct reference to the will of God. And this brings me to the other objection which I promised to notice; that it is a libel on the Deity to suppose that He would send mouths without sending meat to put into them -- that, in short, the principle of population is an evil, and therefore inconsistent with the benevolence of God. One would really think, sir, that there were no such thing as evil in the world -- either physical or moral. As long as any evil exists, the argument of the honourable gentleman is a dangerous one, and may easily be carried a great deal too far. In our present state of ignorance as to the final causes of many things which we see upon the earth, the existence of any evil appears to us inconsistent with the divine benevolence. The principle of population is an evil, it is true, but certainly by no means an irremediable one; and he who can reconcile the benevolence of God with the existence of war, pestilence, famine, poverty, and crime might be able, one would think, to reconcile it also with the principle of population. But if we admit, as we must do, that in the present condition of our knowledge the existence of these evils under an all-wise and benevolent ruler is a mystery which we cannot explain, let us at any rate allow as much to the principle of population as we do to war, pestilence and famine, and not conclude that it does not exist, because there is a difficulty in explaining it which it only shares with all the other evils which afflict humanity.

So much for the religious objection; and with respect to the word unnatural, I should be inclined to reverse the proposition of the gentleman who made use of the word, and instead of saying that it is unnatural and therefore cannot be true, I should say that it is true and therefore cannot be unnatural.

If the gentleman says that the principle is repulsive to his feelings, I answer that this is the first time I ever heard that feeling is the test of truth; that a proposition is true or false according as we happen to like or dislike it, and that there can be no such things as unpleasant truths.

READING 5

As is well known, the teachings of the classical school did not go unchallenged. The groups that criticized the classical economists can be divided roughtly into the socialist, the historical, and the national schools. The socialists argued that social harmony could not be achieved by individuals pursuing their self-interests, and that collective effort in the production and distribution of income should replace individual action. The historical school opposed the classicals' excessive use of the deductive method, which, they said, had to be supplemented by historical research. The nationalists emphasized the concept of the nation as a vital link between the individual and the world. They also justified protectionism under certain circumstances.

Henry Charles Carey (1793-1879), an early American economist, belongs with certain qualifications to the nationalists. He was born in Philadelphia of Irish parents. Carey strongly reacts against those classical economists who base their theories on the law of diminishing returns. His major purpose, it seems, was to prove that the Lord had created a harmonious universe. His dislike of Malthus and Ricardo was in large measure due to his observation that these economists had pointed to disharmonies in life on earth.

Carey tried to disprove the two Malthusian ratios of population and subsistence. He argued that population does not increase geometrically because man's reproductive capacities (fecundity) diminish as he becomes more civilized. He also set out to disprove the law of diminishing returns, which lies behind the theory that food production increases arithmetically. In taking up land, he argued, farmers go from the poorer soils to the richer, just as they go from mediocre to more perfected tools. Therefore the output on the marginal farm (the most recently cultivated) was not decreasing but increasing. Needless to say, Carey's beliefs were influenced by the North America during the first half of the nineteenth century.[5]

---

[5] Source: H. C. Carey, Principles of Social Science (Philadelphia: Lippincott, 1858), Vol. I, pp. 96-104.

H. C. Carey, Principles of Social Science (Philadelphia: Lippincott, 1865), Vol. III, pp. 263-265, pp. 302-308.

DIMINISHING RETURNS AND POPULATION
Henry Charles Carey

What, under such circumstances, is his course of operation, is exhibited
in the following sketch of that of a single supposed individual and his
descendants, during a period of time that the reader may, if he will,
extend from years to centuries. By thus taking a supposititious case,
and placing the settler on an island, we are enabled to eliminate the
causes of disturbance that have, everywhere in real life, resulted from
the vicinity of other individuals equally deficient in the machinery required for the subjugation of nature -- and therefore driven, by fear of
starvation, to robbery and murder of their fellow-men. Having thus, by
aid of the system pursued by .the mathematician, studied what would be the
course of man left undisturbed, we shall then be prepared to enter into
an examination of the disturbing causes to which it is due that his course
has been, in many countries, so widely different.

The first cultivator, the Robinson Crusoe of his day, provided, however,
with a wife, has neither axe nor spade. He works alone. Population
being small, land is, of course, abundant, and he may select for himself,
fearless of any question of his title. He is surrounded by soils possessed in the highest degree of qualities fitting them for yielding large
returns to labor; but they are covered with immense trees that he cannot
fell, or they are swamps that he cannot drain. To pass through them, even,
is a work of serious labor, the first being a mass of roots, stumps, decaying logs, and shrubs, while, into the other, he sinks knee deep at
every step. The atmosphere, too, is impure, as fogs settle upon the low-
lands, and the dense foliage of the wood prevents the circulation of the
air. He has no axe, but had he one he would not venture there, for, to
do so, would be attended with risk of health, and almost certain loss of
life. Vegetation, too, is so luxuriant, that before he could, with the
imperfect machinery at his command, clear a single acre, a portion of it
would be again so overgrown that he would have to recommence his Sisyphean
labor. The higher lands, comparatively bare of timber, are little fitted
for yielding a return to his exertions. There are, however, places on
the hill, where the thinness of the soil has prevented the growth of trees
and shrubs -- or there are spaces among the trees that can be cultivated
while they still remain; and, when pulling up by the roots the few shrubs
scattered over the surface, he is alarmed by no apprehension of their
speedy reproduction. With his hands he may even succeed in barking the
trees, or, by the aid of fire he may so far destroy them that time alone
will be required for giving him a few cleared acres, upon which to sow
his seed, with little fear of weeds. To attempt these things upon the
richer lands would be loss of labor. In some places the ground is always wet, while in others, the trees are too large to be seriously in-
jured by fire, and its only effect would be to stimulate the growth of
weeds and brush. He therefore commences the work of cultivation on the
higher grounds, where, making with his stick holes in the light soil
that drains itself, he drops the grain an inch or two below the surface,

and in due season obtains a return of twice his seed. Pounding this between stones, he obtains bread, and his condition is improved. He has
succeeded in making the earth labor for him, while himself engaged in
trapping birds or rabbits, or in gathering fruits.

Later, he succeeds in sharpening a stone, and thus obtains a hatchet, by
aid of which he is enabled to proceed more rapidly in girdling the trees,
and in removing the sprouts and their roots, a very slow and laborious
operation, nevertheless. In process of time, he is seen bringing into
activity a new soil -- one whose food-producing powers were less obvious
to sight than those at first attempted. Finding an ore of copper, he
succeeds in burning it, and is thus enabled to obtain a better axe, with
far less labor than had been required for the inferior one he has thus
far used. He obtains, also, something like a spade, and can now make holes
four inches deep, with less labor than, with his stick, he could make
those of two. Penetrating to a lower soil, and being enabled to stir the
earth and loosen it, the rain is now absorbed where before it had run off
from the hard surface, and the new soil thus obtained proves to be far
better, and more easily wrought, than that upon which his labor has heretofore been wasted. His seed, better protected, is less liable to be
frozen out in winter, or parched in summer, and he now gathers thrice the
quantity sown. At the next step, we find him bringing into action another
new soil. He has found that which, on burning, yields him tin, and, by
combining this with his copper, he has brass, giving him better machinery,
and enabling him to proceed more rapidly. While sinking deeper into the
land first occupied, he is enabled to clear other lands upon which vegetation grows more luxuriantly, because he can now exterminate the shrubs
with some hope of occupying the land before they are replaced with others
equally useless for his purposes. His children, too, have grown, and they
can weed the ground, and otherwise assist him in removing the obstacles
by which his progress is impeded. He now profits by association and combination of action, as before he had profited by the power he had obtained
over the various natural forces he had reduced into his service. Next,
we find him burning a piece of the iron soil which surrounds him in all
directions, and now he obtains a real axe and spade, inferior in quality,
but still much superior to those by which his labor has been thus far
aided. With the help of his sons, grown to man's estate, he now removes
the light pine of the hill-side leaving still untouched, however, the
heavy timber of the river bottom. His cultivable ground is increased in
extent, while he is enabled, with his spade, to penetrate still deeper
than before, thus bringing into action the powers of the soils more distant from the surface. He finds, with great pleasure, that the light
sand is underlaid with clay, and that, by combining the two, he obtains a
new one far more productive than that he first had used. He remarks, too,
that by turning the surface down, the process of decomposition is facilitated, and each addition to his knowledge increases the return to his
exertions. --With further increase of his family, he has obtained the
important advantage of increased combination of action. Things that
were needed to be done to render his land more rapidly productive, but
which were to himself impracticable, become simple and easy when now
attempted by his numerous sons and grandsons, each of whom obtains far
more food than he alone could at first command, and in return for far less
severe exertion. They next extend their operations downwards, towards
the low grounds of the stream, girdling the large trees, and burning the
brush -- and thus facilitating the passage of air so as to fit the land,
by degrees, for occupation.

With increase of numbers there is now increased power of association, manifested by increased division of employments, and attended with augmented power to command the service of the great natural agents provided for their use. One portion of the little community now performs all the labors of the field, while another gives itself to the further development of the mineral wealth by which it is everywhere surrounded. They invent a hoe, by means of which the children are enabled to free the ground from weeds, and to tear up some of the roots by which the best lands -- those last brought into cultivation -- are yet infested. They have succeeded in taming the ox, but, as yet, have had little occasion for his services. They now invent the plough, and, by means of a piece of twisted hide, are enabled to attach the ox, by whose help they turn up a deeper soil, while extending cultivation over more distant land. The community grows, and with it grows the wealth of the individuals of which it is composed, enabling them, from year to year, to obtain better machinery, and to reduce to cultivation more and better lands. Food and clothing become more abundant, while the air on the lower lands is improved by the clearing of the timber. The dwelling, too, is better. In the outset, it was a hole in the ground. Subsequently, it was composed of such decayed logs as the unaided efforts of the first settler could succeed in rolling and placing one upon the other. As yet, the chimney was unknown, and he must live in perpetual smoke, if he would not perish of cold, as a window was a luxury then unthought of. If the severity of the weather required him to close his doors, he was not only stifled, but passed his days in darkness. His time, during a large portion of the year, was therefore totally unproductive, while his life was liable to be shortened by disease produced by foul air within, or severe cold without, his miserable hut. With increase of population all have acquired wealth, resulting from the cultivation of new and better soils, and from a growing power to command the services of nature. With this increase of power there has been a further increase in the power of association, with steady tendency to the development of individuality, as the modes of employment have become more and more diversified. They now fell the heavy oak and the enormous pine, and are thereby enabled to construct additional dwellings, each in regular succession better than the first. Health improves, and population increases more rapidly. A part of it is now employed in the field, while another prepares the skins, and renders them more fit for clothing -- and a third set makes axes, spades, hoes, ploughs, and other implements calculated to aid the labors of the field, and in those of construction. The supply of food increases rapidly, and with it the power of accumulation. In the first years, there was perpetual danger of famine, but now there being a surplus, a part is stored to provide against failure of the crops.

Cultivation extends itself along the hill-side, where deeper soils, now laid open by the plough, yield larger returns -- while down the slope of the hill each successive year is marked by the disappearance of the great trees by which the richer lands have heretofore been occupied -- the intermediate spaces becoming meanwhile enriched by the decomposition of the enormous roots, and more readily ploughed because of the gradual decay of the stumps. A single ox to the plough can now turn up a greater space than in the outset could be done by two. A single ploughman can now do more than on the ground first cultivated could have been done by hundreds of men armed with pointed sticks. The community being next enabled to drain some of the lower lands, copious harvests of grain are obtained from the better soil now first cultivated. Thus far the oxen have roamed the

woods, gathering what they could, but the meadow is now granted to their
use, the axe and the saw enabling the family to enclose them, and thus to
lessen the labor attendant upon obtaining supplies of meat, milk, butter,
and hides. Heretofore their chief domestic animal has been the hog, which
could live on mast, but now they add beef, and perhaps mutton, the lands
first cultivated being abandoned to the sheep. They obtain far more meat
and grain, and with less labor than at any former period; a consequence
of their increase in numbers and in the power of association. Numerous
generations having already passed away, the younger ones now profit by the
wealth they had accumulated, and are thus enabled to apply their own labor
with daily increasing advantage -- obtaining a constantly increasing return,
with increasing power of accumulation, and decreasing severity of exertion. They now bring new powers to their aid, and the water no longer is
allowed to run to waste. Even the air itself is made to work, windmills
grinding the grain, and sawmills cutting the timber, which disappears
more rapidly; while the work of drainage is in course of being improved
by help of more efficient spades and ploughs. The little furnace makes
its appearance, and charcoal being now applied to the reduction of the
iron yielding soil, it is found that the labor of a single day becomes
more productive than before had been that of many weeks. Population
spreads itself along the faces of the hills and down into the lower lands,
becoming more and more dense at the seat of the original settlement; and
with every step we find increasing tendency to combination of action for
the production of food, the manufacture of clothing and of household uten-
sils, the construction of houses, and the preparation of machinery for
aiding in all these operations. The heaviest timber -- that growing on
the most fertile land -- now disappears, and deep marshes are now drained.
Roads are next made to facilitate the intercourse between the old settlement and the newer ones that have been formed around it, and to enable the
grower of corn to exchange for wool, or perhaps for improved spades or
ploughs, for clothing or for furniture.

Population again increases, with still further development of wealth and
power, and therewith is acquired leisure for reflection on the results
furnished by the experience of themselves and their predecessors. From
day to day, mind becomes more stimulated into action. The sand in the
neighborhood being found to be underlaid with marl, the two are, by aid
of the improved machinery now in use, brought into combination; thereby
producing a soil of power far exceeding that of those heretofore in cultivation. With increased returns to labor all are better fed, clothed,
and housed, and all are incited to new exertions, while with improved
health and with the power of working in-doors and out-of-doors, according
to the season, they are enabled to apply their labor with greater steadi-
ness and regularity. Thus far, however, they have found it difficult to
gather their crops in season. The harvest time being short, the whole
strength of the community has been found insufficient to prevent much of
the grain remaining on the ground until, over ripe, it was shaken out by
the wind, or in the attempt to gather it. Not unfrequently, indeed, it
has been totally ruined by changes of weather after it had been fit for
harvesting. Labor has been superabundant during the year, while harvest
produced a demand for it that could not be supplied. The reaping-hood,
however, now takes the place of the hand, while the scythe enables the
farmer to cut his hay. The cradle and the horse-rake follow, all tending
to increase the facility of accumulation, and thus to increase the power
of applying labor to new soils, deeper or more distant, more heavily
burdened with timber, or more liable to be flooded -- and thus requiring

embankment as well as drainage. New combinations, too, are formed. The
clay is found to be underlaid with the soil called lime, which latter,
like the iron yielding soil, requires decomposition to fit it for the task
of combination. The road, the wagon, and the horse facilitate the work by
enabling the farmer readily to obtain supplies of the carbon-yielding soil,
called coal, and he now obtains, by burning the lime and combining it with
the clay, a better soil than at any former period -- one yielding more corn,
and requiring less severe labor from himself. Population and wealth again
increase, and the steam-engine assists the work of drainage, while the
railroad and the engine facilitate the transportation to market of his products. His cattle being now fattened at home, a large portion of the produce of his rich meadow-land is converted into manure, to be applied to
the poorer soils that had at first been cultivated. Instead of sending
food to fatten them at market, he now obtains from market their refuse in
the form of bones, by help of which to maintain the powers of his land.
--Passing thus, at every step, from the poor to the better soils, there is
obtained a constantly increasing supply of food, and other necessaries of
life, with corresponding increase in the power of consumption and accumulation. The danger of famine and disease now passes away. Increased returns to labour and daily improving condition rendering labor pleasant,
he is seen everywhere applying himself more steadily as his work becomes
less severe. Population further increases, and the rapidity of its increase is seen to be greater with each successive generation -- while with
each is seen an increase of the power of living in connection with each
other, by reason of the power of obtaining constantly increasing supplies
from the same surface. With every step in this direction the desire for
association and for combination of action is seen to grow with the growth
of the power to satisfy it, and thus are their labors rendered more productive and the facilities of commerce augmented -- with constant tendency
to the production of harmony, peace, and security of person and property,
among themselves, and with the world -- accompanied by constant increase
of numbers, wealth, prosperity, and happiness.

Such has been everywhere, where population and wealth have been permitted
to increase, the history of man. With growth of numbers there has been
increased power of combination among men for obtaining control over the
great forces existing in nature -- setting them free and then compelling
them to aid him in the work of producing the food, the clothing, and the
shelter required for his purposes, and to facilitate him in obtaining power to extend the sphere of his associations. Everywhere he is seen to
have commenced poor and helpless in himself, and unable to combine his
efforts with those of is fellow-men -- and everywhere, consequently, the
slave of nature. Everywhere, as numbers have increased, he is seen to
have become, from year to year, and from century to century, more and
more her master -- and every step in that direction has been marked by
rapid development of individuality, attended by increased power of association, increased sense of responsibility, and increased power of progress.

That such has been the case with all nations and in all parts of the earth,
is so obvious that it would seem almost unnecessary to offer any proof of
the fact, nor could it be so but that it has been asserted that the course
of things has been directly the reverse -- that man has always commenced
the work of cultivation on the rich soils of the earth, and that then
food has been abundant -- but that, as population has increased, his suc-
cessors have found themselves forced to resort to inferior ones, yielding
steadily less and less in return to labor; with constant tendency to

over-population, poverty, wretchedness, and death. Were this so, there
could be no such thing as universality in the natural laws to which man is
subjected, for in regard to all other descriptions of matter, we see him
uniformly commencing with the inferior, and passing, as wealth and population grow, to the superior -- with constantly increasing return to labor.
He is seen to have commenced with the axe of stone, and to have passed
through those of copper, bronze, and iron, until he has finally arrived at
those of steel -- to have passed from the spindle and distaff to the
spinning-jenny and the power-loom -- from the canoe to the ship -- from
transportation on the backs of men to that in railroad cars -- from rude
hieroglyphics painted on skins to the printed book -- and from the wild
society of the savage tribe, where might makes right, to the organized
community in which the rights of those who are weak in numbers, or in
muscular power, are respected. Having studied these facts, and having
satisfied ourselves that such has been his course in reference to all
things other than the land required for cultivation, we should be disposed
to believe that it must there also prove to have been the case, and that
the theory referred to -- by virtue of which man is rendered more and more
the slave of nature as wealth and population grow -- must be untrue.

ON HUMAN FECUNDITY
Henry Charles Carey

"Be fruitful and multiply," said the Lord, "and replenish the earth, and
subdue it." That it may be subdued, men must multiply and increase -- it
being only by means of association and combination with his fellow-men,
that man acquires power for guiding and directing the forces of nature to
his service. In obedience to the divine command it is, then, that matter
tends to take upon itself, more and more, the human form -- passing from
the simple forms of clay and sand, through those more complex, exhibited
in vegetable and animal life, and ending in the highly complex ones of the
bones, muscles, and brains of men.

The tendency to assume the various forms of life, is greatest at the lowest point of organization -- the progeny of microscopic beings counting,
at the close of the single week, by millions, even when not by billions,
whereas, the period of gestation in the whale and the elephant, is long,
while the product rarely exceeds a single individual. Such are the extremes, but the rule holds good at every stage of progress, from the coral
insect to the ant, and from the ant to the elephant -- thus furnishing the
law, that fecundity and development are in the inverse ratio of each other.
In virtue of that fixed and certain law, man, "the crown and roof of all
things," should increase less rapidly than any other animal whatsoever,
and -- carrying out the same idea -- the fecundity of the human race itself should diminish, as the peculiarly human faculties are more and more
stimulated into action, and as the man becomes more and more developed.

The periods within which the existing population of the principal nations
duplicates itself, varies greatly -- France requiring more than a century,
and Great Britain more than half a century, while the duplication of
American numbers is accomplished in little more than thirty years.

So far as regards the ultimate destiny of the human race, it is, however,
of small importance whether, in obedience to fixed and immutable laws, the
duplication has been arranged to take effect in 30, 50, or 100 years --
the only difference being, that under the first, there must be, some 700
years hence, a million of persons on the earth for each one that now exists, whereas, in the other, rather more than 2000 years would be required
for producing the same result.

What, now, would be the effect of such increase? Obviously, so to crowd
the earth, as eventually to leave but standing room for the population.
With the near approach of such a state of things, food must have been becoming more scarce -- enabling the owner of land, to dictate to the laborer on what terms he might cultivate the land -- the one becoming more
completely master, and the other more entirely enslaved.

Having once admitted that the procreative tendency is a positive quantity,
always ready to be excited into activity, and existing to such extent as

to insure a duplication in any certain period, it cannot afterwards be
denied, that slavery is to be the ultimate condition of the great mass of
the race; nor, that the tendency in that direction is greater now than
at any former period -- the history of the world presenting no instance of
increase as great as that exhibited in England, Ireland, and America, in
the last hundred years. Neither can it, in that case, be denied, that man
is ultimately to be subdued by the earth -- his liability thereto being in
the direct ratio of his obedience to the divine command with which this
chapter was commenced.

Can such things be? Can it be, that the Creator has been thus inconsistent
with himself? Can it be, that after having instituted, throughout the
material world, a system, the harmony of whose parts is so absolutely perfect, He has, of design, subjected man, the master and director of all, to
laws whose effects can be no other than that of producing universal discord? Can it be, that while furnishing every where else, evidence of the
union in Himself of the qualities of universal knowledge, perfect justice,
and exhaustless mercy, He has here -- in reference to his last and greatest
work -- assumed a character so entirely the reverse? Even in man, true
greatness is always consistent -- always in harmony with itself. Can it
be, then, that after having given to man all the faculties required for
assuming the mastery of nature, it has been a part of His design, to subject him to absolute and irreversible laws, in virtue of which he must
inevitably become nature's slave? Let us inquire.

The law of balance between the nervous and sexual functions is strongly
corroborated by the facts of comparative physiology, some of which have
been before referred to. The queen ant of the African termites lays
80,000 eggs, and the hair-worm as many as 8,000,000,in a single day.
Carpenter says, "that above 1,000,000 eggs are produced at once by a single
codfish, whereas, in the strong and sagacious shark, but few are found."
The higher ranks of reptiles are still less fertile; and among the mam-
malia, those which quickly reach maturity produce large and numerous lit-
ters -- those, on the contrary, which are longer in attaining the reproductive age, and are better provided with brain, producing annually but a
single litter. Higher in rank are those producing singly -- the series
terminating with the elephant, who, in virtue of his nobler nervous sytem,
and its accompanying reasoning powers, presents himself as least prolific
of them all.

The general law of life, throughout all the classes, orders, genera,
species, and individuals, may thus be stated:

The nervous system varies directly as the power to maintain life:

The degree of fertility varies inversely as the development of the nervous
system -- animals with larger brains being always the least, and those
with smaller ones, the most prolific:

The power to maintain life, and that of procreation, antagonize each
other -- that antagonism tending perpetually towards the establishment of
an equilibrium.

Chemical analysis, though less accurately and conclusively ascertained
than might be wished, presents itself in aid of the views thus suggested
-- exhibiting to us the fact, that the sperm cells of the fecundating

fluid, and the neurine, or essential portion of the cerebral substance, possess in common one element -- unoxydized phosphorus -- by which they are specially characterized and distinguished. Of this peculiar substance, no less than 6 1/2 per cent. enters into the solid contents of the brain of adults. In advanced age, it falls to 3 3/4; and in idiots, it is less than 3.

Here, however, as in the argument drawn from the relative size of the brain of the various races of the species, the evidence afforded by experience, and by physiological laws, is more conclusive than that obtained by examination of the structure. Nothing connected with this question is better known -- nothing more fully recognised -- than the general antagonism of the nervous and generative systems. Intense mental application, involving great waste of the nervous tissue, and corresponding consumption of the nervous element for its repair, is accompanied by a proportionately diminished production of sperm-cells -- the excessive production of these latter being, in like manner, followed by defective cerebral energy. In the degree usually regarded as disease, the process is marked first by headache, followed by stupidity, leading to imbecility, and terminating in insanity.

How this antagonism of action affects the female system, is less clearly open to scientific examination, although it appears highly probable, that the provision of nervous matter, as well as of nutriment, to the embryo, limits the supply of nervous matter to the maternal system. So far as mere substance is concerned, this must have some force, wheresoever and whensoever it applies. It is, however, more probable, that the uterine function, beginning with puberty, and continuing until the commencement of old age, is the more efficient counteractive of cerebral force in the sex -- the state of health, and eminently that of disease, furnishing strong evidence to this effect.

Further, there is abundant reason for believing, that certain kinds of nervous action are more efficient than others, in counteracting the activity and force of the instincts, and the functions which they serve, although the physiology of the brain is not, as yet, sufficiently advanced to render us adequate service here -- neither its anatomy, nor its chemistry, yet answering to all the questions which social science puts to them. It being, however, satisfactorily established, that the various parts of the cerebral mass have different offices assigned to them, it is probable, even on this ground, that they have varied relations, both of assistance and of counter-balance, to the action of the viscera. The employment of the mind in passional, imaginative, scientific, moral or devotional applications, has effects upon the propensities, that, as we know, are widely different. Some of them, certainly, minister to their growth, while others as decidedly counteract it. Experience here affords valuable instruction, not only for the conduct of life, but as furnishing important data for inquiry -- all its teachings having an obvious bearing upon the question now before us.

The application of the several points that, as we think, have been secured, would seem to be as follows:

The human race being in a state of transition, we have all the reasons thus far offered, for believing that the existing ratio between its ability to multiply, and its power to maintain life, is not a constant quantity -- the causal law being one, but its effects being modified by almost incessant changes in the conditions upon which it operates. In certain states of society, we find reproduction going ahead of the supply of food -- admitting that we take, for the terms of the problem, the apparent for the true law, in accordance with the views of Mr. Malthus. In other conditions of society, as in the case of the North American Indians, no such disproportion existed, previously to the European immigration. Only in certain states of society, claiming to be held as civilized, does history give any color to the assumption opposed to our theory of balance and harmony -- the preponderance of population in a country like Ireland being, however, well accounted for, as the necessary provision of a relatively redundant life, to meet the waste occasioned by societary and individual disorder. This, however, is not the normal condition of human existence -- not the orderly result of the supreme law which rules in the constitution of things. It is the casual conformity of constitutional forces to accidental exigencies.

Looking, now, to the constant advancement, and ultimate perfection, of civilization, what is it we may expect from the operation of the self-adjusting law, whose existence we thus have sought to establish? All the facts of the past tend to prove, that mere muscular labor, unenlightened toil, accompanied by a general feeling of security, and unattended, therefore, by those cares which stimulate to action the nervous system of the savage, favors fertility, or permits it in the highest degree known to experience -- that fertility being attended by great mortality. Civilization tending, however, towards the substitution of the natural forces for human labor, the life of the masses will not, in the future, be subjected to the lowest forms of drudgery -- the necessary result of this being, either that physical vigor will decline, and thus reduce fertility, or, that the diversion of energy from the muscular to the nervous system, will serve to diminish the ratio of procreation. Such result must be obtained, let the change of conditions be in whichsoever it may happen, of these directions. It is, however, to the latter of these changes, that we tend -- amelioration in our societary condition being the consequence of those improvements which tend to enlarge the sphere of intellectual activity, and stimulate the nervous system. The more society tends to take its natural form, the more does mind mingle with muscle in the labor of producing and converting the commodities required for man's support -- all these minglings tending, in happy proportion, towards diminution of fertility, and towards increase in the power for the maintenance of human life. Such being the case, we have here a self-acting law that, while explaining the past, foreshadows the future -- enabling us to see it, in the distance, working its way steadily and progressively, towards the accomplishment of ends whose beneficence is in perfect harmony with our ideas of the supreme wisdom, justice, and mercy, of the great Being by whom the laws were made.

Will the assumed progress be in intelligence generally -- in all the forms of mental acquirement which most decidedly direct the vital energy from the generative to the nervous structure? The general advancement of mind -- the multiplication of the means of culture -- the improvement of educational agencies, which levels instruction towards both the mental and pecuniary abilities of the masses -- the great enlargement of intellectual commerce resulting from a growing diversity as the demand for human services -- the increased facility of intercourse with distant men, whether in person or by correspondence -- and thousands of other changes that could be named, point, all, in this direction.

Will it be in individual morals and social justice? Real enlightenment,
resulting from the causes above described -- from the development of a
scientific agriculture, and consequent increase of power to command the
service of the earth and all its parts -- from the growing power of association and combination -- must, of its own proper force, increase its
growth in this direction. The more that growth, the greater must be the
tendency towards that prudential self-government, and towards that physical change in the appetencies and powers of the system, required for the
establishment of a perfect harmony between the growth of human life and
that of the raw materials of food and clothing needed for its maintenance.
Factitious civilization, attended by consolidation of the land -- decline
of agriculture -- diminution of the power to command the services of the
great natural forces, and growing power in the soldier and the trader to
control the societary movement -- must as certainly promote a growth in
the reverse direction. The more that growth, the greater must be the
tendency towards a reckless disregard of the duties and responsibilities
of life -- the greater must be the development of the mere sensual powers
at the expense of the intellectual -- the greater must be the discord between the increase of human life and that of the materials required for
life's support -- and the stronger must become the belief in the doctrine
of over-population. Seeking for proof of this last, we need but look to
all the countries that follow Britain in the effort to substitute trade
for commerce -- the highest evidence being found in Britain herself. Look-
inf for proof of the former, we shall find it in every country that adopts
the ideas of Colbert -- preferring the establishment of commerce to aug-
mentation of the power of trade.

That men of great mental activity are generally unprolific, has frequently
been remarked, and there will not, probably, be a single reader of this
volume who cannot find around him evidence of the truth of the proposition.
Occasionally, it becomes possible to trace the movements, in this respect,
of large bodies of men, and whenever it is so, we meet with facts tending
to the establishment of the idea that extinction of families follows
closely upon high development of the mental faculties.

Twenty years since, the number of British peers was 394, of whom no less
than 272 were the result of creations subsequent to 1760. From 1611 to
1819, no less than 753 baronetcies had become extinct; and yet, the total
number created had been less than 1400. Facts precisely similar to these
are found on looking to the noble families of Europe generally -- "Amelot,"
as we are told by Addison, "having reckoned that in his time 2500 nobles
who had voices in the council," whereas, there were not, at the time he
wrote, more than 1500, "notwithstanding the admission of many new families
since that time. It is very strange," as he continues, "that with this
advantage, they are not able to keep up their number, considering that
the nobility spread through all the brothers, and that so very few are
destroyed in the wars of the republic."

So, too, is it, when we turn to ancient Rome -- Tacitus telling us, that
"about the same time Claudius enrolled in the Patrician order, such of
the ancient senators as stood recommended by their illustrious birth,
and the merits of their ancestors. The line of these families, which
were styled by Romulus, 'the first class of nobility,' was almost extinct.
Even those of more recent date, created in the time of Julius Caesar, by
the Cassian law, and under Augustus, by the Saenian, were well nigh

exhausted."

Coming to more recent times, we find that of the 15 occupants of the
Presidential chair in this country, seven have been entirely childless,
while the total number of their children has been but little more than 20.
Looking abroad, the same great fact meets us almost everywhere -- Napoleon,
Wellington, the Foxes, Pitts, and other distinguished men, not having, as
a rule, left behind them the children required to fill the void created
by their decease. How it has been with Chaptal, Fourcroy, Berzelius,
Berthollet, Davy, and the thousand other distinguished names, scientific,
literary, and military, that have flashed before the public eye since the
days of Marlborough and Prince Eugene, we have no means of knowing with
any certainty; but the little that we have learned in regard to them,
has led to the conclusion that, could the whole be ascertained, it would
be found that the existing representatives of such men do not number more
than half as many as they did themselves.

That mental activity, of whatsoever kind, is unfavorable to reproduction,
will be found equally true, whether we examine the records of political,
military, or trading life. In proof of this, we may take the following
facts cited by Mr. Malthus, in regard to the city of Berne:--

"In the town of Berne, from the year 1583 to 1654, the sovereign council
had admitted into the Bourgeoisie 487 families, of which 379 became extinct in the space of two centuries, and in 1783 only 108 of them remained.
During the hundred years from 1684 to 1784, 207 Bernoise families became
extinct. From 1624 to 1712, the Bourgeoisie was given to 80 families.
In 1623, the sovereign council united the members of 112 different families, of which 58 only remain."*

Many other facts similar to these, in relation to the freemen of various
towns and cities of England, are given in a recent work on population --
the whole tending to prove that the excitement of trade is as unfavorable
to procreation as is that of science, or of politics.

Look where we may, we shall find evidence that the reproductive power in
man, is no more a constant quantity than is any other of his powers. It
may be stimulated into excessive activity by such a course of action as
tends to reduce him to the condition of a mere animal -- annihilating the
feeling of pride in himself, and of responsibility for his actions to his
fellow-men, or to his Creator. It diminishes as his various faculties are
more and more stimulated into action -- as employments become diversified
-- as the societary action becomes more rapid -- as land becomes divided
-- and as he himself becomes more free. Such, we believe, is the self-
adjusting law of population.

READING 6

Karl Marx (1818-1883) was born in Thiers, Germany, but spent much of his
adult life in England. During his formative years he familiarized himself
with the philosophy of Hegel, the socialism of several French authors, and
British political economy. His doctrines are built on these three foundations. Marx is usually regarded as the first non-utopian "scientific"
socialist. He limited himself to a critical appraisal of capitalism.

His views on population do not really constitute a population theory but
an attempt to explain unemployment. Marx stated again and again that
laborers are supplanted by machines and other equipment. The capitalist
owner of the means of production exploits the worker by paying him a subsistence wage and keeping him in the factory for long hours. Much of the
huge profit thus made is plowed back and a fast rate of expansion and
accumulation of productive equipment is achieved. But the new machines
and other equipment replace the laborers.

Marx always regarded the machine as a competitor of the worker, making
him invariably superfluous. Thus the industrialization process creates a
surplus of population relative to the number of jobs. The workers then
join what Marx calls the "industrial reserve army", which is the unemployed section of the labor force living in misery. In Marxian phraseology
the argument runs as follows:

The employer-entrepreneur divides his investable funds into two parts.
One part is used to buy machines and equipment, the other to pay wages.
Hence Marx's distinction between constant and variable capital, the latter
being the wage fund used to hire labor. With the accumulation of total
capital in a capitalist society, says Marx, the variable component (wage
fund) expands at a slower rate than constant capital. Marx here alludes
to the rapid accumulation of productive assets which took place in Britain
at the time he was living and writing in London. Therefore, Marx concludes,
the demand for labor, which is determined by variable capital, also declines relatively (although it might continue to grow in absolute terms).
This relative fall in demand is responsible for surplus population (unemployment).

It is clear, however, that even within the Marxian scheme, labour redun-
dancy would ensue only if there were an absolute shrinkage of the variable capital, unless a substantial and continuous population growth is
assumed. In fact, Marx supposed just that.

By tacitly assuming that population would always continue to expand in
this, like in so many other aspects, he remained a prisoner of Ricardian
economics -- Marx implicitly admitted that workers could themselves reduce the relative surplus population by diminishing their fertility. In
this respect he actually came "dangerously" close to what Malthus,

Ricardo, and John Stuart Mill had openly advocated, namely, that labor could raise its wages and welfare by holding back its own supply. Marx, however, did not develop this point. He was not interested in pragmatic considerations of how a net gain in welfare could be achieved. From the start he wanted to demonstrate that there was no hope for labor as long as the existing "capitalist" framework existed. He therefore urged that it should be overthrown and replaced by the dictatorship of the proletariat.[6]

---

[6] Source: K. Marx, Capital (Chicago: Kerr, 1919) Vol. 1, pp. 689-711.

THE PROGRESSIVE PRODUCTION OF A
RELATIVE SURPLUS- POPULATION UNDER CAPITALISM
Karl Marx

The accumulation of capital, though originally appearing as its quantitative extension only, is effected, as we have seen, under a progressive qualitative change in its composition, under a constant increase of its constant, at the expense of its variable constituent.

The specifically capitalist mode of production, the development of the productive power of labour corresponding to it, and the change thence resulting in the organic composition of capital, do not merely keep pace with the advance of accumulation, or with the growth of social wealth. They develop at a much quicker rate, because mere accumulation, the absolute increase of the total social capital, is accompanied by the centralisation of the individual capitals of which that total is made up; and because the change in the technological composition of the additional capital goes hand in hand with a similar change in the technological composition of the original capital. With the advance of accumulation, therefore, the proportion of constant to variable capital changes. If it was originally say 1:1, it now becomes successively 2:1, 3:1, 4:1, 5:1, 7:1, etc., so that, as the capital increases, instead of 1/2 of its total value, only 1/3, 1/4, 1/5, 1/6, 1/8, etc., is transformed into labour-power, and, on the other hand, 2/3, 3/4, 4/5, 5/6, 7/8 into means of production. Since the demand for labour is determined not by the amount of capital as a whole, but by its variable constituent alone, that demand falls progressively with the increase of the total capital, instead of, as previously assumed, rising in proportion to it. It falls relatively to the magnitude of the total capital, and at an accelerated rate, as this magnitude increases. With the growth of the total capital, its variable constituent or the labour incorporated in it, also does increase, but in a constantly diminishing proportion. The intermediate pauses are shortened, in which accumulation works as simple extension or production, on a given technical basis. It is not merely that an accelerated accumulation of total capital, accelerated in a constantly growing progression, is needed to absorb an additional number of labourers, or even, on account of the constant metamorphosis of old capital, to keep employed those already functioning. In its turn, this increasing accumulation and centralisation becomes a source of new changes in the composition of capital, of a more accelerated diminution of its variable, as compared with its constant constituent. This accelerated relative diminution of the variable constituent, that goes along with the accelerated increase of the total capital, and moves more rapidly than this increase, takes the inverse form, at the other pole, of an apparently absolute increase of the labouring population, an increase always moving more rapidly than that of the variable capital or the means of employment. But in fact, it is capitalistic accumulation itself that constantly produces, and produces in the direct ratio of its own energy and extent, a relatively redundant population of labourers, i.e. a population of greater extent than suffices for the average needs of the self-expansion of capital, and therefore a surplus-population.

Considering the social capital in its totality, the movement of its accumulation now causes periodical changes, affecting it more or less as a
whole, now distributes its various phases simultaneously over the different
spheres of production. In some spheres a change in the composition of capital occurs without increase of its absolute magnitude, as a consequence
of simple centralisation; in others the absolute growth of capital is
connected with absolute diminution of its variable constituent, or of the
labour-power absorbed by it; in others again, capital continues growing
for a time on its given technical basis, and attracts additional labour-
power in proportion to its increase, while at other times it undergoes
organic change, and lessens its variable constituent; in all spheres, the
increase of the variable part of capital, and therefore of the number of
labourers employed by it, is always connected with violent fluctuations
and transitory production of surplus-population, whether this takes the
more striking form of the repulsion of labourers already employed, or the
less evident but not less real form of the more difficult absorption of
the additional labouring population through the usual channels. With the
magnitude of social capital already functioning, and the degree of its increase, with the extension of the scale of production, and the mass of the
labourers set in motion, with the development of the productiveness of
their labour, with the greater breadth and fullness of all sources of
wealth, there is also an extension of the scale on which greater attraction
of labourers by capital is accompanied by their greater repulsion; the
rapidity of the change in the organic composition of capital, and in its
technical form increases, and an increasing number of spheres of production becomes involved in this change, now simultaneously, now alternately.
The labouring population therefore produces, along with the accumulation
of capital produced by it, the means by which itself is made relatively
superfluous, is turned into a relative surplus population; and it does
this to an always increasing extent. This is a law of population peculiar to the capitalist mode of production; and in fact every special historic mode of production has its own special laws of population, historically valid within its limits alone. An abstract law of population exists
for plants and animals only, and only in so far as man has not interfered
with them.

But if a surplus labouring population is a necessary product of accumulation or of the development of wealth on a capitalist basis, this surplus
population becomes, conversely, the lever of capitalistic accumulation,
nay, a condition of existence of the capitalist mode of production. It
forms a disposable industrial reserve army, that belongs to capital quite
as absolutely as if the latter had bred it at its own cost. Independently
of the limits of the actual increase of population, it creates, for the
changing needs of the self-expansion of capital, a mass of human material
always ready for exploitation. With accumulation, and the development of
the productiveness of labour that accompanies it, the power of sudden
expansion of capital grows also; it grows, not merely because the elasticity of the capital already functioning increases, not merely because
the absolute wealth of society expands, of which capital only forms an
elastic part, not merely because credit, under every special stimulus, at
once places an unusual part of this wealth at the disposal of production
in the form of additional capital; it grows, also, because the technical
conditions of the process of production themselves -- machinery, means of
transport, etc. -- now admit of the rapidest transformation of masses of
surplus product into additional means of production. The mass of social
wealth, overflowing with the advance of accumulation, and transformable

into additional capital, thrusts itself frantically into old branches of
production, whose market suddenly expands, or into newly formed branches,
such as railways, etc., the need for which grows out of the development
of the old ones. In all such cases, there must be the possibility of
throwing great masses of men suddenly on the decisive points without injury
to the scale of production in other spheres. Over-population supplies
these masses. The course characteristic of modern industry, viz., a decennial cycle (interrupted by smaller oscillations), of periods of average
activity, production at high pressure, crisis and stagnation, depends on
the constant formation, the greater or less adsorption, and the re-forma-
tion of the industrial reserve army or surplus population. In their turn,
the varying phases of the industrial cycle recruit the surplus population,
and become one of the most energetic agents of its reproduction. This
peculiar course of modern industry, which occurs in no earlier period of
human history, was also impossible in the childhood of capitalist production. The composition of capital changed but very slowly. With its accumulation, therefore, there kept pace, on the whole, a corresponding growth
in the demand for labour. Slow as was the advance of accumulation compared with that of more modern times, it found a check in the natural limits
of the exploitable labouring population, limits which could only be got
rid of by forcible means to be mentioned later. The expansion by fits
and starts of the scale of production is the preliminary to its equally
sudden contraction; the latter again evokes the former, but the former
is impossible without disposable human material, without an increase in
the number of labourers independently of the absolute growth of the population. This increase is effected by the simple process that constantly
"sets free" a part of the labourers; by methods which lessen the number
of labourers employed in proportion to the increased production. The
whole form of the movement of modern industry depends, therefore, upon
the constant transformation of a part of the labouring population into unemployed or half-employed hands. The superficiality of Political Economy
shows itself in the fact that it looks upon the expansion and contraction
of credit, which is a mere symptom of the periodic changes of the industrial cycle, as their cause. As the heavenly bodies, once thrown into a
certain definite motion, always repeat this, so is it with social production as soon as it is once thrown into this movement of alternate expansion and contraction. Effects, in their turn, become causes, and the varying accidents of the whole process, which always reproduces its own conditions, take on the form of periodicity. When this periodicity is once
consolidated, even Political Economy then sees that the production of a
relative surplus population -- i.e., surplus with regard to the average
needs of the self-expansion of capital -- is a necessary condition of
modern industry.

"Suppose," says H. Marivale, formerly Professor of Political Economy at
Oxford, subsequently employed in the English Colonial Office, "suppose
that, on the occasion of some of these crises, the nation were to rouse
itself to the effort of getting rid by emigration of some hundreds of
thousands of superfluous arms, what would be the consequence? That, at
the first returning demand for labour, there would be a deficiency. However rapid reproduction may be, it takes, at all events, the space of a
generation to replace the loss of adult labour. Now, the profits of our
manufacturers depend mainly on the power of making use of the prosperous
moment when demand is brisk, and thus compensating themselves for the interval during which it is slack. This power is secured to them only by
the command of machinery and of **manual** labour. They must have hands ready

by them, they must be able to increase the activity of their operations
when required, and to slacken it again, according to the state of the market, or they cannot possibly maintain the pre-eminence in the race of competition on which the wealth of the country is founded." Even Malthus
recognises over-population as a necessity of modern industry, though, after
his narrow fashion, he explains it by the absolute over-growth of the labouring population, not by their becoming relatively supernumerary. He
says: "Prudential habits with regard to marriage, carried to a considerable extent among the labouring class of a country mainly depending upon
manufactures and commerce, might injure it . . . From the nature of a population, as increase of labourers cannot be brought into market in consequence of a particular demand till after the lapse of 16 or 18 years, and
the conversion of revenue into capital, by saving, may take place much more
rapidly; a country is always liable to an increase in the quantity of the
funds for the maintenance of labour faster than the increase of population.
After Political Economy has thus demonstrated the constant production of a
relative surplus-population of labourers to be a necessity of capitalistic
accumulation, she very aptly, in the guise of an old maid, puts in the
mouth of her "beau ideal" of a capitalist the following words addressed to
those supernumeraries thrown on the streets by their own creation of additional capital:- "We manufacturers do what we can for you, whilst we are
increasing that capital on which you must subsist, and you must do the
rest by accommodating your numbers to the means of subsistence."

Capitalist production can by no means content itself with the quantity of
disposable labour-power which the natural increase of population yields.
It requires for its free play an industrial reserve army independent of
these natural limits.

Up to this point it has been assumed that the increase or diminution of
the variable capital corresponds rigidly with the increase or diminution
of the number of labourers employed.

The number of labourers commanded by capital may remain the same, or even
fall, while the variable capital increases. This is the case if the individual labourer yields more labour, and therefore his wages increase and
this although the price of labour remains the same or even falls, only more
slowly than the mass of labour rises. Increase of variable capital, in
this case, becomes an index of more labour, but not of more labourers employed. It is the absolute interest of every capitalist to press a given
quantity of labour out of a smaller, rather than a greater number of labourers, if the cost is about the same. In the latter case, the outlay of
constant capital increases in proportion to the mass of labour set in
action; in the former that increase is much smaller. The more extended
the scale of production, the stronger this motive. Its force increases
with the accumulation of capital.

We have seen that the development of the capitalist mode of production and
of the productive power of labour -- at once the cause and effect of
accumulation -- enables the capitlist, with the same outlay of variable
capital, to set in action more labour by greater exploitation (extensive
or intensive) of each individual labour-power. We have further seen that
the capitalist buys with the same capital a greater mass of labour-power,
as he progressively replaces skilled labourers by less skilled, mature
labour-power by immature, male by female, that of adults by that of young
persons or children.

On the one hand, therefore, with the progress of accumulation, a larger
variable capital sets more labour in action without enlisting more labourers; on the other, a variable capital of the same magnitude sets in
action more labour with the same mass of labour-power; and, finally, a
greater number of inferior labour-powers by displacement of higher.

The production of a relative surplus-population, or the setting free of
labourers, goes on therefore yet more rapidly than the technical revolution of the process of production that accompanies, and is accelerated by,
the advance of accumulation; and more rapidly than the corresponding
diminution of the variable part of capital as compared with the constant.
If the means of production, as they increase in extent and effective power,
become to a less extent means of employment of labourers, this state of
things is again modified by the fact that in proportion as the productiveness of labour increases, capital increases its supply of labour more
quickly than its demand for labourers. The over-work of the employed part
of the working class swells the ranks of the reserve, whilst conversely
the greater pressure that the latter by its competition exerts on the
former, forces these to submit to over-work and to subjugation under the
dictates of capital. The condemnation of one part of the working class to
enforced idleness by the over-work of the other part, and the converse,
becomes a means of enriching the individual capitalists, and accelerates
at the same time the production of the industrial reserve army on a scale
corresponding with the advance of social accumulation. How important is
this element in the formation of the relative surplus-population, is
shown by the example of England. Her technical means for saving labour
are colossal. Nevertheless, if tomorrow morning labour generally were reduced to a rational amount, and proportioned to the different sections of
the working class according to age and sex, the working population to
hand would be absolutely insufficient for the carrying on of national production on its present scale. The great majority of the labourers now
"unproductive" would have to be turned into "productive" ones.

Taking them as a whole, the general movements of wages are exclusively
regulated by the expansion and contraction of the industrial reserve army,
and these again correspond to the periodic changes of the industrial cycle. They are, therefore, not determined by the variations of the absolute number of the working population, but by the varying proportions in
which the working class is divided into active and reserve army, by the
increase or diminution in the relative amount of the surplus-population,
by the extent to which it is now absorbed, now set free. For Modern Industry with its decennial cycles and periodic phases, which, moreover,
as accumulation advances, are complicated by irregular oscillations following each other more and more quickly, that would indeed be a beautiful
law, which pretends to make the action of capital dependent on the absolute variation of the population, instead of regulating the demand and
supply of labour by the alternate expansion and contraction of capital,
the labour-market now appearing relatively under-full, because capital is
expanding, now again over-full, because it is contracting. Yet this is the
dogma of the economists. According to them, wages rise in consequence of
accumulation of capital. The higher wages stimulate the working population to more rapid multiplication, and this goes on until the labour-market becomes too full, and therefore capital, relatively to the supply of
labour, becomes insufficient. Wages fall, and now we have the reverse of
the medal. The working population is little by little decimated as the
result of the fall in wages, so that capital is again in excess relatively

to them, or, as others explain it, falling wages and the corresponding increase in the exploitation of the labourer again accelerates accumulation,
whilst, at the same time, the lower wages hold the increase of the working-
class in check. Then comes again the time, when the supply of labour is
less than the demand, wages rise, and so on. A beautiful mode of motion
this for developed capitalist production! Before, in consequence of the
rise of wages, any positive increase of the population really fit for work
could occur, the time would have been passed again and again, during which
the industrial campaign must have been carried through, the battle fought
and won.

Between 1849 and 1859, a rise of wages practically insignificant, though
accompanied by falling prices of corn, took place in the English agricultural districts. In Wiltshire, e.g., the weekly wages rose from 7s. to
8s.; in Dorsetshire from 7s. or 8s., to 9s., etc. This was the result
of an unusual exodus of the agricultural surplus-population caused by the
demands of war, the vast extension of railroads, factories, mines, etc.
The lower the wages, the higher is the proportion in which ever so insignificant a rise of them expresses itself. If the weekly wage, e.g., is 20s.
and it rises to 22s., that is a rise of 10 per cent; but if it is only
7s. and it rises to 9s., that is a rise of 28-4/7 per cent., which sounds
very fine. Everywhere the farmers were howling, and the London Economist,
with reference to these starvation-wages, prattled quite seriously of "a
general and substantial advance". What did the farmers do now? Did they
wait until, in consequence of this brilliant remuneration, the agricultural labourers had so increased and multiplied that their wages must fall
again, as prescribed by the dogmatic economic brain? They introduced more
machinery, and in a moment the labourers were redundant again in a proportion satisfactory even to the farmers. There was now "more capital" laid
out in agriculture than before, and in a more productive form. With this
the demand for labour fell, not only relatively, but absolutely.

The above economic fiction confuses the laws that regulate the general
movement of wages, or the ratio between the working class -- i.e. the
total labour-power -- and the total social capital, with the laws that
distribute the working population over the different spheres of production
If, e.g. in consequence of favourable circumstances, accumulation in a
particular sphere of production becomes especially active, and profits in
it, being greater than the average profits, attract additional capital,
of course the demand for labour rises and wages also rise. The higher
wages draw a larger part of the working population into the more favoured
sphere, until it is glutted with labour-power, and wages at length fall
again to their average level or below it, if the pressure is too great.
Then, not only does the immigration of labourers into the branch of industry in question cease; it gives place to their emigration. Here the
political economist thinks he sees the why and wherefore of an absolute
increase of workers accompanying an increase of wages, and of a diminution of wages accompanying an absolute increase of labourers. But he sees
really only the local oscillation of the labour-market in a particular
sphere of production -- he sees only the phenomena accompanying the distribution of the working population into the different spheres of outlay
of capital, according to its varying needs.

The industrial reserve army, during the periods of stagnation and average
prosperity, weighs down the active labour-army; during the periods of
over-production and paroxysm, it holds its pretensions in check. Relative

surplus-population is therefore the pivot upon which the law of demand and
supply of labour works. It confines the field of action of this law within
the limits absolutely convenient to the activity of explitation and to the
domination of capital.

This is the place to return to one of the grand exploits of economic apol-
ogetics. It will be remembered that if through the introduction of new,
or the extension of old, machinery, a portion of variable capital is transformed into constant, the economic apologist interprets this operation
which "fixes" capital and by that very act sets labourers "free", in exactly the opposite way, pretending that it sets free capital for the labourers. Only now can one fully understand the effrontery of these apol-
ogists. What are set free are not only the labourers immediately turned
out by the machines, but also their future substitutes in the rising generation, and the additional contingent, that with the usual extension of
trade on the old basis would be regularly absorbed. They are now all
"set free", and every new bit of capital looking out for employment can
dispose of them. Whether it attracts them or others, the effect on the
general labour demand will be nil, if this capital is just sufficient to
take out of the market as many labourers as the machines threw upon it.
If it employs a smaller number, that of the supernumeraries increases;
if it employs a greater, the general demand for labour only increases to
the extent of the excess of the employed over those "set free". The im-
pulse that additional capital, seeking an outlet, would otherwise have
given to the general demand for labour, is therefore in every case neut-
ralised to the extent of the labourers thrown out of employment by the
machine. That is to say, the mechanism of capitalistic production so
manages matters that the absolute increase of capital is accompanied by
no corresponding rise in the general demand for labour. And this the
apologist calls a compensation for the misery, the sufferings, the possible death of the displaced labourers during the transition period that
banishes them into the industrial reserve army! The demand for labour is
not identical with increase of capital, nor supply of labour with increase
of the working class. It is not a case of two independent forces working
on one another. Les des sont pipes.Capital works on both sides at the
same time. If its accumulation, on the one hand, increases the demand for
labour, it increases on the other the supply of labourers by the "setting
free" of them, whilst at the same time the pressure of the unemployed
compels those that are employed to furnish more labour, and therefore
makes the supply of labour, to a certain extent, independent of the supply
of labourers. The action of the law of supply and demand of labour on this
basis completes the despotism of capital. As soon, therefore, as the
labourers learn the secret, how it comes to pass that in the same measure
as they work more, as they produce more wealth for others, and as the
productive power of their labour increases, so in the same measure even
their function as a means of the self-expansion of capital becomes more
and more precarious for them; as soon as they discover that the degree of
intensity of the competition among themselves depends wholly on the pressure of the relative surplus-population; as soon as, by Trades' Unions,
etc., they try to organise a regular cooperation between employed and unemployed in order to destroy or to weaken the ruinous effects of this
natural law of capitalistic production on their class, so soon capital
and its sycophant, political economy, cry out at the infringement of the
"eternal" and so to say "sacred" law of supply and demand. Every combination of employed and unemployed disturbs the "harmonious" action of this
law. But as soon as (in the colonies, e.g.) adverse circumstances prevent

the creation of an industrial reserve army and, with it, the absolute dependence of the working class upon the capitalist class, capital, along
with its commonplace Sancho Panza, rebels against the "sacred" law of
supply and demand, and tries to check its inconvenient action by forcible
means and State interference.

The relative surplus population exists in every possible form. Every labourer belongs to it during the time when he is only partially employed or
wholly unemployed. Not taking into account the great periodically recurring forms that the changing phases of the industrial cycle impress on it,
now an acute form during the crisis, then again a chronic form during dull
times -- it has always three forms, the floating, the latent, the stagnant.

In the centres of modern industry -- factories, manufactures, ironworks,
mines, etc. -- the labourers are sometimes repelled, sometimes attracted
again in greater masses, the number of those employed increasing on the
whole, although in a constantly decreasing proportion to the scale of
production. Here the surplus population exists in the floating form.

In the automatic factories, as in all the great workshops, where machinery
enters as a factor, or where only the modern division of labour is carried
out, large numbers of boys are employed up to the age of maturity. When
this term is once reached, only a very small number continue to find employment in the same branches of industry, whilst the majority are regularly discharged. This majority forms an element of the floating surplus-
population, growing with the extension of those branches of industry. Par
of them emigrates, following in fact capital that has emigrated. One consequence is that the female population grows more rapidly than the male,
teste England. That the natural increase of the number of labourers does
not satisfy the requirements of the accumulation of capital, and yet all
the time is in excess of them, is a contradiction inherent to the movement of capital itself. It wants larger numbers of youthful labourers,
a smaller number of adults. The contradiction is not more glaring than
that other one that there is a complaint of the want of hands, while at
the same time many thousands are out of work, because the division of
labour chains them to a particular branch of industry.

The consumption of labour-power by capital is, besides, so rapid that
the labourer, half-way through his life, has already more or less completely lived himself out. He falls into the ranks of the supernumeraries
or is thrust down from a higher to a lower step in the scale. It is precisely among the work-people of modern industry that we meet with the
shortest duration of life. Dr. Lee, Medical Officer of Health for Manchester, stated "that the average age at death of the Manchester ...
upper middle class was 38 years, while the average age at death of the
labouring class was 17; while at Liverpool those figures were represented
as 35 against 15. It thus appeared that the well-to-do classes had a
lease of life which was more than double the value of that which fell to
the lot of the less favoured citizens." In order to conform to these circumstances, the absolute increase of this section of the proletariat must
take place under conditions that shall swell their numbers, although the
individual elements are used up rapidly. Hence, rapid renewal of the
generations of labourers (this law does not hold for the other classes of
the population). This social need is met by early marriages, a necessary
consequence of the conditions in which the labourers of modern industry
live, and by the premium that the exploitation of children sets on their

production.

As soon as capitalist production takes possession of agriculture, and in proportion to the extent to which it does so, the demand for an agricultural labouring population falls absolutely, while the accumulation of the capital employed in agriculture advances, without this repulsion being, as in non-agricultural industries, compensated by a greater attraction. Part of the agricultural population is therefore constantly on the point of passing over into an urban or manufacturing proletariat, and on the look-out for circumstances favourable to this transformation. (Manufacture is used here in the sense of all non-agricultural industries.) This source of relative surplus-population is thus constantly flowing. But the constant flow towards the towns presupposes, in the country itself, a constant latent surplus-population, the extent of which becomes evident only when its channels of outlet open to exceptional width. The agricultural labourer is therefore reduced to the minimum of wages, and always stands with one foot already in the swamp of pauperism.

The third category of the relative surplus-population, the stagnant, forms a part of the active labour army, but with extremely irregular employment. Hence it furnishes to capital an inexhaustible reservoir of disposable labour-power. Its conditions of life sink below the average normal level of the working class; this makes it at once the broad basis of special branches of capitalist exploitation. It is characterised by maximum of working time, and minimum of wages. We have learnt to know its chief form under the rubric of "domestic industry". It recruits itself constantly from the supernumerary forces of modern industry and agriculture, and specially from those decaying branches of industry where handicraft is yielding to manufacture, manufacture to machinery. Its extent grows, as with the extent and energy of accumulation, the creation of a surplus population advances. But it forms at the same time a self-reproducing and self-perpetuating element of the working class, taking a proportionally greater part in the general increase of that class than the other elements. In fact, not only the number of births and deaths, but the absolute size of the families stand in inverse proportion to the height of wages, and therefore to the amount of means of subsistence of which the different categories of labourers dispose. This law of capitalistic society would sound absurd to savages, or even civilised colonists. It calls to mind the boundless reproduction of animals individually weak and constantly hunted down.

The lowest sediment of the relative surplus-population finally dwells in the sphere of pauperism. Exclusive of vagabonds, criminals, prostitutes, in a word, the "dangerous" classes, this layer of society consists of three categories. First, those able to work. One need only glance superficially at the statistics of English pauperism to find that the quantity of paupers increases with every crisis, and diminishes with every revival of trade. Second, orphans and pauper children. These are candidates for the industrial reserve-army, and are, in times of great prosperity, as 1860, e.g., speedily and in large numbers enrolled in the active army of labourers. Third, the demoralised and ragged, and those unable to work, chiefly people who succumb to their incapacity for adaptation, due to the division of labour; people who have passed the normal age of the labourer; the victims of industry, whose number increases with the increase of dangerous machinery, of mines, chemical works, etc., the mutilated, the sickly, the widows, etc. Pauperism is the hospital of the active labour-army and

the dead weight of the industrial reserve-army. Its production is included in that of the relative surplus-population, its necessity in theirs;
along with the surplus-population, pauperism forms a condition of capitalist production, and of the capitalist development of wealth. It enters
into the faux frais of capitalist production; but capital knows how to
throw these, for the most part, from its own shoulders on to those of the
working class and the lower middle class.

The greater the social wealth, the functioning capital, the extent and
energy of its growth, and, therefore, also the absolute mass of the proletariat and the productiveness of its labour, the greater is the industrial
reserve-army. The same causes which develop the expansive power of capital, develop also the labour-power at its disposal. The relative mass of
the industrial reserve-army increases therefore with the potential energy
of wealth. But the greater this reserve-army in proportion to the active
labour-army, the greater is the mass of a consolidated surplus-population,
whose misery is in inverse ratio to its torment of labour. The more extensive, finally, the lazarus-layers of the working class, and the industrial reserve-army, the greater is official pauperism. This is the absolute general law of capitalist accumulation. Like all other laws it is
modified in its working by many circumstances, the analysis of which does
not concern us here.

The folly is now patent of the economic wisdom that preaches to the labourers the accommodation of their number to the requirements of capital. The
mechanism of capitalist production and accumulation constantly effects
this adjustment. The first word of this adaptation is the creation of a
relative surplus-population, or industrial reserve-army. Its last word is
the misery of constantly extending strata of the active army of labour,
and the dead weight of pauperism.

The law by which a constantly increasing quantity of means of production,
thanks to the advance in the productiveness of social labour, may be set
in movement by a progressively diminishing expenditure of human power,
this law, in a capitalist society -- where the labourer does not employ
the means of production, but the means of production employ the labourer
-- undergoes a complete inversion and is expressed thus; the higher the
productiveness of labour, the greater is the pressure of the labourers
on the means of employment, the more precarious, therefore, becomes their
condition of existence, viz., the sale of their own labour-power for the
increasing of another's wealth, or for the self-expansion of capital. The
fact that the means of production, and the productiveness of labour, increase more rapidly than the productive population, expresses itself,
therefore, capitalistically in the inverse form that the labouring population always increases more rapidly than the conditions under which capital can employ this increase for its own self-expansion.

We saw in Part IV, when analysing the production of relative surplus-value:
within the capitalist system all methods for raising the social productiveness of labour are brought about at the cost of the individual labourer; all means for the development of production transform themselves into
means of domination over, and exploitation of, the producers; they multi-
late the labourer into a fragment of a man, degrade him to the level of an
appendage of a machine, destroy every remnant of charm in his work, and
turn it into a hated toil; they estrange from him the intellectual potentialities of the labour-process in the same proportion as science is

incorporated in it as an independent power; they distort the conditions
under which he works, subject him during the labour-process to a despotism
the more hateful for its meanness; they transform his life-time into
working-time, and drag his wife and child beneath the wheels of the Jugger-
naut of capital. But all methods for the production of surplus-value are
at the same time methods of accumulation; and every extension of accumulation becomes again a means for the development of those methods. It
follows therefore that in proportion as capital accumulates, the lot of
the labourer, be his payment high or low, must grow worse. The law, finally, that always equilibrates the relative surplus-population, or industrial reserve army, to the extent and energy of accumulation, this law
rivets the labourer to capital more firmly than the wedges of Vulcan did
Prometheus to the rock. It establishes an accumulation of misery, corresponding with accumulation of capital. Accumulation of wealth at one pole
is, therefore, at the same time accumulation of misery, agony of toil,
slavery, ignorance, brutality, mental degradation, at the opposite pole,
i.e. on the side of the class that produces its own product in the form
of capital.

This antagonistic character of capitalistic accumulation is enunciated in
various forms by political economists, although by them it is confounded
with phenomena, certainly to some extent analogous, but nevertheless essentially distinct, and belonging to precapitalistic modes of production.

The Venetian monk Ortes, one of the great economic writers of the 18th
century, regards the antagonism of capitalist production as a general
natural law of social wealth. "In the economy of a nation, advantages and
evils always balance one another (il bene ed il male economico in una
nazione sempre all, istessa misura): the abundance of wealth with some
people, is always equal to the want of it with others (la copia dei beni
in alcuni sempre eguale alla mancanza di essi in altri): the great riches
of a small number are always accompanied by the absolute privation of the
first necessaries of life for many others. The wealth of a **nation** corresponds with its population, and its misery corresponds with its wealth.
Diligence in some compels idleness in others. The poor and idle are a
necessary consequence of the rich and active", etc. In a thoroughly bru-
tal way about 10 years after Ortes, the Church of England parson, Townsend,
glorified misery as a necessary condition of wealth. "Legal constraint
(to labour) is attended with too much trouble, violence, and noise, ...
whereas hunger is not only a peaceable, silent, unremitted pressure, but
as the most natural motive to industry and labour, it calls forth the
most powerful exertions." Everything therefore depends upon making hunger
permanent among the working class, and for this, according to Townsend,
the principle of population, especially active among the poor, provides.
"It seems to be a law of nature that the poor should be to a certain degree improvident" [i.e. so improvident as to be born without a silver
spoon in the mouth], "that there may always be some to fulfil the most
servile, the most sordid, and the most ignoble offices in the community.
The stock of human happiness is thereby much increased, whilst the more
delicate are not only relieved from drudgery...but are left at liberty
without interruption to pursue those callings which are suited to their
various disposition ... it [the Poor Law] tends to destroy the harmony
and beauty, the symmetry and order of that system which God and Nature have
established in the world." If the Venetian monk found in the fatal destiny
that makes misery eternal, the raison d'etre of Christian charity, celibacy, monasteries and holy houses, the Protestant prebendary finds in it

a pretext for condemning the laws in virtue of which the poor possessed
a right to a miserable public relief.

"The progress of social wealth", says Storch, "begets this useful class
of society ... which performs the most wearisome, the vilest, the most
disgusting functions, which takes, in a word, on its shoulders all that is
disagreeable and servile in life, and procures thus for other classes
leisure, serenity of mind and conventional [c'est bon!] dignity of character." Storch asks himself in what then really consist the progress of
this capitalistic civilisation with its misery and its degradation of the
masses, as compared with barbarism. He finds but one answer: security!

"Thanks to the advance of industry and science", says Sismondi, "every
labourer can produce every day much more than his consumption requires.
But at the same time, whilst his labour produces wealth, that wealth would,
were he called on to consume it himself, make him less fit for labour."
According to him, "men" [i.e. non-workers] "would probably prefer to do
without all artistic perfection, and all the enjoyments that manufactures
procure for us, if it were necessary that all should buy them by constant
toil like that of the labourer ... Exertion today is separated from its
recompense; it is not the same man that first works, and then reposes;
but it is because the one works that the other rests ... The indefinite
multiplication of the productive powers of labour can then only have for
result the increase of luxury and enjoyment of the idle rich."

Finally, Destutt de Tracy, the fish-blooded bourgeois doctrinaire, blurts
out brutally: "In poor nations the people are comfortable, in rich nations
they are generally poor."

READING 7

The following article is the editor's translation of a speech the Swedish economist Knut Wicksell (1851-1926) gave in the Hague in 1910 at an international conference of Neo-Malthusians.[7] The lecture was given in German and later published in a German Neo-Malthusian periodical called Die Neue Generation (The New Generation).

Throughout his career Wicksell seems to have believed that the population problem was the most important social question. In the earliest editions of his Forelasningar i nationalekonomie (Lectures on Political Economy) he had devoted an entire chapter to the subject. The English translation of the lectures, however, was made from the third edition, in which the chapter on population had been left out.

In 1909 Wicksell published a revision of this chapter as a separate pamphlet entitled Laran om Befolkningen (The Theory of Population). In it he presents theoretical considerations with regard to the optimum concept that are very similar to the contents of the address he gave in the Hague. Building upon J. S. Mill, Wicksell formulates the concept of the optimum population. That particular size that maximizes real output per worker is called the optimum population for a given nation with a closed economy.

According to Wicksell, a growing population has two effects. It raises productivity because it makes possible a better division of labor and greater specialization. It decreases productivity by worsening the relationship between physical resources and the human production factor. Before the optimum is reached, the first factor prevails; population growth increases per capita output. Once the optimum is exceeded, the second factor is more important; further population expansion reduces the per capita output.

---

[7] Source: K. Wicksell, "Das Optimum der Bevolkerung", Die Neue Generation (October 1910), pp. 383-391.

THE POPULATION OPTIMUM
Knut Wicksell

People generally speak of _the_ population question; but in reality, there are at least two such questions which should be carefully separated although they are related to each other in several ways.

The first of these questions is nothing more than the well-known "Malthusian Dilemma". Since man's natural capacity to procreate exceeds by a wide margin what any civilized country needs to maintain an approximate balance between the number of births and deaths, and if we want at the same time to avoid an otherwise necessary increase in death rates, then we have no other choice but to prevent the number of births from reaching their natural level.

And here begins the problem that we, as Neo-Malthusians, have set ourselves namely, to reach that goal in such a manner as will serve human happiness better and with less negative effects than the method which Malthus himself recommends, namely the postponement of marriage. Malthus had, by the way, a rather light-hearted idea of the consequences. He says, in essence, that postponement of marriage would undoubtedly lead to greater immorality, such as prostitution, etc., all consequences he feels himself forced to reprove as a moralist, but he hoped that our judge in heaven, able to weigh sin against temptation, would render a milder judgement. This really is a rather antiquated way to discuss social questions.

But there exists another population problem, one which belongs more properly in the sphere of economics and which for this reason should attract the attention of economists. To have gained a firm conviction about the ways and means of keeping a population within precise limits is by no means enough; for we should first ask ourselves what those limits are. In other words: if we take a country with specific economic conditions, and a given size, location, fertility of the soil, etc., and also an average of level of technical knowledge of its population, then the question arises as to what population size and density would then guarantee everyone the maximum share of well-being and would thus, economically speaking, be the best. It is possible for a country to maintain for centuries a constant population and yet be terribly overpopulated, so that it suffers from all the ills of overpopulation throughout the entire period. On the other hand, if for some reason a sudden population growth is urgently needed, then the Neo-Malthusian method of population control would be as inappropriate as the old Malthusian method; in such circumstances there should be no reduction of numbers and, presumably, there would not be any.

The importance of this observation can hardly be denied and since it is of a strictly scientific character it is probable that people will ask me what the experts have to say about the guidelines leading to a decision whether the existing population of a country is as large as it should be, too small or too large. Unfortunately, however, one hears not a word, not

a single word, from the experts about this. They are mute on this issue.
One can peruse the entire economic literature from now until next Christ-
mas without finding this salient point even mentioned by economists.

Some of these economists really seem to think -- even if they do not openly
admit it -- that the greatest possible population is naturally the best,
even if -- had they read and understood one line of Malthus -- they should
be well aware of the fact that on the contrary, the largest population is
the worst of all for a country. Others, who are a little more cautious,
will perhaps admit that a population can grow too rapidly and that it
might eventually become too numerous in the far distant future. But very
few among them will have the slightest doubt that their own country should
be much more populated than it is at present. And yet if Malthus' assertion is correct that population always strives to reach the maximum (that
is, the worst population size) then the suspicion arises that the current
situation is the second worst is strengthened.

When science is so confused on this point we can hardly expect the laymen
to be better informed, and in fact, they are not. Only a few weeks ago
several well-known French statesmen including M. D'Estournelles de Constant,
have busily inquired about the means to promote a faster population growth
in France. But I ask you: has it been proven that the French population
should grow at all; by whom and in what way has it been proven that the
greater mass of Frenchmen would be better off if their numbers were greater? Probably the reverse would be true. Probably the material and moral
living conditions of the French would be much better if the country's
population were only one-half or perhaps one-fourth of the present number.

If we assume that this fact were indeed proved; would M. D'Estournelles
de Constant and his friends take it upon their conscience to advise population growth even though this would cause the economic well-being of the
population to decline?

Now let us examine the case of England and Germany. In the history of
the entire world there is probably nothing which can be compared with the
technical and economic development of England and Germany (although perhaps I should refer only to their development in the second half of the
19th century). And what are the results? Not too long ago a German statistician (P. Mombert)[1] felt himself called upon to assert that approximately one-half of the current German population must be viewed as under-
nourished. And in England, too, it is certain that the majority of the
population does not come close to the condition which could have been expected after such a magnificent and encompassing industrial development.
Does the number of people have nothing to do with these deplorable facts?
Would this obvious failure have been so great if the population had experienced a slower growth or had not grown at all? Doesn't it almost go
without saying that with no population growth, such development as took
place could not have helped but leave its traces by causing a very substantial increase in the welfare of the great masses? If this is so,
would not the most certain and perhaps the only way to better the living
conditions of the masses be to reduce the number of people as soon as
possible to the same level as that of fifty years ago?

---

[1] The German economist-demographer P. Mombert has written numerous
studies on population problems the most important being: Bevolkerungs-
lehre (Jena: Fischer, 1929), 490 p. (editor's footnote).

However, Mr. Kautsky, one of the leaders of the German socialists, tells
us in his latest book that, for his political party a population question
does not exist at all.[1] He says that if the socialist system came into
being the people could multiply themselves faster than ever for at least
another century. I don't believe that he is correct in this instance,
but that is not the point. The question is not what the people could do,
but what they should do. If one accepted the socialist system and all
that can be expected of it with the greatest optimism, then would the
German people, for example, be happier with 70 or 100 million people rather
than with a population of only 35 million (as they had fifty years ago)?
That is the question, and that question is certainly extant. It may perhaps be solved one way or another but it cannot be shaken off; it cannot
be ignored.

It is not my intention, and time does not allow me, to give you more than
the bold outlines of the solution to this gigantic problem. Naturally,
when population grows, two opposing forces become operative. On the one
hand, the productivity of labor diminishes when everyone has a smaller
share of land, or natural resources in general, to work with. On the
other hand, the united human efforts, the division of labor, the cooperation, the organization of industry, etc., are always important and under
certain circumstances of considerable importance in the subjugation of the
forces of nature. At the point where these tendencies cancel each other
out is indeed the true optimum population. However, this stage is not
fixed. The profusion of new discoveries and the growth of technical knowledge will most often, if not always, displace it. However, to argue
that this stage has not yet been reached because new inventions are still
to come shows a very unclear way of thinking. It can have been entirely
exceeded at that particular time. A little boy receives a new pair of
shoes every six months, every time receiving a size larger than before.
If, however, the shoes were every time one size too small he would obviously suffer throughout his entire growth period from tight shoes. And so
it is with this case. The population of a century ago had probably exceeded its optimum considerably. The population living in those years
would perhaps now be the optimum, and the current population may, for all
I know, be the optimum in another 100 years. But in any case, that is no
reason to multiply the current number of people or even to keep it constant. We do not live in the future, nor do we live today from the successes of future inventions.

Mr. Kautsky gives as the sole basis for his opinion, by which he denies
the existence of the population problem, the assurance that if modern
agricultural techniques were universally applied, the total harvest per
"morgen"[2] could be doubled and even tripled. But this proves nothing as
long as one does not know whether this result could be obtained with a
relatively larger or relatively smaller input of labor. Naturally, his
assertion would be crucial if the aim were to improve productivity per
"morgen" of land and not the condition of men. Insofar, however, as it
is (or should be) our intention to further human happiness, we must rather
pay attention to inventions which raise total agricultural output per

---

[1] The work in question was probably: "Vermehrung und Entwicklung in
     Natur und Gesellschaft" (editor's footnote).

[2] "Morgen" is a unit of cultivation varying from 0.6 to 0.9 acres
     (editor's footnote).

worker, and not per "morgen". Such inventions exist, even outstanding
ones, but they commonly require the possibility of more land per worker
and therefore a diminution, rather than a further concentration, of the
rural population. It has been noted that, in Argentina, two men are said
to be able, with the help of modern agricultural machinery, to plow, sow,
and harvest not less than 500 "morgen" or wheatland. The crop yield comes
to about 100 tons of wheat annually. This is not a very large harvest per
"morgen", it is even a rather small one; however, it is a considerably
larger output per worker than has ever been witnessed at any time in any
part of the world. The same rule will undoubtedly hold true in industry.
The most far-reaching and most successful inventions are always those
which replace human energy by inanimate energy, while inventions which
replace non-human energy by human energy or use man's energy more intensively, have understandably limited possibilities for efficient use. In
order to be able to make a claim to usefulness such inventions must often
assume that each individual would or must be satisfied with a smaller share
of output. The latter category of inventions will nevertheless be valuable to landowners as well as industrial entrepreneurs (perhaps to an even
greater degree as population grows and cheap labor becomes available).
Here we have the origin of the common complaint that agriculture and sometimes even industry, suffers from a "lack of labor". But this point will
not be agreeable to a socialist, such as Mr. Kautsky. Thus I believe that
we are correct in asserting that all real progress which was realized
during the past century, or the last fifty years, was realized not because
of, but in spite of, a simultaneous growth in population, and that with a
smaller population the level of aggregate output would have been somewhat
smaller, but that per capita output would have been considerably higher
than it is today.

Next to these purely materialistic considerations we have to add the asthe-
tic importance of having population which is not too dense. It is important that every individual should have the possibility of enjoying the
beauty and grandeur of nature and to satisfy the need to be sometimes
alone, a need to which Mill alludes so admirably in his "Reflections on
the Stationary State" (Principles Book 4, Chapter 6). Professor Marshall,
the well-known English economist almost makes fun of Mill's sentimentality
and emphasizes instead "the growing enrichment of human life when the
backwoodsman finds neighbors who settle around him, and the backwood settlements gradually grow into villages." But surely there must be a golden
mean between new settlements in the woods and the ghettos of the poor in
our big cities.

I have, I believe, said enough to convince you that a problem exists which
is well worth the mutual interest of the politicians and the economists.
It is a rewarding, if difficult, issue which has been irresponsibly neglected until now. When all of you return to your homelands, I would en-
treat you to try to get your scholars involved in this question. Please
ask them the following questions: "Professor, what do you think of the
optimum population with respect to our own country? Do you think that
we have not yet reached it, or just reached it, or overstepped it considerably at the present time?" I am certain that none of them will have a
suitable answer ready. Very probably they will only give you a look of
utter incomprehension. If you do not cease your questions you will slowly
force your men of science to look for an answer to your question, and this
answer will, I believe, arouse their concern a bit too. In any case, if
you manage to destroy the common superstition (unfortunately also shared

by many economists) that the optimum population is related to the greatest population density you will have done a good job. They are two entirely different concepts. The densest population (the maximum) is the most unfavorable (the pessimum) for a country.

READING 8

Professor Edwin R. A. Seligman (1861-1939) was born in New York City and studied economics and law at Columbia University as well as at the Universities of Berlin, Heidelberg, and Paris.

From 1885 to 1931 he taught economics at Columbia University. According to Seligman the real issue is no longer a conflict between food and numbers. What counts is who wins the race between population and labor on the one hand and productivity on the other. In a progressive economy (U.S., United Kingdom, etc.) capital goods increase faster than population. Besides, the quality of the labor force has continually improved and the state of technical and organizational knowledge has progressed. With increasing labor efficiency, employees become more valuable to their employers, which permits wages and salaries to rise. The rise in prosperity, moreover, says Seligman, sets into motion forces that depress fertility. For these two reasons, there is, according to Seligman, no longer much reason for Malthusian fears. Unfortunately, Seligman does not explain why higher levels of socioeconomic development result in lower fertility levels. Data for Northwestern Europe generally show declining birth rates after 1870. This was due to such factors as growing urbanization, the rising costs of rearing children, the prohibition of child labor (thus making it impossible for the child to contribute to the family income), and the improved status of women.[8]

---

[8] Source: E. R. A. Seligman, Principles of Economics (8th ed., New York: Longmans, Green, 1919), pp. 63-66.

POPULATION, PRODUCTION AND INCOME DISTRIBUTION
Edwin R. A. Seligman

With reference to population, however, two considerations have been advanced to offset the contentions of Malthus, -- the biological and the
socio-economic arguments. The biological argument asserts that the power
of reproduction itself diminishes with more complex and civilized beings,
and points to the small families of the higher classes and to the increasing sterility of the New England women. This argument, however, is by no
means indisputable; and it is above all uncertain whether the diminishing
ratio is natural or artifical, -- that is, whether or not it is a result
of volition. The socio-economic argument claims that, as a consequence
of general social as well as economic reasons, the size of families varies
inversely with wealth, and thus keeps down the ratio of increase. With
the poorest classes every child is regarded as a prospective bread-winner,
and to that extent not only a help in the near future but an additional
support for old age. This leads to early and often improvident marriages
and large families. In the next stratum of society the demands of education and of the maintenance of a social position induce more deliberation
in marriage, and effectively bar the probability of so numerous a progeny.
Finally, where wealth is abundant, the desire carefully to train a few
rather than to half train many children, as well as the wish to escape the
nervous strain of a numerous offspring, conspire to restrict the number of
children. The French peasant is not so different from the average American or European resident of a large city. The economic motive may be
slightly stronger with the former, the other social motives slightly
stronger with the latter; but in essence they are alike. Here again, however, the argument is not anti-Malthusian; for the phenomena just described are the results of prudential considerations, and really fall under the head of the preventive agencies mentioned by Malthus.

It might seem, then, that Malthus was right in his premises; and since
the preventive considerations are proverbially weak in the poorer classes,
it might be claimed that he was also justified in his gloomy forebodings.
This conclusion, however, does not follow. The real antithesis is proxi-
mately at least not between population and food, but between population
and wealth, or productive efficieny. Through a proper organization and
utilization of improved methods, production of wealth in general may be so
augmented as to permit an increase both in population and in prosperity.
This has happened, for instance, all through the nineteenth century, even
in the older countries of Europe; the industrial revolution has not only
multiplied national wealth, but has greatly increased population, while
reducing misery, vice and crime. It might be contended, indeed, that this
is exceptional, because the increased numbers have after all been dependent ultimately upon the food supply which they have secured from the
newly opened areas of North and South America; and it might be added that
the population of these countries is increasing so rapidly that sooner or
later they also will have no surplus food to export. Even granting this
contention, however, and looking forward to the distant time when all the

huge and now uncultivated areas of the earth's surface will be utilized
for food production, it still remains true that the increase of wealth
may for almost indefinite periods keep ahead of population. For, as was
intimated in the last chapter, a really intensive capitalistic system of
agricultural production has never yet been attempted on a large scale. If
there is enough wealth to put into the soil, it can be transmuted into
food. The diminishing returns from land can be arrested by the increasing
returns of a rapidly augmenting efficiency of industry in general. The
food may indeed cost more, but there will be more wealth with which to
buy it.

Not only can wealth be made to increase faster, but, as we have seen, the
increase of wealth will in itself set in motion those economic and sociological forces which tend to reduce the rate of increase of population.
Thus from both sides the antithesis of wealth and population may be weakened. Under favorable conditions population may increase gradually, and
wealth rapidly.

It is clear, however, that these favorable conditions include those of
distribution as well as production. The communists against whom Malthus
wrote were mistaken, but not for the reason alleged by him. They thought
that a mere change in the distribution of wealth would suffice to bring
prosperity. They failed, just as the socialists of today still fail, to
realize that even an ideal distribution is valueless without enough to
divide, and that their schemes would dangerously impair productive efficiency. On the other hand, the wages-fund doctrine of the English classical economists erred, as we shall learn, chiefly in that it overlooked the
connection between wages and production, and took no account of the fact
that, given a greater productive efficiency, more workmen and higher wages
are perfectly compatible.

The problem of population as a whole is, then, not one of mere size, but
of efficient production and equitable distribution. That is, it is a problem not of numbers alone but of wealth. Since man is the chief labor
force, large numbers indeed, other things being equal, mean greater national strength and power. But the reverse may be true if other things are
not equal. A small nation with greater productive efficiency, like England, will outrank a more populous country, like India. Smaller numbers
with a fairly equable distribution of wealth are preferable to a dense
population living in the extremes of misery and opulence. Mere numbers
are therefore not the vital point. The world has alternated in its opinion and action. In classic antiquity, where the absence of advanced industrial methods soon set a limit to production, over-population was a
real danger, tempered first by emigration and then by infanticide. In the
middle ages population was sparse, and yet, because of undeveloped production, kept down by famine and disease. With the growth of enterprise
in the fifteenth and sixteenth centuries, increase of population was favoured but not always secured. The conditions at the close of the eighteenth century seemed to lend color to the fears of Malthus; but for well-
nigh a century the concern in the advanced industrial countries has been
not of an unduly rapid but of an unduly slow increase of population;
until in France today it has become a problem not of excessive fecundity
but of race suicide.

The doctrine of over-population has therefore lost its terrors for modern
society. The stress has been shifted from food to wealth and efficiency.

Productive efficiency, however, depends not only upon character and education, intellectual, industrial and ethical, but also upon social organization and economic methods. The problem of population, in short, is today a part of the broader problem of the production and distribution of wealth. In this sense it is a result rather than a cause. If we increase productive efficiency and secure an approach to distributive justice, population will adjust itself to the new conditions either by increasing automatically up to the level of comfortable subsistence or by being voluntarily kept down to that level.

PART TWO

THE POPULATION DEBATE
IN THE INTERWAR YEARS

READING 9

John Maynard Keynes (1883-1946) does not need much introduction. He was
born in Cambridge, England, where his father taught logic and economics at
Cambridge University. After completing his education and a short period
in the civil service, Keynes became a professor of economics at Cambridge.

After the First World War the population problem once more drew attention.
During the conflict England's dependence on overseas supplies of food and
raw materials had been laid bare. As some of the customary channels of
international trade had been interrupted, nations like England, Germany,
and the Netherlands had faced very difficult times. After the war the
United Kingdom was plagued by heavy unemployment. This had many causes,
such as overexpansion in certain industries during the war in order to
meet the war-time needs, the loss of international markets that had been
neglected, the rise of new, sharply-competing industrial nations such as
the U.S.A. and Japan, and the overvaluation of the pound sterling, which
made English commodities relatively expensive abroad.

Such considerations, however, cannot be disconnected from the population
issue. There was no denying the fact that England's rapidly growing population had become dependent on a complex and fragile system of international trade and that further demographic growth only worsened the situation. Keynes had already commented on this situation in his essay The
Economic Consequences of the Peace, in which he argued that until 1914
Europe's prosperity had depended upon an intricate system of international trade on favorable terms. Food and raw materials were cheaply imported from the U.S.A. and other countries and manufactured goods were
sold at relatively high prices. The "Malthusian Devil", to use Keynes's
terminology, was forgotten. World War I, however, shattered this system
and made Europe aware that it could not even feed its dense populations.

In the following reading Keynes follows a different line of thought.
The enormous annual increments in the labor force due to high birth rates
fifteen and more years earlier required heavy investments to maintain
existing ratios between capital and labor and hence productivity levels.
Keynes wonders whether Britain could make the needed effort in saving
the investment. The article was produced in 1922 and appeared in the
"Manchester Guardian Commercial."[9]

---

[9]Source: J.M. Keynes, "An Economist's View of Population," Manchester
Guardian Commercial (August, 1922) pp. 340-341.

AN ECONOMIST'S VIEW OF POPULATION
John Maynard Keynes

A belief in the material progress of mankind is not old. During the
greater part of history such a belief was neither compatible with experience nor encouraged by religion. It is doubtful whether, taking
one century with another, there was much variation in the lot of the un-
skilled labourer at the centres of civilization in the two thousand years
from the Greece of Solon to the England of Charles II, or the France of
Louis XIV. Paganism placed the Golden Age behind us; Christianity
raised Heaven above us; and anyone, before the middle of the eighteenth
century, who had expected progressive improvement in material welfare
here, as a result of the division of labour, the discoveries of science
and the boundless fecundity of the species, would have been thought very
eccentric.

In the eighteenth century, for obscure reasons which economic historians
have not yet sufficiently explored, material progress commenced over
wide areas in a decided and cumulative fashion, not experienced before.
Philosophers were not laggard with an appropriate superstition, and before the century was out Priestley was fashionable when he wrote that,
by the further dividion of labour, --

> "Nature, including both its materials and its laws, will be more
> at our commend; men will make their situation in this world abun-
> dantly more easy and comfortable; they will prolong their existence
> in it and will grow daily more happy."

It was against the philosophers of this school that Malthus directed
his Essay. Its arguments impressed his reasonable contemporaries, and
the interruption to progress by the Napoleonic wars supplied a favourable atmosphere. But as the nineteenth century proceeded, the tendency
to material progress (from causes better understood than those which
first initiated the movement in the early eighteenth century) reasserted
itself. Malthus was forgotten or disbelieved. The cloud was lifted;
the classical Economists dethroned; and the opinions of the Vicar of
Wakefield who "was ever of opinion that the honest man who married and
brought up a large family did more service than he who continued single
and only talked of population," and of Adam Smith who held that "the most
decisive mark of the prosperity of any country is the increase of the
number of its inhabitants," recovered their sway, until, both before and
since the war, -- to judge from the utterances of English Bishops,
French politicians, German economists and Bolshevik Russians, -- public
opinion does not differ very much from what it was in 1790.

Nevertheless the interruption to prosperity by the war, corresponding
to the similar interruption a hundred years before, has again encouraged
an atmosphere of doubt; and there are some who have a care. The most

interesting question in the world (of those at least of which time will
bring us an answer) is whether, after a short interval of recovery,
material progress will be resumed, or whether, on the other hand, the
magnificent episode of the ninettenth century is over.

In attempting to answer this question it is important not to exaggerate
the direct effects of the late war. If the permanent underlying influences are favourable, the effects of the war will be no more lasting than
were those of the wars of Napoleon. But if, even before the war, the
underlying influences were becoming less favourable, then the effects of
the war may have been decisive in settling the date of transition from
progress to retrogression. In this case the future historian, though
he may take 1914 as the dividing date between two eras, may possibly prefer the last quinquennium of the nineteenth century as the culminating
period of the economic forces which had been driving the modern world.

I hesitate to give the pessimistic answer. It is hard to detect the
underlying influences whatever they may be. But there are certain
observations which an economist is entitled to make.

Progress during the nineteenth century was an affair of acceleration.
It depended essentially on perpetual expansion; its organization pre-
sumed this; and it could not have taken the same form in a stable
society. Some of the expanding elements are not capable of further
expansion to the same extent as before. The exploitation of new
natural resources, though not yet exhausted, has not the same possibilities as a hundred years ago. The economies of large-scale operations
and the principle of increasing return are diminishing in importance,
because in many cases no important additional economies are any longer
obtainable from further increasing the scale. On the other hand, we may
still regard the possibilities of scientific improvements as unlimited,
in spite of the fact that we now have steam, electricity, and oil behind
us, instead of to come.

On the balance of considerations, however, it would not be prudent to
assume that we can continue to expand the material resources of the
world in the same geometrical progression during the next fifty years
as during the past fifty. The economic argument, therefore, would urge
us to slow down the acceleration and to prepare the social structure
for a return to conditions of quantitative stability.

On the other side press the forces of Population. Malthus taught an
essential truth when he laid down the most criticized of all his dicta,
namely that Population always tends to increase in a geometrical progression. This must not be taken so literally as to imply that the
birth-rate is always the same. It means that the birth-rate is cumulative. As the population increases any given excess of the birth-
rate over the death-rate means a constantly greater increase in absolute
numbers. It is certain that sooner or later this state of affairs must
come to an end. An accelerating Society may persist for a shorter or a
longer period, but it cannot last; and in a given area, such as Great
Britain or Europe, expansion will be brought to an end sooner than in
the world as a whole.

The great impending peril to human happiness arises out of the combination of this situation with the fact that the life of a man, sixty
or seventy years, is very long compared with the rate at which his
surroundings are changing. New births do not exercise their full effects on Society until many years after they occur; and when once a
disequilibrium exists and the population is definitely excessive, many
years must elapse before the balance can be restored, except by violent
methods.

Two instances are sufficient to illustrate this. The population of
Vienna is described below in an article by Professor Pibram. Circumstances have suddenly arisen which render the pre-existing population
largely superfluous; yet it is difficult to see how it can be sufficiently reduced by any painless method except after an interval of decades. This is a problem about which the Viennese have been for the
last four years balmeably happy-go-lucky. In my opinion the proposals
of Professor Pribram, though they are in the right direction, are far
too moderate.

The other example is on a greater scale and is to be derived from Dr.
Brownlee's figures for the age distribution of the population of England
and Wales. It primarily illustrates the "time-lag," referred to above,
due to the length of human life. People now living of the age of
sixty and upwards are the survivors of those born in 1860 and earlier,
when the population was not much above half what it is now, with the
result that the burden of old people which we are now carrying is only
half of what it would be in a stable population of the same size. But
there is another anologous figure not less important. If we assume, for
the sake of simplicity of illustration, that the working life of a man
is from 17 to 67, the number of additional workmen offering themselves
for employment annually depends, with due allowance for rate of survival,
on the difference between the birth-rates 17 years ago and 67 years ago.
That is to say, the annual changes in the supply of labour at the present
moment do not depend on anything that is happening now or even recently,
but on events some of which took place in 1855 at the time of the
Crimean War and none of which took place later than 1905. Thus they
depend on influences which are mainly irrelevent to present circumstances; and however great the disequilibrium which results, compensating forces cannot produce their full effect for twenty years and
more, unless they are actually destructive of life. Such violent compensation is in fact highly improbable; and what is much more likely
to occur is a slow but steady lowering in the standard of living which
will not occur suddenly, at a given moment, in melodramatic fashion,
reported in the newspapers, but will proceed by slow and scarcely
perceptible degrees.

In Great Britain we are supporting a body of unemployed much beyond
what we can afford to support permanently. A large part of this unemployment is due to the depression of trade from which in due course
we shall recover. But it is necessary to remember that the number of
males between 20 and 60 is, in spite of war casualties, 1,300,000 more
than it was in 1911, a number considerably in excess of the total unemployed. It is not sufficient, therefore, that our trade should recover to its pre-war volume of activity, -- which is generally the

utmost for which we now hope; it must be on a substantially larger scale,
approximately 15 per cent larger than in 1911, if we are not to lose ground
Moreover, for many years to come, regardless of what the birth-rate may be
from now onwards, upwards of 250,000 new labourers will enter the labour
market annually in excess of those going out of it. To maintain this
growing body of labour at the same standard of life as before, we require
not only growing markets but a growing capital equipment. In order to
keep our heads above water, the national capital must grow as fast as the
national labour supply, which means new savings at the rate of ₤400,000,000
to ₤500,000,000 per annum. Whether we can reckon on the continuance of
this, in view of the change in many of the circumstances which, during the
nineteenth century, were specially favourable to saving is at least doubtful.

Thus there certainly exists a problem. And the same problem as I have
outlined above for Great Britain is present in an even acuter form in
some other parts of Europe. Possibly unforeseeable developments may intervene to help us out. Possibly natural forces tending back towards equilibrium may come into action of themselves in good time. But failing the
unforeseen the problem is, I think, of much greater magnitude than can be
solved by Dr. Brownlee's expedient of emigration, which is only an expensive palliative.

Indeed the Problem of Population is going to be not merely an economist's
problem, but in the near future the greatest of all political questions.
It will be a question which will arouse some of the deepest instincts and
emotions of men, and feeling may run as passionately as in earlier strug-
gles between religions. The issue is not yet joined. But when the instability of modern society forces the issue, a great transition in human
history will have begun, with the endeavour by civilized man to assume
conscious control in his own hands away from the blind instinct of mere
predominant survival.

READING 10

The following reading contrasts sharply with Keynes's pessimism. Its author is Eugene Gustave Dupreel, born (1879) in Malines, Belgium. He taught sociology at the Free University of Brussels. This reading consists of selections from a paper he presented in 1920 at the Institute of Sociology of the University of Brussels.

Dupreel was a French-speaking Belgian sociologist. The relatively low birth rates in France after 1870 (relative to Germany) and the heavy losses suffered by France during World War I created strong pronatalist currents in that country. One finds in the literature of that period many attempts to explain why high demographic growth rates are advantageous. About the ultimate consequences of such rates -- a greater population density -- little is said, although in a much later work (Sociologie Generale, 1948), Dupreel does make a clear distinction between (1) a large population, (2) a dense population, and (3) a growing population.

Dupreel's main theme here is that population growth is highly stimulating and conducive to socioeconomic progress. Man needs strong external factors to exert himself. Without some strong stimulus, apathy and inertia tend to prevail. Population growth is precisely such a factor. If it occurs in a society that finds itself in an equilibrium position, the initial result is likely to be a certain disorder; but during the movement towards a new equilibrium, a burst of innovations occurs and people take new initiatives. These activities lead to a new more profitable equilibrium position.[10] Traces of Dupreel's theories can be found in the works of Alfred Sauvy (General Theory of Population, 1969) and Albert Hirschman (The Strategy of Economic Development, 1958). Hirschman's position is that rapid population growth can stimulate economic development because it gives rise to repercussions and counter-pressures that more than offset the initial disadvantages.

---

[10] Source: E. Dupreel, Les Variations Demographiques et le Progres (Brussels: Imprimerie Scientifique et Litteraire, 1922).

DEMOGRAPHIC CHANGE AND PROGRESS

Eugene G. Dupreel

The author of this document has assembled a series of sociological
analyses which converge to demonstrate that social progress and civilization are a product of the numerical increases of societies.

A—DEMOGRAPHIC CHANGE AND THE CHOICE OF PROFESSIONS.

A large number of children per family is the regular cause for an increase in population. But certain differences have always been noticed
between the behavior of members of large families and that of small
families with only one or two children. One conspicuous difference is in
the choice of professions.

In a situation of equal income, the child who has grown up in a small
family finds himself in a privileged situation; his parents are prepared
and willing to make more sacrifices for him than the heads of large
families can make for their children. Because of this an only child, for
example, may choose among a larger number of careers; those careers which
demand a costly and time-consuming preparation are therefore more open to
him than to others. He will thus enter professions judged the most desirable either by himself or by his parents.

It would be an error to believe that in the choice of a profession, the
parties concerned make a rigorous and objective analysis of the advantages and disadvantages, or that they decide according to the real value
of the available careers. Observation reveals, to the contrary, that
certain characteristics of these careers are much more influential than
others. The most annoying disadvantages are the most immediate, those
nearest in time. Young people, and even more so their parents, are
highly sensitive to the social position associated with the earliest
stages of a particular career. Those who have the greatest freedom
of choice will value especially those which do not involve difficult or
particularly humiliating beginnings, but which to the contrary provide
an early and lasting social prestige. Examples are administrative careers
and the liberal professions; in them, both the young civil servant and
the student are from the outset considered to be on a par with the
social class in which they are likely to remain throughout their lives.
At least they stand at the threshold of this class, with the prospect
of entering into it without descending below the level at which their
family had maintained itself until then.

On the contrary, much more frequently something trying marks the beginning of the child who grows up with many brothers and sisters. Necessity is paramount, impossible sacrifices make him forget certain preferences; careers that bring immediate prestige, being the most envied,

are the least accessible, barred by the lack of money and time. It is
necessary to choose other professions whose beginnings are unattractive
and which involve association with inferior social classes. Such are
certain business and industrial careers, characterized at the outset by
manual labor or by relatively menial associations. Another form of difficult beginning is migration. The two forms are often combined: one
being born into the middle class, is only willing to appear as a manual
laborer in a locality different from where he grew up and there he was
known.

But, on the other hand, careers of the first type, those in which one
benefits immediately from all the social prestige they imply, are the
most stratified. The advantages from the beginning are counterbalanced
by a relative slowness in advancement and by all sorts of limitations,
notably the material ones. Business and industrial careers are less
restricted and allow, notwithstanding the mediocrity of their beginnings,
an indefinite climb up the ladder of success and fortune, and they
yield the esteem which follows these two results. These careers are
thus more flexible.

The results from all this will be that men who come from small families
will limit themselves to activities that scarcely do more than maintain
and reinforce the existing institutions and structures of society.
Men from large families but with otherwise identical origins are led
to adopt professions and life styles that reward the spirit of enterprise, courage, and daring. The lowering of status from which they
will have suffered at first will create in them the ambition first to
return to and then to pass beyond the point of departure.

The spirit that the normal evolution of small families introduces into
a society will be a spirit of dignity and preservation; the spirit
created by the descendants of large families will be a spirit of initiative and creativity....Effects of demographic variations on the
social hierarchy in general or on the relationships of equality and inequality between individuals and groupes....

Numerical increase tends to upset social barriers and formal inequalities
which existed in the society before the increase started. This proposition...is based on two premises, one which we propose to call social
advancement.

Social advancement: The demographic structure of a people does not
depend in the same manner upon the different social strata of a population. The so-called inferior classes are those which have a predominant influence on this regime. This becomes immediately evident if one
considers that these classes are usually the most numerous; but there
are also causes of a more complex order. The upper classes depend
strictly, for the number of their members, on the size of the lower
classes. For example, one could not conceive of an aristocracy
growing indefinitely without altering its status, while the laboring
classes remained stationary. Either it would certainly lose much of
its prestige by the redistribution of the same privileges over a far
larger number (that is, by relative impoverishment), or--and this has
been a common phenomenon in history--a part of its members would become
impoverished and would intermingle with the lower classes. The normal
starting point of an overall increase in numbers is, therefore, an increase of the lower classes of the population.

But by the same law that we have just invoked, if prosperity permits the
common people to grow in number, there is room for an increase in size
of the upper classes; and the vacant spots can be occupied by people
coming from the lower social strata: a net upward social mobility will
result.[1] This upward movement will assert itself in very different ways;
one of the most frequent is a fact that we have already made use of in the
preceding analysis [the author refers to paragraphs not here included]:
A population which increases expands its administrations; it calls for
more civil servants, and advancement in the administrative hierarchy is a
cause of upward mobility; the son of a peasant or worker ends his career
in well-paid jobs and his family has definitely become part of the middle
class.

Success in commercial and industrial enterprise is another aspect of the
same phenomenon. A growing population transforms a large number of small
businessmen or small entrepreneurs into wealthy and respected people,
managing important business firms and producing in their turn more middle-
class members. Thus, a social ascension generalizes itself. The phenomenon repeats itself so often that it appears to be built-in optimism and
confidence in the future spread which encourages ambition and provides an
incentive to work and to take risks. To improve one's condition is the
goal of each person and the characteristic shape of the social effort;
that is what we propose to call "social advancement"... If one takes a
snapshot of a society where this "social advancement" is intense, one
will find each person on the move toward a social situation judged better,
and the single common measure of the level attained by each one will be,
in the long run, no longer the status of the family, or its origins, but
instead a person's life style and what conditions it -- money ...

In societies with a stationary population, the social system and the
psychological atmosphere tend to become entirely different. Upward mobility from the lower classes ceases or slows down; the chances to get
ahead or to become rich by starting with nothing become thin; optimism
and confidence in the future do not prevail; the dominating preoccupation
becomes not to rise in the world, but to avoid retrogression. People
grow concerned with the preservation of what they have and with emphasizing the situation in which they originally found themselves. Staying
essentially at the level where he is born, each person attaches himself
to what symbolizes this level. Hence the importance of birth, of trans-
mittable titles, of closed relationships and everything that accentuates
separation from the lower strata. Continuous possession, its indefinite
transmission from generation to generation in a society in equilibrium
where change is exceptional, leads to a system of castes and to the
corresponding psychology ...

---

[1] Dupreel inserts here the unexamined assumption of rising prosperity
(editor's footnote).

B—GENERAL CONSIDERATIONS.

Analyses of the kind which have just been outlined lead one to perceive that there are common characteristics in all societies with growing populations, and that the combination of these characteristics corresponds sufficiently with what one means by the concepts social progress and civilization. It is in growing societies that there are the best chances to find a generalized tendency to innovate, as well as a sufficient effort to conserve those innovations and to combine them with one another in a manner to provoke, on the one hand, an increasingly more nearly perfect adjustment of certain means to certain ends and, on the other, an indefinite renewal of the means and ends which people have in view.

Societies in a state of stagnation or numerical decrease present rather the opposite characteristics: be it the unchanging repetition of a certain way of doing things, be it even a progressive impoverishment of social activity in volume and in variety.

Let us ask ourselves what is the profound nature of this phenomenon; what is the common mechanism that operates in all the forms of social activity that we have passed in review. If the demographic factor has repercussions on all societies and on all aspects of their activities, it must act more or less directly on all the members of these societies: can this action be singled out?

Let us consider a growing society at a given moment of its existence. Among its members, some are already established; these are the old-timers. Others get in, and these newcomers are in greater number than those who depart. As we have already noticed, every society tends to be self-sufficient without the newcomers; it is normally adapted to its dimensions. The immediate effect of the newcomers' arrival[1] is to provoke an increase in the burdens and a relative decrease in the advantages that everybody enjoys. The newcomers provoke, therefore, a discomfort, they are the cause of a relative loss suffered by the old-timers.

For their part, the newcomers, who arrive in a society where jobs are taken and all positions filled, take root and prosper there only at the price of extra efforts by which they manage to assert themselves and to be a part of it. The most immediate and consistent effect of an increase in the members of a society is, therefore, a relative disadvantage shared between all individuals which manifests itself in the difficulties affecting the old-timers as well as the newcomers.

---

[1] The author probably refers here to the net increments to the labor force or entrants in excess of outgoers (editor's footnote).

But this initial disadvantage is overcome; otherwise the increase in population stops and the phenomenon we are attempting to understand no longer
exists. The obstacle is overcome by mutual concessions, by an intensification of efforts, and by initiatives which the novelty of the situation
provokes and which for that matter issue principally from the newcomers
themselves. The phenomenon of progress, set in motion by the numerical
increase, can therefore be divided into three phases: (1) a relative
disadvantage; (2) efforts to overcome it (greater intensity of effort
and initiatives); and (3) new equilibrium with an advantage over the old
state of affairs.

In static societies, this mechanism has fewer chances to operate; the
individual is always pigeon-holed in the same functions; he himself car-
ries on without improving upon the work of his predecessors. Nothing
pressing incites him to make extra efforts or to accept or prompt innovations. Of innovations he perceives only the disorder they entail and the
discomfort they invariably cause him. This leads us to pass from the
formal aspect of the question to the psychological.

In all societies man has always been spontaneously inclined to head only
toward immediate advantages; the sacrifice of an actual advantage in
order to obtain a distant reward appeals a great deal less to him. If
nothing forces it to make changes, the human species confines itself to
routine as do all known living species. The aversion of middle-class
families to employment that entails an initial lowering of social status,
which our first analysis stressed is only a typical example of this fundamental psychological inertia.

What numerical increase introduces are the necessity for each person to
accept relative disadvantages, which is the price to be paid for future
advantages; and the need to overcome the psychological inertia that leads
people to shun risks and the provisional disadvantages and initial detri-
ments that accompany all innovations.

The relative discomfort and scarcity, the first results of numerical increase, force individuals to exercise certain influences over each other
as well as themselves. This reciprocal action manifests itself in three
aspects characterized by these words: <u>concession</u>, <u>submission</u>, and <u>pres-
sure</u>.

The newcomer strains his talents to offer to the old-timers advantages
which they denied themselves until then (concessions); in order to be
accepted in society, the entrant conforms to its rules and conventions
with an ostensible and systematic punctuality (submission); just as he
adjusts himself to the wishes and whims of the old-timers. It is the
young and the newcomers who maintain the conventions, notably the moral
laws, by their eagerness to adjust themselves as soon as their education
has vanquished their primary indocility. Finally, the newcomer uses all
the means at his disposal to hold his ground and to advance in social
rank (pressure; pressure of children on the parents, of young people on
their protectors, and of those on society in favor of their dependents,
etc.). Reciprocally, one could show that the three types of pressure are
found among the old-timers as well, to the extent that they are the indirect cause of the population growth, or simply to the extent that they
resign themselves to it. The most obvious case is that of the family:
the parents make sacrifices for their children (concessions); they are

less free than those who have no parental responsibilities to question
the conditions their employers offer to them or to question society's
laws (submission); in the final analysis, they exercise pressure on
society in favor of the young.

Our point is that while multiplying all these interrelations of concession,
submission, and pressure between individuals, old-timers, and newcomers,
numerical growth increases the "social tension" of the society under consideration. It tightens the bonds of the members; it makes of each one
of them a center of initiatives and introduces into the community as a
whole the need to combine and structure these initiatives. What is usually called the progress of civilization reduces itself to this double
phenomenon: individuals who strain their talents to innovate and who
strive to take advantage of the forthcoming initiatives by combining them.

The character of stationary societies, where all positions are stereotyped
and where all lines of work have become well adjusted to one another in
the course of time, becomes repetitious; these societies are normally
characterized by a progressive decrease in social tension. Each person,
holder of a social status fortified by time, without hope of social ascent
and afraid to see his lot deteriorate, rejects every new concession, shows
repugnance toward every disrespectful form of obedience, and does not care
to exercise pressure on others... .

READING 11

Professor E. M. East (1878-1938), a genetist and agricultural economist who taught at Harvard University, published in 1924 a work in which we find the earliest calculation of the carrying capacity of the earth, or the population maximum.[11]

In his estimate of future demand, East considers only the population factor. Population expands exponentially at a regular yearly percentage rate. The growth in absolute numbers, however, keeps swelling as the growth rate is applied to an ever larger base. But rising incomes also affect the future demand for agricultural products, and East neglects this factor.

Turning to the supply side, East estimates that on this planet thirteen billions acres are available for cultivation. This estimate has not changed much since East made his calculations. The total land area of the world is about 32 billion acres, excluding Antarctica. Half of that is too cold or too arid for growing crops. Between three and four billion acres are already used for agricultural purposes. About five billion acres are used for meadows and pastures, and some nine billion acres are forested. It is at the expense of the latter two categories that cropland can be increased, although not without considerable investment. East's estimate that 2.5 acres are needed to sustain one person is now too high because hybrids and the use of large applications of chemical fertilizers have increased present yields to levels far above those in 1920.

Professor East also draws a picture of what the world will look like at the end of the twentieth century if population growth continues. East's prophesies are gloomy although they may now seem relatively optimistic compared with some contemporary forecasts of world-wide doom.

---

[11] Source: E. M. East, Mankind at the Crossroads (New York: Scribner's, 1924, pp. 67-71; pp. 346-347.

FOOD AND POPULATION
Edward M. East

Mankind has had an average annual increase during the past century of about
0.7 per cent, and the increase at present is as great as at any time during
the past. My own estimate of this current material increase, from a careful study of all available data, is about 12 millions. In other words,
there are almost two new Belgiums to feed just now with each additional
year, and the number is increasing like a compound-interest table. And my
own estimate is conservative, since Knibbs, one of the most eminent of our
contemporary population statisticians, estimates the current increase at
1.16 per cent, or nearly 20 millions a year. By his calculation the world
must provide for a new France at every biennium.

What do these huge figures mean in terms of food and land? Pitkin has
recently calculated them in his carefully written book Must We Fight
Japan?, which because of its seemingly jingoistic title has not had the
serious consideration it deserves. Arguing from the army rations of the
civilized world, he shows that the average adult requires a thousand
pounds of dry foodstuffs per year. Allowing for natural loss and provision
for seed, then, every year the farmer must provide the world with some
23,000 million pounds of foodstuffs more than they ever provided before if
the people are to be fed. Translating these figures into land requirements
is still more staggering. On the average it takes from two to three acres
to support a man. Thus every season the tillers of the soil must prepare,
plant, cultivate, and harvest nearly 40 million acres more than they did
the year before unless they can persuade mother earth to give up more of
her bounties than has been her habit of yore. And, with few exceptions,
every new plot of virgin soil subdued is just a little worse than that
which went before.

It is easy to see that a rate of natural increase such as this could not
possibly have been in force during earlier periods of the world's history,
unless it be assumed that periodic catastrophes far beyond anything of
which there is record have practically wiped out the human race. It takes
merely the evaluation of a problem of compound interest to show that a
single pair of human beings would have produced the present world population in less than 1800 years. Even the low rate of increase in France
(.0016) just before the war, when France was being held up to scorn by
ill-informed publicists as a decadent nation, would take our hypothetical
Adam and Eve back to only 10,000 years before Christ.

The current rate of growth, according to Knibbs, doubles the population
every 60 years. If it were possible to maintain it, therefore, our great-
grandchildren would live to see some 7,000 millions struggling for life,
while in the year 3000 A.D. there would be the stupendous number of 34,000
million souls. Thus, says Knibbs, it is certain that however great human
genius or effort may be in enlarging the world's food-supplies, this rate
cannot be maintained for many centuries.

There are various methods by which to confirm this conclusion. A production calculation is perhaps as convincing as any. Excluding the arctics,
the land area of the world is 33,000 million acres. The International
Institute of Agriculture at Rome has determined the proportion of cultivated land to total area in the most populous countries, which are generally
the countries with the greatest relative amount. On the average it is
about 40 per cent. If a similar proportion of the land area of the entire
globe is assumed to be the maximum limit for arable land, there are 13,000
million acres available for food production.

The number of people this huge world farm can support will vary with the
progress of the art of agriculture, with the provision for transportation
and for storage, with the security of property, with the efficiency of
human effort, with the type and the amount of food consumed per capita,
and with the margin of safety necessary to tide over the years when the
crops are poor.

I have made a rather extended study of this matter, based on the assumption that there will be sane beneficent governments, adequate means of
distribution, constant efficient effort equal to that of western Europe
during periods of peace, agricultural production equivalent to a return
per acre midway between the average and the best in the world today, and
a standard of living on a parity with what is found in the more densely
populated countries of Europe. This study has led to the conclusion that
a reasonable maximum for the world's future population is one person for
each 2.5 acres on 40 per cent of the land area of the globe. This gives
a figure of 5,200 millions, a population which at the present rate of
increase would be reached in just a little over a century.

Let us emphasize this result. Under the most optimistic assumptions as to
production and distribution of food that it is reasonable to make, the
world can support but 5,200 millions of people; and these people must
content themselves with the limited dietary and the few material necessities which form the current standards among the peasantry of Europe.
Furthermore, if the present rate of increase could continue unabated,
babies now alive would live to see this event come to pass. The world
would be filled with people without faith or hope, a seething mass of dis-
contented humanity struggling for mere existence, within the span of a
single lifetime...

These calculations allow the same proportion of the population of the
future to be supported by sea food as is supported at present, and it is
a grave question whether more than this is possible. It is easy to see
a food source of limitless extent in the tremendous water area of the
globe - an area four times that of the land. But one feels constrained
to discount too great an optimism when he looks into the facts. Plants
are as much the primary foods of the sea as of the land, and scarcely any
of the important species can be used directly. There is a carnivorous
succession through several mouths before they come to our tables as mack-
erel or salmon, with much waste in the process. Most of these plants are
probably found in the shallow waters less than 200 feet in depth, for
light is essential in their elaboration. It has been estimated that the
plant growth in such situations is about equal to primary food production
on land, and the depth maps of the sea show that this area is roughly
equal to 5 per cent of the land area of the globe...

Let us look forward and draw a picture of the world as it would be at the
end of the century with a continued expansionist policy. Food exportation
had ceased some thirty years before, except for the exchange of specialties;
all temperate regions had then reached the era of decreasing returns in
agriculture. The tropics are being populated as fast as their submission
to the hand of man makes it possible. Gradual reduction in population
increase has occurred, due to the intensity of the struggle; yet there
are 3,000 million people in the world. Migration has ceased; the bars
have been put up in every country. Those nations where there is still a
fair degree of comfort wish to retain it as long as possible. Food is
scarce and costly. Man works from sun to sun. When crops are good there
is unrest but no rest, there is privation and hardship; when crops are
bad there is mass starvation such as China and Russia had experienced long
before. Agricultural efficiency has risen 50 per cent during the past
half-century through the pressure of stern necessity, yet the food resources of each individual are smaller than ever before. Where war occurs
it is a war of extermination, for only by extermination can the conquerors
profit; where peace remains it is under the shadow of a struggle as grim
as war. Morale has weakened, and with it morals. The death-rate has
risen until it equals the birth-rate. And the potential fecundity of the
human race still remains at about 60 per thousand annually. It is not a
pretty picture, but I do not believe it to be overdrawn. It is a portrait
of the China and India of today, and the China and India of today will be
the world of tomorrow when the world as a whole reaches the same population status.

READING 12

The following paper was grouped with other writings in a publication entitled <u>Population Problems in the United States and Canada</u>. It was written by A. B. Wolfe, born 1876, Professor of Economics at Ohio State University from 1923 to 1946.

In this paper Wolfe restates and develops Wicksell's concept of the optimum population, which is now carefully formulated in terms of per capita income. We also find in this paper an early version of the capital adjustment theory, i.e., the extra public investments on infrastructure, housing, land reclamation, and so forth which population growth imposes on a society. Wolfe also expresses a more general environmental concern. Wolfe criticizes the light-hearted super optimists and the pronatialist nationalists, of whom there were an increasing number in the 1920's and 1930's (especially in France and the Fascist countries). Nationalists favor a dense and growing population, which, in their view, maximizes national power. But they disregard the welfare of the individual human being, considering a person to be a means rather than an end.

Wolfe finally argues that the economists and sociologists of his day have devoted too little attention to the various obstacles to a rational population policy and the motivational factors that induce people to limit the size of their families.[12]

---

[12]
    Source: L. J. Dublin (ed.), <u>Population Problems in the United States and Canada</u> (Boston: Houghton, Mifflin, 1926), pp. 63-76.

THE OPTIMUM SIZE OF POPULATION
Albert B. Wolfe

The outstanding feature of current literature on population is the interest it reveals in the potentialities of growth. Biologists and statisticians are vying with one another to show us with what astounding speed
the present rate of increase, if continued, would carry us to the physical limit of subsistence. The 'geometrical ratio' has been rediscovered.

One brief but riotous century has doubled the world's population. The
total number of people now on the earth is put conservatively at 1.7 billion. At the present rate, numbers double every sixty years. A continuation of this rate would result at the end of each of the next four centuries in populations of 5, 17, 60, and 171 billion respectively. If our
own present rate of doubling every five decades were to continue, persons
now living would see a population in the United States of 250 million.
Unless, therefore, this increase is quickly and greatly retarded, the
saturation point is only a few generations off at most, not thousands of
years away as is popularly supposed.

Much time has been wasted in estimates of the exact number of millions
this country can support. Disputation over a few score millions is unimportant, for in the absence of an improbable revolution in agriculture,
we shall soon be confronted with the pointed choice of reducing either
our birth-rate or our standard of living.

Practically, an essential part of the population problem is to get the
people to see that they are confronted with a condition, not a theory.
Fixed attitudes and prejudices are hard to break down, and the public is
not easily impressed with what it has been taught to regard as at most a
remote danger. The American farmer will not soon believe that overpopulation is imminent. There are, moreover, speculative and other interests
which profit by population increase. And there are many timid, optimistic folk, dominated by traditional moral and religious sentiment, whose
rationalizing proclivities prevent them from facing the issue squarely.
To avoid admitting early danger of overpopulation, they institute an
imaginary migration to the jungles of South America, or grasp at the straw
of synthetic food and intra-atomic energy. It goes without saying that
no bank would lend money to a business man whose plans for future solven-
cy were as visionary as those of the optimists who think we need not worry
over population increase.

The population problem needs restatement for two reasons: first, because
however convincing the calculations of statisticians may be to the adequately informed, their warnings make little popular impression; and
second, because we should not be satisfied with avoiding absolute over-
population. We should aim at a policy which will secure such adjustment
between population and natural resources as will enable us to live as well
as possible. Even if it could be demonstrated that this country could

support 500 million people by eliminating waste and giving up meat, cui bono? The standard of living would continue to fall and the problem of numbers continually get worse. The only happy people would be the sword-rattling generals. Those who today argue that we can find a way to support double or treble our present population are simply falling victim to our unthinking American worship of size and growth, without inquiry into the human values involved. A sane theory of population should consider these values.

Usually the problem is presented as a 'safety-first' proposition, and it gets no hearing. If the matter were presented as an ever-present problem of efficiency, it would get a hearing. And if a reasonably rational adjustment of population to resources can be obtained, the two problems - that of avoiding overpopulation, and that of securing the highest practicable per-capita economic efficiency - will be solved at the same time.

Fundamentally, the problem is one of factoral proportion - of securing the most efficient numerical ratio between natural resources and labor power, or, more briefly, between land and population. For simplicity of statement, it is here assumed that capital may be regarded merely as a device for increasing labor power.

Given a fixed supply of natural resources and a fixed technique of production, per-capita product must diminish when population increases beyond a certain point. This static law of diminishing returns, more accurately called 'the law of factoral proportion', is so completely established, both by general experience and by experiment station records, that few persons question it.

But this static law of factoral proportion is useful only as a starting-point in analyzing relations between population and resources. It is based on assumptions contrary to fact. Productive technique is not constant; it is constantly improving. And our natural resources are not fixed; they are constantly decreasing, because we are using up at a whirlwind rate supplies which it took the slow ages to store. Even if, to simplify analysis, we regard resources as constant, it is obviously not easy to predict the exact outcome, at any given time, of variations in the other two factors, population and technique. The endless and mostly barren controversies over the Malthusian theory have been made possible primarily by this highly dynamic quality of the problem. This aspect of the problem is also responsible for much of the incorrigible optimism of those who feel that it is wrong to 'tamper with conception,' and who seem to think that a dense mass of stereotyped beings represents a higher order of good than a smaller number of individuals.

Nearly all these anti-Malthusian optimists rest their case on two misconceptions: they think the earth is a great deal larger than it is; and they believe that 'progress' can work miracles. Migration and invention - these are the two means of escape which they invariably hold sufficient. They see vast empty spaces. The State of Texas, especially, appeals to their imagination. Most of them have never been there. They do not study the rain map, the temperature chart, or contour intervals. They have a naive faith in mechanical progress. For them, invention will 'set aside' and 'indefinitely postpone' the law of diminishing returns. Progress will find a way. Man is master of his fate. Thus we are invited to soar into the lyrical regions of 'two-story agriculture' and to listen to the

music of solar engines throbbing in the white sunlight of the deserts.
The chemists will make our food in the laboratories and we can continue
to beget unlimited offspring to the glory of God.

All this faith, however, overlooks certain important facts. The essential
considerations commonly lost sight of are the following:

(1) Only inferior lands, limited in extent, remain for settlement.
(2) Progress itself involves a paradox, for, as Julius Wolf long ago
pointed out, it is inconceivable that technical advance can maintain the
pace it set in what Wallace called 'the wonderful century' and which J.
M. Keynes thinks may prove to have been 'a magnificent episode' in history.
In the main, future improvements are to be 'looked for in the fourth dec-
imal place.' There was a 'pace that killed Athens.' There are reasons
for believing that we cannot maintain our own pace.
(3) The engineering and the economic problems are confused. Some things
technically possible are possible economically only at prohibitive cost
and a lower standard of living.
(4) There is a limit to the degree to which cheapened manufactures can
offset increasing costs in the extractive industries.
(5) Per-capita agricultural yield should be calculated on the basis of
all the labor engaged, both directly and indirectly, in the production
of agricultural commodities -- as, for example, in the manufacture of farm
machinery and fertilizers and in the transport of farm products.

If these considerations, which are discussed at length in the next three
chapters, were given the weight they deserve, there would be less foolish
optimism, and less sentimental and doctrinaire opposition to controlled
fecundity. Only by formulating population theory accordingly can we have
a rationally economic population policy, that is to say, a policy which
will first of all retard growth before we are hopelessly beyond the optimum ratio of numbers to resources, and which will take as its aim the
attainment and maintenance of that ratio.

In what follows, the real population problem will be considered to be
that of attaining, and maintaining, the most productive ratio between
population and natural resources. Productivity is to be measured by the
per capita income of ultimate consumers' goods. This ratio is called the
optimum, and a population of this most efficient size the optimum population. Economically, the desideratum is not to wring from the earth the
largest possible total product, but to obtain, in return for whatever expenditure of effort the people may regard as normal and proper, the largest, permanently practicable, per-capita product.

The notion of the optimum is frankly a utilitarian and an individualistic
concept. It assumes that the function of the economic process is to serve
individuals. The nation may be regarded as a productive unit, but must
not be thought of as an end. Doctrines and policies which have in the
past sought to encourage unlimited population growth have usually, except
in new countries, been based upon political, rather than economic, interests, and have all but lost sight of the welfare of individuals. A realistic population policy must, of course, take into account political facts.
Nationalistic sentiments and frictions are today undoubtedly the most
serious obstacle to a population policy aimed at securing maximum individual income. They counsel a 'safety-first' policy, and safety is supposed to reside in overwhelming numbers. Perhaps the toughest and the

most fundamental problem the world has to solve is to harmonize national safety with per-capita efficiency. Economically, this is the basic significance of the problem of international peace.

In the absence of an effective method of adjusting international differences, we are, as the world now reasons, caught on the horns of a dilemma. If we do not breed like rats, regardless of economic consequences, we shall be in danger of attack by other, and envious, nations, in which unlimited multiplication will have afforded both a reason and a means for aggression. And if we do so breed, we shall reach the subsistence level in which death will continuously reap a fat harvest without any foreign assistance. Economically, each nation will be caught in a vicious circle. It will have to have a teeming population from which to recruit the cheap labor necessary to retain its foreign markets; and the militant protection of these same markets will be necessary because of the teeming population which will starve if they are lost.

An optimum policy, aiming at the maximum per-capita income, will require, on the contrary, stringent restriction of population growth. This will involve not only a reduced birth-rate, but drastic regulation of immigration, perhaps even virtual suppression. Certain international adjustments and modifications of nationalistic attitudes are bound to be necessary. When a country is at or near its optimum, an exclusion policy is entirely justifiable, for it is no country's duty to take in the surplus children of another. The only ground on which it could be held to be so would involve a serious impairment of sovereignty and a sort of world communism of natural resources. The ultimate result of a policy of unrestricted intermigration, such as popular leaders in some countries demand, would be to reduce all countries to the standard of living of the lowest. Humanity, in every sense of the term, will be best served if each nation is held responsible for the poverty caused by its own sentiments and superstitions. This conclusion involves no assumption, such as frequently mars discussion and clouds the real issue, of hereditary inferiority on the part of any race or people.

The whole political and international aspect of the subject needs extended treatment, rather than passing notice, for it is possible that just on this issue of control of migration the wealthier nations may find themselves in a disagreeable position. Japan and Italy, for instance, might refuse to join in any plan for international peace which did not embrace international control of migration. Acceding to this impairment of sovereignty, we should have to lower our bars. Not acceding to it, we should have to give ear to the militarists. In either case a rational population would be impossible.

There is, therefore, some cogency in Harold Cox's suggestion for a league of low birth-rate nations. An international conference on the population problem ought to be held before long. At the least, it would do no harm to have a few population experts at the next disarmament conference.

Since the central impetus to population policies has in the past been political, and since economists have conceived the problem mainly as one of avoiding absolute overpopulation, the theory of the optimum has not been worked out. The term itself is seldom met with in economic literature.

The first query that will be raised will doubtless be how, in view of the large number of variables involved, we can know when we have arrived at the optimum. The problem is difficult, it must be admitted. But it must be emphasized that even if only the roughest sort of measurement is possible, the ideal of the optimum as the criterion of a rational policy still retains its validity. Various indexes of prosperity might be outlined, but space does not permit. It should be noted, however, that statistics of national wealth, or of net value-product, are of little service. The inventory of wealth may increase without an increase in the inventory of consumers' goods. Monetary value, also, even when stated in terms of an index of stable prices, may increase, with a decrease in actual real income. The fully accurate index of prosperity would be an index of the inventory of consumers' goods produced each year. In the absence of an approximation to such an index, we shall have to rely upon a price index of money income, less savings and reinvestment.

Once the optimum were attained, the expenses attendant on population growth would be avoided. Additional housing, public utility extensions, and land reclamation would no longer be essential. Increase of land values and rents would be checked. Slower use and decreased waste of natural resources would retard the increase in the cost of raw materials. Distribution of income would undergo some change. Wages would be higher and interest lower. Business would become less speculative. Costs of consumers' goods would tend to fall.

The number of people needed to constitute the optimum population will depend upon various circumstances. The quality of the human stock, the level of health and vitality, and demographic constitution are obvious factors. Both the death-rate and the birth-rate would be lower, and the average length of life higher, than now. There would be more old people, but fewer children below the working age. On the whole, however, the proportion of non-workers might be higher than at present.

The state of the arts is, of course, highly important. Technical improvements may do three things: they may provide new and more refined commodities, they may save labor, and they may for a time offset the tendency to higher cost of raw materials. Generally speaking, a nation may utilize its technical progress either to support more population or to raise the standard of living of the existing population. If invention saves labor, several alternative results may be chosen. The same population with the same per-capita effort can have a larger income. Or they can have the same income with less work. Or, with the same work and the same income, they can elect to increase population. Or, with the same work, a lesser population can have a larger income. Given only rational control of population, the outlook for a high level of per-capita income and culture in the future is exceedingly attractive.

A wise people, preferring more leisure to maximum income, might elect to fix its numbers at a point below the physical optimum. By so doing, they would avoid some of the expense now thrust upon us by increasing density. Some of our so-called utilities are merely devices for mitigating, often inadequately, the discomforts incident to agglomeration. There are also moral losses connected with increasing density, which we may well wish to avoid. Increasing density means diminution of freedom, more intricate and expensive organization, loss of community self-reliance, and the multiplication of centralized and peremptory social controls. It means

also -- and this is not to be counted lightly -- a distinct aesthetic loss,
at least to those who do not judge the beauty of a landscape by the amount
of corn and hogs raised on it, and who still hope that some of our wild
life and wild places may be preserved.

Many obstacles will impede the adoption of a rational policy. International friction and militaristic sentiment have already been mentioned.
Hardly less effective are religious sentiment, ignorance, and uncritical
optimism. Many people fear birth-control because they are told that it
will increase extra-marital immorality. They do not stop to consider
whether if this were so (which is open to doubt) it might not be a low
price to pay for the moral advances gained by avoiding the hideous immorality of enforced maternity, and by easing that population pressure which
bids fair to be a fruitful cause of international discord. Finally, there
is the eugenics-Nordic complex. Few clever phrases have ever been more
productive of loose thinking, and of unsubstantiated hypotheses taken as
eternal verities, than 'race suicide'.

Practically, the population problem is in large measure a problem in social
psychology; for the attainment of a rationally adjusted birth-rate depends
upon the attitude of the whole people. If their attitude is to be that of
the Roosevelts and the reactionary clergy, the optimum may as well be regarded as a wild and impossible dream. It is probable, however, that the
public will understand the idea of an optimum relation between numbers
and resources, when it is adequately presented, and that the theory of
the optimum can be made the basis for a change in popular attitude toward
the danger of overpopulation. Certainly there is ample evidence that, as
soon as the mediaeval statutes against contraceptive knowledge are removed, the birth-rate will decline, perhaps by the required amount, without further discussion.

Then, with rising standards of living and broadened democratic opportunity,
much that the biological eugenists attribute to poor heredity, and the
believers in innate Nordic superiority to deficiencies in quality of non-
Nordic stocks, will be found to be due to lack of opportunity. The trend
of present-day psychology, with its virtual discarding of instincts, and
its increasing emphasis on the learning process, marks a change in scientific insight which many biologists and some anthropologists are slow to
recognize, but which, to say the least, should make us all wary of accept-
ing uncritically the tradition of innate, organically inherited differences of capacity in races and classes. While, with the advent of a
rational policy as to numbers, the problem of quality will not disappear,
it will be much less pressing than to many it now appears to be.

The theory of population is, however, in an unsatisfactory state. While
the problem is fundamentally economic, it involves many factors which
economists often overlook. The essentially psychological element in the
problem has been handled crudely by the economists and inadequately by
the sociologists. Here statisticians and biologists can be of little
assistance. It is too far a cry from fruit flies in a jar to human beings
who have had a taste of rational self-direction. There is an implied fatalism in statistical curves -- a fatalism unjustified by the underlying
facts. We are likely to forget the human motives which lie back of the
phenomena summarized in our logarithmic charts. The future trend of a
curve can be predicted only if we know these motives and the future
changes which they are likely to undergo. But psychological factors are

not always predictable. Herein lay the defect of Malthus's analysis.
Herein also lies a great defect of current population literature.

One can read the Essay from cover to cover without encountering a passage
which indicates that Malthus ever thought that women have anything to do
with population. Much the same blindness still persists. It is a fault
of population theory that it is man-made. This also puts a black mark
against traditional optimistic attitudes, and against cameralistic and
mercantilistic population policies from Frederick the Great down to our
own time. Such attitudes and such policies never count the vital costs of
a high birth-rate -- the costs to the women of the race. Many economists
and most biologists fail to consider this. Yet the very essence of economy is to balance real costs against real income. A valid population
theory, as well as a rational population policy, must take account of the
way in which half the race, hitherto practically ignored, will probably
calculate the costs against the satisfactions of large families. Neglect
to consider the interests and attitudes of the potential mothers of the
race impairs the objectivity of any population theory.

There are powerful influences tending to perpetuate the dangerous rate of
increase -- ecclesiastical policy, for example, commercial avarice, and
militaristic illusion. But, fortunately, there are equally powerful influences which will retard population growth. The whole movement for a
real democracy, the modern woman movement, the universal demand for a more
worthy standard of living, the growth of rationalism and of individualism
-- forces almost unknown to Malthus, because barely started in his time --
are factors which no serious student of the problem may overlook. There
is evidence that the workers, even the socialists, no longer regard the
Malthusian warning as a mere subterfuge of exploitative capitalism. There
is abundant indication that women are taking a hand in determining their
own population policy. Happily, it is fairly clear that their decision
will be in line with what statistical analysis and economic experience
show to be essential, either for avoiding absolute overpopulation or for
attaining the optimum. The question is whether this harmony of individual
and social interests will be allowed to express itself freely soon enough
to avoid the unpleasantness which tables of population increase, crop
yields, and reserve resources indicate to be lurking just under the horizon.

READING 13

An important characteristic of the interwar period was the resurrection of nationalism. Together with political nationalism came demographic nationalism. The fascist nations such as Italy especially encouraged population growth by granting family allowances and tax rebates for prolific parents, by supressing use and knowledge of birth control and by using heavily pronatalist propaganda in the press. The fascists urged their people to procreate extensively for the obvious reason of providing the manpower for the policies of territorial conquest and domination they were planning.

The Italian demographer Corrado Gini (1884-1965), who taught statistics, economics, and demography at the universities of Cagliari, Padua, and Rome, was a pro-fascist, and his conclusions were inevitably natalistic. He believed that Italy needed more people. He presented the following paper, consisting of a series of comments on the optimum population concept, at the World Population Conference in Geneva in 1927.[13]

To Gini, a denser population (in Italy, of course) would work miracles. It would stimulate intensive agriculture (which, as Wicksell pointed out, is no advantage at all), it would bring about land reforms, and it would stimulate thrift and increase the savings ratio. All of these activities would result in a growing per capita income. In addition, Gini believed that a higher population density would make the arts and sciences bloom.

In our view, Gini's arguments are little more than pseudo-scientific rationalizatons and justifications for the pronatalist policies that were then advocated by the fascist rulers of Italy. Such rationalizations are still quite common and can be found in the works of some contemporary writers.

---

[13]

Source: World Population Conference, Proceedings, (London: Arnold, 1927), pp. 118-122.

CONSIDERATIONS ON THE OPTIMUM DENSITY OF A POPULATION
Corrado Gini

The first point to make clear when we speak of an optimum population density is for whom does this density represent the optimum: is it for the
individual or the State? It is true that the State is an aggregate of
individuals, but not only of individuals today but also of posterity.

Now that which may be regarded as the best for those actually existing in
the State may not be equally so for the State considered as an entity in
itself.

It is true that the life of present-day individuals stretches out into
the future, and that family affection, ties of friendship and relationship
often result in as great a concern in what will take place after the individual's death as in his own immediate affairs. These emotions do not
sway all, and, even in those who are affected by them, the influence exerted is not always the decisive one. At all events, and bearing in mind
all the considerations above mentioned, there can be no doubt that the
concern of individuals for future events is much weaker in intensity and
limited in time than the interest of the State.

Thus, indeed, in judging as to what must be regarded as the optimum of
population, as in judging any other phenomenon of which the future issue
may be different -- if not indeed contradictory from its immediate effect
-- the State is inclined to attribute a greater importance to future
results than is ever accorded them by individuals.

A striking example of this divergence in appreciation is afforded by the
point of view regarding a reduction of the birth rate.

From many points of view, this undoubtedly represents an advantage for
the generation in which it takes place, and possibly for that immediately
succeeding, inasmuch as it diminishes for the former the burden of children, thus enabling them to be better educated and to grow more robust and
better fitted for the trials of life. On the other hand, by reducing the
population, it enfeebles the military strength of the State, and, by
starting the nation on a downward path on which experience has shown it is
difficult to pull up, it may even definitely compromise national development in the near or distant future. We can readily understand that the
individual lends a readier ear to the first considerations, while the
latter cannot be disregarded by the State.

Obviously, then, the point of view of the individual must be harmonized,
and actually was, is, and will be harmonized with the national point of
view.

But the point of equilibrium depends upon a multiplicity of circumstances
and, above all, on the inclinations of the individual, so that it would

be vain to attempt to determine it a priori in a general way, regardless
of the particular national psychology. Admitting for a moment that we
may fix the point of equilibrium between the individual and national points
of view for a certain population of given psychological tendencies --
even yet a judgment regarding the optimum density of a population would
work out very differently according to time and place.

In quiet times, when neither near nor remote menace of war appears on the
horizon, it is quite evident that the requirements of national defence
lose importance as compared with considerations of immediate economic
advantage. And it is also clear that, even for military requirements
themselves, the question of the actual mass of the population will be
relatively less or more important according to the size and technical
development of armaments. The consideration of the size of the State
may, however, be decisive.

It can matter little to Belgium, and evidently nothing at all to Luxem-
burg, for example, from the point of view of national safety, whether its
own population remains stationary or grows even by fifty per cent. On the
other hand, for nations like Italy, or France, whether they count sixty
rather than forty million inhabitants may be a decisive fact. Whenever a
State rises to dimensions or to a power which are well beyond those of
possible competitors, the numerical question of population from the military point of view may lose much of its importance. This is the case today regarding, for example, the United States, and it might tomorrow be
the case in Russia. Geographical position is another of those considerations which may decisively influence our conclusion. A nation isolated
from others by the sea, trusting for security to naval forces, needs a
much smaller number of men for its defence than a continental Power, and
may thus be indifferent to an approach more or less rapid towards the
static condition of population. Those nations, on the other hand, whose
frontiers lie inland, tend to attribute to a highly numerous population
much greater military importance, particularly if their boundaries are
without natural defence.

The optimum demographic density may further be dependent on the characteristic of the territory and on the social life. In a dense population it
is evidently easier to maintain order. Density stimulates intensive agriculture, the subdivision of big estates, and thus secures the disappearance
of malaria; it leads to the construction of aqueducts, canals, and similar works contributing to the public profit. It further makes profitable
the construction and use of railway communications, tramways, riverways,
harbors, and ports, even in localities which are naturally little adapted
thereto, and it contributes powerfully to the development of the higher
forms of culture, such as conferences, theatres, concerts, congresses,
all of which presuppose a crowd of spectators in order to make them possible. It gives to the market for artistic, scientific, and political
publications the size which alone enables them to take firm root, and to
spread the thought of the nation beyond its national frontiers.

And so it comes about that the population density required to enable a
people to expand its aptitudes to the full is highest when external difficulties are greatest, when geographical climatic conditions are the least
favourable, and where public order is most difficult to enforce and culture slowest in developing.

Many of these circumstances are met with in Italy. This probably explains why the great increase of the population which has been observed during and since the war -- although it happened in a period of disturbance and worldwide economic crisis -- has rather accelerated than slowed down economic reconstruction in comparison with other countries, such as France and the Balkan States, which were equally tried by war.

Strong currents of emigration are by many regarded as a sure sign that the desirable density of a country has been exceeded. From my point of view this is a mistake. The fact that many migrate from a country means nothing more than that many promise themselves more favourable conditions or a pleasanter life in other lands. But, quite apart from the possibility of mistaken appreciations, it may happen, and frequently it does happen, that their departure actually does harm to the nation, which was not, in point of fact, oversupplied with men.

An emigrant's savings, which often enrich the families left behind by him, in part compensate and in part mask the harm which emigration has done; it sometimes happens that the difficulties which are feared by many from the reduction of the outflow are belied by the facts. This at least has occurred in Italy. The reduction of emigration to almost negligible numbers, not only has not damaged the country, but it has considerably advanced the agricultural economy of those regions from which the stream of emigrants was chiefly fed.

It is to this that is due the fact of great significance that in many regions the price of the landed property has risen greatly since the war, and this particularly in the case of the less valuable lands, which need for their productivity a larger supply of labor and which in the past were neglected on account of rural emigration.

Another error which, in my opinion, is often made in judging the optimum density of population is due to the failure to appreciate duly the influence which variations in that density may have on the accumulation of wealth.

It is an admitted fact that as population grows the national income grows, but many believe that, if the total amount of property to which work is applied remains unchanged in quantity or slightly increased, the national income will not grow proportionately to the population, so that the per capita income would diminish and either the standard of living or the amount of savings would inevitably decline.

This argument would be flawless if the stimulus to work and to save were as great in the case of a stationary population as in that of one increasing more or less rapidly. But this hypothesis does not correspond to facts. The fact that when the population is growing the family fortune is inadequate to allow of the children living on the same standard as their parents is a most effective inducement to them to work more and to save more. Therefore, as the population increases, productive effort and thrift increase pari passu, and this increase added to the increased mass of workers, and often to the other favorable circumstances above examined arising from the greater density of the population, may determine an increase of total income greater than the increase of population.

The comparison of the economic progress realised by France and by Germany

in the pre-war period does not favor the theory that it is a stationary
population which promotes the most rapid growth of the average per capita
income.

Thus we see that, in general, population density acts as a stimulus to
national qualities, and more especially that the increase of that density
acts as a stimulus to work and savings. But these stimuli may be more or
less needed, and their effect may be greater or less, according to the
psychology of the population. Where the individuals of a nation are gifted
with a high degree of initiative, a very high form of civilization may be
obtained even with a meagre population; although we cannot hide from ourselves that in all epochs it was in the most densely populated zones that
the highest manifestations of the civilization of the period have appeared. Other nations, on the other hand, may, in order to reach up to their
full measure, need the stimulus of a dense population, to which, be it
noted, they respond admirably. Finally, a nation may be so torpid as to
remain passive even under such a stimulus, and for these the increment of
population density may, instead of being a spur to progress, become a
source of permanent economic crises. The Scandinavian people, Italians,
and the population of some parts of China, may perhaps be adduced as
examples of the three types sketched.

In conclusion, the question of optimum density of population is not a
theoretical question which can be solved by generic formulae, but is one
which presents itself in the most varied forms in various times and regions,
and which in every age and every region is open to a different solution
in accordance with the greater or less prevalence which is given by the
varied instructions of the several peoples to the individual or to the
national point of view.

READING 14

This century's interwar period (1918-1939) was a time of increasing participation of non-Western scholars in the population debate. Professor
Radhakamal Mukerjee of the University of Lucknow, India (born 1889) was
perhaps the most distinguished among them. He wrote a number of books
and articles in which he contributed to population economics in general
(see for instance his Political Economy of Population) and to a better
understanding of India's dilemma in particular.

In his view, continued population growth in a traditional agricultural
society such as India in the 1930's with a high rural density would lead
to very serious problems. Nearly all available land had been converted
to cropland, hence there was little room to expand the cultivated area.
The constant increase in rural population led to excessive parcelling of
the land with a consequent increase in uneconomic holdings. If in 1935,
says Mukerjee, the average Indian had been provided with 2800 calories a
day, some 48 million people would have been deprived of food supplies.
The Indian scholar estimated India's ultimate carrying capacity to be
477 million people, a figure that was in fact reached early in 1965. By
that time, however, a more intensive application of fertilizers, the use
of hybrid seeds, new and better tools, and new irrigation facilities had
raised the population ceiling.

Mukerjee also briefly discusses the determinants of marital fertility and
the need for smaller families.[14]

[14] Source: R. Mukerjee, "The Population Problem in India", The Asiatic
Review, Vol. XXXIII (October, 1937), pp. 709-714; 720-725.

THE POPULATION PROBLEM IN INDIA

Radhakamal Mukerjee

POPULATION INCREASE AND AGRICULTURE

It was Malthus who first warned mankind of the danger of population outstripping the means of subsistence, and enunciated the law of diminishing
returns so important for a country like India which depends mainly on
agriculture. Over-population did not strike Malthus as a possibility
because population would not, according to him, overstep its limits owing
to poverty, war and pestilence. But even in Oriental countries the notion
that population automatically regulates itself by external checks has become incompatible with modern social ideals. In fact, with the spread of
democratic ideas and institutions in the East, the notions of optimum and
over-population have become highly significant along with a desire to
regulate population policy. The entire outlook in modern population study
is thus changed, the emphasis being now shifted to the means of social
control of numbers and the aims and objects of such regulation, due regard
being paid to the qualitative and selective aspects of population changes.

The whole of India with an area half that of the United States has a population almost three times as large. In the sixteenth century the population of India stood roughly at 100 millions, and in the middle of the
nineteenth century at 150 millions. In 1931 the population was 353 millions; now it is approximately 377 millions. Population has increased
roughly from 20 to 50 millions in the United Provinces; from 5 to 25 millions in North and South Bihar; and from 10 to 51 millions in four provinces of the Gangetic Valley, giving some of the world's highest records
of rural aggregation.

With a rapid population increase, the total percentages of cultivated to
cultivable area have now reached the phenomenal figures of 75 to 95 per
cent in the Ganges Valley. Forests, meadows and marshes, all are now in-
vaded by the plough as a result of population increase, which also leads
to the scarcity of fodder and grazing grounds. For the same reason holdings have been fragmented to tiny bits. Continuous subdivisions of holdings restrains the cultivator from adopting improved methods of cultivation, constructing wells and even intensive farming. In the United Provinces during 1928-33 the net area sown diminished by 100,000 acres and
the double-cropped area by 400,000 acres as compared with the average for
1920-25. In Bihar also the net area diminished by 250,000 acres in the
same period. "Nor can it be asserted," observes the Census Superinten-
dent, "that the yield per acre of land has increased to any extent through
new and improved methods of exploitation." Similarly, Bengal's net cultivated area has decreased during the last decade. It was 2.4 million acres
on an average between 1915-20. Between 1920-25 and 1928-33 it stood at
2.3 millions. Except in Assam, Burma and Sind a high proportion of
available cultivated area has been brought under the plough, ranging from
65 per cent in Bihar and Orissa to 86 per cent in Bombay.

Throughout Northern India there is now little room for expansion of cultivation. Settled conditions have long been established, permitting the
extension of the frontiers of cultivation into the forest and marsh, ravine-
stricken jungle and sand-dune. The possibilities of large canal irrigation
schemes have been almost exhausted. Much new uncultivated land can no
longer be brought under the plough as a result of the construction of new
canal systems. The Malthusian law of diminishing returns is now operating
in agricultural development, not only by soil exploitation, but also by
water acting as a limiting agent.

INSUFFICIENCY OF FOOD PRODUCTION

In an appendix[1], I give the index numbers of variation of population and
food supply in India during the last quarter of a century. It is true
that on the whole the increase of total agricultural production has out-
stripped population growth between 1910 and 1935, but the margin is less
in the case of food production, only 4 per cent, which is further reduced
to 2.5 when we compute the food supply actually available for consumption.
The increase of food production has been chiefly due to the phenomenal expansion of cane, barley and jowar, which have almost doubled in output.
During the period 1910-35, rice, the cereal of about two-thirds of the
population, increased in aggregate output only by 6 per cent. Wheat has
shown a steady decrease since 1925; while barley (103 per cent), jowar
(25 per cent), maize (15 per cent) and gram (16 per cent) increased steadily. The difference between the indices for population and food production or available food supply is getting narrower and narrower.

In the same period India's increase of mineral and industrial production
has no doubt gone much ahead of increase of numbers, the figures respectively being 17 and 57, but mineral and industrial production occupies a
relatively small place in contrast with agricultural production in the
economic life of India and in relation to India's population and standard
of living. The relative percentages of contribution to total national
income from agriculture, industrial and mineral production are 79.8, 18.1
and 1.3 respectively.

By using Lusk's coefficient of comparison with those of an average man and
woman we estimate "the average and total man value" of India's population
of 1931 in the following table:

Ages	Population in Millions (1931)	Man Value per Head	Total Man Value in Millions
0 to 15 (39.9 per cent) ...	141.2	0.7	98.84
Males of 15 and upwards ...	109.2	1.0	109.20
Females	102.6	0.83	85.15
	353.0	0.835	293.19

Allowing 2,800 calories per man per day (calculating on the basis of
2,400 and 3,000 calories respectively for rice and wheat eaters and de-
ducting 200 calories for wastage during distribution), the total requirement of the Indian population will amount approximately to 292 billion
calories per annum. Estimating on the basis of 100 calories per oz. per

---

[1] Not included here (editor's footnote).

average food grain, India's aggregate food supply available for consumption in 1931 (60.1 million tons) would yield 215.4 billion calories, to which should be added 34 billion calories from an approximate milk supply of 113,000 million lbs. and 0.7 billion calories from the total fish supply, roughly estimated at 700,000 tons. The amount of energy contributed to Indian food requirement from all sources is accordingly 250.1 billion calories as compared with her minimum need of 292 billion calories. Between 1931-35, India added 24 millions mouths to feed and increased her food supply to 280.4 billion calories approximately (her sugar adding a quota of 26.1 billions   India thus has now fallen short of food for 48 millions of her average men -- i.e., for 12 per cent of her present population. The following important facts and conclusions emerge out of the study:

1. India's population in 1931   353   millions
2. India's population capacity on the basis
    of her food supply in 1931   291   millions
3. India's food shortage in 1931   42   billion calories
4. India's present population   377   millions
5. India's addition to food supply between
    1931 and 1935   30.3 billion calories
6. India's present food supply   280.4 billion calories
7. India's present food needs   321.5 billion calories
8. India's present population capacity   329   millions
9. India's present food shortage   41.1 billion calories
10. Present number of average men estimated
    without food, assuming that others obtain
    their normal daily ration   48   millions

India's total waste lands, which are available for cultivation but either not taken up or abandoned, comprise 162 millions of acres which might provide about 29 million tons of food grains given unremitting pressure of population. Under the most complete expansion of cultivation, which will not be possible without the adoption of vast measures of land reclamation and irrigation and the strenuous efforts and practices characteristic of the Chinese peasantry, India's total population capacity cannot be above 447,000,000 persons. Immediately after 1921 India's present population capacity was overstepped and by the middle of the century, assuming that the present real increase continues, India will in all probability overstep 447,000,000, her ultimate population capacity under the existing farming and living standards and industrial conditions of the people.

FAMINES AND EPIDEMICS

The biological effects of over-population in India have been a direct correspondence of birth rate and inverse correspondence of death rate with favourable harvests and a gradual adjustment of natality and mortality, so that an equilibrium density or an average abundance is reached. These were the unclassified Malthusian "positive" checks of population which are now operating in large areas in India in a somewhat modified manner. The mortality from famines has been estimated by William Digby as 4,485,000 between 1850-75 and 23,740,000 between 1875-1900. Thus during the latter half of the last century the total toll of life on this account was represented by the figure of 28.25 millions. In the famine of 1901, the worst of recent years, one million people perished. The incidence of mortality from famine or scarcity diseases has not yet been investigated. In areas

which have just been under the grip of scarcity, the increase in mortality
from diseases like dysentery, diarrhoea and fever as well as from wasting
and deficiency diseases needs enquiry. The Report of the Famine Commis-
sion (1910) abundantly shows that mortality due to privation is followed
by a further rise in mortality due to cholera, diarrhoea and fever owing
to the reduced power of the people to resist infections.

Though famines have now lost their rigour, drought and agricultural scarcity are accompanied by a high death rate and low birth rate. Epidemics
thus continue to play their important role in checking population growth;
the mortality from the main epidemic diseases between 1901 and 1931 was
about 67.25 millions. In some congested districts in the United Provinces
the trend of vital statistics over a period of 60 years indicates that the
damage done by epidemics to these populations is severer than elsewhere.
A more significant phenomenon is a slackening of birth rate after a dis-
trict's saturation density is overstepped. The absence of an agricultural
surplus, and malnutrition, which affects especially women and children,
lower the birth rate temporarily and alter the age and sex distribution
for a long period to the long-run detriment of the birth rate.

A state of chronic food shortage, punctuated by spells of unfavourable
seasons, particularly affects the very young and old women, and notably
those in the child-bearing age, when the ancient practices of infanticide,
abortion and abstinence from intercourse have been largely discarded. The
result of this is high infantile and maternal mortality. The reduction
of the number of women at the reproductive period, worn out by a long
struggle with food deficiency and by frequent child-bearing, is one of the
demological causes of the slackening of the birth rate in the heavily
congested plains of India... Meanwhile the peasantry in the absence of
epidemics multiply heedlessly. More mouths to feed also accompany more
hands to work, but the hands are idle. The ancient traditions of forbear-
ance and self-control, Malthus's moral restraints, are inoperative amongst
the masses. Malthus emphasized the postponement of the age of marriage
accompanied by strict continence. In India one of the significant factors
in the population problem is the social sanction and encouragement of child
marriage.

THE SMALL FAMILY HABIT

In the past, India developed the planned family system and the small
family was the general rule. As in China or Japan in the past, the
limited family habit depended upon innumerable social canons and regulations, which governed daily life and practice including conjugal relationship. Such customs included the postponement of marriage for large sections of the population and prolonged abstinence from intercourse for
married persons, who were bound to conform to certain religious injunctions
in this regard. Hypergamy, a heavy bride-price, and an expensive and elaborate marriage ceremony also contributed towards less frequent marriages.
A large section of the population, again, lived a single life in maths,
monasteries and convents. The greater the number of these in a period of
religious revival in India the smaller was the number of births. Infanticide, especially the exposure of female babies, was also a common practice
in India among the castes who practised hypergamy. Prostitution, which
Malthus also regards as a check on the growth of numbers, has been associated in South and Western India with temple girls forming an honoured
priesthood, devoting itself to devotional song and dance. Early abortion

was also not uncommon, and there is also evidence that in the villages
some crude and casually found methods of birth control are in use among
the women.

Birth control is now adopted in the higher social circles in Bombay, Bengal and Madras, and it is not unknown in some rural areas. Contraception
of a crude kind has, for instance, been observed among the Goundans of
Salem, apparently in order to prevent the undue growth of families and
consequent fragmentation of holdings and weakening of the joint family
system and influence. The small family tradition, the postponement of
marriage, and the social emphasis on celibacy checked unrestricted increase of numbers. The results of the Mohammadan conquest proved, however,
disastrous for the small family system in India. Infant marriage, which
was unknown in the epic and Buddhist literature and did not play any part
until the Gupta period, began to prevail and to be widely adopted, especially in the central areas which were most powerfully affected by the Mohammadan influences, touching on one side or the other a line drawn from
Sind to Rajmahal.

Infant marriage was promoted by the desire of the family to get its girls
safely mated to suitable husbands in an age when there was danger of an
improper alliance due to the Mohammadan contact. But since then child
marriage has been practised mostly by the lower social strata. The Brah-
mins, Kayasthas and the intermediate castes are less addicted to this
practice, except in the Central India Agency and Hyderabad. Since it is
these lower castes who also allow their widows to marry again, the result
has been an unrestricted multiplication in their case. As the industrial
revolution promoted population increase in Europe in the 19th century and
in Japan in the 20th, so the continued subdivision of holdings making
agriculture less and less remunerative, and de-industrialization due to
the decline of cottage industries and handicrafts, are today discouraging
thrift or home-spun prudence and promoting multiplication in India.

Climate also is a factor in over-population by reducing the age of puberty.
In India girls attain puberty between 12 and 15 years and reproduction has
not been unusual at 13. Violations of the Law of Consent are not unusual.
"Cases are not uncommon," says a witness before the Age of Consent Committee, "in which girls bring forth six or seven children before they attain
their eighteenth year." The lactation also appears to be reduced and there
are shorter intervals between childbirths among low castes than among high
castes. Social customs and taboos do not adequately protect the Indian
mother against the demands of the house, the field and the cattle-shed.
Though child-bearing is frequent, the woman is not relieved from toil and
drudgery. "Enquiries into a large number of cases," observes the Age of
Consent Committee, "show that when the marriage of young people is con-
summated at an early age, say, when the boy is not more than 16 years or
the girl is 12 or 13, a fairly large percentage of wives die of phthisis
or some other disease of the respiratory organs or from some ovarian com-
plication within ten years of the consummation of marriage."

NEED OF POPULATION RESTRICTION

Apart from the neglect of female children, too early and frequent maternity, ignorant midwifery, dangers of childbirth, and disorders and diseases
continuing as a result of bearing too many and too frequent children have
all contributed (in the absence of selective epidemic diseases) towards a

higher death-rate amongst females than amongst males in India, especially
in the reproductive ages. The risk which the Indian woman runs at her
first child-bearing is aggravated later when her strength has been broken
by her having borne too many children at too short intervals. The net
result is a deficiency of females in India as a whole and in the higher
castes in particular, which is on the increase. It is because early
marriage and maternity are so widespread and their effects are so disastrous upon health, mortality and the biological condition of the population that appropriate and cheap devices of birth control derived by the
rural population from materials in its own domestic surroundings are necessary, so that contraception may be applied until the man has attained the
age of, say, 21 or 23, and the woman the age of 20 or 22.

It is sometimes suggested, and that on the basis of historical experience,
that there is only one way in which we can seriously reduce the Indian
birth rate; that is, by raising the standard of living. If under the
term "the standard of living" man's family and marriage habits and social
tradition connected with the increase of his family are included, the suggestion is not wide of the mark. But, with a mere economic conception of
the standard of living, to depend upon an uplift of the standard of living
for an automatic decrease of the birth rate is putting the cart before the
horse. The introduction of improved seeds, fertilizers and implements,
change in marketing methods, or even a reform of land tenure -- these are
all thwarted in India by the fractionalization of holdings and cheap and
inefficient labour in the countryside, which are the indirect results of
population increase. The offensive against illiteracy is similarly baf-
fled because population outruns the capacity of education. The dead
weight of illiteracy among the backward castes and the Muslims of India
makes the problem of its removal a formidable one, both from financial
and administrative points of view. As population continues to outrun the
educational facilities that are provided it is clear that the pressures
of population cannot be viewed merely in relation to the food supply. As
a matter of fact, in India the present attitude of most provincial governments in deferring schemes of village education and sanitation, amelioration, and uplift, and in lowering for the time being the accepted standard, is entirely due to an expanding population which makes readjustments
more and more difficult.

A rational family planning and education of the masses in birth control
must be accepted as one of the important means, though not the only means,
of combating population increase. The small family system, deliberately
planned and integrated with other habits and traditions which regulate
different sides of domestic life, must now be adopted in India as the
social and ethical norm; and such a custom as polygamy, which by encouraging a large family has become an obvious economic misfit, must be de-
clared illegal. At the same time, without better farming and increase of
the agriculturist's income, industrialization, and absorption of farm
hands and casual labourers in small industries and workshops, an improvement of the standard of living of the masses -- which alone can create the
mental attitude that is the sole bulwark of the small family habit --
cannot be effected. Birth control is after all a special measure. It can
effectively regulate population increase and help towards a solution of
the population problem in India only when the customs and attitudes of
the masses towards the family support it. Why should Indian peasant women,
who will in the future obtain education, leisure and a few luxuries of
life, and lose only, say, 5 or 10 per cent of their infants in the first

year, bear at the same rate as now when they lose 20 or 30? The present
fertility has the accompaniement of mud hovels shared with cattle and
goats, one-third of the babies dying in infancy, thin gruel and a loin
cloth for the survivors, widespread abortion and appalling maternal mortality. As the desire grows for better food and higher standards of living,
and for giving the children better opportunity for advancement; as women
gain in enlightenment and self-consciousness, and as men rid themselves of
the over-awing authority of religious injunctions of remote spacious times
which have now become obvious misfits, the prejudice against "interference
with nature" will yield to economic necessity.

Modern education, medicine, and public hygiene have reached the Indian
village, and as these spread more, birth control will shock the people
less, and what Ross calls "an adaptive fertility" will relieve the present
heavy population pressure. Nothing is more important than this adaptive
fertility for securing in India the economy of reproduction, the absence
of which has made it more and more difficult to raise the standards of
farming and living, led to chronic unemployment in the fields and in the
cities, and brought about an appalling waste of life spilling on all sides.
On the other hand, it is only when the fertility of India's work-a-day
millions becomes somehow adapted to the present situation of definite and
increasing food shortage through their forethought and a new attitude in
the matter of the family, that India can look for a fresh advance in improved agriculture, education and mass sanitation in her villages. These
will be followed up as in the West by a reduction of mortality and increase
of average longevity and thus as more and more of human fertility is left
to lie fallow, there will be an enrichment of the equipment and experience
of life.

PART THREE

DECLINING FERTILITY
AND ECONOMIC STAGNATION

READING 15

In the interwar period, European and North American birth rates declined rather sharply and it seemed that for a number of these countries a stationary population was not far off.

Economic thinking in the 1930's became strongly influenced by the theoretical work of national income theorists who attempted to explain the great economic depression of the 1930's. They argued that a main cause of the economic collapse was the decline in aggregate demand of which investment demand was a major component. In a paper, Some Economic Consequences of a Declining Population, read before the Eugenics Society in 1937, John Maynard Keynes analyzed the reasons for the decline in investment demand. He assumed that investment demands depends on population, per capita income, and the extent to which the production process in a given country is capital intensive or roundabout. With the slackening rate of population increase, this important outlet for investment tends to disappear. According to Keynes's calculations, the British population had, between 1860 and 1913, increased by some 50%, absorbing about half the investment flow of that period.

In his presidential address to the American Economic Association in 1938, the American economist Alvin H. Hansen added that the volume of private investment was also governed by the opening up and development of new territories such as those of the Western Hemisphere. In the 19th century, for example, the United Kingdom poured forth massive investments in the economic development of the New World. There were no vast new territories left, however, and thus another important avenue of investment was now closed.

Neither Keynes nor Hansen argued in favor of pronatalist policies designed to increase the birth rates. Instead, they endorsed such measures as a more even distribution of income to reduce savings and enhance private consumption, low interest rates to encourage borrowing for investment purposes, and an acceleration of government spending to enlarge the public component of aggregate demand.

The English economist Sir Roy Harrod (born 1900) went far beyond this. As is evident from the following paper,[15] he gave a very pessimistic analysis of the implications of the slowing down of population growth. In his view a system of lavish family allowances should be set up in order to influence birth rates upwards. His argument provoked a rather sharp reaction from Professor Jewkes.

---

[15] Source: R. F. Harrod, "Modern Population Trends," The Manchester School, Vol. X (April, 1939), pp. 1-20.

MODERN POPULATION TRENDS

Sir Roy Harrod

It is not my intention, nor would it be within my power, to present a new demographic theory or fresh findings in the field of vital statistics. In this I rely upon the work of others. Rather, I propose to review the contemporary situation, as it has been painted for us by the experts, and to consider its social and economic implications both by way of cause and effect.

The time is ripe for such a review. The magnitude and duration of the fall in fertility in this and other countries are sufficiently great to suggest that they will entail wide-sweeping changes both in the internal structure of countries and in the balance of power in the world. They even suggest that the complete extinction of the human species in, what is from the anthropological point of view, the near future can no longer be ruled out as an idle and absurd speculation. Each year that passes enables us to view the decline in better perspective and this points to the wisdom of postponing the formation of definite conclusions and a settled point of view in regard to the problem. On the other hand each year that passes will make the reversal of existing trends by conscious planning more difficult. So that it may be that in these present and immediately coming years we are at the very crisis and climax of human history, that this is the tide in the affairs of men, and that if we do not take it at the flood, albeit a flood which is beginning to ebb fast, the human experiment on this planet will peter out.

Not only have we new facts, strange and wonderful, to consider, but also vital statisticians, among whom the name of Mr. R. Kuczynski must be particularly honoured, have devised means of presenting us with a clearer conspectus of those facts. At the risk of traversing ground, which may be familiar to some of you, I will give a brief account of the new methods of measuring population trends and an outline of recent history.

The most popular and frequently mentioned concepts in this field are the birth-rate and the death-rate. The word rate has a scientific flavour which flatters the knowledgability of its user. Moreover by subtracting the death-rate from the birth-rate, the natural rate of increase of the population is obtained, and this appears to be precisely what some one interested in the trend wants to know. Yet in fact, if used for this purpose, these rates may be highly deceptive. The fact that in recent years births have exceeded deaths in this country and the birth-rate exceeded the death-rate, has obscured the more important fact that since that year the adults of the right age to produce children have continually failed to have enough children to replace themselves.

The reason for this deception is that the age-composition of a population is seldom normal and has not been normal in recent years. It cannot be normal if the rate of reproduction has recently been changing. The birth-

rate relates the total number of children born to the total population.
It is of more interest to relate the number born to the number of women
within the child-bearing period. But even this ratio may not give the
required information. The fertility of women differs in the different ages
of the child-bearing period, and, if the number of women between 40 and 45
exceeded the number between 40 and 35 and the number of women between 40
and 35 exceeded that between 35 and 30, the ratio of the number of births
to women between 30 and 45 to the number of women between 30 and 45 would
under-estimate the fertility of women between 30 and 45 owing to the preponderance of numbers in the less fertile ages. Similarly the ratio of
births to the number of women in the whole child-bearing period may give
a false indication of the true fertility of women. A movement of the
former magnitude in one direction may co-exist with a movement of the
latter in the opposite direction.

A similar difficulty occurs with the death-rate. Certain ages, particularly old age and infancy, are peculiarly subject to mortality. If an
abnormally high proportion of the total population belongs to these age-
groups the death-rate will over-estimate the incidence of death, and if
an abnormally low proportion belongs, the death-rate will under-estimate
the incidence of death. That is the position at present. The death-rate
has in a number of recent years stood at about 12 per thousand. It is
easy to see that if the age-composition were normal this would represent
an average length of life of about 80 years, which we know to be absurd.
If only we could persuade the Life Insurance companies to give us a policy
on this basis! But they, with their financial axe to grind, have had to
be more careful in their death statistics. The Life Tables which they use
based on the recorded number of deaths of people of each year of age per
thousand of the total population of that year of age and give a true
picture of the situation. This index of mortality was for long in advance
of anything available for natality. If provident parents had commonly
taken the precaution of insuring their children to cover the expenses of
prospective grand-children, the position might have been different!

Vital statisticians did endeavour for many years to grapple with the problem presented by an abnormal age-composition. But they failed to take up
the clue provided by the Life Tables. It must be admitted that the insuf-
ficiency of statistical data made things difficult for them. Experiments
were made with the ratio of births to marriages and with standardised
death-rates; but these do not give satisfactory results. The Registrar-
General still publishes a standardised death-rate which assesses what the
death-rate would be, given present mortality and a population of an age
composition equal to that which obtained in 1901. But as the age-
composition in that year was still less favourable to death than it has
recently been -- the number of births had then recently been at about its
peak -- the resulting standardised rate has been lower than the crude
death-rate, but the crude death-rate itself under-estimates the incidence
of mortality.

For the purpose of obtaining a true view of the trend we must resort to
the gross reproduction rate and the net reproduction rate. Ideally the
gross reproduction rate should be computed as follows. Each year of the
child-bearing period must be taken separately and the number of girls
born to women of that year of age per thousand women of that year computed (specific fertility rate). These numbers are added together and the
sum divided by 1,000. If the resulting number is equal to one, this means

that the present population is exactly replacing itself, subject to the
condition that none of the children die before reaching the end of their
child-bearing period. If the number is equal to two, fertility is such
that present women are providing two for every one of themselves in the
present generation. If the number is equal to a half, every two present
women are only providing one successor to take their place. And so on.
If the number is two the population may be said to be doubling itself in
each generation. The length of a generation is equal to the average age
of mothers at childbirth, but this average must be computed not from the
actual figures of births as recorded, but from the specific fertility
rates worked separately for each year of the child-bearing age. Thus
starting from the beginning of the child-bearing period, the numbers born
per thousand of each year are added until a number is reached equal to
half the sum of all specific yearly fertilities. The year of age at which
this number is reached may be taken to be the average age of mothers or
the length of a 'generation'.

This gross reproduction rate entirely neglects the incidence of death.
It is none the less of great importance in two ways. (i) Changes in it
give the true measure of changes in fertility. (ii) It indicates the
maximum that can be done to alter a given trend of increase or decrease
by reducing mortality.

The net reproduction rate takes deaths into account.   To compute this,
it is necessary to ascertain from the Life Tables the fraction of girls
born which survives to each year of the child-bearing period. The
specific fertility rate for each year must be multiplied by the fraction
appropriate to that year, and the net specific fertility rates for each
year so derived must then be added together and divided by one thousand
to obtain the net reproduction rate. As before, if this is equal to one,
the present population is exactly replacing itself; but of course higher
gross specific fertilities are required to obtain this number one, to allow
for the wastage among the young due to death. If the net reproduction rate
is equal to two, the present generation of women of the child-bearing age
are bearing so many girls, that the mean number of them who live through
the child-bearing is twice as great as their own number. And so on.

The net reproduction rate in England and Wales for the years 1934-6 was
.76 and gross reproduction rate .87. This means that to every 100 women
of the child-bearing age only 87 were born and of these, if mortality
remains as at present, only the mean number of 76 will survive to contribute the reproductive quota. We are destined to lose one quarter of our
population per generation on the average unless mortality decreases or the
average size of the family increases. But the absolute limit of what can
be obtained by a decline of mortality alone is shown by the gross reproduction figure. Even if no deaths at all occurred among women before the
end of their child-bearing period -- and such a reduction of mortality is
hardly to be hoped for -- the population would be destined to decline at
the rate of 13 per cent per generation. Ultimately an increase of child-
bearing is the only way in which our race can be saved from extinction.

A reduction of mortality in the older years of life can contribute nothing
towards reducing the downward trend. It might vouchsafe a temporary increase in total numbers but would have no effect on the number of those
under 50; this would continue its decline uninterrupted and by the consequent decline in births inevitably reduce the total in the long run.

The figures quoted cannot claim absolute accuracy owing to our lack of statistical information. The age of mothers at the birth of their children has not hitherto been recorded by the Registrar-General. But our knowledge of the age-composition derived from various sources, and inference from the specific fertility differentials in other countries, where fuller information is available, allows an approximation to be made, which is regarded by the experts as likely to be close. The recent passage of the Population (Statistics) Act will secure the relevant information about the age of mothers.

The prospective loss of a quarter of our population in each generation is an average figure; the calculation does not show what will happen in each of the coming years. For while the reproduction rates truly show what the present generation is doing towards replacing itself, the actual rate of decline will continue to be affected by the changing age-composition. And just as in recent years that composition has been abnormally favourable to a natural increase, it will for corresponding opposite reasons, be abnormally unfavourable in coming years, and the actual decline during a number of years must be expected to be more rapid than a quarter per generation.

Next it may be expedient to quote some illustrative figures. The gross reproduction rate for England and Wales in 1870-2 was 2.34 and the net reproduction rate, 1.52. Comparing these with recent figures we see that the average mid-Victorian family was approximately three times as large as the average modern family, and there is no evidence that this mid-Victorian rate was substantially higher than that which had obtained during the previous century. On the other hand the number of surviving children was only about twice as great. This closing of the gap between the gross and net rates measures a remarkable and welcome reduction in infant mortality. But the gap is now so nearly closed that we have little contribution towards survival to expect from a further narrowing.

In Sweden we find analogous figures, a decline in the gross rate from 2.14 to .81 in the same period and a decline in the net rate from 1.45 to .7. In Germany the gross rate was as high as 2.45 in the period 1881-90; it had declined to .82 in 1933, but a subsequent rise to 1.06 is recorded; the net rate fell from 1.44 to .7 with a subsequent rise to .87. In France, despite its bad name for a low birth-rate, the gross rate does not appear to have fallen below 1 nor the net rate below .88.

In Italy in 1922, when the rates in the afore-mentioned countries had already accomplished a substantial part of the downward journey, the gross rate was still 2, but it fell to 1.4 during the following decade, despite the existence of a fascist regime; the net rate stood at 1.18 in 1933. In Poland in the same period the gross rate fell from 2.1 to 1.43 and the net rate from 1.5 to 1.11. In Bulgaria, a country of high birth-rates, a fall in the gross rate from 3.24 (1902-3) to 1.86 (1930-2) is recorded, and a fall in the net rate from 1.87 to 1.27.

Similar declines are observed overseas. In the United States the gross rate was 1.41 in 1920 and 1.04 in 1930-4; the net rates were 1.15 and .94. In Australia the gross rate stood at 1.67 in 1908-13 and at 1.03 in 1935; the net rates were 1.39 and .95. In New Zealand the gross rate was 1.54 in 1911-15 and 1.04 in 1936; the net rates were 1.35 and .96.

In European Russia, a country of high birth-rates, the downward movement
is not so marked but appears to be present: gross rate in 1896-7, 3.44;
in 1926-7, 2.72;   in 1929, 2.4;   net rate in 1896-7, 1.65;   in 1926-8,
1.7.   The immense improvement in mortality offsets the declining birth-rate.

These figures are impressive both by the breadth of the area covered and
the magnitude of the declines. They are extracted from the contribution
of Mr. R. Kuczynski to Political Arithmetic. The countries have been
selected not because they are especially illustrative of the downward
tendency, but because information about them is fullest.

The decline seems to have gained momentum first in France and England and
to have spread more or less rapidly to other countries roughly in the order
of their spiritual propinquity to the countries of origin and their degree
of material well-being. It is extremely rash to prognosticate. We do
not know if the movement in the countries of origin has yet reached its
limit. It appears not unreasonable to suppose that where the downward
movement started late it has not yet done so.

In order to form sensible judgments about the causes and significance of
this phenomenon, it is necessary to revert to certain elementary considerations about the processes of nature. Worthy humanitarians plead that
an improvement in the conditions of the people would soon re-stimulate
the birth-rate, but it is very doubtful if that view is tenable.

The physical mechanisms and instincts and emotions, which sustain reproduction in the human as in other surviving animal species, are adapted
to the severity of the environment. The gross human reproduction rate
has for millennia of man's history stood substantially above one, to allow
for the wastage due to plague, pestilence, famine and war; but it has not
stood so far above unity as that of many animal species.

The environment has undergone great changes from time to time; the generalized and therefore readily adaptable nature of man's instinctive endowment has stood him in this as in other fields in good stead. His capacity
for social organisation, giving rise to clearly defined and tenacious institutions, has also been of service.

The practice of infanticide is an example. It is to be noted that while
this has been widely practiced as a recognised social custom for long
periods and over large areas, it was never pushed too far. The instinct of
parental tenderness though not so strong as to have been a bar to infanticide when that was needed to check over-population, was probably the factor
responsible for checking its excessive application. It is fairly clear
that, if it had been practised throughout the periods when it was allowed
with the intensity with which contraception is practised today, the human
race would not now be inhabiting this planet. And that reflection gives
rise to grave misgivings. If parental tenderness exerts a smaller check
upon contraception than it does upon infanticide, is it not probable that
we are doomed to extinction in the near future?

Social institutions with regard to property are highly relevant to reproduction. The system of serfdom with the hereditary attachment of families
to a given plot of land, the tribal-communal system, the well-being of each
member varying with the power of the group as a whole to aggrandize itself,

the system of private property with free exchange and testamentary rights, each impose their own appropriate inducements and deterrents to the rearing of families; and these institutions themselves may have waxed and waned under the varying incidence of the lethal factors in the environment.

Then there are religious and moral sentiments. The sense of assured security and prospect of indefinite progress in the nineteenth century allowed us to suppose that we could debate the rival merits of traditional marriage and other arrangements purely as contributions to present human happiness. The Christian ideal of family life could be pitted against Ibsen's claim for the paramountcy of the individual's right to fulfil his own best capacities by breaking the tie of incompatible partnerships. But in truth overshadowing any such argument is the question what arrangement will secure sufficient but not excessive reproduction. We do know if any arrangement yet offered as ideal will meet the situation presented by the modern environment.

A history of marriage and the evolution of moral sentiment, relating these to the varying incidence of population requirements, which clearly governed them, has, curiously enough, still to be written. We have not yet had even the barest outline of the story. Only with this knowledge at our disposal can we build anew a rational and surviving ideal of modern marriage or its equivalent. If we pause too long, we may find ideals and moral sentiments imposed upon us by the process of natural selection, the ideals with an insufficient admixture of philoprogenitivity being rapidly weeded out, by the decline of the societies where they prevail.

Towards the end of the eighteenth century and during the nineteenth the environment in this country became for a variety of reasons considerably more clement. The agricultural revolution followed by the growth of overseas trade supplied a greater abundance of nutritive and protective foods and medical progress together with the improvements in sanitation and cleanliness made great inroads upon the incidence of death. Malthus was quick to appreciate the threat of over-population and had good grounds for doing so. While partly mistaken in his diagnosis of factors likely to stimulate the birth-rate and failing to appreciate that the current increase of population was almost entirely due to the fall in the death-rate, he set out clearly the relation of the reproductive instincts to the pressure of the environment in governing the trend of population, and his work is fundamental to the subsequent development of thought upon the subject. Furthermore had the gross reproduction rate not begun to fall in the later part of the nineteenth century and continued to do so at a rate which he could not be expected to predict, we should now be experiencing an intolerable strain of over-population.

What then are the causes of this great decline? It might seem appropriate to divide these into (i) causes making people desire to have smaller families, and (ii) causes enabling them to limit the size of families with smaller violence to natural instincts. It is clear that these must not be regarded as forces which simply have to be added together to deduce the consequent movement. They are intimately inter-related. To illustrate this, I will put forward an extreme hypothesis, which may quite well be true, namely, that the causes referred to under the second head are responsible for the whole movement.

Easy contraception is undoubtedly a new factor in man's environment and one that clearly bears the hall-mark of paramount importance. Methods of birth-control there have always been, natural and artificial. The modern improvements in artifical methods contain the factors of (i) doing less violence to instinctive desire, (ii) doing less violence to natural sensitiveness, (iii) requiring less forethought and self-control and (iv) increased cheapness. Since further large progress in all these respects is expected, it would be very rash to assume that the effect of the increased facilities in reducing births had yet reached its limit. The superiority of the modern contraceptive in doing less violence to natural instincts than natural birth-control and abortion (to say nothing of infanticide) is not open to question.

Those who would challenge the view that this new factor is the sole cause of the decline point to the causes coming under the other head and claim for them an operative power of their own reinforcing that of improved contraception and even, in the view of some, having considerably more importance. Such are the increased availability of alternative interests, cheaper travel and recreations of various kinds, the increased cost of education and the decline of certain moral sentiments. But with regard to these it may be asked why they did not come into force earlier. Are they truly independent causes? The action and reaction of different elements in the environment must be more deeply studied.

Man has a remarkable capacity for diverting his mind from desires which cannot be fulfilled. It is arguable that none of the desires which are or might be included in the foregoing categories are necessary desires in the sense of being a congenital ingredient in the human composition. It is arguable further that none of them are as strong as the desire not to employ natural birth-control. Consequently it is arguable that if the only alternative to the large family had continued to be natural birth-control or some equally unsatisfactory method of artificial contraception, these ulterior desires would never have been allowed to take root; that parents would in fact have continued to have large families and diverted the inventiveness of scientists to devising means for enlivening and enriching the home. This argument cannot be pressed to the point of fully cogent demonstration; but neither can it be shown to be wrong. It is a matter of judgment: and I submit that a man of good judgment may well believe it.

The influence of social custom is also relevant. The best method of spending his time is largely dictated to the individual by the majority or the leaders of fashion. Thus if a given way of life comes to command itself to the majority of people, the others tend to acquiesce from imitativeness or to avoid being held in low esteem or because the means of satisfying their private fancies are not available or are too expensive, because not mass-produced.

A similar argument may be applied to the alleged influence of the cost of education. Why has education been allowed to become so expensive? Would it have been allowed to become so expensive but for contraceptive facilities? A man may say that he prefers to have few children and to give them the best possible chance in life. But would he say that if the mans of preventing children were not more satisfactory than those prevalent a hundred years ago? And why did he not say it a hundred years ago? It is not to be supposed that parental tenderness has increased during that period. And the same argument may be applied to the change in moral sentiment.

I hope that this sociological excursus may be excused on the ground that
these considerations are relevant to the specifically economic causes and
possible remedies of the decline in reproduction. The fact that the
decline has occurred in a period and in countries in which the standard
of living of the mass of people has been higher than ever before decisively rules out the view that the low size of families is due to the lack of
means of parents. The reduction has occurred in a period in which the
parents have had far more means of life than before. And in passing I may
add that the view that the low reproductivity is due to the fear of war,
the unwillingness of mothers to bear children only in order to be cannon-
fodder, is equally untenable. The most notable fall in reproduction occurred in the decade after the last war, when the fear of another war
stood, for reasons which may have been unjustified, as its lowest point.

Poverty is a relative term expressing the ratio between means of subsistence available and the standard of living which their holder regards
himself as entitled to. An increase of means will not make the potential
parent feel himself better able to afford another child if it synchronizes
with a still greater expansion of what he regards as the necessaries of
life. Such an expansion has occurred in recent decades throughout a wide
range of income classes and is welcome in itself. There is no reason to
suppose that it has reached its limit. Indeed there may be some psychological law, which would be quite consistent with the progressive tendency in man to which history bears evidence, by which as opportunity increases
ambition increases still more quickly. If this is so, it is impossible to
hope that further improvements in the condition of the people will be
favourable to reproduction; rather the reverse. Indeed some relapse might
be more favourable; but since it is impossible to wish that the human
species should be saved by such a retrogression, except as a last resort,
some other way out must be sought.

While the decline in reproduction has coincided with increased means of
livelihood, there may be some truth in the view that the cost of a child
including the expense of education at the conventional standard appropriate to the social status of the parent has increased still more. Along
with this must be reckoned the factor, which may be of considerable importance to the majority of the lower income classes, that the prospective
value of a child as an earning asset has greatly receded. Here again
there appears to be no limit to the possible expansion in this cost --
the standard of what a parent thinks he ought to do for his child may
rise indefinitely -- and here again it would be retrogressive to wish for
a reversal of this trend in the interests of reproduction. But in this
case there is clearly a way out; the burden of the cost may be shifted
off the parents' shoulders.

The view that this would stimulate reproduction is not inconsistent with
the hypothesis, set forth above, that contraception is the cause of the
high cost of education and not the high cost of education, the cause of
contraception. This point may serve to illustrate the subtle interrelation of causes already referred to. Consider the extreme hypothesis
that the cost of education would not have been allowed to grow at all but
for the increased facility of contraception. (This is an extreme hypothesis, since it may well be argued that the mere progress of science and
technology requires a more elaborate education to maintain efficiency.

A more moderate hypothesis is that the conventional cost has grown much more than it would have been allowed to do in the absence of improved contraception. The conclusions flowing from the extreme hypothesis may be applied mutatis mutandis to the more moderate one).

Even on the extreme hypothesis, the cost of upbringing and education may have a causal role, in this manner. Suppose that the cost of upbringing and education were rigidly fixed by social convention so firmly that no change in the environment would effect any change in this cost. Modern contraception would then have come into an environment different in an important respect and the effect of its impact would have been different. In these circumstances the parent could not argue that he preferred to limit the size of his family in order to do more for the children he already had; for there would be no means of doing more for them, the pre-existent level of nurture, education and endowment being at once the maximum and minimum that was socially possible. In such an environment the effects of modern contraception would have been less potent. Thus one may hold (i) that modern contraception is the sole cause of the decline, in the sense that if it had not occurred, no decline would have occurred (extreme hypothesis), and, at the same time, (ii) that the presence in the environment of the possibility of expanding expenses of nurture and education has made the restrictive effect of modern contraception greater than it would otherwise have been by a given amount; and that consequently the cost of education may properly be regarded as a true cause of the decline in reproduction by that amount.

It appears to follow that if this particular feature could somehow be taken out of the environment, the restrictive effect of modern contraception could be pro tanto reduced. It may be well to concentrate attention on the proposal for family endowment, although it should be borne in mind that the special adaptation of housing programmes, town and country planning and the provision of social services to meet the needs of larger families are highly relevant.

Family endowment, if it is to have a significant effect on reproduction, must be on a generous, even lavish, scale; and it must be graduated to meet the socially endorsed conventional standard of cost of upbringing and education in each income stratum. On the face of it this would involve a vast and intolerable financial burden. Having this in mind I shall propose a scheme especially devised to meet the requirements of the foregoing argument.

Happily we have on our side the parental instinct, which has resisted the temptation of infanticide through many centuries and, while it has yielded much more to the temptation of contraception, has not yet succumbed completely. We may probably rely on most parents having one or two children; the strain begins to be felt when it is a question of the third or fourth. The family allowance should be confined to children in excess of two and it should be so generous as to exceed the conventional expenses of a child in the appropriate social class and to exceed what parents are able to expend on each of the other two. Thus the present position would be reversed; the parents could feel that by having another child the allowance would not only cover their extra expenses but even enable them to do more for the children they already have. It may be argued that, human nature being what it is, not all the money would necessarily be spent on the children. But since the production of a child would be the sine qua non

of obtaining the money, the scheme would serve its purpose of stimulating
reproduction; and humanitarians could console themselves with the reflection that in all cases the children would be better cared for than they
would be in its absence, and in most cases considerably better cared for.
And there is no reason why some part of the allowance should not be paid
in kind.

In view of Professor Lancelot Hogben's extremely valuable work in stimulating interest in this subject, it is greatly to be regretted that he
gives the weight of his authority to the crude fallacy contained in the
following sentences:- "The phenomena of differential fertility dispose of
the illusion that mere spending capacity favours a high reproductive capacity. Hence it is not likely that any changes in the distribution of
spending power by such means as family allowances will suffice to re-
establish the survival minimum." While we may accept the first sentence,
it is to be hoped that the foregoing arguments will enable the reader to
see that the second is a non sequitur.

In order to make the words generous and lavish more vivid, I venture to
put forward scales of payment. Research into the actual expenditure by
parents on their children in different social classes might provide a
firmer basis for a scheme. The canon is that the allowance per child in
excess of two should substantially exceed what the parents actually spend
on each of those two. I propose £40 per annum for each child in excess of
two to parents below the income tax limit during the period of child dependence, and a quarter of the parents' income up to a maximum allowance
of £400 per annum (income = £1,600) to those above the income tax limit.
It is not practicable to propose an inducement which will have much effect
on the very rich; but the lower and middle-salaried classes and the professional classes, representing a valuable element in our stock, would
certainly be moved by the prospect of assistance on this scale.

The cost of the scheme would be low in the early years, since children
already born need not be assisted, reaching its maximum after 15 years.
In budgeting for it, the assumption should be that it would raise the net
reproduction rate to 1. If it were found to exceed all hopes and over-
stimulate reproduction, the allowances for children not yet born could
then be scaled down. I defer the question of how the money is to be found

I now pass to a brief consideration of the economic effects to be expected
if the decline continues unabated. The prospect appears to me to be
wholly gloomy.

1. Considering the matter from the traditional point of view of the laws
of diminishing and increasing returns, I judge that there is likely to be
a net loss in production per head. The economies of large scale have not
yet reached their limit in this country and a contraction of the market
would lead to diminished efficiency in many fields. On the other hand in
the case of production from the land, it must be remembered that we draw
upon a world market, and the diminution of our demand alone is not likely
to bring about a substantial fall in the cost of agricultural output. If
the world shrinkage of population is taken into account, some net gain
may be registered, but the revolution of methods now proceeding, consequent upon the application of science to agriculture, throws some doubt
on whether the law of diminishing returns works very strongly in the
backward direction away from the present equilibrium. Some, looking at

the matter from a purely strategic point of view, might welcome the possibility of maintaining a larger proportion of our people on home-produced
supplies; but from the same strategic point of view the loss of man power
will more than offset this gain.

2.   In the coming decades we shall have a rapidly aging population and the
maintenance of the older members will be an increasing burden on those
actively employed.

3.   Mr. Henderson, attaches great importance to the reduction of mobility
of labour within the country, which we already feel to some extent, and
which will become more important as the decreased rate of increase in the
population gives place to an at first gradual and eventually rapid net
decrease.   The relative number of workers which each industry requires is
bound to change from time to time, and may change more rapidly if society
continues to advance, since a smaller proportion of consumption consists
of necessary articles and a larger proportion is devoted to quasi-luxuries
the demand for which is less stable.

If the population is advancing a big shift in the relative importance of
industries may occur without any industry undergoing an actual decline.
In that case the problem of immobility is less severe, since the required
adjustment can take place without anyone being compelled to leave his
industry.   Even if the advance is less rapid and some absolute shrinkage
is entailed by a big relative shrinkage, still the problem may not be un-
manageable if this can be secured mainly by superannuation of the old.
But if the population is itself shrinking, the relative decline of some
industries may entail a large absolute decline and the necessity, if an
adjustment is to be secured, of many changing their occupation in middle
life.   And this comes at a time when, owing to the progressive and welcome
rise of working class standards above bare subsistence and the proper provision of unemployment benefit and assistance, it becomes progressively
less easy to persuade labour to make the required shift.   This increase
in immobility must be expected to increase unemployment.

4.   Planners with their eyes on the slums may welcome some reduction in
numbers.   But the fact that the reproduction rate has been well below the
replacement level for more than 15 years makes it almost certain that
they will have their wish;   what has already happened points to some decline in any event.   But the enormous and continued decline which is due
unless the reproduction rate is raised in the near future will give the
planners more problems than it relieves them of.   Our country will present the mournful aspect of a deserted and derelict area, its houses
uninhabited and its equipment unused.

5.   The fifth point is one on which I wish to place special emphasis.
Popular thought supposes that a decline in numbers would relieve the unemployment situation.   The immobility argument points in the opposite
direction.   There is a still more fundamental consideration in favour of
the view that a declining population will intensify unemployment.

The increase of population has provided one of the most important sources
of demand for fresh capital.   Each new head requires its quota of productive capital equipment together with consumption capital in the form of
housing, etc.   Failing this source of demand new capital can only be
required if and in so far as more capital can be associated with each

unit of labour in the productive process. If the demand for new capital is insufficient to absorb the savings which accrue when the economic system is working to full capacity, the system will run down.

During the nineteenth century the natural annual rate of increase of population stood between 1 and 1-1/2% and only fell below 1% in the present century. And, since the infant does not develop his full consumer's demand until later in life, we have continued to benefit from the higher rate of increase of an earlier period. If the total national capital were assessed as four times annual income, the nineteenth century rate of increase would provide by itself a demand for the utilization of savings equal to about 5% of income. This might well absorb a half of the available supply. When the increase of population ceases, this source of demand will come to an end. The situation will be worse if part of the existing capital has to be liquidated. This trouble comes upon us at a time when the channels of overseas investment are closed and not likely soon to be re-opened and technical inventions are not notably of a capital-requiring kind.

The stock remedy for a deficient demand for new saving is public loan expenditure; and the stock objection to this remedy is the increase in the burden of indebtedness on future generations which such a policy entails. If the aggregate output of wealth were increasing at least as quickly as this burden of indebtedness the objection would not be very weighty. But there is serious danger that, when the population begins to decline rapidly, aggregate output will not increase at all. The more the population declines the greater the need will be for public works to absorb redundant savings; but equally the more intolerable will be the growth in the burden of indebtedness. The problem may become so acute as to threaten the institution of private property itself.

It is incumbent on me, in conclusion, to refer to the finance of endowment. There is much to be said for an insurance or pooling scheme, each income stratum having its own pool; for otherwise it may be difficult to overcome the objection of a democratic public opinion to giving sufficient and therefore graduated allowances to those enjoying incomes above the manual wage-earning level. By the pooling scheme each income class would carry its own burden, the less prolific helping the more prolific.

But I cannot refrain from mentioning another proposal. If only the pace of re-armament slackened it would seem most appropriate from various points of view to finance the endowments by public loan. The loans would supplement the deficiency in the demand for new savings to which the decline of population gives rise. If they availed to stimulate population they would prevent an excessive increase in this deficiency and so limit the need for public loan expenditure in the future. If they availed to stimulate population they would reduce the burden which any increase of indebtedness inflicts on the future. And they would meet the criticism which, as economists may recall, Alfred Marshall made of the individualist system, that it tends to invest too small a proportion of its resources in human capital.

READING 16

Professor John Jewkes (born 1902) taught economics at the University of Manchester (1936-48) and Oxford University (1948-69). On several occasions he lectured for periods at universities in the U.S.A. such as Chicago and Princeton.

In the following article he warns against the validity of long-term estimates concerning population change. Jewkes notes the undeniable fact that the record of all past forecasts has been poor and he observes that social scientists must resist the temptation to trust simple extrapolations. It was quite common in the 1930's to extrapolate the ongoing decline in fertility and conclude that mankind was about to disappear. The Caucasians would be the first to go, it was postulated, followed speedily by other races who would copy Western fertility patterns. Jewkes was correct in noting that current trends often change and that unforeseen events happen. Toward the end of the second World War, fertility rose sharply in the Western World, to decline again after 1957. In the less developed countries the death rate fell to unexpectedly low levels after World War II.

In this paper Jewkes eloquently replies to Harrod's arguments and points to the undeniable benefits that smaller families confer. The author also comments upon the various possible financial schemes designed to raise fertility to replacement levels.[16]

[16] Source: J. Jewkes, "The Population Scare", The Manchester School, Vol. X (1939) pp. 101-121.

THE POPULATION SCARE
John Jewkes

In the past, political arithmeticians and economists who have been coura-
geous enough to embark upon long distance forecasts of changes in population and of their economic consequences have been notoriously unfortunate.
Gregory King estimated that the population of England would slowly grow
to eleven millions by 2,300 A.D. Malthus, writing at a time when the
population of England and Wales was around nine millions was palpably in
error as to the limits of growth possible without a fall in the standard
of living. "On the possibility of increasing very considerably the effective population of this country, I have expressed myself in some parts of
my work more sanguinely perhaps than experience would warrant. I have
said that, in the course of some centuries, it might contain two or three
times as many inhabitants as at present and yet every person be both
better fed and better clothed."

In the latter part of the nineteenth century the fear of "a devastating
torrent of babies" was stilled, partly by contemporary facts, partly by
the growing realisation that if there was a 'law' of diminishing returns
there was also a 'law' of progressive inventiveness on the part of man.
But the Malthusian devil was loosed for a time after the war. Mr. Keynes,
perhaps under-estimating the regenerative economic power of the post-war
world and apparently misinterpreting the available statistics bearing
upon diminishing returns, believed that we were confronted, in Europe at
least, with a long period of population pressure. The Old World could not
expect to continue to draw upon the fertility of the New and the post-
war breakdown of economic relations would, apparently, hurry on tendencies
well established even before the war. "Before the eighteenth century
mankind entertained no false hopes. To lay the illusions which grew popular at that age's latter end, Malthus disclosed a Devil. For half-a-
century all serious economical writings held that Devil in clear prospect.
For the next half-century he was chained up and out of sight. Now perhaps
we have loosed him again."

Mr. Keynes had his followers. Wright, quoting Mr. Keynes and Dean Inge
with approval in 1925, explains that these writers "tell us in effect,
that we are living, and that our parents have been living, for fifty years,
in a fool's paradise, believing that they were building up our economic
life upon solid foundations, and preparing the way for a happier posterity,
whereas, in reality, they were squandering our family estates and wasting
the gains of civilization on a mere increase in numbers."

The resurrection of the Malthusian devil turned out, however, to be merely
an exhumation, and since 1930 increasing emphasis has been placed upon
imminent under-population, if not of actual race suicide. The subject has
become a popular one. Estimates of future population have been courageously projected forward for a century with the most startling results.
The quaintest explanations have been advanced for decreases in the birth-

rate and for differences in experiences in different countries. It would perhaps be unfair and futile to quote some of the more extreme forms in which the danger of under-population has been expressed. But eminent economists have recently added their authority to the case for public alarm and remedial action. Mr. Harrod, for instance, has written; "so that it may be that in these present and immediately coming years, we are at the very crisis and climax of human history, that this is the tide in the affairs of men, and that if we do not take it at the flood, albeit a flood which is beginning to ebb fast, the human experiment on this planet will peter out."

The wheel, then, has come full circle. But, in view of their regrettable record in thinking of long-distance population problems, it seems important that, in this case at least, economists should avoid spectacular inter-pretations of available estimates; they should regard with the gravest suspicion any estimates made over more than a relatively short period and should give full weight to the possible appearance of new and unsus-pected economic or social forces or events which might invalidate estimates projected into an unknown future.

I

What is the substance of the alarm now being so authoritatively expressed? The net reproduction rate in Great Britain is below 1, so that the popu-lation is inevitably destined to fall in the absolute unless the rate is increased. But the likelihood is that the actual decline by 1971 will be relatively insignificant. We know that it is virtually certain that mor-tality rates will continue to fall in the future. The really uncertain elements are future fertility rates, and although this is a less important item, migration rates. But it does not appear to be without significance that the birth-rate in this country was, for the first time since 1870, constant between 1933 and 1938. And it would appear reasonable to assume that, at least for a number of years, migration to this country would be on the increase. If we take the estimate made by E. Charles, which ignores migration and assumes that mortality continues to fall whilst fertility remains at the 1931 level, the population of England and Wales is as follows: (in thousands) 1935, 40,563; 1945, 42,338; 1955, 43,651; 1965, 43,744; 1975, 43,021; and in 2035, 33,585.

That estimate has at least as strong a sanction as any other. Its proba-bility value is as high as that of any other. Even if rather more pess-imistic assumptions are accepted it is still reasonable to anticipate that any absolute decline in the population by 1971 will be relatively small.

Why then the scarifying urgency of contemporaneous population discussions? The answer usually given seems very unsatisfactory. It is commonly argued that we must now make a final and irrevocable decision as to what is to be done about population; that if the net reproduction rate is not raised now, then we do inevitably embark on a slippery slope from which there can be no recovery and which inexorably ends in national extermination. This surely is the point that Mr. Harrod seeks to stress where he talks of "this ... tide in the affairs of men" which "if we do not take it at the flood ... the human experiment on this planet will peter out." But it is a point which is far from being obvious.

If a community of 100 people has a net reproduction rate of .75, we can roughly assume that, at the end of one generation, it will total 75 and at the end of two generations 55. Why should it not, having reached 55, now decide that any further fall is undesirable and take steps to raise the net reproduction rate to 1? Why would it necessarily be more difficult to do this at the end of the second generation than earlier? Curiously enough, although the "slippery slope" argument is most vital for the really alarmist view of the population problem, no very convincing reasons appear to have been advanced to support it. Mr. Carr-Saunders has argued that if for long periods families are kept small "all the habits connected with the small family system will harden into customs." But I cannot see that present-day habits would be any easier to break down than customs in the future. He has also suggested that housing conditions would adjust themselves to the small family. But a declining population will surely safeguard us against a housing shortage. More recently he has suggested that, if in the future a rather sudden increase in the size of the family took place, it would constitute a heavy burden in addition to that created by the more than proportionate increase in the number of older people in the community. Reference will be made to this argument later. But it should be clear that if there are serious drawbacks to a declining or a smaller population it would be much easier to raise the community to take action in the future when these consequences would be before our eyes than to do so now when the vast majority of people believe, and I think correctly, that we are becoming unduly pessimistic about them. I can see no reason why a community, if it consciously embarks upon the experiment of allowing the population to fall, does substantially weaken its power to call a halt and to stabilize at a lower level.

In most present-day discussions of population, no distinction is made between the alleged drawbacks of the actual process of a fall in population and the alleged drawbacks of a smaller, as against a larger, population. There may be economic aches and pains associated with the transition from one size of population to another. But that is quite distinct from the relative social and economic efficiency of two populations of different sizes. Yet the arguments regarding the two are bundled together and, in particular, it is frequently implied that no community could ever experiment with a reduction of population because, in the transitional period, the forces making for a decline accumulate an impetus which cannot be controlled and which, in effect, will prevent any stability being reached save at zero population. If that view is correct it ought to be substantiated. It implies that public policy regarding population can only work in one of two directions, either increasing or maintaining the population. Conscious control working for a fall is out of the question. It is just at this point that the sceptics, who have been so often right, join issue with the population experts, who have been so often wrong. The doubters are not convinced that a smaller population will have any very serious drawbacks; they are frequently of the opinion that the opposite would be true. Why not, therefore, let the population fall? If the transitional problems prove to be serious then would be the time to take steps to raise the net reproduction rate to 1.

II

Mr. Harrod, in his recent article, presents a gloomy picture of the economic effects of a fall in population. They appear to me to constitute an insecure basis upon which to erect the social policy which he advocates. Certain of these economic effects are transitional aches and pains; if

we assume that the population could be stabilized at a lower level, they
are, therefore, temporary in character.

Mr. Harrod argues that "in the coming decades we shall have a rapidly aging population and the maintenance of the older members will be an increasing burden on those actively employed." On the other hand, he omits to
point out that there will be a smaller number of children to be maintained
by the actively employed. Enid Charles, even on the basis of a forecast
that the population of England and Wales will fall to 19 millions by 2035,
also estimates that the number of persons aged 15-59 years, which was 64.3
per cent of the total population in 1935, will be 62.3 per cent in 1970
and 60.1 per cent in 2035. This is a decline of insignificant magnitude.
Other estimates give more optimistic conclusions. Thus Colin Clark argues
that "owing to changing age composition, the economic productivity of the
population is going to rise during the next generation" and that, even
after 1975, the decline in the proportion of occupied males will be comparatively small. The other important possible reactions must, however,
be taken into account here. First, if the average size of family falls,
it is not unlikely that there will be an increase in the proportion of
females who are not unduly embarrassed by heavy family responsibilities
and who, therefore, will be able to increase the total occupied population.
Second, the increasing length of life means not only that people live
longer but that they are capable of carrying on effective work to a later
age. A great deal of play has been made with the idea of a 'nation in
carpet slippers' but in fact, in the future, we can confidently expect
that the average person will be able to delay the donning of his carpet
slippers. The proportion of the occupied to the total population would
then tend to increase. The presumption, therefore, is that the nation will
gain, and not lose, within the next thirty years, from the changing proportion of occupied to non-occupied persons.

There is, secondly, the argument that, were the population is declining,
secular changes in the relative importance of industries will creater
greater dislocation of the labour market and make for increasing labour
immobility and unemployment. The validity of this argument, of course,
is not to be doubted. It really constitutes a case for a rapidly increasing population, since a stationary population is also at some disadvantage
here. But this surely is a factor of minor importance, certainly not one
which should count heavily in reaching fundamental decisions relating to
population policy. The upward pressure of population, even in Great
Britain in the nineteenth century, scarcely exceeded 1 per cent per annum.
Population in Great Britain in the next thirty years will probably decline
by less than .25 per cent per annum. Normal retirement of personnel from
an industry through old age or death is about 2 per cent per annum. And
it must not be overlooked that a rapid increase in population leading to
a swift growth of certain industries may, under free enterprise, produce
dislocation in the labour market because of the faulty or short-sighted
judgment of individual workers. The nineteenth century was not free from
periods of severe maladjustment in the labour market, ranging from the
plight of the hand-loom weavers down to the periodic gluts of labour in
the building trades. In any case a policy of encouraging a large domestic
population can bring little relief to industries mainly concerned with
export. Cannan's balanced perspective is surely the correct one: "(the
approach of a declining population) will provide more rather than less
reason for promoting mobility of labour ... we shall have to take more,
rather than less care, than at present to secure that arrangements which

seem superficially desirable do not hinder that mobility." But when Mr.
Harrod seeks to magnify this point and assert that mobility of labour is
likely to decrease in the future, and hence increase unemployment, it
appears that he embarks upon extremely dangerous surmise. It may be true,
as he suggests, that the growing importance of semi-luxury trades will increase the instability of demand and hence the need for greater mobility.
It is probably true that the Unemployment Insurance Scheme has reduced
mobility. And there are many other points that might have been added.
For instance, since female labour is particularly immobile, any increase
in its relative importance will increase general labour immobility. On
the other hand, there are many factors which might normally be expected
in the future to increase mobility. A higher proportion of workers are
being trained in more general forms of industrial skill, particularly in
machine-tending. In the future, we shall probably never have again the
problem of a dislocated labour market in the degree to which we suffered
from it after 1920; our export trades are relatively smaller; our industries less intensely localized. It is only to be expected that, with
increasing experience, the placing work of the Employment Exchanges will
become more efficient: certainly their recently enlarged experiments in
the re-training of unemployed workers hold out enormous possibilities.
I am not suggesting, of course, that mobility of labour in the future will
be greater. In the midst of these, and many other counteracting and im-
ponderable factors, my answer would be that I don't know. But then, I
submit, neither does anyone else.

I turn now to the economic reasons for deploring a return to a smaller
population. Mr. Harrod believes that a small population will result in
a "net loss of production per head. The economies of large scale have
not yet reached their limit in this country and a contraction of the market would lead to diminished efficiency in many fields." This, of course,
is a crucial decision and Mr. Harrod, presumably, has evidence, which could
not be given in one short paper, to back this decision. My own impression
would be exactly the contrary. Most industries in this country consist
of a relatively large number of independent firms and of an even larger
number of independent technical units. Moreover, these units are of varying efficiency. I cannot think that the output per head would decrease in
coal mining, in iron and steel, in cotton, in clothing, in engineering,
in food or in building, if (say) the 20 per cent least efficient firms
were closed down. It is difficult to think of any one important industry
or public service which could not seize upon the full economies of large
scale production with (say) a market of 20 million persons in an area as
small as that of Great Britain. On the other side the cost of congestion
in our main centres of population in the way of traffic delay and the time
spent in reaching and returning from work must be considerable. Clearly,
innumerable and most intricate problems involving economic, social and
administrative issues would have to be settled here before any judgment,
having any claim to scientific responsibility, could be arrived at. I
suggest that we are not yet in a position to exercise that judgment.

Mr. Harrod seeks, even, to snatch away from us the consolation that at
least a diminished population will, by forcing the less efficient lands
out of cultivation, increase agricultural productivity. He believes that
"the application of science to agriculture throws some doubt on whether
the law of diminishing return works very strongly in the backward direction." It may be true, although I am not aware of the evidence, that increasingly scientific methods in agriculture will somewhat lessen the

consequences of inherent differentials in productivity between one piece
of land and another. But those differences still remain substantial. Even
in a country as small as our own, Mr. Kendall has shown recently what substantial variations there are in fertility, and the decline in arable area
in the past ten years, county by county, confirms what most people up to
now have regarded as a truism, that the least fertile lands goes out of
cultivation first. In the United States the yield per acre varies greatly
for the same crop from one State to another. Certainly the decline in
arable acreage in the United States since the war has taken place in the
naturally less fertile lands. It is just as dangerous now to under-
emphasize the importance of the law of diminishing returns as it was, in
the time of Malthus, to over-emphasize it.

Mr. Harrod is particularly alarmed lest a decline in population, by leading to a deficient demand for new saving, will increase unemployment.
This, again, is partly a problem of transition, although it is not wholly
unrelated to the question of the size of the population. His conclusions
are based upon a number of forecasts of probable secular changes in habits
of saving and outlets for investment.

(a) "The channels of overseas investment are closed and are not likely
soon to be re-opened." If by 'soon' is meant a decade the statement may
have some probability value. But if 50 or 75 years is meant, and that is
the period of which Mr. Harrod must think in terms of his population policy, it would seem to have none. Who is to say that, within the next
quarter of a century, there may not be enormous international investment
in China, in South America, in Africa?

(b) "The new technical inventions are not notably of a capital requiring
kind." Here again forecasting seems to be dangerous. But many will be
surprised that the statement should be made even of the last decade. It
is true that there are, at present, no spectacular openings for investment
such as that provided in this country in the nineteenth century by the construction of railways, but, after all, there has been practically no railway building for the past half-century. On the other hand, we have had
enormous growth of investment in road transport and in the generation and
distribution of electricity. Moreover a considerable number of industries
provide illustrations of extremely heavy investment: branches of the
chemical industry; the hydrogenation of coal; mechanization in bottle-
making and flour-milling. But it is not so much the general rule as the
average case that is important. There is a universal tendency towards
mechanization at present which there is no reason to believe will slacken
off in the future. Estimates of the rate at which capital equipment is
accumulating must inevitably be hazardous, but Douglas, in the only elaborate calculation that has been made, indicates that, in the United States,
between 1899 and 1922 there was certainly no tendency for the annual percentage rate of increase of capital equipment to slow down. And the fact
that, in the United States, between 1922 and 1929 the output of durable
goods and capital equipment was increasing much more rapidly than that of
non-durable and consumption goods should at least lead us into caution
when forecasting future technical changes.

(c) A decline in population, of itself, might be expected to create a
tendency towards long-period unemployment. When population is increasing
the multiplication of capital goods of the existing types is a task which
the entrepreneur confidently foresees; he has a fairly definitely pre-

ordained function. If the population is falling, the supply of capital
goods will be maintained only if different kinds of capital goods are
being brought forward. Recognizing Mr. Harrod's eminence in this field
of economics I express doubt on his conclusions on this point only with
the greatest reluctance. But I am not convinced that, in fact, the tendency mentioned above is particularly likely to become actual since possible counteracting forces cannot be ruled out.

There is the whole question of the rate of industrial invention. For many
reasons this might be expected to increase rather than decrease in the
future. Improvements in the general standard of education enlarge the
field of the intellectually trained from whom new ideas may spring. The
increase of mechanical mindedness which normal life demands of us all
may be the forcing ground for further mechanical developments. The increasing proportion of the national income devoted to industrial and
scientific research might have the same effect. Moreover, once a general
body of scientific knowledge exists, each new invention is not only of
value in itself; it becomes possible, very often, to link it with earlier
techniques and apply it almost universally. Thus the internal combustion
engine makes possible, for the first time, controlled flight in the air
but the engine can also be harnessed to the boat, the road vehicle, the
stationary machine. The conveyance of impressions by waves makes possible
the transmission of sound and of form and colour but also opens up the
possibility of more complete use of existing wire telephony. Each new invention is not merely the establishment of a new plant; it is a fertilizer
which leads all the existing trees to push out all their boughs and
branches a little further. It is at least tenable that, in the future,
the consequences of a declining population upon possible avenues for investment might well be offset by the force of invention alone.

There is, too, the question of the increasing use of durable consumption
goods. It may well be that an increasing proportion of the capital equipment of the community is now taking this form and will continue to do so.
The equipment of homes with labour-saving devices; the association of
leisure pursuits with the use of machines, such as television or motor
cars; the replacement of hand-work by the typewriter and the dictaphone;
the more complete control of temperature and air condition within buildings,
including the domestic house; the replacement of the mass-provided public
services, such as the public service vehicle, and cinema by the more convenient (but probably more expensive from the capital point of view) private motor car or home cinema; here are enormous potentialities over a
long period in the case of which the consumer will be clamouring for the
new technique. A rapid increase in the capital intensity of private possessions is certainly not out of the question. The possibilities are the
greater here since the existing inequality in the distribution of wealth
means that there are numerous forms of private capital equipment now in
possession of the rich which, as it were, are on show to the rest of the
community who may frequently seek, by economy on consumers goods, to take
advantage of that kind of equipment. So the dinner parties disappear and
the eight-cylinder car is bought, or the consumption of beer declines and
the motor cycle replaces it.

As a population declines it acquires, almost as a legacy, an increasing
quantity of equipment per head such as more factories, more roads. Some
of that equipment will almost certainly not be found worthwhile to maintain. But other equipment, notably roads, would almost certainly be main-

tained. The cost of depreciation per head of the population would rise.
An increased part of national savings would, therefore, be directed into
these channels; an increased proportion of the population would find employment in these fields.

Finally, it must be borne in mind that, over the next thirty years in
Great Britain the decline in population will be small; that the decline
in the number of adults (who exercise the important demand for capital
equipment) will go on more slowly than in the case of the population as a
whole and that this decline will be foreseen with some confidence and will
therefore not be so serious, from the angle from which we are at present
discussing it, as might otherwise be the case.

(d) If Mr. Harrod is thinking over a long period of the relation between
the demand for new capital and the savings accruing, he must not leave out
of account the possibility of secular changes in habits of savings. Mr.
Clark, indeed, has recently startled us all by the statement that "net
private saving has ceased or become negative." Whether that statement is
true or not, it appears that changes in habits of saving are not impossible
and it is possible that they would be in a direction which would lessen
the evils feared.

Finally, Mr. Harrod feels that "our country will present the mournful
aspect of a deserted and derelict area, its houses uninhabited and its
equipment unused." That is a value-judgment which many would not be prepared to accept. Others might be more prepared to mourn the fantastic
pushing and jostling of our larger centres of population and the de-
humanising influence of constantly living in a large crowd which many of
our cities enforce upon a large section of the population.

III

There are certain social and economic advantages associated with a smaller
population which are generally understood, or, at least, used to be understood, which are, perhaps, worth repetition.

(1) The smaller family has in the past half-century been one of the important devices by which the more brutalizing forms of poverty have been
reduced. Bowley and Hogg have shown that, excluding the effect of unemployment, the proportion of families, in five representative towns, below
the poverty line had fallen, by 1924, to one-fifth of its pre-war level.
Of this improvement, they argued, one-third could be attributed to the
fall in the number of dependents per family. Recent social surveys have
shown that 11 per cent of the families in London below the poverty line
(in Southampton, 17 per cent; Northampton, 9 per cent; Warrington, 28
per cent; Reading, 23 per cent; Bolton, 9 per cent; Bristol, 20 per
cent and Stanley, 32 per cent), were cases where the natural head of the
family was in full work but his income was insufficient to provide even
the barest necessities of life. I cannot help but feel that, in these
cases, it would be better for everybody concerned if the number of dependents had been smaller.

(2) There are, at the moment, certain forms of our social equipment which
are, by the general admission of enlightened folk, inadequate but in the
case of which improvement is hampered by public ignorance, indifference
or selfishness. Outstanding illustrations are houses, schools, hospitals,

pre-natal clinics, playing fields, parks and libraries. A fall in population will automatically tend to increase the services available to each
individual.

(3) The same is true of other long-lived equipment, such as roads, where
an increased supply per unit of population would generally be regarded as
of both economic and social value.

(4) Stationary, or even declining populations, escape some of the wastes
invariably associated with expanding economies. Periods of rapid economic
expansion may lead to numerous industrial mistakes, ill-conceived or over-
optimistic enterprise, the uneconomical exploitation of raw materials and
the mal-distribution of labour. It must not be overlooked that rapidly
growing communities, such as Great Britain in the nineteenth century and
the United States after 1880, have suffered the most violent economic dis-
locations which virtually stationary populations, such as France after
1861, appear to have largely escaped.

(5) The experience of countries such as Sweden and Switzerland, leads
many people to the view that a smaller community can more easily maintain
administrative efficiency and the whole atmosphere of democracy. In the
smaller country the personal contact of the citizen with leaders is closer;
the feeling of democratic responsibility is more immediate; the guiding
political and intellectual spirits of the age are less submerged by the
task of running the administrative machine.

(6) The smaller family has brought inestimable non-economic gains. The
release of women from the burden of unwanted and excessive child-birth
constitutes perhaps the greatest step forward in human liberty that history has to record. The spacing of births may well have had as great an
influence on the health of individuals as any great medical discovery of
the past century. And the restraint that can now be exercised over births
has given to the institution of marriage potentialities in the way of a
long, free, full and equal companionship in most phases of life between
men and women out of which may well arise the supreme achievement of the
art of living and feeling.

IV

Mr. Harrod's anxiety to prevent any fall in the population leads him to
put forward a scheme of family allowances of a novel kind. The parental
instinct, it is argued, may be relied upon to lead most parents to have
one or two children; the allowances would apply only to the third and
subsequent children. And the allowances must be generous enough to more
than meet the full costs of nurture and education of the additional child
so that, in effect, the conditions made possible for the existing children in the family would be improved. For each child over two, the parents
would receive per annum a sum equal to one-quarter of their income. So
that parents with an annual income of ₤160 would, when their family increased to three and then to four children, find their total incomes increased to ₤200 (i.e. ₤160 + ₤40) and then to ₤240. Similarly with parents with an annual income of ₤1600; their income would increase to
₤2000 (i.e. ₤1600 + ₤400) and then to ₤2400.

It is suggested that two alternative methods of financing such a scheme
might be possible: the funds might be raised by taxation or loan or,

alternatively, there might be a pool in each income class, the single and
small family people, in effect, transferring a part of their income to the
large families. The first method, whether the funds arise from general
taxation or loans, seems to me both politically unthinkable and socially
undesirable. The very heavy expenses that the middle-classes must meet in
bringing up their children is largely due to the heavier costs of education
in which they are incurred. A part of that cost is due, of course, to a
real superiority in the education of middle-class children over that received by others. But a part of it is a payment which middle-class parents
pay that their children may enjoy the privilege of passing through, exceptionally expensive, although not necessarily exceptionally efficient, educational institutions, mere attendance at which confers a label of great
value in their subsequent careers. The parents are, in fact, buying monopolies for their children. That, in a democracy, is not a pursuit which
should be openly financed by the State. The inequality in educational
opportunity is one of the most striking social anomalies of our times. To
give it a further sanction by making special arrangements under which the
parents in the higher income groups could be certain of providing a better
education for their children than could those in the lower income group
would be socially retrogressive. Quite apart from the real merits of the
case, moreover, the fact that the rich man was obtaining ₤400 per year for
doing something for which the poor man received only ₤40 a year would provide a weapon for political propaganda which no political party would dare
to face.

Income pooling in each income class, if it were acceptable to the members
of the classes, would not suffer from this defect. But even pooling might
be expected to have its opponents. It would almost certainly produce a
violent re-distribution of income within each class. We have, of course,
no information of how all those receiving (say) ₤800 a year are distributed as between single persons and married persons with one, two, three or
more children. But let us assume the following percentage distribution of
the population (which in fact assumes a net reproduction rate below 1).

Single	Married Income Receivers with Children								Total
	0	1	2	3	4	5	6	7	
18	19	22	17	11	6	4	2	1	100

Let us further assume that Mr. Harrod's scheme is completely under way,
that for each child over the second ₤200 is payable; that the funds necessary for this purpose are raised from the single and the married with no
children or only one child, the single paying 50 per cent more than these
who are married but are without children and three times as much as those
who have one child. It is assumed that married persons with two children
neither receive from nor subscribe to the pool. Then it can easily be
calculated that the following annual deductions would have to be made from
those with an income of ₤800 per year.

	Married Person	
Single Person	No Children	One Child
Ь252	Ь168	Ь84

When it is remembered that these deductions would be in addition to other
taxation and that the pool deductions would be heavier if a distribution
had been taken showing a net reproduction rate of about 1, it is clear
that the scheme would involve an extraordinary re-distribution, the economic consequences of which on personal initiative and habits of saving and
consuming might be equally spectacular. It would constitute a plunge into
the unknown.

Another rough way of calculating the total transfer of income involved for
all income classes can be made as follows. The annual number of births
at present in Great Britain is about 700,000 and the net reproduction rate
.75. About 230,000 extra births are necessary to raise the rate to 1.
But all these extra births would not have to be paid for. Assume that
only 170,000 children are paid for and that the average allowance per child
is only Ь80 and that allowances are paid for the first fifteen years of
the child's life. Then the transfer in the first year would be Ь13$\frac{1}{2}$
millions and would rise to Ь204 millions a year at the end of fifteen
years.

How far this scheme might affect the birth-rate it is not easy to say.
The single young man with Ь800 a year who finds that, if he remains single,
his income will be Ь550 but that if he can marry and accumulate three
children his income will rise to Ь1,000 might perhaps hurry on to this.
Alternatively, faced with the prospect of having to live on less than
Ь800 until he was married and had two children, and finding it difficult
to save as a bachelor because of his contribution to the pool, he might
give up the unequal struggle and decide to remain a bachelor. Some people
who would normally on a salary of Ь800 have had one child and could or
would not have more might decide that it was preferable not to have a
child at all with an income of Ь632 than to have a child with an income
of Ь716. On the whole, the scheme might, however, be expected to increase
the birth-rate but simultaneously create a crop of economic and social
dangers.

(1) At the lower income levels the pool payments would throw very great
hardship on the single man and the small family. If, as is certainly not
unlikely, the single man with Ь160 had to pay Ь50, that would constitute
an intolerable burden, even if it were only temporary.

(2) In certain classes of society, where the birth-rate is even now very
high, such as the very poorest quarters in a dock area, the scheme would
probably increase the birth-rate very rapidly, consequently depress the
standard of living of those in that income group who had small families,
and thus push the prudent section of the population below the poverty
line in order to meet the allowances to be paid to the imprudent.

(3) If the scheme were successful and the net reproduction rate were to
rise higher than 1, presumably the allowances would be reduced. This would

frustrate the legitimate expectations of those who had been led to increase
the size of their family by the possibility of an allowance but had not yet
qualified for allowance. And frequent changes of allowance would create
several series of families being paid varying amounts for performing just
the same services.

(4) In so far as parents were influenced by the lure of the allowance
they would seek to qualify in the minimum period. The relative disadvantage of having one or two children and the possibility that the allowances
might suddenly be discontinued would lead people who did intend to have
at least three children to have them as quickly as possible. This would
destroy the wise spacing of births.

(5) The administrative problem of such a scheme seems altogether formidable. At what age is it to be considered that financial pressure upon
single men is no longer of value? Are single women to pay into the pool?
If so, who is to decide whether they remain unmarried because they choose
not to marry or because they can't find a husband. Are the allowances in
each income group to be operated independently so that, if the net reproduction rate rises to 1, the allowance will be discontinued in one group
whilst continuing to operate elsewhere? What is to happen if parents move
from one income group to another? Would exemptions be given to parents
where the small family was prudent on medical grounds?

(6) Important repercussions on the family institution itself might be
expected. The financial would be one of the elements which would now intrude into every decision about marriage. Or the inducements to further
child-bearing offered by the lavish family allowances might well appear
stronger to a father than to a mother and thus create family discord.

V

I arrive at a single and negative conclusion: that scientific knowledge
of the economic and social consequences of changes in the size of population is still too fragmentary to justify our framing of any population
policy, much less one which constitutes a drastic revolution in the distribution of income. It is true that more, much more, is known concerning
population movements now than half-a-century ago. But it is equally clear
that other questions can be formulated to which answers cannot be provided
with confidence. And beyond this there are factors, which we cannot even
yet formulate precisely, but which we are dimly and obscurely aware might
in the long run be of overwhelming significance. It is necessary to give
the benefit of the doubt to what we do not know. At the present time the
need is for patient and unambitious research into population problems and
not for large scale and precipitous experiment or even for Royal Commis-
sions. Another big mistake by economists on this subject would certainly
put them out of court for the rest of this century.

PART FOUR

THE POPULATION ARGUMENT AFTER WORLD WAR TWO

READING 17

Frank W. Notestein (born 1902) was formerly director of the Office of Population Research at Princeton. He was also President of the Population Council and served as a consultant to the United Nations.

Dissociating himself from the optimum type of theory as well as from those scholars who anticipated an identical course of both birth and death rates in all countries, Notestein focuses his attention first on those socio-economic conditions in which both vital rates tend to change from high to low levels. In other words, he gives an account of the demographic transition (the shift from a high birth and death rate equilibrium to a low birth and death rate equilibrium) and discusses some probable explanatory factors.

Examining the case of Northwestern Europe and North America, Professor Notestein concludes that in these areas fertility declined in response to the ongoing social and economic evolution. Mortality dropped as a result of improvements in scientific medicine and public health practices, which were actually by-products of the scientific revolution and the modernization process. Both of these advances started with the Renaissance and the Reformation and accelerated after 1750.

In most less developed countries the death rates were reduced through the introduction of medical and public health facilities developed in the high-income nations. Birth rates, however, remained high in these less developed countries.

After a review of the negative economic and social implications of the high rate of population growth in traditional agricultural societies, Notestein expresses the fear that the rising demographic pressure may complicate the task of developing an economy to the extent that it actually prevents such an economy from making a decisive break with the past. As a result, one cannot quite rely on the forces of modernization and economic development to push such nations through the demographic transition.

Measures to enhance socio-economic development, he concludes, must be supplemented with direct and indirect population policies which have a dampening effect on fertility.[17]

17
  Source: F. W. Notestein, "Economic Problems of Population Change", Eighth International Conference of Agricultural Economists, Proceedings (London, Oxford University Press, 1953), pp. 13-31.

ECONOMIC PROBLEMS OF POPULATION CHANGE

Frank W. Notestein

For practical purposes, too much of the work done on the economic problems of population is dominated by points of view that lie at opposite poles. At one extreme the optimum population theorists treat the subject as if the major problem were that of deciding on the number of people needed to maximize per capita income or some other goal of their choice. This work is done, or proposed, almost as if the essential questions would be solved once such a number were ascertained. Problems of transition are neglected as if they did not exist -- as if numbers could be changed at will and without repercussions on the economy and society. The abstraction is a dangerous one. It neglects the fact that the nature of the social-economic changes selected to achieve the desired population size partly determines the population size that is desirable. Processes of population change are neither completely flexible nor **frictionless.**

The opposite extreme is equally unfortunate. It tends to treat population growth as following an established and predictable course. In this view, which is usually implicit rather than explicit, all that is necessary is to extract a prediction from some authority, and then set about the problems of meeting the economic needs of the predicted population -- set about it, that is, on paper, not in fact. This procedure also suffers from a fatal defect. There is no immutable course of population growth that can be forecast. Future trends will depend on many things, important among which will be the nature of the steps taken to meet the economic problems of population growth. The nature of the economic changes ahead will be quite as important in determining the size of the population as will the nature of the population growth in determining the magnitude of the economic problems.

One extreme overlooks the processes of population change, and the other treats them as independent of the situation in which they arise. Both fail, therefore, to focus attention on the major questions which are those of the interrelated processes of social, economic, and demographic evolution. The result has been a good deal of rather idle speculation. There is not very much point, for example, in finding the extent to which India or China is 'overpopulated' when the avoidance of continuing population increase would apparently involve a catastrophic loss of life.

Those who treat population as independent of its social-economic setting have contributed even more to the confusion in matters of food and population. Will mankind's numbers eventually outrun the possibility of obtaining a minimum adequate supply of food, minerals, and energy? This question of ultimate carrying capacity is meaningful only in a very restricted way. Any reasonable consideration of the subject will show that the highest conceivable limit would be reached if growth, even at current rates, were to continue for any span of time that could be considered significantly long in the history of the human race. The point is important

because it establishes a principle. Growth must stop sometime, and it must
do so either by a reduction of the birth-rate or by an increase of the
death-rate. If man covets low death-rates in the future, as he always has
in the past, he must eventually reduce birth-rates. The principle established, however, the question becomes one of means and timing, and the
real problems are those of process.

Difficulties also arise when the analysis relates to the needs of a predicted population in the near future. By disregarding the social and
economic processes involved we can think almost exclusively in engineering
and scientific terms. We can talk about the marvels of science and technology as if there were no intervening terms. In a word, we can forget
that we are social scientists who should know that both the application
of new knowledge and the processes of new discovery depend on social settings that have been infrequently present in the world. We forget that we
already know much more than we apply, and that we shall not see science and
technology smoothly applied in some never-never land of economic, social,
and political vacuum. There is great danger that social, economic, and
political difficulties will intervene to bring drastic checks to population increase long before the theoretical possibilities of advanced technology are exhausted. It is in this sense that the problems of social-
economic organization and change, rather than those of technology, seem
the important ones.

This is the thesis, and a warning of the bias with which my paper proceeds.
To make the case it will be necessary to see what we know of the processes
of change, to find the major gaps in our knowledge, and to ask the meaning
of our knowledge and ignorance for research and action.

THE EUROPEAN SETTING

Europe and the industrial countries of the New World furnish us with the
most important information. They provide the longest statistical record,
and they have gone furthest in the transition toward a balance of low
birth- and death-rates. An understanding of their experience gives us
considerable information about the kinds of processes likely to be found
in other parts of the world as technological development gets under way.

First of all it must be recognized that Europe's population growth during
the past three centuries was unique in the world's history. Her population multiplied fivefold, and the population of European extraction increased probably more than sevenfold throughout the world. The major
source of this increase was a reduction of mortality. The decline of the
death-rate was gradual for a long time, as public order and the agricultural, commercial, and industrial revolutions lifted incomes, and as
sanitary and medical knowledge advanced. In the late nineteenth century
a precipitous decline in mortality got under way and has continued to the
present with the virtual elimination of deaths from contagious and infect-
ious diseases. The expectation of life at birth probably was below 35
years in the mid-sixteenth century. Today in advanced countries it is
seldom below 65 years and it exceeds 70 years in the best modern experience.

Meanwhile birth-rates remained generally unchanged until the last quarter
of the nineteenth century. Although they were lower than in Colonial
America, or in the Orient today, they were high by present standards.
Indeed, they had to be high. We may take it for granted that all popula-

tions surviving to the modern period in the face of inevitably high mortality had both the physiological capacity and the social organizations
necessary to produce high birth-rates.

Peasant societies in Europe, and almost universally throughout the world,
are organized in ways that bring strong pressures on their members to
reproduce. The economic organization of relatively self-sufficient agrarian communities turns almost wholly about the family, and the perpetuation
of the family is the main guarantee of support and elemental security.
When death-rates are high the individual's life is relatively insecure and
unimportant. The individual's status in life tends to be that to which
he is born. There is, therefore, rather little striving for advancement.
Education is brief, and children begin their economic contributions early
in life. In such societies, moreover, there is scant opportunity for women to achieve either economic support or personal prestige outside the
roles of wife and mother, and women's economic functions are organized in
ways that are compatible with continuous childbearing.

These arrangements, which stood the test of experience throughout the
centuries of high mortality, are strongly supported by popular beliefs,
formalized in religious doctrine, and enforced by community sanctions.
They are deeply woven into the social fabric and are slow to change.
Mortality dropped rather promptly in response to external changes because
mankind has always coveted health. The decline of fertility, however,
awaited the gradual obsolescence of age-old social and economic institutions and the emergence of a new ideal in matters of family size.

The new ideal of the small family arose typically in the urban industrial
society. It is impossible to be precise about the various causal factors,
but apparently many were important. Urban life stripped the family of
many functions in production, consumption, recreation, and education. In
factory employment the individual stood on his own accomplishments. The
new mobility of young people and the anonymity of city life reduced the
pressures toward traditional behaviour exerted by the family and community.
In a period of rapidly developing technology new skills were needed, and
new opportunities for individual advancement arose. Education and a rational point of view became increasingly important. As a consequence the
cost of child-rearing grew and the possibilities for economic contributions by children declined. Falling death-rates at once increased the
size of the family to be supported and lowered the inducements to have
many births. Women, moreover, found new independence from household obligations and new economic roles less compatible with child-rearing.

Under these multiple pressures old ideals and beliefs began to weaken,
and the new ideal of a small number of children gained strength. A trend
toward birth restriction started in the urban upper classes and gradually
moved down the social scale and out to the countryside. For the most
part this restriction of childbearing was accomplished by the use of folk
methods of contraception that have been widely known for centuries throughout the world. However, they were not widely used until the incentive
for birth restriction became strong. Later, presumably in response to
the new demands, the modern and more efficient methods of contraception
were developed and gained widespread acceptance. By the middle nineteen-
thirties birth-rates throughout the modern West had reached very low levels
The transition to an efficient recruitment of life on the basis of low
birth-rates and low death-rates was virtually completed. Because the

decline of the birth-rate lagged behind that of the death-rate, pending the reorientation of attitudes and beliefs about childbearing, the transition produced an unparalleled period of population growth.

In brief, this is the standard interpretation of the demographic transition. There are other views but they will not stand close scrutiny. One of them is that modern technology has reduced reproductive capacity by producing better diets. This theory fails, among other things, to account for the finding that when the urban women of today do not practice contraception they conceive about as readily as their predecessors did two centuries ago. Neither can the invention of modern contraceptive methods be thought of as the fundamental cause. The trend toward decline was well under way before modern methods had any appreciable importance.

The cases that do not fit easily into the standard interpretation are also important to an understanding of the decline in fertility. Birth-rates have declined outside the urban-industrial setting and, on occasion, have failed to decline in it. American birth-rates were dropping early in the nineteenth century, but the drop was from extremely high levels to those more nearly characterizing Europe. In France, however, rural birth-rates apparently were dropping in the eighteenth century. An early rise of rationalism and a secular point of view may have been involved, but this explanation raises more questions than it answers. Similarly, birth-rates were falling rapidly between the world wars in the Balkans, and notably in Bulgaria which is almost wholly agricultural. Here we may note the presence of popular education, an awareness of the outside world, rapidly improving health, and an extreme shortage of land newly intensified by international restrictions on migration.

Ireland is the most outstanding and difficult case. It is the only country that reduced its population during the last century. The main factor was wholesale emigration beginning after the potato famine. Its birth-rate, however, also fell sharply. The decline came in an essentially rural culture and almost exclusively by means of rising age at marriage and increasing spinsterhood. There has been very little control of fertility within marriage. Here, then, is a rural society in which the motives for reducing fertility became so strong that reproduction was controlled by a measure of self-restraint that other populations have been unwilling to accept. The situation seems so unusual as to make its repetition in other parts of the world unlikely.

On the other side of the matter, birth-rates have failed to decline in a number of urban settings, notably in Egypt and the Far East. In these instances, however, the city dwellers do not represent major proportions of the total population. We may note, moreover, that health conditions are poor, there is little popular education, the middle classes are weak, and often much of the labour force is transient, retaining its familial roots in the countryside. It is also true that the higher economic groups are controlling their reproduction to some extent.

It is evident that urbanization provides no mystical means for the reduction of fertility. The small family ideal and strong motivation for the reduction of births have arisen in a variety of conditions. At present we cannot either list all of the factors involved or attach precise weights to the factors we can list. There is, however, good reason to believe that among the important factors are: the growing importance of the individual rather than the family, and particularly the extended family group; the development of a rational and secular point of view; the growing aware- ness of the world and modern techniques through popular education; improv- ed health; and the appearance of alternatives to early marriage and child- bearing as a means of livelihood and prestige for women.

Some of these factors have been present in most of the situations in which fertility has declined in rural areas. Many have been absent where urban fertility has failed to decline. But it is in the urban-industrial society that all have been present in greatest force. Looking at the scene as a whole, it is difficult to escape the conclusion that the development of modern technology lies at the root of the matter. The societies that de- veloped the technology which produced the declines in mortality were ul- timately transformed by the very requirements of that technology in ways that brought forward the small family ideal and the practice of birth restriction.

The population of the modern West may or may not increase considerably in the future. When death-rates are low, rather small changes in the proportions married and in the number of children born to married women can make the difference between growth and decline. But the almost auto- matic increase of the transitional period seems to be over. From the point of view of problems of food, one important fact should be noted: these populations can check their growth by a further restriction of births any time the wisdom of such a course becomes generally obvious.

EVIDENCE FROM NON-EUROPEAN EXPERIENCE

One of the crucial questions in demographic analysis is whether that part of the world's population whose fertility remains very high would react as Europeans did if submitted to similar circumstances. There can be no cer- tain answer. On the evidence thus far considered we may note only that the principles drawn upon in our account are very general ones -- hence probably widely transferable under appropriate circumstances.

This view is strengthened by Japan's experience, which does not differ in essentials from that of Europe. Here, too, the death-rate led the birth- rate in decline. Moreover, the urban-rural and regional differences in fertility are reminiscent of those in the West. Perhaps the greatest difference lies in the fact that a relatively large part of the decline in fertility was due to rising age at marriage. However, contraception is practised extensively in the urban centres, and currently abortion is rife throughout the nation. During its period of modernization the popu- lation has grown from about 30 to more than 84 millions. Moreover, al- though birth-rates have declined sharply since 1920, the transition is by no means complete. By the time it is complete the period of modernization may have lasted from a century to a century and a half and have resulted in a three-to-fourfold multiplication of numbers.

The hypothesis that the principles of the European analysis are transfer- able to other peoples receives indirect support of another sort. Where, as in Formosa and Ceylon, economic development has taken a different course, the population trends have also been different. In both cases colonial Governments have facilitated a rapid expansion of production in agriculture and rather little has been done about non-agricultural pro- duction. In both cases efficient government, rising production, and effective public health programmes have reduced death-rates sharply.

Between 1905 and the early years of the last war, the Japanese transformed
Formosa from one of the most unhealthy regions in the Far East to one of
the healthiest. Without benefit of sulfa drugs, antibiotics, or modern
insecticides, the death-rate was reduced to 20 per 1,000 by 1940. Since
the war, and with the assistance of funds, medical supplies, and technicians from the United States, the death-rate has been further reduced.
In Ceylon the essentials of the story are not too much different for our
purposes. The early reductions in death-rates were somewhat less impressive, but the recent ones even more spectacular. Under the impact of a
vigorous antimalarial programme, the death-rate dropped from 20 per 1,000
in 1946 to 13 in 1950.

Meanwhile nothing much has happened to the birth-rate of either area. That
of Formosa has, if anything, risen, and that of Ceylon probably has remained rather steady. The 1940 figure was 44 per 1,000 in Formosa, and
the 1950 figure was 40 per 1,000 in Ceylon. Moreover, this effective
stability of birth-rates is exactly what one would expect on the basis of
our European analysis. In both regions agricultural development has been
accomplished with a minimum of disturbance to the existing social order.
Foreign technicians have provided the necessary initiative and supervision.
There has been little general education and little occasion to learn new
skills in an unfamiliar setting. Even in the field of public health the
control of disease has meant an emphasis on doing things for people, rather
than on teaching people to do things for themselves. In short, the programmes of agricultural development administered by outsiders have enhanced
production and improved health, but they have also left relatively untouched the details of social organization, and the customs, attitudes,
and beliefs of the population which throughout the centuries have served
to maintain high birth-rates.

The results in the cases under consideration are rates of natural increase
that have exceeded 2 per cent per year for a considerable time and that
are currently running to nearly 3 per cent. Such rates, if maintained,
double the stock every 23 years. The case of Puerto Rico is in principle
the same. The natural increase is about 3 per cent per year and there are
already more than 650 persons per square mile. Thus far rapid agricultural development under colonial and semi-colonial management appears to
have delayed the demographic transition. It has speeded the decline of
the death-rate, and done so with almost startling efficiency in the past
decade. But it appears to have delayed the sorts of social change from
which the restriction of childbearing might be expected to emerge.

Both the Japanese experience and the different course of events produced
by a different sort of economic development in such areas as Ceylon,
Formosa, and Puerto Rico tend to confirm the hypothesis that the principles drawn from the European demographic transition are widely applicable
throughout the world.

THE PROBLEMS OF DENSELY SETTLED AREAS OF HIGH FERTILITY

To say that the principles drawn from the European analysis apply to the
world's present areas of high fertility is, of course, a far cry from
saying that we may expect events to take a similar course. Possibly they
will in the parts of the world that, like Europe at the beginning of its

transition, are relatively lightly populated in relation to the resources potentially available. But in the densely settled regions of Asia the initial conditions are strikingly different from those of Europe a century ago. It is to these regions, containing more than half of the world's population, that we shall devote our attention because they present the major problems both of food supply and of population change.

It would, of course, be advantageous if the transition to low birth- and death-rates could come as an automatic by-product of economic development. Difficult social, political, and moral questions could then be avoided. Economic development is generally wanted, at least in principle, and is urgently needed to meet the immediate problems of poverty and disease. With an automatic demographic transition, changes that are immediately wanted could become the unrecognized carriers for the changes that are ultimately necessary. However, many factors suggest that the regions under discussion face no such easy prospect.

Much remains unknown about the actual demographic situation, and still less is known about the details of the economy and of the resources available. Moreover, the situation is by no means uniform from region to region. For our purposes, however, the general picture is clear. The populations are heavily agrarian; probably more than three-quarters of the people are dependent on agriculture. The amount of cultivated land per person is extremely small, and significant extensions would be expensive. The vital rates are not known precisely, but there is good reason to believe that birth-rates are generally above 40 per 1,000. This figure is higher than any ever recorded in western Europe. In spite of universally high birth-rates, population growth is by no means universally rapid. Indeed, by Western standards it has been rather slow, because death-rates are in general extremely high. Again, exact figures are not available for the major populations. However, the expectation of life at birth is probably not as much as thirty-five years in India, and may be even lower in China.

Starting from this position, what is the magnitude of the economic task if the transition to low birth- and death-rates is to come as the by-product of a successful programme of economic development? Since no special effort would be made to induce declining birth-rates, our previous analysis would lead us to expect no immediate or substantial change.   Birth-rates would remain for several decades at about their present level -- say 40 per 1,000 population. Moreover, efforts to reduce death-rates would be fostered. Few people would hold that a demographic situation was at once sufficiently relaxed to make unnecessary any effort to reduce the birth-rate, and so desperate that reasonably available techniques for preventing death should be withheld. What, then, would happen to population increase?

A death-rate of more than 20 per 1,000 would be most unlikely under the assumed conditions of economic development which would provide progressively rising per capita incomes and reasonable health protection. A birth-rate of 40 and a death-rate of 20 yield an increase of 20 per 1,000, or 2 per cent per year. This rate doubles a population in 35 years and trebles it in 52 years. Formosa experienced such a rate of increase during the period of Japanese control and, as we have seen, in several regions the current increase is even more rapid. Under our assumption of a programme of economic development, which is to be continuously successful in improving living conditions, birth-rates would eventually begin to fall. In the early stages, however, the reduction would be offset by the continued

decline of the death-rate. It seems likely that, under these imaginary
conditions, the rate of population growth would be between 2 and 3 per
cent per year for several decades -- perhaps for two generations.

A programme of economic development sufficiently successful to yield progressively increasing per capita income would therefore need to be a programme that improved living conditions for populations growing at between
2 and 3 per cent per year. At least this would be the case under our assumption that no special efforts were required to reduce birth-rates or
to check the decline of the death-rate. Such an expansion of the economy
is no mean undertaking even when land and other resources are relatively
abundant, populations are literate, and the incomes are high enough to
facilitate capital accumulation. But it is a staggering task in the absence of such conditions.

Let us consider some of the problems that would be faced in the Orient.
It may be taken for granted that the labour force in agriculture ought
not to expand. If per capita incomes are to increase, the need is for more,
not less, land per worker. The increase should be drained off to the non-
agricultural sector of the economy. Such a transition would involve an
enormous effort. It would mean that a sector of the economy on which less
than one-quarter of the population is dependent would have to absorb the
total increase. On this reckoning a 2 per cent rate of increase in the
total population would require the non-agricultural sector of the economy
to expand at an average annual rate of 5 per cent per year for the first
thirty years. Among other things, such an increase would require a rapid
expansion in non-agricultural investment and in non-agricultural skills.
Meanwhile, a relatively constant agricultural labour force would have to
increase its production at rates well above 2 per cent per year in order
to provide an improving food supply for populations growing at 2 per cent.
Heavy investment in agriculture would also be required. Under these imaginary conditions a 4 per cent annual rate of expansion in total production would scarcely seem adequate.

Moreover, there would be long-run problems of sheer size involved. It
seems most unlikely that the regions concerned could expand their agricultural production rapidly enough to provide adequate diets for two
billion people in thirty-five years. To do so might well require trebling
agricultural production. England and Japan solved their analogous problems
by selling their industrial and commercial services to the world in exchange for food, but their populations constituted no substantial part of
the world's total. Here, however, we are dealing with more than half of
the world's population. The problems of securing the necessary resources,
production, and markets for trade on this scale would seem insuperable.

Unfortunately this is not the end of the difficulty. Much might be accomplished if there were ideal conditions of social-economic organizations,
appropriate skills, and populations well oriented to the factory and market economy. The actual situation is the vastly different one in which
new Governments are endeavouring to rule huge numbers of uneducated peasants who are increasingly aware of their difficult position. Great unrest, great uncertainty, and great yearning for a better life are present,
and complicate the attainment of the discipline needed to build a strong
economic machine.

It may be argued that the picture is overdrawn. We have dealt with an annual increase of 2 per cent, whereas in most of the regions under consideration the rate of population growth has been less than 1 per cent. But recall the problem. We are not discussing what will occur. Instead we are considering what would be required if reliance were to be placed on the automatic processes of social-economic change to bring the transition to low birth- and death-rates.

With existing high birth-rates and modern methods of controlling disease, a smaller rate of increase -- say 1 per cent -- would mean either: (a) that gains in production were too small to permit the attainment of reasonable health in spite of efforts in that direction or (b) that mortality was intentionally held high to relieve the pressure of population increase. The latter could scarcely be envisioned except as a temporary means of avoiding the perpetuation of the former. In reality, therefore, both alternatives come to the same thing. They amount to holding death-rates up, as a substitute for reducing birth-rates. That amounts, in turn, to admitting that rates of economic development that permit increases of only 1 per cent are inadequate to yield sustained improvements in living conditions if birth-rates stay high.

The conclusion is one that an examination of the past records of India, Java, and Egypt amply justifies. Indeed, as their records show, the dangers are greater than we have indicated. Programmes of economic development that just manage to meet the needs of gradually expanding numbers run the risk of being worse than useless. Being insufficient to change the conditions of life, they run the risk of expanding the base populations without reducing their capacity for still further growth.

To me it seems evident that almost insuperable difficulties are involved in achieving the sort of economic development required to permit reliance upon the automatic processes of social-economic change for the transition to low birth- and death-rates. The difficult initial conditions, and the new efficiency with which disease can be controlled, require measures that will speed the reduction of birth-rates, if programmes of economic development are to achieve their objectives. But this conclusion has an embarrassing consequence. If it is valid, the already difficult task of economic development becomes more complicated than ever. The objective is no longer restricted to the increase of production. It now also becomes that of speeding the processes of social change in directions that yield falling birth-rates, which in turn will permit more rapid increases in per capita income. In effect, we must move from economics to sociology and back again, travelling always in a political world.

Moreover, the problem is that of stimulating social change without inducing a measure of social disorganization that leads to catastrophe. By definition, the stimulation of social change involves weakening loyalties to the institutions and beliefs that have served to give stability and continuity. When these bonds are weakened, internal pressures may well become explosive. The very efficiency of modern medical techniques enhances this risk. It is now quite possible to keep people alive in spite of appalling living conditions. There is much less danger than there used to be that the failure to enhance production will lead to the curtailment of population growth by epidemic and starvation. Now the danger is that even the best efforts will fail to improve living conditions among populations newly aware of their disadvantaged positions.

Rising internal pressure and the weakening of traditional social bonds can easily result in political explosions; indeed, they are doing so. It is not at all unlikely that political explosion, and the economic disorganization which accompanies it, will provide the major check to population increase in the future. Populations living close to the level of subsistence, yet dependent on increasingly complex economic organizations, are vulnerable to the failures that complexity entails in times of disorganization. Today, the risks appear to be those of political upheaval, its attendant economic disorganization, and the resulting catastrophic loss of life. To be sure, times of upheaval can also be times of rapid social change that could assist in the resolution of long-run problems. Before the fact, however, the direction of the change is difficult to predict. Moreover, the loss of life could be great. In view of this risk, the advocate of social upheaval must be completely convinced of the futility of a humanitarian policy of social evolution.

It is in this tense situation that the resolution of long-run problems requires the stimulation of social change. The difficulties are insidious. No Government and no international organization can afford to take the long view when pressed by immediate emergencies. The situation two decades from now attracts little attention when a major catastrophe looms this year. Hand-to-mouth action is literally essential; yet it may intensify future problems.

The problems are by no means limited to demographic matters. It seems likely, for example, that immediate increases in the production of food can best be obtained by steps that involve minimum disturbance of the existing social-economic organization, interference with vested interests, and difficulty in obtaining community co-operation. In short, immediate gains in production can probably be maximized by minimizing the changes in the institutional organization of the economy. Yet, in the long run, fundamental changes in the institutions, attitudes, and beliefs are probably as essential to the attainment of high economic productivity as they are to stimulating the decline of the birth-rate. The social organization of a peasant society is ill-adapted to the achievement of high technological proficiency. There is much easy talk about the necessity for each society to follow a line of development consonant with its own values, but those who seek to reap either the productive possibilities of modern technology or the lasting benefits of good health will, in all probability, have to undergo a reorientation of their value structures. At least such a reorientation has occurred in all populations that have made substantial progress toward these goals.

The difficulty is that the need for immediate efficiency requires a minimum of disturbance, whereas long-run success requires rapid social-economic evolution. In the West and in Japan the possibility of a severalfold multiplication of population permitted the necessary compromises between immediate and eventual needs. The apparent impossibility of such multiplication in the regions under discussion is the major source of the difficulty. Hence the need for attaining new efficiency in the processes of social change.

It is this line of reasoning that led to our initial proposition that the important economic problem of population is not either that of locating some ideal goal in terms of size, or that of finding the means of attaining adequate living conditions for some inevitable rate of increase. The

real problem is that of population change. Within the limits of the possible, what course of events will minimize human suffering?

IMPLICATIONS FOR RESEARCH

To answer such a question our knowledge is at present wholly inadequate in
the fields of economics, sociology, and demography. In demography our
theory of the broad processes of population change seems to have been sufficiently tested to prove its general validity. It is adequate to delin-
eate the nature of the problem at hand. But it does not answer the concrete questions on which information is needed either for purposes of prediction or for the formulation of policy. It does not do so because it
tells us almost nothing precise about costs, magnitudes, and rates of
change; and it gives us a minimum of information about the effects of
particular courses of action. Yet the formulation of wise policy will require as detailed knowledge as it is possible to secure. Whatever the
situation may be in economics, in demography it seems to me that there is
less need for work on the over-arching theory of change than for knowledge
at lower levels of generality.

We may illustrate the needs in the case of fertility. We have argued that
reduction of the risk that economic development may fail to achieve its
goal requires an early decline in fertility. In effect this means endeavouring to reduce the birth-rates within the peasant society. Both theory
and experience indicate that such a reduction is difficult to bring about,
but also that it is not necessarily impossible. What do we need to know
to permit an intelligent effort to be made? There are two broad lines of
approach. In the first place, direct measures may be taken. In the second
place, background factors of the economy and society can be manipulated to
some extent.

One direct measure is to lift the age at marriage. What would be the best
measures of community education, legislation, and incentive taxation to
take in this direction? The problems are suitable ones for experiment, but
we know almost nothing about them.

Direct efforts can also be made to reduce childbearing by spreading the
practice of birth control in its various forms. We know that resistance
is great but that, under suitable conditions, something might be accomplished. Although people in most peasant societies want large families,
the truly huge family is not always considered desirable, particularly by
the mothers. Some interest in the possibility of limiting childbearing is
always present. The extent of such interest does not make itself evident
currently, because the majority of the population takes it for granted
that the restriction of childbearing is not really a practical matter. An
intensive programme of public education, coupled with competent technical
advice, might accomplish a good deal. But here again the questions are
what precise programmes, with what results, and at what costs. The questions are readily amenable to investigation and experiment. It is within
the bounds of possibility that the wise use of modern methods of communication and training to promote higher marriage age and the practice of
birth control would bring a considerable reduction of the birth-rate even
in peasant societies.

The problems will not be easily solved because local willingness to attack
them energetically presupposes an understanding of their importance. Dom-

inant beliefs and attitudes often are not congenial to the spread of such
an understanding. Little enthusiasm can be expected for activities designed to reduce the birth-rate if, as is often the case, the community
thinks it needs more children instead of fewer, and views action taken to
limit childbearing as immoral. In this situation the second type of approach, which endeavours to stimulate interest in family limitation by
manipulating the background factors, may prove to be even more important.
We may give only a few examples of the sorts of questions needing examination.

If, as our analysis suggests, the dominance of the extended family is an
important element in supporting high birth-rates, what can be done to
weaken that institution? An obvious approach is to provide more effective
means of fulfilling the functions now served by the extended family. Many
of these fall in the field of elementary economic security. What are the
alternative possibilities and what are their costs? At present it is often
economically advantageous to have many children. How could the lines of
interest be changed in the most acceptable form by means, for example, of
taxation and of changes in property institutions? These questions have
not been seriously examined.

For the purpose of inculcating an innovative point of view and a rationa-
listic approach to life, could not something be done about the ways in
which agricultural innovations are introduced to the community? Could not
the community organizations for the improvement of agriculture be utilized
in ways that would give added prestige to families with educated children?
In short could not existing interest in better crops be used to extend
interest in other forms of economic and social change?

There would seem to be even more direct possibilities connected with public
health activity. Could health programmes be used to transform the existing
ideal of many children into the ideal of a few healthy children? In general, would it not be possible to construct programmes of agricultural development and public health in ways that would stimulate many of the social
changes that came as a by-product of urban-industrial development in Europe? Very little work has been done on this problem.

There are any number of such questions. How can programmes of land development be managed to increase the mobility of young people, thereby weakening the pressures toward traditional behaviour exerted by the elders of
the family and community? It is the women who best understand the difficulties of bearing and rearing large numbers of children. What measures
can be taken to enhance their status? What economic and social alternatives to early marriage and abundant childbearing could be provided for
them? Are cottage industries so important to the economy as to be worth
the dangers of adding new economic functions that are fully compatible with
high reproductive performance?

Although we have argued that urban-industrial development will not be sufficient to bring the demographic transition, it is also clear that it will
be necessary in economic terms and useful in relation to population trends.
How can such development be guided in ways that speed the rise of marriage
age and the restriction of childbearing?

What are the possibilities in the field of popular education? How can its
scope and content be arranged to stimulate an innovative and rational view

of life, to enhance the importance of the individual as opposed to the extended family group, to improve the status of women, and to substitute the ideal of a healthy prosperous family for that of a large family? What are the possibilities, and what are the costs?

Perhaps the most fundamental of all questions are those of the allocation of scarce resources to meet unlimited needs. How much of the product of economic development can be allowed to go into immediate consumption, and how much must be deflected to capital equipment, education, health, and the provision of elemental security? The answers may well be essentially political, and the decisions are inevitably hard. They are being taken every day, implicitly. Nevertheless, there are differences of opinion as to what existing programmes may be expected to accomplish in the near future, and whether, if they succeed in their immediate aims, they may not do more harm than good in the long run. Such differences of opinion are eloquent testimony to the complexity of the problems and to the paucity of our knowledge.

We have confined our suggestions about the scope of needed research to questions of human fertility because that is the fundamental variable. In many situations, however, migration also offers a possibility of relief during the period of transitional growth. Here, too, our information on the economic, social, and demographic aspects of specific plans is grossly and needlessly defective.

Little in the way of concrete action may be expected until the political leadership of the regions concerned becomes aware of the need for curtailing population growth. In a number of regions such an awareness shows signs of developing at the highest levels, but it is not as yet broadly based. Widespread studies by local scholars of the processes of population change under a variety of conditions of economic development could do much to stimulate interest. The subject is charged with emotion, and citizens of prosperous nations are inevitably open to suspicion as to their disinterestedness. It seems likely that local political leaders can be brought to an understanding of the relation of population growth to health and prosperity most effectively through the work of their own scholars studying the practical problems of population, social, and economic development.

Given an understanding of the problems by local leaders, and a large store of detailed information about the costs and potential results of a wide range of possibilities, the problems may yet find their resolution. It is quite possible that we can learn to speed the reduction of fertility with something of the efficiency with which we already reduce mortality. If so, we shall greatly enhance the chance that economic development can mean sustained improvements in health and living conditions for the world's poorest peoples.

If there is a moral to this analysis for the economist, it lies in the fact that he should stray from the well-worn and familiar paths if he is to be truly useful. His problems are not simply those of production, distribution, and consumption within the framework of well-established institutions. In view of the demographic situation, his hopes for long-run success in ameliorating living conditions must lie in speeding the change of institutions. In short, to be useful the economist must also be a general social scientist, for, in view of the demographic situation, the key problems are the interrelated ones of social, economic, and political change.

READING 18

Harvey Leibenstein (born 1922), formerly associated with the University of
California at Berkeley and now teaching at Harvard, was the first author
to set forth a conceptual framework explaining completed family size.

In his book Economic Backwardness and Economic Growth, he presents a systematic analysis of the costs and benefits of an added child. Childbearing is treated as one course of action among others and prospective parents
balance the benefits against the costs of the additional birth with particular attention to their income and market prices.

Leibenstein divides utilities, or benefits, from children into consumption
utility, production utility, and security utility. For most parents children are a source of pleasure. Besides, children can have economic value
as they can help on the farm or otherwise contribute to the family income.
In certain societies parents can also rely on their children for security
in old age. Discussing disutilities, or costs, Leibenstein divides them
into the direct costs of rearing children and the indirect costs. The
best known variety of indirect, or opportunity, costs is the sacrifice of
potential income that the wife could have earned had she been able to join
the labour force. But children tie the mother to the home and earnings
are thus foregone. Besides, extra children tend to diminish social and
spatial mobility. A smaller family finds it easier to move socially and
geographically.

In the course of the development process, incomes rise and fertility declines. Leibenstein hypothesizes that in the process of modernization an
increasing proportion of the population moves to urban centers to work in
industry and in the service sector. The production and security utility
of the added child declines, whereas both his direct and indirect costs
increase. The negative relationship between income and fertility is
thus explained.[18]

---

[18]
   Source: H. Leibenstein, Economic Backwardness and Economic Growth
(New York: John Wiley & Sons, 1957), pp. 161-165.

THE ECONOMIC THEORY OF FERTILITY

Harvey Leibenstein

And now to the theory proper.

The object is to formulate a theory that explains the factors that determine the desired number of births per family. Of course, family size depends also on how many of the births survive. Our central notion is that
people behave in the same way as they would if they applied rough calculations to the problem of determining the number of births they desire.
And such calculations would depend on balancing the satisfactions or utilities to be derived from an additional birth as against the "cost", both
monetary and psychological, of having an additional child. We distinguish
among three types of utility to be derived from an additional birth and
two types of cost. The types of utility are: (1) the utility to be derived from the child as a "consumption good", namely, as a source of personal pleasure to the parents; (2) the utility to be derived from the
child as a productive agent, that is, at some point the child may be expected to enter the labor force and contribute to family income; and (3)
the utility derived from the prospective child as a potential source of
security, either in old age or otherwise.

The costs of having an additional child can be divided into direct and
indirect costs. By direct costs we refer to the conventional current expenses of maintaining the child, such as feeding and clothing him at conventional standards until the point is reached when the child is self-
supporting. By indirect costs we refer to the opportunities foregone due
to the existence of an additional child. These are represented by such
lost opportunities as the inability of mothers to work if they must tend
to children, lost earnings during the gestation period, or the lessened
mobility of parents with large family responsibilities.

We may discern three changes that occur during the course of economic development that affect the utilities and costs of an additional child. It
is convenient to refer to these as (1) the income effects, (2) the suvi-
val effects, and (3) the occupational distribution effects. That is to
say, economic progress is characterized by increases in per capita income,
increases in the chances of survival, and changes in the occupational distribution, and each tend to alter the motivations toward having additional
children. To analyze our problem, we examine what happens to the utility
and cost aspects as these three effects play their roles during economic
growth.

Consider each of the effects in turn. The income effects are summarized
in figure 10-3 below. It depicts the relations between alternate levels
of per capita income and the utilities and costs of an additional child.
The curves marked a, b, and c depict how the three types of utility to be
derived from a child are likely to change as per capita income increases.
The relations (a) between the consumption utility and per capita income

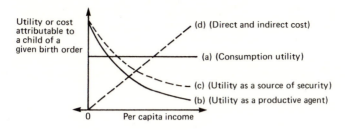

Figure 10-3

is difficult to determine, since it is hard to say whether parents get
greater or less satisfaction out of an additional child if their income
is greater rather than smaller. Arguments can be found for both views.
If other sources of satisfaction and direct possibilities for personal ful-
fillment are exceedingly limited, it seems reasonable to suppose that a
great deal of satisfaction is to be derived from a child. Usually an exceedingly high prestige is attached to the bearing of male children in
backward economies. On the other hand, the complementary goods necessary
for a child's development (and hence the satisfaction derived from observing such development) are more readily available with higher incomes. It
is possible that with respect to children of the higher birth orders,
greater utility is derived at lower income levels rather than at higher
ones, but in the absence of more definite information, it is assumed that
the consumption utility does not change in any significant way with changes
in income.

The relation (b) between the value of a child as a contributor to family
income and changes in per capita income is fairly clear. As per capita
income increases, there is less need to utilize children as sources of
income. At the same time the level of education and the general quality
of the population implied by a higher income per head mean that more time
must be spent on child training, education, and development, and therefore,
less time is available to utilize the child as a productive agent. Therefore, the higher the income, the less the utility to be derived from a
prospective child as a productive agent.

As incomes rise, the possibilities for parents to provide for their own
old age, to insure themselves, and the ability of the state to provide
adequate insurance unquestionably increase. As a result, the need for
children as a source of security declines. Hence, the shape of the curve
marked c.

The conventional costs of child maintenance increase as per capita income
increases. The style in which a child is maintained depends on the position and income of the parents; therefore, we expect such costs to rise
as incomes rise. The indirect costs are likely to behave in a similar
manner. Opportunities for engaging in productive or in various time-
consuming consumption activities are likely to grow as income increases;
therefore, the opportunity costs of having to tend to an additional child
rise accordingly as income increases.

The survival effect is, of course, closely related to income expenditures and costs. In a sense it is not a unique aspect of the situation. It is a consequence of the increased expenditure for the maintenance of children. However, we would not expect the relationship between increased expenditure and survival to be either a proportional or a linear one. First, not all direct costs result in increased survival. Second, when mortality rates are high, decreases in mortality are easier to attain. As mortality rates decline further improvements can be achieved only at progressively greater costs per unit increase in the expectation of life.

The survival effect on the three types of utility curves depicted in figure 10-3 is of special interest for our purposes. In general, increased survival rates raise the utility curves, since for each birth there are more prospective years of life and, therefore, more expected years of satisfaction. This is true also with respect to the utility of children as a source of family income and as a source of old-age security. It is important to note, however, that the survival effects will not be in proportion to the increase in the survival rates, a fact that turns out to be exceedingly important for our theory.

Indeed, what we have here is something that may be called "overcoming the infant mortality hump." Infant mortality rates are very much higher than average mortality rates, sometimes as much as fifteen times above the average rate. As mortality rates decline the infant mortality rate declines, at first, much more rapidly than the others. The initial survival effect is a considerable increase in the number of children per conception who conquer the high infant mortality hurdle. The economic costs of children decline since a higher proportion reaches the productive age groups where they make at least some contribution toward their maintenance. Therefore, the initial survival effect is to enhance the productive value of an additional birth. However, as mortality rates continue to decline, the relative impact on the infant age group lessens compared with the impact on the higher age groups. The decline in mortality rates in the relatively high age groups will have less effect on the prospective utility of a child than similar declines in the low age groups. As a source of parental income, increased survival in the higher age groups is unimportant since in those age groups the children have their own family financial responsibilities. Also, as a source of parental old-age security, increased survival in the high age groups is unimportant since most parents cannot hope to live to the point where their children fall into the very high age groups. Thus we see that beyond some point the survival effect must become progressively smaller as a force that motivates the desire for additional children.

The occupational distribution effect consists mostly in adding to the direct and indirect costs of children. As incomes increase, so do the degree of specialization and the degree of economic (and possibly social) mobility. The number entering narrower, more specialized, and more urban activities also increases. The new occupational environment limits opportunities for child labor, requires more costly training for children, and necessitates smaller family obligations on the part of the parents so that they can take advantage of the new and different economic opportunities.

This last point is related to the "social capillarity thesis" about which much has been written in demographic literature. As summarized in the United Nations report, this theory is roughly as follows:

The desire to improve one's position in the social scale has been stressed
as an important motive for family limitation. The argument is particularly
associated with the name of Dumont, who in the latter half of the nineteenth century devoted an extensive series of studies to this phenomenon,
which he termed "social capillarity" (capillarite sociale). Just as a
column of liquid must be thin in order to rise under the force of capillarity, so also must a family be small to rise in the social scale. He
and many others have argued that during the period when family size declined, the mobility between social classes increased greatly, and new
attitudes toward social mobility developed. Whereas formerly most men took
their social position for granted, concern with improving one's own position or that of one's children became an ever-pressing preoccupation in
those countries where family limitation spread. The effect of social mobility on fertility appears to be attributed in general to the fact that
rearing children absorbs money, time, and effort which could otherwise be
used to rise in the social scale. Social mobility is thus more feasible
with one or two children than with a larger number.

The "social capillarity" theory is, of course, only part of the picture.
But it illustrates well the notion that the increased specialization implied by the growth in per capita output and the consequent changes in
the occupational distribution imply concomitantly a set of social and
economic circumstances in which the opportunity costs (that is, the economic opportunities foregone as a result of having to tend to children)
of a large family increase rapidly. It is worth noting that the "social
capillarity" type of opportunity costs probably depends more on the rate
of growth of per capita income than on the level of per capita income.
The greater the rate of per capita income growth, the greater the extent
of the new economic and social opportunities that open up, and the more
attractive the possibilities of economic and social mobility. Therefore,
the more rapid the rate of growth, the more of a burden children and
family responsibilities are likely to be. Hence, if this were the only
factor at work, we would expect that the more rapid the rate of growth,
the greater the motivation for family limitation.

READING 19

Colin Clark (b. 1905), a statistician and economist, is presently teaching at Monash University in Melbourne, Australia. Clark is one of the
few remaining Western economists who are still enthusiastically pronatalist. Dense and growing populations promote prosperity and national
strength and stimulate innovation and discovery, he says. Like the
Mercantilists of the 16th and 17th century, Clark believes that numerical
density and growth induce men to exercise their power and ingenuity
which results in scientific and socioeconomic progress.[19] In reality
it seems rather that the various forms of progress are due to non-demographic factors, otherwise the most crowded areas should be the most
innovative and progressive while in fact the opposite is often true.

Clark also states the view that the earth can sustain 28 billion people
if all arable land can be made as productive as that in the Netherlands.
Such a project, however, would require enormous investments in land
improvement and education, which would take many decades to realize
even if the funds could somehow be found. In addition, the number of
people the earth can feed at one time is only part of the question.
We must also ask how long 28 billion people can be maintained year in
and year out, since every living person consumes depletable raw materials. And finally, as Wicksell has pointed out, the maximum population
is by definition always the worst. What matters is not that the upper
limit, set by the limits of food supplies, is 28 billion or some other
number. What really counts is that living human beings, whatever their
number, can lead satisfactory and fulfilling lives. The fact that the
optimum number is far removed from the maximum number does not need
much explanation.

Clark also maintains that communities that run out of land reserves can
produce manufactured products and exchange them for food. But this implies that there will always be nations with agricultural surplusses
willing to buy thos industrial products. In fact, the number of nations
with food surplusses is small and declining. Clark finally contends
that if a country is too small to industrialize it can stimulate emigration in order to prevent excessive crowding. The problem here is
identical to the one discussed above. As more and more nations are
running out of space, the number of countries willing to receive immigrants is steadily falling.

---

[19] Source: C. Clark, "World Population", Nature, Vol. CLXXXI,
(May, 1958), pp. 1235-1236.

WORLD POPULATION
Colin Clark

If not impeded, the probability of conception in fertile human couples
appears to average 0.1 per menstrual cycle, higher for first conceptions,
but otherwise irrespective of age. From a minimum of 3 per cent, the
proportion of infertility rises rapidly with age from 25 onwards. Infertility, at any given age, appears greater among coloured than among
white races. The assertion that natural human fertility rises with
undernourishment rests upon no evidence whatsoever.

This probability of conception allowing for some miscarriages, and some
temporary sterility during lactation implies the birth of a child for
every 21 years of married life, as observed in England a century ago, or
in some peasant communities now.
'Total fertility', defined as the number of children born to an average
woman by the end of her reproductive period, in the circumstances most
favourable for reproduction, when every woman marries young, and with
surplus males waiting to re-marry any widows, assuming the onset of infertility on the average twenty years after marriage, should be 8 (that
is to say, $20/2\frac{1}{2}$). This rate is indeed found among those (very few)
Irish women who are married young, to young husbands, and who are not
widowed; rates of 6 or 7 are found among primitive nomadic peoples, and
among peasant populations in Asia and Latin America; considerably lower
figures are found in Africa, where the percentage of infertility is
unaccountably high. The highest total fertility ever recorded was 10,
for the early French-Canadian settlers; but they were a group specially
selected for vigour and hardihood. Evidence from India indicates that
the consummation of marriage below the age of seventeen tends, in the
long run, to reduce rather than to increase total fertility.

Writing in 1798, Malthus taught that populations always tend to increase
up to the limits of their food-producing capacity, whereupon population
growth must necessarily be checked, if not by late marriage (which he
recommended) then either by 'misery' or by 'vice'. In the same year
Jenner was publishing his proposals for vaccination against smallpox,
which probably did more than any other single factor to bring about the
great rise in population in the nineteenth century. Malthus, however,
stated that Jenner's work was a waste of time, because the "principles of
population" indicated that, even if he were successful, it was inevitable that some other disease would spring up to take the place of smallpox. Instances of populations growing rapidly until they reach the
limits of food supply have occurred, but exceptionally, and certainly
not generally in the history of mankind.

For the greatest proportion of mankind's time upon Earth our ancestors
lived the life of nomadic hunting peoples, which involves high mortality, with few people surviving to the age of forty. In these circumstances, a total fertility of 6 or 8 will only just suffice to maintain
the population. This is observed among some primitive tribes to-day.

The present world average rate of population increase is 1 1/2 per cent per annum, as against 1 per cent in the nineteenth century. From approximate figures of world population (errors in them will not affect the order of magnitude of our results) we deduce, between the first and the seventeenth centuries A.D., an average growth-rate of only 0.05 per cent per annum; and from the beginning of the human race to the beginning of the Christian era 0.005 per cent per annum. These low growth-rates, while populations were far smaller than those now supported by the same agricultural methods in the same areas, were clearly not due to the world's inability to produce food.

In a settled peasant community, population increases at the rate of about 1/2 per cent per annum, but only so long as there are no widespread epidemics, and peace and order can be preserved. "Better fifty years of Europe than a cycle of Cathay"; India and China for thousands of years have been slowly building up population, and then losing most of it again in recurring periods of war and disorder. In Europe, where total fertility may have been reduced to 5 by the custom of later marriage, population growth proved to be slow, too. The Black Death was only the first of a cycle of epidemics which checked the growth of population all over Europe. In France, which also suffered greatly from the Hundred Years' War, the population-level of the fourteenth century was not regained until the eighteenth. Egypt, and many other regions in the Middle East, had less population in the nineteenth century than they had had 2,000 years earlier. The spread of malaria, sometimes adduced as a cause, is better regarded as a consequence of social disorder; Anopheles only secures a hold when irrigation channels are neglected. Sustained growth of population, at the rate of 1 per cent per annum or more, which began in the British Isles and Scandinavia with the improvement of medical knowledge in the late eighteenth century, began in China only with the establishment of peace under the Manchu Empire in the seventeenth century, in India with the establishment of the British Empire, in Latin America not until the nineteenth century, and in Africa not until the present century.

Prospects did not look good at the time when Malthus wrote. Real wages were low and did not rise until the middle of the nineteenth century. Nevertheless, the British courageously refused to listen to Malthus. Had they done so, Britain would have remained a small eighteenth century-type agrarian community; and the United States and the British Commonwealth would never have developed. No great degree of industrialization would have been possible. The economics of large-scale industry demand large markets and a first-class transportation system, only obtainable with a large and growing population.

The country which did listen to Malthus was France, where size of family began to decline early in the nineteenth century. "If population limitation were the key to economic progress," as Prof. Sauvy said at the World Population Conference, "then France should be the wealthiest country in the world by now." France, which seemed to be on the point of dominating the world in 1798, has since seen her influence steadily decline; and the recurring inflations which France has suffered are an economic consequence of the excessive burden of pensions and other overhead costs which an ageing country has to carry.

When we look at the British in the seventeenth and eighteenth centuries,
at the Greeks in the sixth century B.C., the Dutch in the seventeenth
century, and the Japanese in the nineteenth century, we must conclude
that the pressure of population upon limited agricultural resources
provides a painful but ultimately beneficial stimulus, provoking unen-
terprising agrarian communities into greater efforts in the fields of
industry, commerce, political leadership, colonization, science, and
(sometimes but not always, judging from Victorian England) the arts.

But if a country fails to meet the challenge of population increase, it
sinks into the condition known to economists as 'disguised unemployment'
or rural overpopulation. The simpler forms of agriculture using hand
tools (as in China or Africa), can economically occupy 50 able-bodied
men per sq. km. (246 acres), or 20 men per sq.km. using draught animals.
A man working for a full year, using hand tools produces at least two
tons of grain-equivalent (expressing other products as grain at their
local exchange values); twice that with draught animals. Minimum subsistence requirements can be estimated at 275 kilos of grain-equivalent
per person per year (225 kilos of grain plus a few other foods and
textile fibres). So one agricultural worker, even with hand tools, can
produce subsistence for seven or eight people, that is to say, he can
feed himself and his dependants at better than subsistence-level, and
have some food to exchange for clothing, household goods, etc., so
that an urban population can begin to grow up. (One Canadian grain
grower, however, could feed 750 at subsistence-level.) Where, however,
the densities of agricultural population exceed these limits, as in
southern Italy, India, Egypt, etc., the marginal product of this additional labour is very low, and the consequence is that many men consume only a subsistence diet, are idle for a considerable part of their
time, and have little surplus to exchange for industrial products.

Lord Boyd-Orr's statement that "a life-time of malnutrition and actual
hunger is the lot of at least two-thirds of mankind" is simply an
arithmetical error, based on confusing two columns in a statistical
table. Malnutrition exists in the world, but it is impossible to state
its extent until physiologists can be more precise about food requirements, and statisticians about agricultural output and body-weights.

Countries the population of which has outrun their agricultural resources can industrialize, and exchange manufactures for imported food,
as did Britain and Japan, and as India can--if they have a large population and a good transport system. Experience in both India and the
U.S.S.R. has shown that, with modern engineering knowledge, capital
requirements for establishing an industrial community are less than was
previously supposed. This solution, however, is not open to the smaller
and more isolated islands away from the main channels of world trade.
If they become overcrowded they must seek relief in emigration, which
from an island such as Porto Rico is as high as 2 per cent of the population per annum.

Some fear, however, that the agricultural resources of the world as a
whole may soon be exhausted. The world's total land area (excluding
ice and tundra) is 123 million sq. km., from which we exclude most of
the 42 1/2 million sq. km. of steppe or arid lands, discount anything
up to half the area of certain cold or sub-humid lands, but could

double 10 million sq.km. of tropical land capable of bearing two crops
per year. We conclude that the world possesses the equivalent of 77
million sq.km. of good temperate agricultural land. We may take as our
standard that of the most productive farmers in Europe, the Dutch, who
feed 385 people (at Dutch standards of diet, which give them one of
the best health records in the world) per sq.km. of farm land, or 365
if we allow for the land required to produce their timber (in the most
economic manner, in warm climates--pulp requirements can be obtained
from sugar cane waste). Applying these standards throughout the world,
as they could be with adequate skill and use of fertilizers, we find
the world capable of supporting 28 billion people, or ten times its
present population. This leaves us a very ample margin for land which
we wish to set aside for recreation or other purposes. Even these
high Dutch standards of productivity are improving at a rate of 2 per
cent per annum. In the very distant future, if our descendants outrun
the food-producing capacity of the Earth, and of the sea, they will by
that time be sufficiently skilled and wealthy to build themselves
artificial satellites to live on.

'Total fertility' is an accurate measure of reproductivity, but we
cannot measure it directly until the generation in question has reached
the end of its reproductive period. In interpreting current data, a
difficult mathematical problem is involved, because the probability
of any given family producing a child depends upon: (1) the mother's
age, (2) the duration of the marriage, (3) the number of children already born; and these three variables are highly intercorrelated.
Crude measurements, such as birth-rates and reproduction-rates (so-
called), can give gravely misleading results when there have been
temporary fluctuations in the marriage-rate, or in the age-structure
of the population. Henry has devised an elegant mathematical technique
whereby, from the birth data of a single year, it is possible to in-
tegrate the probabilities for all future years that a family containing n children will expand to (n + 1). By multiplying together these
probabilities the ultimate total fertility of the generation can then
be estimated.

During the past century reproductivity has fallen heavily in all the
economically advanced countries. During the past two decades, however,
there has been a dramatic reversal of this trend in several countries,
particularly in France, and in the Unites States the British Commonwealth countries, the populations of which are now growing faster than
India's; but not in England. Mortality-rates throughout the world,
after declining fairly steadily for a century, greatly accelerated
their fall in the 1930's and 1940's, through the discoveries of sulpha-
drugs and penicillin. We must therefore certainly expect a further
acceleration in the rate of growth of world population.

We have as yet little understanding of the economic, social, historical
and religious factors lying behind either the past decline in fertility,
or its recent recovery. Most familiar generalizations have proved to
be erroneous. It used to be held that it was the wealthier, more educated and more urbanized communities which most reduced their fertility. This was true in the past; but in the English-speaking and
Scandinavian countries the educated are now beginning to have larger
families than the uneducated. The urban-rural difference in reproductivity disappeared in France fifty years ago, and is now disappearing

in Britain and the United States. We have little understanding of
those profound motives which make people willing to face the hardships
and inconveniences of bringing up a family, motives often of a religious
or similar character. An irreligious community is rarely a reproductive
one.

READING 20

Leibenstein's cost-benefit approach to fertility decisions (see reading 18) emphasizes the long run effects of a secular rise in income on family size decisions. Taking the less developed low-income countries as his starting point, he concludes that in the long run economical progress with its concomittant rise in income levels ultimately depresses income levels.

Professor Gary Becker (born 1930) now at the University of Chicago focuses on the more developed affluent societies in which children do not contribute to the income of their parents.[20] Their economic benefits are zero but they do provide psychic income or satisfaction. Using a utility maximization model subject to budget constraints he argues that rising disposable incomes result in higher fertility. Treating the demand for children analogously to the demand for consumer durables such as houses and cars he concludes that when the consumers' income increases his demand for children will increase as well. The empirical fact that in reality the more affluent families are often smaller than the low income ones is according to Becker due to unequal access to contraceptive information and devices. In a society where access to contraceptive knowledge and facilities would be completely equal, income and family size would be positvely correlated.

Becker also distinguishes between quantity elasticity and quality elasticity. As incomes rise, people not only consume durable goods in greater quantity (inferior goods being the exception to the rule) but they also require higher-quality products which yield extra satisfaction. The same holds for children. With rising incomes the concern with child quality is intensified and parents spend increasing amounts on higher-quality rearing and education. Becker concludes that the quantity income elasticity is positive but low while the quality elasticity is high. Hence as incomes increase people do to some extent respond by having larger families but the main part of the added income set aside for children is devoted to higher-quality rearing and education.

In comment we may observe here that Becker only considers the short term effect of income changes. As long as tastes and preferences do not change rising disposable incomes will in fact tend to affect fertility positively. In the longer run, however, rising incomes tend to modify people's value systems and attitudes. Higher income levels are usually associated with socio-economic progress which presents new needs and opportunities such as increased access to education and information as well as greater social and spatial mobility. These phenomena affect people's fertility negatively via a change in their preferences and values.

---

[20] Source: G. S. Becker, "An Economic Analysis of Fertility", Demographic and Economic Change in Developed Countries ed. National Bureau of Economic Research (Princeton: Princeton University Press, 1960), pp.209-217

AN ECONOMIC ANALYSIS OF FERTILITY

Gary S. Becker

The inability of demographers to predict western birth rates accurately
in the postwar period has had a salutary influence on demographic research. Most predictions had been based either on simple extrapolations
of past trends or on extrapolations that adjusted for changes in the age-
sex-marital compostion of the population. Socio-economic considerations
are entirely absent from the former and are primitive and largely implicit
in the latter. As long as even crude extrapolations continued to give
fairly reliable preductions, as they did during the previous half century,
there was little call for complicated analyses of the interrelation between socio-economic variables and fertility. However, the sharp decline
in birth rates during the thirties coupled with the sharp rise in rates
during the postwar period swept away confidence in the view that future
rates could be predicted from a secularly declining function of population compositions.

Malthus could with some justification assume that fertility was determined primarily by two primitive variables, age at marriage and the
frequency of coition during marriage. The development and spread of
knowledge about contraceptives during the last century greatly widened
the scope of family size decision-making, and contemporary researchers
have been forced to pay greater attention to decision-making than either
Malthus or the forecasters did. Psychologists have tried to place these
decisions within a framework suggested by sociological theory, but most
persons would admit that neither framework has been particularly successful in organizing the information on fertility.

Two considerations encouraged me to analyze family size decisions within
an economic framework. The first is that Malthus' famous discussion
was built upon a strongly economic framework; mine can be viewed as a
generalization and development of his. Second, although no single
variable in the Indianapolis survey explained more than a small fraction
of the variation in fertility, economic variables did better than
others. Section I develops this framework and sets out some of its
implications. Section II uses this framework to analyze the actual
effects of income on fertility. Section III speculates about some
further implications of the discussion in I and II.

I. THE ECONOMIC FRAMEWORK

General Considerations

In societies lacking knowledge of contraception, control over the number
of births can be achieved either through abortion or abstinence, the
latter taking the form of delayed marriage and reduced frequency of
coition during marriage. Since each person maintains some control over
these variables, there is room for decision-making even in such societies.

Other things the same, couples desiring small families would marry
later and have more abortions than the average couple. Yet the room
for decision-making would be uncomfortably small, given the taboos
against abortion, the strong social forces determining the age of marriage, and the relative inefficiency of reductions in the frequency of
coition. Chance would bulk large in determining the distribution of
births among families.

The growth of knowledge about contraception has greatly widened the
scope of decision-making, for it has separated the decision to control
births from the decision to engage in coition. Presumably, such a widening of the scope of decision-making has increased the importance of environmental factors, but which of the numerous environmental factors are
most important? To simplify the analysis of this problem I assume initially that each family has perfect control over both the number and
spacing of its births.

For most parents, children are a source of psychic income or satisfaction,
and, in the economist's terminology, children would be considered a
consumption good. Children may sometimes provide money income and are
then a production good as well. Moreover, neither the outlays on children nor the income yielded by them are fixed but vary in amount with the
child's age, making children a durable consumption and production good.
It may seem strained, artificial, and perhaps even immoral to classify
children with cars, houses, and machinery. This classification does not
imply, however, that the satisfactions or costs associated with children
are morally the same as those associated with other durables. The satisfaction provided by housing, a "necessity," is often distinguished
from that provided by cars, a "luxury," yet both are treated as consumer
durables in demand analysis. Abstracting from the kind of satisfaction
provided by children makes it possible to relate the "demand" for children to a well-developed body of economic theory. I will try to show that
the theory of the demand for consumer durables is a useful framework in
analyzing the demand for children.

Tastes

As consumer durables, children are assumed to provide "utility." The
utility from children is compared with that from other goods via a utility function or a set of indifference curves. The shape of the indifference curves is determined by the relative preference for children, or,
in other words, by "tastes." These tastes may, in turn, be determined
by a family's religion, race, age, and the like. This framework permits,
although it does not predict, fertility differences that are unrelated
to "economic" factors.

Quality of Children

A family must determine not only how many children it has but also the
amount spent of them--whether it should provide separate bedrooms, send
them to nursery school and private colleges, give them dance or music
lessons, and so forth. I will call more expensive children "higher
quality" children, just as Cadillacs are called higher quality cars than
Chevrolets. To avoid any misunderstanding, let me hasten to add that
"higher quality" does not mean morally better. If more is voluntarily
spent on one child than on another, it is because the parents obtain

additional utility from the additional expenditure and it is this additional utility which we call higher "quality."

Income

An increase in income must increase the amount spent on the average good, but not necessarily that spent on each good. The major exceptions are goods that are inferior members of a broader class, as a Chevrolet is considered an inferior car, margarine an inferior spread, and black bread an inferior bread. Since children do not appear to be inferior members of any broader class, it is likely that a rise in long-run income would increase the amount spent on children.

For almost all other consumer durables, such as cars, houses, or refrigerators, families purchase more units as well as better quality units at higher income levels, with the quantity income elasticity usually being small compared to the quality elasticity. If expenditures on children responded in a similar way, most of the increased expenditures on children would consist of an increase in the quality of children. Economic theory does not guarantee that the quantity of children would increase at all, although a decrease in quantity would be an exception to the usual case. Thus an increase in income should increase both the quantity and quality of children, but the quantity elasticity should be small compared to the quality elasticity.

Malthus, on the other hand, concluded that an increase in income would lead to a relatively large increase in family size. His argument has two major components. First, an increase in income would cause a decline in child mortality, enabling more children to survive childhood. If a decrease in births did not offset the decrease in child mortality, the number of children in the average family would increase. His second argument is less mechanical and takes greater account of motivation. An increase in income increases fertility by inducing people to marry earlier and abstain less while married.

My analysis has generalized that of Malthus by relating the quantity of children to the quality of children and by permitting small (even negative) quantity income elasticities as well as large ones. My conclusion that in modern society the quantity elasticity is probably positive but small differs from his for the following reasons. First, child mortality has fallen so low that the ordinary changes in income have little effect on the number of survivors out of a given birth cohort. Moreover, it is doubtful that even a large decline in child mortality would have much effect on family size, for parents are primarily interested in survivors, not in births per se. Therefore, a decline in child mortality would induce a corresponding decline in births. Second, births can now be controlled without abstinence and this has greatly reduced the psychic costs of birth control. "Human nature" no longer guarantees that a growth in income appreciably above the subsistence level results in a large inadvertent increase in fertility.

Cost

In principle the net cost of children can be easily computed. It equals the present value of expected outlays plus the imputed value of the parents' services, minus the present value of the expected money return

plus the imputed value of the child's services. If net costs were
positive, children would be on balance a consumer durable and it would
be necessary to assume that psychic income or utility was received from
them. If net costs were negative, children would be a producer durable
and pecuniary income would be received from them. Children of many
qualities are usually available, and the quality selected by any family
is determined by tastes, income, and price. For most families in recent
years the net expenditure on children has been very large.

Real incomes per capita in the United States have increased more than
threefold in the last 100 years, which must have increased the net expenditure on children. It is possible that in the mid-nineteenth century
children were a net producer's good, providing rather than using income.
However, the marginal cost of children must have been positive in families receiving marginal psychic income from children; otherwise, they
would have had additional children. Even in 1850, the typical family
in the United States was producing fewer children than was physically
possible. Some more direct inferences can be drawn from the data on
Negro slaves, an extreme example of a human producer's good. These data
indicate a positive net expenditure on male slaves during their first
eighteen years. Slave raising was profitable because the high price that
an eighteen-yearold could bring more than offset the net cost during the
first eighteen years. Presumably, in most families expenditures on
white children during their first eighteen years were greater than those
on slaves. Moreover, after eighteen, white children became free agents
and could decide whether to keep their income or give it to their parents.
The amount given to parents may have been larger than the costs before
eighteen, but it is more likely that costs before eighteen dominated
returns after eighteen. This conclusion does not imply that monetary
returns from children were unimportant, and indeed, they are stressed
at several points in this paper. It does imply, however, that a basic
framework which treats children as a consumer's good is relevant not
only for the present, but also for some time in the past.

A change in the cost of children is a change in the cost of children of
given quality, perhaps due to a change in the price of food or education.
It is well to dwell a little on this definition for it is widely mis-
understood. One would not say that the price of cars has risen over
time merely because more people now buy Cadillacs and other expensive
cars. A change in price has to be estimated from indexes of the price
of a given quality. Secular changes in real income and other variables
have induced a secular increase in expenditures on children, often in-
terpreted as a rise in the cost of children. The cost of children may
well have risen (see pp. 227-28) but the increase in expenditure on
children is no evidence of such rise since the quality of children has
risen. Today children are better fed, housed, and clothed, and in increasing numbers are sent to nursery schools, camps, high schools, and
colleges. For the same reason, the price of children to rich parents
is the same as that to poor parents even though rich parents spend more
on children. The rich simply choose higher quality children as well as
higher qualities of other goods.

It is sometimes argued that social pressures "force" richer families to
spend more on children, and that this increases the cost of children to
the rich. This higher cost is supposed to explain why richer families
have fewer children than others and why richer societies have fewer

children than poorer ones. However, since the cost of different goods is given in the market place, social pressures cannot change this, but can only change the basket of goods selected. That is, social pressures influence behavior by affecting the indifference curve structure, not by affecting costs. To put this differently, social pressures may affect the income elasticity of demand for children by rich (and poor) families, but not the price elasticity of demand. Therefore, the well known negative relationship between cost (or price) and quantity purchased cannot explain why richer families have had relatively few children. Moreover, nothing in economic analysis implies that social pressures would make the quantity income elasticity of demand for children negative. Thus my conclusion that the quantity income elasticity if relatively small but positive and the quality elasticity relatively large is entirely consistent with an analysis which emphasizes social pressures.

Suppose there was an equal percentage decline in the price of all qualities of children, real income remaining constant. Although economic theory suggests that the "amount" of children consumed would increase, it does not say whether the amount would increase because of an increase in quantity, quality, or both--the last, however, being most likely. It also has little to say about the quantitative relationship between price and amount. There are no good substitutes for children, but there may be many poor ones.

Supply

By and large, children cannot be purchased on the open market but must be produced at home. Most families are no longer self-sufficient in any major commodity other than children. Because children are produced at home, each uncertainty in production is transferred into a corresponding uncertainty in consumption, even when there is no uncertainty for all families taken together. Although parents cannot accurately predict the sex, intelligence, and height of their children, the distribution of these qualities is relatively constant for the country as a whole. This uncertainty makes it necessary to distinguish between actual and expected utility. Thus suppose a group of parents received marginal utility equal to U_m from a male child and U_f from a female child. The expected utility from an additional child equals $EU = PU_m + (I - P)U_f \cong \frac{U_m + U_f}{2}$, where P, the probability of a male is approximately equal to 1/2. They would have additional children whenever the expected utility per dollar of expected cost from an additional child were greater than that from expenditures elsewhere. The actual utility is either U_f or U_m, which differs from EU as long as $U_f \neq U_m$. In fact, if U_f (or U_m) were negative, some parents would receive negative utility.

A second important consequence of uniting consumption and production is that the number of children available to a family is determined not only by its income and prices but also by its ability to produce children. One family can desire three children and be unable to produce more than two, while another can desire three and be unable to produce fewer than five. The average number of live births produced by married women in societies with little knowledge of contraception is very high. For example, in nineteenth-century Ireland, women marrying at ages 20-24 averaged more than 8 live births. This suggests that the average family more frequently had excess rather than too few children.

Relatively effective contraceptive techniques have been available for
at least the last 100 years, but knowledge of such techniques did not
spread rapidly. Religious and other objections prevented the rapid
spread of knowledge that is common to other technological innovations in
advanced countries. Most families in the nineteenth century, even in
advanced Western countries, did not have effective contraceptive information. This information spread slowly from upper socio-economic groups
to lower ones.

Each family tries to come as close as possible to its desired number of
children. If three children are desired and no more than two are available, two are produced; if three are desired and no fewer than five are
available, five are produced. The marginal equilibrium conditions would
not be satisfied for children but would be satisfied for other goods, so
the theory of consumer's choice is not basically affected. Families
with excess children consume less of other goods, especially of goods
that are close substitutes for the quantity of children. Because quality
seems like a relatively close substitute for quantity, families with
excess children would spend less on each child than other families with
equal income and tastes. Accordingly, an increase in contraceptive
knowledge would raise the quality of children as well as reduce their
quanity.

READING 21

In 1952 Sir Charles Darwin (born 1887), a well known British scientist
and descendant of the great nineteenth century naturalist, published a
work entitled The Next Million Years in which he argued that the prosperity a large part of the world then enjoyed could not be of lasting
nature. We live, he said, in a "Golden Age" characterized like former
periods of an identical nature by a food surplus due to technical advances. Periods of prosperity, however, tend to abolish the various
checks on population and numbers grow up to the new population ceiling.
Then the "Golden Age" is over and "Average History" recurs. Average
history is characterized by heavy pressure of population on resources
with many people unable to survive because of high mortality conditions.

The present address, delivered in Vevey, Switzerland, in 1960, summarized
Darwin's views at that time. Darwin denies that economic development
and increases in per capita income reduce fertility. This, it will
be remembered, is the essence of the theory of the demographic transition.
The fact that in most countries of the western worl the birth rate rose
after World War II proved to him that economic progress stimulated fertility. In a sense Darwin returns to the views of the 18th century
economist Cantillon and the classical economists such as Malthus who had
argued that economic betterment (due to higher yields per acre, improved
wages, etc.) tended to increase completed family size and thereby population. As a result, says Darwin, our relatively high living standards
are not sustainable in the long run. Darwin also discusses some difficulties of population control.[21]

---

[21] Source: E. Bignami, J.C. Corthesy (eds.), Humanity and Subsistence
(Lausanne: Librairie Payot, 1961), pp. 88-95.

THE FUTURE NUMBERS OF MANKIND

Sir Charles Darwin

The serious thought of the world at the present time is very rightly
concerned with avoiding the dangers which threaten us from atomic bomb
explosions, but not nearly enough thought is being given to what threatens to be quite as formidable a menace to the future prosperity of mankind, and this is the so-called explosion of population. To call it an
explosion is of course radically to alter the time-scale, for whereas
an ordinary explosion is all over in a matter of seconds, this one
started roughly speaking two centuries ago; it has been going on ever
since at an increasing rate, and even now it shows no signs of ending.
Most people are unconscious of it, because we have never seen anything
different ourselves, nor did our fathers before us, nor our ancestors
back for five or six generations, so it is taken for granted that we are
living in a normal state of the world, whereas a little thought will
show that it must be a quite fantastically exceptional state.

It is self-evident that these increases cannot go on forever, but few
seem to realize how soon they must stop. At the present time, our numbers are increasing at such a rate that they will more than double themselves in the next fifty years, and this rate of increase is confirmed
by the censuses of the past century, though indeed the rate of increase
is now even greater than it was before. At the present time there are
about 2,800 million human beings, and by the year 2000 A.D. there will
be 5,000 million. Following the same extrapolation, by 2050 A.D. there
should be 10,000 million and by 2100 A.D., 20,000 million, which would
certainly make the world most uncomfortably crowded. We can see then
that within less than two centuries from now, conditions have simply got
to change in some way so as to stop the explosion. Can we hope to discover any way of doing this which will succeed in maintaining, at least
to some degree, our present prosperity?

It will be well to look at the recent figures more closely. The demographers tell us that every year our numbers are increasing by 40 mil-
lions--and indeed this is a conservative estimate. The increases are
of course unevenly distributed, but not entirely in the way one might
have expected at first sight. Thus it is true that many of the less
well developed countries are showing enormous increases, for example by
the recent destruction of the malaria mosquito, or by the introduction
of modern sanitation. In such countries death control has triumphed,
and it has not been balanced by any corresponding birth control, so that
in some of these countries there are increases above 3% per year. But
it is not only these countries that are increasing, for the United States,
at the present time, is increasing faster than India, though India is
often cited as having the most formidable problems of all.

Not so many years ago, some students of population used to hold a very
comforting doctrine. They could point to the countries of Western

Europe, which were only showing small rates of increase, and they attributed this to their prosperity. They argued that prosperity stopped
the increase, and that if only the other countries of the world were one
by one raised to a European level of prosperity, their increases would
cease, and the whole world would enjoy a millennium of luxury. Unfortunately for this argument we are now seeing that the country which is
indisputably the most prosperous in the world is one of those increasing
at the greatest rate. Granted that the pressure of population is less
in the United States than in many other countries, so that they can afford to expand in comfort, still that concedes the main point of the
argument, in that it is not the prosperity that will stop the increase,
but rather the reverse, so that it can only be expected to stop when
the United States does become crowded like India.

There is one thing about the present increases that must be recognized.
The wonderful new developments of medical science are year by year length-
ening the expectation of life. This is particularly true of the expectation of life for the younger people who can now hope to live till, say,
seventy with much higher probability than ever before. On the other
hand the expectation of life for older people has not been much altered.
It might then be thought that the present increases were due simply to
the fact that fewer people are dying young in each year than in the preceding year, and that the increases will cease when everybody succeeds
in living till seventy. If that happy state should be achieved the
rate of increase would certainly diminish; I am not going to estimate
by how much, but the increases would still be quite formidable. It is
no use thinking that they are primarily due to this greater expectation
of length of life, and that they will cease when everybody lives to the
age of seventy.

These demographic calculations for the coming fifty years are not much
affected by the various possible events which might be suggested by
naive thinking. For example it is natural to ask if a great war might
not upset them, but the immediate answer is that war of the type we have
experienced hitherto would be quite negligible. Thus it took four
years of the First World War to kill ten million people, a number now
replaced in three months. An atomic war would obviously be much more
serious, but the direct effects even of that can be over-estimated.
Take a hypothetical case and imagine that 200 million people were killed.
This would be far the greatest disaster in the whole history of the
human race, but that number would be replaced in about five years. It
is not the killing itself that would seriously affect population numbers,
but it is to be expected that under such conditions the world's economy would collapse, so that a great number would also die from famines.
However it is not possible to make predictions about atomic war. May
we hope that human folly will not go so far as to solve the population
problem by insisting on an atomic war every few years.

There is another thing that might upset prediction, and unlike any of
these calamities it has the advantage of being humane. It has to be
recognized that the instincts of humanity are so strong that no prohibition of the sexual act would be very effective in limiting the increase of our numbers, but this has now been rendered unnecessary through
the development of practices of contraception. Such practices are extending all the time, but they would have to become world-wide if they
were seriously to upset the estimates of our numbers fifty years from

now. In such intimate personal matters it is hardly credible that in
the short period of fifty years the habits of 2,000 million people could
be fransformed in such a radical manner. It would seem that the 5,000
million people in A.D. 2000 are inevitable.

THE NECESSITIES OF LIFE

We have got to accept these enormous increases, and we must therefore
ask the question how the people are going to live. The first thing to
note is that, at the present time, more than half the world do not get
enough to eat, and that the situation is not improving. At the great
conference on Population, held by the United Nations in Rome in 1954,
an example was cited. In the years 1947-53 the world's food production
increased by 8%, which can be claimed as a triumph for agriculture, and
one not often to be repeated. But our satisfaction was diminished when
we learned that during those same seven years the population increased
by 11%. At the end of this period the world was hungrier than at its
beginning.

At this same conference, the agriculturists gave full considerations
to the prospects there might be for increasing food production so as to
match the increasing numbers, and they concluded it would be possible
to double the amount of food produced. This would call for much research
in the improvement of the breeds of agricultural plants, and for a great
outlay of capital on irrigation works, but it could be done by methods
that we do understand how to develop.

To go beyond this would call for the discovery of new methods of food
production, for example the cultivation of the oceans, or the direct
synthesis of food from its inorganic elements, or perhaps the provision
of vast greenhouses growing algae in an atmosphere of carbon dioxide.
All these things are possibilities, but to have any practical importance
the new methods must produce food for something like 1,000 million people,
and it seems at the least unlikely that any wholly new process could
develop to this extent within fifty years. Thus we have no reason to
look at the situation with satisfaction. Even now half the world is
underfed. In fifty years there will be twice as many people, and with
the best success we can reasonably hope for, there will be twice as much
food available. So still half the world will be underfed, but the number will be twice as great.

Food is of course the ultimate necessity for life, but there are many
other things which are also essential if we are to hope to maintain our
present ways of life in which a considerable fraction of humanity live
concentrated in large cities. To make this possible we need large supplies of steel and copper and other metals, also such things as cement
and copious supplies of fresh water, and at the base of them all there
lies the need for enormous quantities of mechanical energy. These things
constitute the capital of the earth and they are being used at an enormous rate. Thus man has mined the earth now for many centuries, but it
is estimated that of all the minerals he has extracted from the earth
more than half have been taken out during the past forty years. It is
then proper to enquire whether we shall not be faced with a shortage of
minerals as great as the shortage of food. The situation would seem to
be precarious, but perhaps not quite as formidable as is the provision
of food. Thus only a few years ago the supply of mechanical energy

looked to be the most serious problem of all in view of the rapid exhaustion of our resources of coal, but it now seems probable that radio-
active energy can replace coal, and that the supplies of uranium can at
any rate last for a thousand years instead of only the century or two
of coal. There is also a good hope that the problem of hydrogen fusion
may be solved, which would provide energy in quite unlimited quantities.
This would of course leave many difficult problems in the replacement
of the various metallic ores, which may soon be running short, but this
is the sort of thing that does lie within the ingenuity of our engineers
to solve. We must expect many troubles that we cannot foresee, but they
do not threaten the same overwhelming difficulty as does the provision
of food for our increasing numbers.

MAN AS AN ANIMAL SPECIES

It is questionable whether we are not looking at the whole subject the
wrong way round. Thus we say that there will be so many people in the
year A.D. 2000, and that therefore we must provide food for that number.
But we must remember that man is an animal, and with this in mind it
may be juster to put the matter the other way about. If we can estimate
the production of food possible by A.D. 2000, will not that tell us the
number of mouths that will be asking for it?

The point may be illustrated by a political speech that was recently reported. The speaker was discussing conditions in Egypt, and he claimed
that the making of the great Aswan Dam was quite essential in order to
relieve the starving millions of Egyptian peasants. But having made his
point, he added that twenty-five years hence they would be back again
in their present starving condition, only there would be a great many
more of them. If I may put the point in relation to our present occasion, we may welcome the new developments here because we can be quite
certain that, no matter what happens in the world, food production will
always be what the economists call a "seller's market".

For hundreds of millions of years our animal ancestors have obeyed the
laws of evolution by natural selection. Each generation always tended
to produce an increased number for the next, and then the excess was
killed off in the struggle for life. It was this struggle that determined the numbers of every species, and if for any reason the struggle
was eased, the numbers at once started to increase, and continued to do
so until, once again, the severity of the competition returned on account of the greater numbers.

With one qualification, to which I shall return later, man has behaved
like any other animal in this respect. Most of the time his numbers
have been held roughly constant by the struggle for life, but just now
the situation has been eased, and we are responding by the present great
increases. The easing has been mainly due to two causes. One has been
the discovery of parts of the world, such as the Americas, which were
inhabited on a scale so low, as compared with Asia and Europe, that
there were vast areas waiting to be filled up. But even more important
has been the Scientific Revolution. This has taught us how we can so
dominate nature that we can provide a prosperous life at densities ten
or twenty times greater than was ever possible before. In response to
these discoveries, we are rapidly filling up the world to a new level,

and this is posing us the problem what to do when this level has been
reached.

In multiplying in this way, man has merely conformed to the universal
law of evolution, which controls all animal life through the operation
of the principles of genetics and natural selection. But in the course
of his history he has evolved that wonderful organ, the human brain, and
through it he has succeeded in breaking one of the laws which otherwise
govern the genetics of all animal life. This is the Law of the Non-inheritance of Acquired Characters, which dictates that each generation
gets all its characteristics from the germ cell created by its parents,
and it derives nothing at all from any of the experiences of those
parents during their lives. This is of course only a rough statement
of the law; it was for long regarded as doubtful, but its validity is
now accepted by all the leading authorities. Man, however, has succeeded
in breaking this law, because he can modify his conduct through education
and by communication with his fellows quite independently of whether he
is genetically related to them.

This new form of inheritance has had an enormous effect on our life. It
first showed its effects ten thousand years ago with the invention of
agriculture, but to take a more recent example, the number of individuals
who have seriously contributed to the Scientific Revolution is not very
great--it would indeed be almost possible to give a list of their names--
and yet it is through these few that our whole race has benefited by
producing the present vast multiplication of our numbers. This power
of our species is quite a new thing in the whole of world history.

I may cite as an example of its effects a conversation I once had with
a leading zoologist. I had asked him whether wild animals showed the
effects of old age in the same manner that we do and that our tame dogs
do. His answer was that there is no such thing as an old wild animal,
because they are all killed by the accidents of life before they can get
old. Yet we have now reached a condition where we consider there is
something wrong with our social organization if we die of anything except
old age.

THE CONTROL OF NUMBERS

Through his understanding of the laws of nature, man has mastered the
rest of the living world, and gained his present extraordinary prosperity,
but this can only continue if he can supplement it by mastering himself.
Can we hope to maintain something of the present prosperity by a conscious limitation of our numbers, or are we condemned to multiply until,
once again, we come under the control of the ruthless operation of
natural selection. In other words, after having operated for hundreds
of millions of years, one of nature's basic laws has been breached to
our great benefit, but we can now recognize that the breach of a second
law is essential if we are to retain the benefit. We must contrive some
conscious means for preventing the excessive multiplication of our race.

The difficulties are formidable. One is a matter of deep genetic theory.
In the general evolution of animal life, the operation of the Mendelian
Law of inheritance is wonderfully accurate, but not quite perfect. In
every animal the inheritance of a very few of the genes has gone wrong
and produced a mutation, that is to say a character differing from that

of the parents. Most mutations are deleterious because of the delicate adjustment of an animal's life to its surroundings. In wild life this means that the individuals carrying these bad mutations are likely not to survive the struggle, but a few beneficial ones do occur also, and the possessors of these are likely to have more offspring than their fellows. Thus natural selection is perpetually keeping each species up to the mark by the destruction of its inferior members, but it is also, though very slowly, improving the qualities of the species. It is not too much to say that a very severe struggle for life is one of the basic conditions which has led to all the wonders of biological evolution.

Man has evolved under exactly these conditions, but at the present time we are free from the insistent pressure of natural selection, and we are hoping that we may retain this abnormal condition. Our present aim seems to be to keep alive all human beings, no matter how inferior their qualities, and we are likely to pay for it by a steady increase in the number of deleterious mutations carried by the members of our race. In the case of the breeder of prize animals, this sort of thing might be avoided by his making a detailed study of the genetic constitutions of his beasts, which he would then follow by strictly controlled matings, but this sort of thing could hardly be applied by the master race to itself. For one thing it seems out of the question that we could ever have detailed knowledge of the genetic constitution of the thousands of millions of individuals of mankind, but even if we could, is it likely that we should tolerate this kind of control exerted against ourselves? So the best that can be said is that the deleterious effects of our mutations will take many generations to show themselves seriously, and that we need not concern ourselves overmuch about the condition of the world thousands of years hence.

There is another difficulty about the conscious control of our numbers that is even more serious, because it may act much more swiftly. It is that any process of limitation threatens to be unstable. Let us suppose that the problem of limiting our numbers has been solved in some entirely satisfactory manner, no matter what. Half the world adopts this practice, and so retains a prosperous life, but the other half refuses to do so. It does not matter what their motive may be; it might be a religious doctrine, or it might be the opinion that the world would be a better place with more people in it, or it might be sheer negligence. The limiters will continue to live in comfort, keeping their numbers constant, but the non-limiters will start multiplying. They will pay for it by having a harder life, perhaps suffering from famines. Nevertheless, after a few decades, there will be twice as many of them as of the limiters, and in the long run it seems inevitable that they should overwhelm the limiters by the sheer weight of numbers.

I have sketched two of the main difficulties facing us if we are to hope to retain something of the prosperity of the world's present Golden Age. When we circumvented the Law of the Non-inheritance of Acquired Characters we raised man from being merely the most efficient member of the animal kingdom into being its master. We have got to discover a way of circumventing another natural law, that of the universal tendency of all species to multiply in numbers, if we are to retain the good things of the world in anything like their present form. The difficulties are enormous, and I can only end by expressing the hope that they will be solved.

READING 22

In 1958 authors A.J. Coale and E.M. Hoover published a study entitled
Population Growth and Economic Development in Low-Income Countries. This
book received wide acclaim and is now considered a classic in its field.
Coale developed his views in subsequent papers and articles, of which
the following is perhaps the clearest and shortest presentation of the
subject.

The theoretical considerations underlying the argument are derived from
growth theory, an area of economics that became particularly active
after World War II. This body of ideas received its inspiration directly from Keynes's The General Theory of Employment, Interest, and
Money. Keynes's ideas, however, matured during the economic depression
of the 1930s. Then the main problem in the Western World was the
underutilization of productive resources. Accordingly, Keynes was preoccupied mainly by the short term problem of full employment of productive factors. His theoretical system concentrates on the macroeco-
nomic variables, especially investment, that determine income and employment. Keynes, in other words, was concerned primarily with the
"income effect" of investment demand on output and income.

Postwar growth theorists such as the Englishman Roy Harrod and the
American Evsey Domar drew attention to the "capacity effect" of investment, i.e., its ability to enlarge the capital stock and thereby expand
the potential national product. In their discussions of the growth-in-
ducing role of investment, growth theorists also put considerable emphasis on the role of what is known as the capital-output ratio. This
ratio represents the relationship between the value of a nation's capital stock and the annual output it produces. In this article Coale
assumes a constant and marginal capital-output ratio of 3:1

From growth theory to the study and analysis of the effects of population expansion on the potential economic growth of low-income countries
is but one step. Additions to population make saving and investment
more difficult, and economic gains due to capital formation, technical
and organizational innovations, and qualitative improvements in the
labor force are swelled up by ever larger numbers.

In the following paper, Professor Coale (born 1918) first discusses the
five major characteristics of low income countries--high birth rates,
declining death rates, accelerating population expansion, a sharply increasing proportion of nonproductive dependents, and the increasing
man/land ratio. He then goes on to discuss the short-term, medium-run,
and long-term implications of further population expansion in low-income nations. Coale argues that fast population growth increases the
dependency ratio and thereby reduces the capacity of families--and hence
the nation--to save. At the same time, expanding numbers create the

need for greater investment efforts to preserve existing (often low)
living standards, leaving little room for investments that increase the
capital/labor ratio and thereby per capita output.[22]

A special variation of this argument is the theory of the low-level
equilibrium trap, not discussed by Coale. This theory states that in
the earlier stages of economic development when per capita income begins
to rise above subsistence levels, the rate of population growth may
catch up. This can be because of such factors as lower infant mortality,
increased survival of women during the reproductive ages, the fact that
fewer couples are separated by death, and earlier marriage. If, then,
the population growth rate begins to exceed that of production, the
system is pushed back to a stable equilibrium position where per capita
income is again equal to subsistence.

---

[22]Source: A.J. Coale, "The Economic Effects of Fertility Control in
Underdeveloped Areas," Human Fertility and Population Problems, ed. R.O.
Greep (Cambridge: Schenkman, 1963), pp. 143-162.

THE ECONOMIC EFFECTS OF
FERTILITY CONTROL IN UNDER-DEVELOPED AREAS

Ansley J. Coale

I am neither a sociologist nor a biologist, and I am not a physician.
In talking before this audience about the economic implications of population, I am in the position of a young man who was an Army Air Force
pilot during World War II. He flew in the early days of the Pacific War
one of the first models of air-borne radar, and had some combat experience with this first radar for aircraft. They brought him back to the
States and took him before the Army War College, and asked him to give
a talk on the tactical uses of air-borne radar. He looked at his audience, which consisted of high-ranking officers, the most junior of whom
were one or two majors, but most of whom were colonels and generals. He
took a deep breath and said, "There must be dozens of people who know
more about the tactical use of air-borne radar than I; however, seeing
none of them here ...." That's why I chose to say something on the
economics of population. Besides, it is a most serious aspect of population today. What I would like to direct your attention to is the relationship between population growth and economic development in the
developing areas. I will not discuss the equally interesting problem
(though perhaps not as crucial a one) of the same relationship in the
industrialized countries.

If one looks at a statistical compendium giving economic facts in the
world today, in a year book or popular article, one cannot fail to be
struck by the stark contrast between the wealthiest countries and the
poorest countries. The countries which have the highest average income--
and it is some ten times greater than in the poorest countries--are those
which are industrialized, or modernized. And the poorest countries in
contrast are those which are characterized by remaining preindustrial,
by retaining an emphasis on extractive industries (primarily agriculture),
and by the use of traditional techniques of production which have scarcely changed in generations. There is then a contrast, perhaps a growing
contrast, between the conspicuous well-being of the modernized countries
and the conspicuous poverty of the preindustrial or underdeveloped
countries.

Our concern here is the relationship between the demographic features--
the characteristics of the population--of these underdeveloped countries
and their economic well-being that contrasts so strongly with that of
the modernized countries.

There is no need to dwell in detail on the demographic characteristics of
the underdeveloped countries. I will mention only the most conspicuous
of these.

First of all, every underdeveloped country is characterized by high
fertility--by a birth rate of 40 per thousand or higher and by a completed size of family of five or six children or more. In general, this

is a fertility which has been sustained at a high level without a perceptible change in the last two or three generations and probably in the
remote past as well.

Secondly, the underdeveloped countries are characterized today by low
or rapidly falling mortality--by death rates which in some instances
are 10 per thousand or lower, by an expectation of life at birth which
in some countries has risen to 50 to 60 years. Moreover, in those
areas where mortality is not low the typical situation is that it is
dropping very rapidly. The reason for this development is in brief that
the underdeveloped areas have been able to import from the countries
which pioneered in the development of scientific medicine techniques
of low cost public health, which even in the absence of substantial
social and economic change have been able to bring the major diseases
under some measure of control. The use of antibiotics, insecticides
and the like and of low-cost sanitation has brought death rates down
very rapidly. This has happened repeatedly in areas where there has
been no sign of major economic development or industrialization. I am
sure most of you are familiar with some of the developments in low cost
public health. There are areas (Ceylon is the most often cited) where
the death rate has been cut in half in less than a decade. In many
instances the expectation of life at birth has risen at least one year
per calendar year. That is, the expectation of life may rise from 40
to 50 years in less than a decade.

The consequence of these first two characteristics (of high fertility
and low or rapidly declining mortality) is that the underdeveloped
areas of the world today are characterized by rapid population growth,
or if the growth is only moderate,it tends in general to be rapidly
accelerating. Given the technical possibility of reducing the death
rate through effective public health techniques and medicine, it seems
to me if the death rate is not low there is every prospect that within
less than a decade it will be low. Only contact with the rest of the
world is essential. In view of the efforts of the World Health Organization, UNICEF, and the private foundations, and of aid programs from
the West, it requires only a receptive attitude on the part of the
underdeveloped country to enjoy the decline in mortality which is technically feasible today at low cost.

The fourth demographic characteristic of low income countries is a very
young age distribution. This is a consequence primarily, in fact almost
exclusively, of the high birth rate. Allusion was made in a previous
talk to the fact that the age distribution of a population (the proportion in childhood and at other ages) is primarily a consequence of
fertility, and depends very little on mortality. It seems a little
anomalous that fertility should predominate, but one way of seeing that
it is not contrary to common sense is to note that a high birth rate
tends automatically to create a large proportion of children in relation
to adults. Whether the death rate is low or high, the fertility level
determines the rate at which children are introduced into the population relative to adults. Moreover, if high fertility existed in the
past, today's parents will be numerous relative to their parents, so
that the proportion of old people will be small. As mortality rates
are reduced, the proportion of children in the population tends to be
increased slightly rather than the opposite, so that the underdeveloped
countries are characterized by very high proportions of children.

Typically, 40 to 45 per cent of the population consists of persons under 15, and as mortality has been reduced and is being reduced today, this proportion is rising slightly rather than changing in the opposite direction. All this entails, as we will see later, a high burden of childhood dependency. Relative to the industrialized countries the number of persons in the dependent ages, compared to the number in the productive ages, is much higher. In other words, the burden of dependency is much higher in the underdeveloped countries than in the industrial countries.

The fifth demographic characteristic--density--is not uniform in different underdeveloped areas. Up until now I have mentioned characteristics which are common to almost all pre-industrial countries. The density of population in the underdeveloped areas is highly varied. It ranges from less than ten persons per square mile in some of the Latin American countries to over 600 per square mile in Korea. In my remaining remarks I shall discuss the relationship between these demographic characteristics and the process of change from a preindustrial society to an industrialized or modernized society. The process of modernization or industrialization is very complex and involves a gamut of social and economic changes, and that would carry us far beyond what I could hope to cover here if I were to attempt to discuss the relations between population change and this complex process in much detail. What I shall do instead is to present a simplified picture of the process of industrialization concentrating on an essential element to which population has a particularly close relationship. The element on which I will concentrate is the need for capital for the accumulation of productive plants and equipment such as fertilizer plants, transportation networks, and new schools and classrooms. Capital in this sense is an essential component in the complex process of industrialization or modernization. I will emphasize this component more than any other, though I shall mention some others, in discussing the implications of population trends for the prospects of successful industrialization. In trying to characterize successful economic development or modernization I will concentrate on two criteria--again something of an oversimplification. One criterion is increase in per capita income, a very important feature of industrialization; the other is the provision (which I shall emphasize less) of productive employment for the growing labor force in the industrializing countries.

A specific question in which I shall frame this discussion is this: What difference will it make to the process of economic development or modernization if on the one hand the fertility of a country now in a preindustrial phase remains at its present high level, or if on the other hand the fertility is reduced very drastically? The specific form of reduction that I want to discuss in order to make the argument concrete is a hypothetical reduction of 50 per cent in a period of about twenty-five years. In other words, we shall try to answer this specific question: How much difference will it make to the success and to the pace of economic development if, on the one hand, an underdeveloped country maintains its fertility unchanged, or if, on the other, it reduces fertility by 50 per cent in twenty-five years?

This latter hypothetical course of reduction is not without precedent. There have been a number of areas in the world where such a reduction has taken place--Japan, for example, and several European countries.

I needn't say that I'm using fertility in the demographers' sense. I'm not talking about an impairment of reproductive capacity, but a reduction in the birth rate.

Before discussing the population implications of these two alternative courses of fertility, I'd like to say that from an economic point of view it appears possible in the short run, even in the most impoverished of the preindustrial countries, to keep up with the growth that would follow from the reduction in mortality that we expect, even if fertility is unchanged. I say this with the possibility of bringing dismay to some of you who think that one should present an alarmist picture, saying that if we don't bring the birth rate down we face inevitable catastrophe in the underdeveloped areas. I think this view is incorrect in the short run. India is certainly a major example of a country with forbidding population prospects. Yet, even in India where if the birth rate is unchanged in the next generation, the population would double, approximately, in twenty-five or thirty years, producing 900,000,000 Indians compared to the approximate 450,000,000 of today--even in that circumstance, there appears to be every technical possibility of somewhat higher per capita incomes at the end of a generation than today. This is because the technical possibilities of increasing production by the importation of more advanced techniques are parallel in a sense to the possibilities of reducing the death rate by importing techniques in the health field.

The productivity, for example, of Indian agriculture is very low per acre as well as per person. However, by the utilization of further irrigation, double cropping, better seeds, consolidation of land holdings, fertilizer, and without any use of tractors or extensive mechanization of that sort, it appears readily feasible to produce outputs more than twice as great as they are today. Moreover, the likelihood of increases in output in the nonagricultural sectors are even better. Hence, I think it is a mistake in dealing with the short run future to say that if something doesn't happen to the birth rate there is going to be inevitable starvation in the underdeveloped areas. In some instances, perhaps this will happen, but if so I think it would be because of a failure of organization and of the economic development program. I say this, in part because there is widespread misapprehension on this point, but also in part because there is a tendency for people who are preoccupied with the population problem to feel there should be no economic aid unless the recipient countries are prepared to do something about their population. To the contrary, the population problem makes the necessity of economic aid even greater, because of the possibility of keeping up with the rapid population growth of the next generation is a real one only if the economic possibilities are realized, and because a decline of fertility is much more probable in a context of spreading education and social and economic change.

What I want to deal with, then, is not the likelihood that there is going to be disaster, starvation and necessary deterioration in living standards in the short run if fertility is not decreased, but how much difference will it make to the pace and success of economic development if fertility is reduced rather than remaining constant. I want to make the declaration in advance that I don't believe there's any necessary disaster in the next generation if fertility is not changed. But having said something which may sound a little unorthodox, let me

emphasize that the goal of merely staying even or perhaps doing only
slightly better than today is not a very inspiring goal with annual per
capita incomes in India at sixty to eighty dollars. If in the next generation incomes are merely maintained, it would scarcely be a good record and would not do much towards promoting a sense of progress, or
social stability or whatever other political purposes economic development migh serve. It would certainly be a humanitarian failure of the first
magnitude if the miserably low economic conditions that exist in these
countries today are not greatly improved.

From a demographic point of view then--let us start with that--from the
point of view of population itself, what difference will it make if on
the one hand fertility were to be cut in half in an orderly way over a
twenty-five year period, or on the other hand fertility were to remain
unchanged? It is possible by a standard analytical technique to convert
these contrasting assumptions about the future course of fertility into
a detailed picture of the development of the size and age structure of
the population. I shall summarize some of the salient differences between the two populations. If a million persons at present experience
the kind of fertility and mortality conditions that prevail in Mexico
or Brazil today, and experience a continuing rise in life expectancy
in the future with no change in fertility, in thirty years there would
be about 2.7 million people; in sixty years about 8.3 million and in one
hundred and fifty years about 245 million people. In other words, if
fertility were to be unchanged, reasonable progress in reducing mortality
would lead to a multiplication by 245 in 150 years. The implications
of a reduction in fertility by 50 per cent would be an increase of population by a factor of two instead of 2.7 in thirty years, by a factor
of 3.4 instead of 8.3 in sixty years and by a factor of 10 instead of
245 in one hundred and fifty years. Note that even a reduction of fertility by 50 per cent still provides a great potential for future growth.
The startling figures of multiplication by 245 and the like that come
from considering the implications of a continuation of current trends,
arise in the rather distant future, in the order of hundreds of years
from now. It strains our capacity to be concerned about posterity when
we worry about events one hundred and fifty years from now. I think most
of us are more concerned about the next generation or so, say the next
twenty-five or thirty years.

Because of the greater interest of the more immediate future, and because
the demographic-economic relations have aspects that differ in the near
and more distant future, I shall organize the rest of this discussion
around three different time periods: the short run (a period of twenty-
five to thirty years or about one generation), a period of medium duration
of another generation, or around thirty to sixty years; and the long
run from sixty years on out to the indefinite future. One reason for
breaking our discussion into these rough time divisions is that during
the first generation, the first twenty-five years or so, the entire difference in the population that would result from these two alternative
courses of fertility, is concentrated in the child population. Literally, it is concentrated in the population under 25. Obviously, something
which affects births in the next twenty-five years cannot affect the
number of people who are over 25 at that time. If there is an orderly
change in fertility, the difference in number of births at first is not
of very large magnitude, so that actually almost all the difference in
the alternative populations twenty-five years hence is in the population

under 15, the child population. What this means is that we can consider
the effect, the demographic effect, of these two alternative trends as
being primarily a matter of age distribution in the first generation.
It is an age distribution effect because the size of the labor force,
the size of the adult population, is not affected, only the size of the
child population, and therefore the principal social and economic implications arise from change in the shape of the age structure and the
reduction of children relative to the adult population.

After a period of twenty-five years or so, an additional implication of
these two alternative courses of fertility begins to develop: from then
on there appears a difference, at first a growing difference, in the
rate of growth of the labor force in the two populations. It is this
period (when the difference in growth rate of the labor force first
becomes conspicuous) that I wish to consider as intermediate. In the
long run the cumulative effect of the difference in rate of growth leads
to an ever more important difference in the size of the two populations,
and therefore in the density of the population compared to the land or
the resources upon which it depends. In sum, we distinguish three
periods: a short run period (the first generation) in which differences in dependency appear as the principal effect of different fertility
experience; then an intermediate period where added to the difference in
dependency is a difference in the rate of growth of the labor force;
and finally in the long run, an ever growing and more and more important
difference in the density of the labor force relative to resources is
added to the age-distribution and rate of growth differences.

Most discussion of "the population problem" is in terms of crowding, or
excessive population relative to resources. This turns out to be the
most difficult problem to analyze, and the most difficult one on which
to reach any certain conclusions. Our frame of analysis will defer the
question of density until later, just as significant differences in
density result from different courses of fertility only in the rather
remote future. We can be much more sure of the economic implications of
the age distribution and growth rate differences that differences in
fertility imply, and we shall begin with these short run effects.

During this first generation there are only trivial differences in the
number of persons of labor force age. In the illustrative numerical
projection that I have carried out, at the end of twenty-five years
there is only a 4 per cent difference in the number of persons 15 to 64.
A strong case can be made that the 4 per cent smaller number of persons
15 to 64 resulting from low fertility does not really mean a lower number of potentially effective participants in economic activity. In the
first place, most of these underdeveloped countries are having a great
deal of difficulty in providing productive employment for their present
labor force, and this difficulty promises to become worse rather than
better. Moreover, when there is a reduction of fertility that amounts
to 50 per cent at the end of twenty-five years, there is every reason
to suppose that the availability of women for employment in the labor
force market will be much greater in the population with reduced fertility than with sustained fertility, because there would be 50 per cent
fewer pregnant women and 50 per cent fewer dependent children for them
to care for. Hence, if additional manpower or womanpower is an economic
asset, I think the 4 per cent difference in numbers is more than offset
by the much greater availability of women for economic activity that

would be the result of reduced fertility. Hence, for twenty-five years
the population with reduced fertility would have at least as great a
supply of available labor. Obviously, it would have exactly the same
resources to work with. I can see no reason to suppose that there
will be more minerals or farm land in existence in response to a different number of children. Thus, there is no difference in available
labor or resources in the first twenty-five years, but a major difference in that the population with reduced fertility would have many fewer dependents to provide for.

The economy that had those fewer dependents would be in a much stronger
position to increase its allocation of resources for productive purposes.
It would feel much less pressure to consume everything that it produced
each year to provide food and clothing and shelter for its larger and
more rapidly growing child population. It would be able to put its
efforts into building more factories, roads and the other essentials
of development. Here I emphasize again the provision of capital as an
essential ingredient of economic development. The economy with reduced fertility would be in a stronger position to provide additional
capital, which is certainly a bottleneck item, an essential item with
the highest priority in the whole process of development. It would
have the same resources and the same labor and would be in a better
position to provide capital and would have been in an increasingly
better position from the very time that fertility started down.

Over a period of the first generation, the population with reduced
fertility because of the age distribution effect, because of the consequent lesser necessity to use almost all of its resources for consumption would be in a stronger position to add to the stock of productive
capital that the economy has for development purposes. More than that,
whatever resources were made available for enhancing the stock of productive tools and equipment could be utilized in a more immediately
productive way if the dependency burden were less. There is less pressure to utilize investable resources for schools, less pressure to
put them into housing, when the families are smaller and the school
population is growing less rapidly. Capital can be used for factories,
irrigation projects, and other purposes that add almost immediately to
national product. More immediately productive uses can be made of capital can be accumulated. We end up with a paradoxical result. In the
first twenty-five or thirty years when one is considering these two
alternative population developments, the population with reduced fertility can achieve a faster growth of total national product than can
the population with sustained fertility. This is before considering
the number of consumers that the national product is going to be divided
among. A tangibly greater total national product would be achieved
with the same degree of sacrifice of current consumption in order to
achieve economic development. The net effect is that on a per capita
basis there is a smaller number of consumers and also a greater product
to divide among them. So much for the short run.

In the intermediate period we consider a time when the labor force grows
more rapidly if fertility is unchanged, and it might appear that some of
the advantage that results from reduced fertility would be offset. To
the contrary, the implication of a faster growth in the labor force is
that in order to keep productivity per worker changing at the same pace
or, to take the simplest case, held fixed, one needs to add to the pro-

ductive equipment, to the stock of useful tools and the like, in a way which is proportionate to the growth of the labor force. In other words, if the labor force is growing 3 per cent a year, one needs, roughly speaking, to add each year 3 per cent to the stock of capital. When the labor force grows more rapidly, in order not to fall behind on per capita output, the pace at which the stock of productive equipment is increased must be stepped up. Meanwhile, the age distribution implications make it more difficult rather than less to do so. We can put this very simply by using a numerical example. If on the one hand you imagine a labor force which is not changing in size and imagine that the economy is investing for nonconsumptive purposes about 9 per cent of its national product, it would add, on the usual economic assumptions, about 3 per cent to the total cumulated stock of tools, so that each worker would every year have 3 per cent more productive equipment to work with. If the population of labor force age were on the other hand growing at 3 per cent (which is about the maximum rate that it is growing in some of the underdeveloped areas today) that same level of annual investment would simply leave the stock of capital per worker unchanged. Actually, a level of 9 per cent is representative of the investment goals in some of the underdeveloped areas today. India, for example, is straining to achieve such a rate of investment. If their labor force were growing at 3 per cent a year that 9 per cent would just enable them to stay even to keep the growth of plant even with the growth of the labor force. Whereas, if the labor force were growing more slowly or in an extreme case not at all, that same level of investment could be used to enrich the endowment that each worker had in productive equipment. After the short run period, in which the age distribution effect dominates, the additional effect of a difference in growth rate is simply to add to the discrepancy in the growth of per capita output and income in the two alternative projections. In the long run this difference in rate of growth has a cumulative effect on difference in size. At first, if we look at the size of labor force alone (and I think it proper to consider this separately because differences in the child population are covered by considering the dependency burden), it is not very different. The first difference we notice in the labor force is a difference in rate of growth, but as time goes on, of course, these different growth rates begin to show up in a substantially different size of the labor force. The size difference reaches a factor of 2 after about seventy years, and then grows cumulatively so that after one hundred fifty years the labor force in a population with sustained fertility would be more than 18 times as big as it would be if the fertility had been reduced.

I said earlier that density is the hardest factor to analyze. I mean one can make a clear economic case for the disadvantages of a higher burden of dependency and for the economic disadvantages of a rapid rate of growth of the labor force. Superficially, density appears to be the simplest element to understand. Overcrowding is easy to visualize, as in the example that continued growth at current rates would produce one person per square foot in six hundred years. However, if you look around the world today, it is not at all clear that within the large range now found, greater density is always an economic handicap. One of the most densely populated areas in the world begins in Boston and extends to Washington, at least. I am not sure that there is any other area in the world of similar extent that has as many people in it. There are 28 million in that 200-mile strip. And it is not at all clear that the density of 2,000 persons per square mile in this region is an

economic handicap. Per capita incomes in this part of the United States
are higher by 25 per cent than in the rest of the country. I am not at
all sure that if the area were less densely settled it would be more
prosperous. Now, of course, everyone knows that this area trades with
the rest of the country, exporting services and manufactured goods and
importing raw materials. But so does Hong Kong. Hong Kong has a density
of 13,000 persons per square mile, yet it has raised its annual product
by nearly 10 per cent for the last decade. It is able to import raw
materials and to export its manufactured services to the rest of the
world and to achieve a more rapid economic development than most of the
low-income countries which are relatively empty and not densely settled.

Now you might say that Hong Kong is a metropolis which is economically
part of China, mainland China, but in fact in the last two or three years
only about 16 per cent of Hong Kong's trade has been with China. Most
of its trade is on the world market. It is exporting goods to the whole
world and importing raw materials from many sources. I do not want to
make too much of these examples, but do want to say that in a trading
world and in an economy which is not primarily extractive, it is not at
all clear what the economic burden of density is.

We can be sure, of course, that for the world as a whole density is an
important consideration, and if we imagine the whole world's population
getting to be as dense as that of Hong Kong there would be no complementary agricultural areas with which the densely populated area could
trade, However, when one looks at an individual country, it is a mistake to consider the implications of population growth wholly in terms
of density, or even primarily in terms of density. It nonetheless remains true that if one looks into the far distant future the density
implications of the rates of growth in the underdeveloped areas today
are literally absurd. Consider Latin America, where the population of
Mexico has been growing now at about 3 1/2 per cent a year for the last
ten years. Three and a half per cent a year doubles the population
every twenty years, doubles it five times in a century, and that means
multiplying by 32, and again by 32 in another century or by a thousand
in each two hundred years. At this rate in 200 years the population of
Mexico would be 35 billion instead of 35 million, and it would be multiplied by a thousand again in the ensuing two hundred years. By such
calculations one estimates that in 1200 years or so our descendents
would outweigh the earth--a density far beyond any practical consideration. There is no doubt that in the long run with continued rapid
growth, density becomes overwhelming. I would like to reiterate, however,
that the proper perspective on density as a national problem is probably
a long run perspective. In any event the differences in density that
would result from these two alternative courses of fertility do not become very pronounced except in the rather distant future--50 or 60 years
away.

We come then to the conclusion, if we examine the implications of these
two alternative courses of fertility, that in the short run there is a
pronounced advantage which attaches to a reduction in fertility, because
it reduces the burden of dependency. In an intermediate period the reduction in fertility would reduce the rate of growth of the labor force
and this would have a further economic advantage by making investment
more productive of per capita increases in output. In the long run if
fertility is not reduced, density reaches absurd levels. At the Office

of Population Research we have made some calculations to translate these
effects into rough numerical terms. Without describing the techniques
of calculation, I shall give you some of the salient results.

We utilized the projected population I have discussed here, and made
for each projected population the same assumptions about the factors
which determine the growth of output. We calculated the income per
consumer that developed for each population projection. I say per consumer instead of per head because in calculating the number of consumers,
we counted each child as only a half a person on the grounds that children do not consume as much. This allowance tends to reduce the difference in income between the projected populations. At the end of ten
years after the reduction of fertility begins output per consumer is
only 3 per cent higher than with fertility unchanged. At the end of
twenty years it is 14 per cent higher, and at the end of thirty years,
41 per cent higher. Note that these figures are not the growth in output per consumer, but rather give the output per consumer with reduced
fertility relative to what there would be if fertility remained unchanged.
In other words, in thirty years there would be 41 per cent higher output
per consumer with reduced fertility than if it were unchanged. At the
end of sixty years the population with reduced fertility would have
doubled the income perconsumer, in ninety years three times, and after
one hundred fifty years it would have an income per consumer six times
as great as the population with unchanged fertility. The economic advantage from reduced fertility in terms of growth in income per consumer is slow at first, but it accumulates to impressive dimensions as
time goes by. I should add that these calculations make no allowance
for density whatsoever: no allowance for diminishing returns, no allowance for the fact that resources become more expensive and that living
space competes with farmland as the population grows. They were made
in terms of the effect on investment of differences in dependency and
the differential effect of the different rates of growth in the labor
force. In one hundred fifty years, leaving out the whole question of
diminishing returns and density, the income advantage from reduced fertility reaches a factor of 6, starting with an advantage of about 40
per cent at the end of one generation.

When a country is striving desperately to raise its per capita income
from the level of $60 to $80 a year to a more reasonable humane level,
a 40 per cent gain is a big one. Also the reduction in fertility makes
the increase in the per capita income greater as well as more certain.

I will add only a word about the implication of these alternative future
courses of fertility for other aspects of development than the increase
in per capita income. Another factor that I want to emphasize especially
is that of productive employment for persons of the normal age for economic activity. One of the problems that all underdeveloped countries
feel most acutely is the problem of underemployment or unemployment.
We have a problem in the United States of unemployment. Five to six
per cent of our labor force is unemployed. This problem has been a
chronic one, though not as severe since World War II as it was before.
Unemployment in the U.S. economy with plants shut down while workers
are out of jobs is a matter of simultaneous idle labor and idle capital
equipment. It is ordinarily attributed by economists to what we call a
"deficiency of effective demand"--the total of the money being spent for
consumption, investment and by the government for various purposes is

not adequate to utilize out productive resources fully, including the
labor force.

In the underdeveloped countries, one also has to deal with something which
is called unemployment though to measure it in terms of proportion of the
labor force is very difficult. It is more precisely termed underemployment. Most economists feel that the fundamental causes are quite different from the causes of unemployment in the industrialized countries. The
difficulty is a lack of adequate organization and of productive equipment to provide work that will produce a reasonable output per worker.
The underemployment usually associated with the underdeveloped economies is the sort of thing one observes in an Indian railway station or
in a Mexican barbershop, or in shops in any city in Indonesia, where in
the railroad station there are more porters than are needed to carry
luggage for any given train, where the barbershop has barbers who are
idle most of the day because there are not enough customers, and where
a large number of retail shops offer essentially the same merchandise,
and the clerks or the proprietors spend most of their day cooling their
heels waiting for the few customers to come in. This is called underemployment because in any one of these activities if there were fewer
people offering their services the output would not be diminished. This
does not show up as the kind of unemployment found in the United States
because there is no one actively looking for a job, there being no real
job opportunities. This kind of failure to have really useful and productive employment is one of the aspects of extreme proverty in the
underdeveloped countries. Even if some of the other aspects of poverty
could be alleviated, this is one that also cries for solution. Quite
aside from the question of low per capita income, as long as the rapidly
growing labor force has job opportunities only of that sort, that is, to
show up as additional porters, farm laborers, or barbers when there are
already too many, the situation is degrading and undignified and not
worthy of a society or economy in the twentieth century.

It is extremely difficult in realistic economic development plans to
provide promise of productive employment even for the persons who are
now unemployed. When one looks forward to a labor force twice as big
thirty years from now, this goal of economic development is seen to be
one of the most difficult. During the period when the dependency burden
is the principal difference between the two projected populations, the
population with reduced fertility has the advantage of more rapid accumulation of capital, which also will make possible a somewhat faster expansion in job opportunities. In the immediate and long run, the slower
growth of the labor force will, of course, make the problem of providing
productive employment for all a lot nearer to attainment, though I still
would not say easy. Add a similar comment about the attainment of other
goals such as providing education: universal primary education, secondary education for all within a generation, and growing universities.
The difference in costs on the one hand and in the availability of resources on the other is enormous between the population which has a
slowly growing child population and the one with the exploding child
population that goes with sustained fertility.

In summary, I think there is no need for alarmist statements about how
if fertility isn't reduced in the next ten years the population of India
or Pakistan will starve, nor for anti-social statements about how if a
country is not prepared to accept the advice of Planned Parenthood, we

should give it no aid. I think one can in a dispassionate and scientific way see very clearly that the reduction of fertility in the next generation, or as soon as it can be achieved, will be a major element in making possible the modernization and industrialization that every country must pass through in order really to join the twentieth century.

READING 23

In 1939 Professor W.B. Reddaway (born 1913) published a study entitled
The Economics of a Declining Population in which he analyzed the advantages and inconveniences of a stationary or slowly declining population.
This book retains its freshness and actuality, especially now that a
number of Western countries seem to be moving toward achieving populations that are not growing.

In the following reading, Reddaway discusses the economic consequences
of greater or lesser population density and of population increase or
decrease. In his view the world population as a whole has already
overstepped its optimum size. World per capita income would be greater
if numbers of people were smaller.

He also belabors the point that densely population countries such as
Great Britain, which maintain their relatively high standard of living
through a complicated system of international trade, become very vulnerable. They export manufactured products and import fuels, raw materials, and food. Such nations can prosper only if raw products and
food can be obtained relatively easily and if markets for their industrial products can be found. These countries' lack of landed resources
implies that they have little or no control over the very foundations
of their prosperity. Further population increase, says Reddaway, has
a negative effect on their balance of payments because the increments
in population require extra imports of food, fuels, and raw materials.
To pay for these imports a country must export more industrial commodities, which themselves require extra imports of raw products and oil
for manufacture.[23]

The rudiments of this type of argument can be found in Wicksell's
Lectures in Political Economy (Swedish edition) and in an earlier work
by Keynes entitled The Economic Consequences of the Peace. Reddaway's
version of the argument, however, is more sophisticated and contemporary.

---

[23]Source: W.B. Reddaway, "Population, Economics of, "Chamber's
Encyclopaedia, Vol. XI 1966, pp. 88-90.

POPULATION, ECONOMICS OF
William B. Reddaway

This subject needs to be considered under two different heads, which
are often confused; firstly, the economic consequences of having a
large or a small population at any one time; secondly, the effects of a
population which is increasing or decreasing over a period. In both
cases one should consider the effects in individual countries, which
differ greatly according to their circumstances, as well as the effect
for the world as a whole. In the first one also needs to distinguish
different meanings of the words 'large' and 'small' which are unintel-
ligible unless the standard of reference is given; thus the population
of Belgium is fairly small compared with that of other countries, but
large in relation to its area.

Large and Small Populations. -- The advantages and disadvantages of a
large population for the world as a whole have long been a subject of
discussion amongst economists. On the one hand there have been the
fears of those who said that the supply of good agricultural land was
limited, so that a large population could only be fed if inferior land
were also cultivated and the good land worked very intensively; both
these courses would mean that mankind produced less as a result of a
day's work, and so would mean a lower average income than could be obtained with a smaller population. On the other side have been the arguments that a large population would give more scope for mass-production,
specialization and the introduction of things like railways, which require a certain minimum of demand to justify them; similarly many 'overhead costs' of society, such as the whole apparatus of government,
would be less onerous if they were shared amongst a large population.

The rival merits of these two arguments cannot be assessed without reference to the size of the population which is assumed. At one extreme,
Robinson Crusoe would undoubtedly have been better off if his island-
world had had some more inhabitants, so that he need not have tried to
be a jack-of-all-trades and production of particular things could have
been done on a larger scale with more specialized equipment; at the
other extreme a world which was all as densely populated as Lancashire
would be a poverty-stricken place. Taking the world as it is in the
20th century, it is most probable that its inhabitants would have a
higher average income if they were less numerous. This is not only because of the limited supply of land: a smaller population would also
mean that each worker had more machinery and equipment with which to
work and that each family had more house-room in which to live. The
advantages to be gained from both these considerations are most marked
in the densely populated countries of the far east, but they are not
negligible anywhere. The losses from the smaller scale of production
etc. need only be trifling when one is considering the whole world as

a market.

Two common fallacies should perhaps be briefly mentioned. They are firstly that a larger population would mean more unemployment, because more people would be seeking work; and secondly that it would mean less unemployment, because the demand for goods would be greater. Unemployment (q.v.) is discussed briefly below, but essentially these arguments cancel out; in practice there is no evidence that unemployment is heavier either in large countries or in small ones.

Increasing and Decreasing Populations. -- Some of the considerations discussed above are relevant in this context too. Thus an increasing population tends, in itself, to reduce the stock of land and capital per head, so reducing the average income. Taking land and capital together, the passage of time will not usually show a fall in the amount available per head, because most countries are continuously accumulating capital, but the rise will have been less than it might have been with a stationary population. This consequence of a rising population is of immense importance to India and other under-developed countries which are trying under economic plans to raise the real incomes of their population by raising the amount of capital per head.

The working out of the above factor may be seen from two different angles. On the side of production, it will be necessary to raise the total stock of factories, machinery and equipment by a fairly considerable amount in each year merely to provide the additional workers with the same facilities for production as the average worker previously used; only the residue of the community's saving will be available for raising the level of mechanization etc. and so increasing output per head. On the side of income-receipt, an increasing population implies large families, so that the father's estate is divided amongst more children than is the case with a stationary one, and the latter then receive less 'unearned' income. In a progressive economy the father will probably have saved something to add to the capital which he inherited, so that the average legacy may rise with each succeeding generation; but large families put a brake on this process.

It is worth noting that just the same factors apply in the field of 'social' or 'communal' capital. A country with an increasing population is continually having to use part of its income to build new schools or hospitals, merely to maintain existing standards; with a stationary population this could have been used for improvements instead.

Unemployment. -- The influence of population trends on unemployment is complex and needs careful analysis. Only a very summary statement is possible here; for a fuller treatment the reader is referred to the bibliography.

In under-developed economies, such as one finds in Asia or Africa, the main reason for unemployment may be stated broadly as lack of suitable land, capital equipment, raw material and other factors, without which labour cannot be effectively applied. In such countries, a rapidly expanding population naturally tends to make the problem worse, since it aggravates the excess of labour in relation to the things with which labour should work. The result may not be actual unemployment, in the sense of people doing nothing all day, but is more commonly seen as

underemployment or 'ineffective' employment, the salient feature being
that the worker (who is often self-employed) produces and earns very
little in the day.

In developed economies of the western type, however, the main risk of
unemployment comes from the more subtle problem of balancing demand and
supply, both for goods and services in total, and for particular items.
If aggregate demand is too small, there is likely to be unemployment;
if aggregate demand is allowed to be too big, there is likely to be inflation and rising prices.

An increasing population has a direct effect on this problem, because
it provides a steady and reliable reason for an increase in demand for
almost everything, including items such as house-room which can only
be provided after a considerable expenditure on capital. Moreover, the
fact that the market always had expanded in the past will give industrialists rosier expectations for the future, and make them more willing
to start expanding their productive capacity, even before the demand has
fully taxed their existing plant.

Other things being equal, therefore, a declining population is more
liable to suffer from unemployment, and an expanding population is more
liable to suffer from inflation. In both cases, however, it is perfectly possible for the evil to be averted by wise governmental policies, and conversely unwise policies may lead to heavy unemployment in
a developed country, even if it has a rapidly expanding population. A
declining population does not necessarily imply that there will be more
unemployment, but rather it calls for more skilful and resolute action
by society to avoid it.

Effect on Public Finances. -- Population trends have an important influence on the public finances, both on the revenue side and on expenditure.

So far as expenditure goes, a declining population implies an abnormally high proportion of elderly people, who, at least in advanced
countries, will mostly draw an old age pension; on the other hand an
increasing population implies an abnormally high proportion of children,
who are mostly educated at public expense, and for whom some countries
provide family allowances. In each case there is compensation in the
shape of a lower expenditure 'at the other end' than would prevail with
a stable population of the same size, and the net effect may be small,
depending on the provisions actually made. However, a changeover from
an upward trend in population to a stationary or declining one will
usually give a period in which conditions are temporarily very favourable for the public finances: this was important in Great Britain in
the years around 1940. The number of retired people was still well
under that which would prevail in a stable population with present
mortality rates, partly because the British population was smaller in
the period when they were born (i.e. about 1870) and partly because far
more people used to die young than happens nowadays. At the same time
the number of British children was also subnormal in the 1940s, because
of the low birthrate since 1930, so that the exchequer saved at the
children's end before having to pay out to a 'normal' proportion of
pensioners. From the budgetary point of view the change from an increasing to a declining population is an insidious affair, bringing

nothing but relief to start with and then burdens.

On the revenue side of the budget the most important point is that an increasing population will imply a rising revenue from almost all taxes. Some forms of expenditure will rise correspondingly (e.e. education and social services generally) but this is not true of others (e.g. defence), and above all it does not apply to the interest on the national debt. The burden of the British debt, which seemed so formidable at the end of the Napoleonic wars, was progressively relieved throughout the 19th century by the growth of the population and of the national income until it became relatively unimportant; a corresponding relief is not to be expected for the debt incurred in the second world war.

Effects of Comparative Variations. -- If we are concerned with a country's population compared with that of other countries, some additional factors appear.

A large population will help to make a country a great power; this brings some economic gains in international trading and concession-hunting (e.g. for oil), but the resulting responsibility for maintaining law and order in the world and bearing the 'white man's burden' entails some economic costs. The economic policy of a great power also has a much bigger influence on the level of world prosperity than that of a small country, and it is correspondingly more nearly the master of its own economic fate and less at the mercy of 'world economic forces' which it is powerless to control. Whether this is really an advantage or not depends on whether the policy of that country is likely to be wiser than the average; in some cases it is just as well that the really decisive factors lie outside the country's influence.

A country with a large population is in some respects better able to secure the advantages of mass production and specialization, because of its large domestic market. This argument must not be pressed too far; if a small country has access to the world market, that will often make up for a small home market, as we see from the success with which Australia can specialize on wool growing, Switzerland on watch making, and Malaya on tin and rubber. In some cases a country may have a flourishing industry which works wholly for export, such as the British manufacturers of plantation machinery. Furthermore some of the gains which we think of under this heading, such as large-scale gas-works, depend on density of population, rather than its aggregate size; Belgium may fare better in this respect than the Soviet Union.

Nevertheless, there are some important cases where a large domestic market is a real advantage in securing mass production. This will be the case wherever tariffs or other restrictions limit international trade. Even with free trade it will also apply to such things as films and books, where a large sale for each one produced is particularly important and the market in other countries will often require a rather different model; a small country is at a specially great disadvantage in this respect if its language is not used elsewhere.

It must of course be remembered in considering the above arguments that population is only one factor which influences the size of the domestic market. The level of income per head may in some cases be much more important, as we see from the fact that 2 million New Zealanders

buy more cars than 400 million Indians; and special local needs may also
be decisive; neither an increased population nor a rise in the level of
income would create a bid demand for refrigerators in Lapland.

Density -- The analysis of 'world' factors brought out the disadvantages
of having too large a population in relation to the supply of fertile
land. This argument will apply in just the same way to a single country,
if for one reason or another its population is primarily agricultural --
as is the case in most of the poverty-stricken countries of the far
east and other 'backward' areas. It is quite possible, however, for
particular countries to escape the evil consequences of a dense population by relying on international trade to supply a large part of
their need for agricultural products, in just the same way as large
towns rely on trade with people outside their boundaries. They may
then enjoy the benefits which can be secured in a closely populated
country, such as cheap gas or electricity, good shopping facilities and
theatres.

For a densely populated country to have a high standard of living two
main conditions must both be fulfilled. It must be able to produce
manufactured goods efficiently, of a kind that are wanted abroad; and
there must be other countries with a surplus of agricultural products
which they are willing to exchange for these manufactured goods on
reasonable terms. The first requires a good stock of capital equipment and a skilled and versatile labour force, using that term to cover
management as well as operatives; the second requires both that there
should be other countries which are not densely populated and that
these should be willing to obtain some of their manufactured goods
from abroad.

In the 19th century the British population was able to multiply four-
fold without encountering the difficulties which had been foretold, but
circumstances were then specially favourable in both respects: Britain
was the leading producer of manufactures, and the newly developed areas
were very willing to supply agricultural products in exchange on favourable terms. Such a situation was unlikely to last forever, and two
world wars plus the growth of economic nationalism have hastened its
disappearance. The result is a 'balance of payments' problem, under
which it is difficult for the country to produce and market abroad
enough manufactures to pay for the imports of primary products which it
must have for its crowded population. This means in effect that the
old difficulty over the pressure of a large population on limited
natural resources has been arrived at by a new route: instead of the
numbers growing faster than agricultural technique could improve, the
possibilities of obtaining additional supplies from outside on favourable terms have contracted. The densely populated country may then
have to meet a greater proportion of its need for agricultural commodities by costly production on poor land at home, or to accept less
favourable terms in its trading with others. Either route threatens
a lower standard of living, unless the loss can be offset by increased
efficiency, and the second may be blocked by other countries' refusal
to spend enough on British goods, however cheaply they are offered.

Under such circumstances a still larger population would be a source
of embarrassment, and its influence is greater than might be expected.
This is mainly because almost the whole of the additional requirements

for agricultural products must be met from abroad, whereas part of the existing ones can be met from domestic production; a subsidiary reason is that the additional exports needed to pay for the extra imports consumed in Britain will themselves require imported materials.

Little needs to be added on the subject of increasing and decreasing populations in a single country, as the 'world' analysis applies, with a modification to take account of external trade similar to that discussed above. International capital movements may also, however, affect the issue. A country with a rapidly expanding population may be able to borrow from abroad to equip the additional people with houses, machines, etc. and so avoid being short of capital for improvements. This was particularly important when 'new' countries were receiving large numbers of immigrants; to some extent these brought capital with them, and in these cases there was no interest payment to be made to people in other countries.

READING 24

The following reading originates from the contemporary Soviet economist-demographer Y. Guzevatyi (born 1921) who has widely traveled outside the Soviet Union and who is well acquainted with demographic thinking in Asia and the West.

The early post-Marxian socialists wrote in strict obedience to Marxist principles. Toward the end of the 19th century, however, the socialist movement split into evolutionary and revolutionary brances. The latter adhered strictly to Marx and Engels whereas the evolutionary socialists opted for patient reform and construction. Evolutionary socialists also felt that the Marxian doctrines were no longer consistent with apparent reality and that accordingly a revision of those principles was in order. The revisionists generally adopted the view that birth control would improve the living standards of agricultural and industrial laborers. The orthodox socialists tended to disagree with this outlook. Yet even some Marxist writers took positions that in a sense represent a departure from Marx. In his work The Impact of Population Increase on the Progress of Society (1880), the German socialist Karl Kautsky recognized the law of diminishing returns, which, he said, could be temporarily postponed but not abolished by technological progress and innovation. The laborers, he asserted, can also improve their bargaining position by holding back their own supply, i.e., by keeping their families small. This objective should be achieved through the use of contraception. Kautsky rejected Malthus's moral restraint.

For his part Lenin tended to deny the law of diminishing returns, or at least his version of it. Continuous technical development nullifies this law, he said. He also strongly rejected the view that social problems could be solved merely by limitation of family size among the industrial and agrarian laborers. Yet he supported abortion and the freedom to use contraception, believing that all medical knowledge should be freely disseminated and that prospective mothers have the right to terminate pregnancy at will.

After the 1917 revolution Soviet demographers and other social scientists continued to be inspired by the writings of Marx, Engels, and Lenin. After World War II, Soviet opinion as expressed in the government-controlled press and by delegates to international meetings took a strong, if not violent, position on what were labeled as "Malthusianism" and "Neo-Malthusianism". Although it was not always clear exactly what these terms meant, it was obvious that they referred to opinions expressed by certain American and European writers. The so-called Neo-Malthusians were compared to racists, cannibalists, and the like. Scientific opinion was only a little more moderate. A Soviet demographer named Ryabushkin delivered a paper at the World Population Conference of 1954 which is perhaps characteristic of Soviet opinion of that period. His views are reproduced here without further comment.

(a) Absolute population problems do not and cannot exist. Labor is
by far the most important factor of production; therefore, increments in
population and labor produce more than proportional increases in production. (Ryabushkin assumes uninterrupted technological advances.)

(b) Relative overpopulation or unemployment does exist under capitalism
and is a real problem. It is inherent in this system and will disappear
only when capitalism no longer exists.

(c) The possibilities of developing a society's productive forces are
limitless.

(d) Large increases in agricultural output per acre are possible and
huge uncultivated lands are still available.

(e) Propositions in favor of lowering birth rates or decreasing population in such low-income countries as India are merely "cannibalistic."

Since 1964, however, such traditional views on population have been
challenged by writers who apparently have a better demographic background and more understanding of the realities outside the Soviet Union.
We are referring here to such social scientists as Boris Urlanis,
Yaropolk Guzevatyi, and M. Kolganov. They recognized that the less
developed countries face a special problem, i.e., a combination of high
birth rates and rapidly declining death rates. The fast population
growth that results is a real obstacle to economic betterment. According to Urlanis, economic solutions must be found, but they must be supplemented by demographic policies aimed at lowering birth rates.

Guzevatyi's article that follows gives an interesting picture of how a
group of contemporary Soviet economic demographers view the population
problem in less developed countries.[24]

---

[24]Source: Y. Guzevatyi, "Population Problems in Developing Countries,"
International Affairs (September, 1966), pp. 52-58

POPULATION PROBLEMS IN DEVELOPING COUNTRIES
Yaropolk Guzevatyi

The social and economic development of the young Asian and African states which have freed themselves from the yoke of colonialism encounters numerous difficulties, among which population problems are increasingly claiming attention. Besides causing serious national preoccupation, they are important factors which cannot be ignored in world politics.

Population growth is known to have accelerated sharply in modern times. In the fifteen years from 1950 to 1965, the rate of average annual population increase doubled in comparison with the first half of the century and the earth's population increased by 800 million, roughly as much as in the preceeding fifty years. Almost nine-tenths of this increase was in the countries of Asia, Africa and Latin America.

This rapid growth in world population (often called the "population explosion") is caused by considerable changes in the population processes in Airo-Asian and Latin American countries. Now, as in the past, these countries have a high birth rate, double or even treble that of the developed industrial states. This is quite natural when one takes into consideration the backward social structure which the emancipated countries inherited from the colonial epoch, a structure characterized by widespread survivals of feudal and primitive relations and an overwhelming majority of illiterate peasant population, often lacking in elementary culture, ossified in prejudices and superstitions.

In such conditions, large families are sanctified by long-standing tradition and are the fruit of early marriage, the active part taken by children in the family's economic life, woman's complete deprivation of social rights and, above all, the absence of any material or cultural stimuli to a conscious approach to family planning.

However, notwithstanding the high birth rate, the growth of the population in the colonial countries before their national liberation was comparatively moderate, since it was kept down by a high mortality rate. Hunger and unhygienic living conditions facilitated the spread among the popular masses of all sorts of serious diseases such as smallpox, cholera, malaria, tuberculosis, and various forms of avitaminosis and helminthiasis. Under the colonial regime there was no serious fight against such diseases, and medical care for the population was practically nonexistent. Infantile mortality was very high. In Togo, for instance, half the newborn children died before the age of one year.

With the appearance of effective anti-epidemic means, especially antibiotics, a steady decrease in the death rate began. This was considerably accelerated after the liquidation of colonial and semi-colonial regimes, when in the course of state construction the national governments were able to implement measures for improving sanitation and the health services.

If a high birth rate is maintained, it is obvious that even a small drop in the death rate leads to a rapid increase in the natural growth of the population.

Natural Growth of Population in Asia and Africa
(Average annual percentage*)

Continent	1930-1940	1950-1960
Africa	1.21	2.33
North Africa	1.5	2.39
Tropical and South Africa	1.1	2.3
Asia	1.31	2.11

*Source: 1963 Report on the World Social Situation, United Nations, New York, 1963, p.6.

The population of Asia rose in the first half of the 20th century by 370 million, and in the next 14 years by 500 million. The population of the Afro-Asian countries is still continuing to grow rapidly. The following data (in millions) testify to the population growth in some Asian and African countries: India--12, Pakistan--over 2, Indonesia--over 2, Philippines--1, Thailand--0.9, U.A.R.--approximately 0.8, Nigeria--over 0.7.

The history of the industrial states has shown that the eonomic and cultural development of the liberated countries will gradually strengthen the material and psychological requisites for lowering the birth rate. These requisites are first and foremost the disintegration of the patriarchal system, especially as regards family relations, under the influences of agrarian transformations and industrialization. The new opportunities that young people get as a result of the spread of education, greater participation by women in production, study, social and political life, have as one of their most important consequences a rise in the marriage age and a lowering of the birth rate. The desire for a reasonable limitation of the number of children is the result of increased demand for cultural and material values. Finally, the lowering of the birth rate is, in a way, a reaction to the drop in infantile mortality, since a high birth rate is a sort of compensation for high infantile mortality.

However, the inevitable changes in the way of life and family traditions during the revolutionary transformation of society constitute a slow process, and the tendency towards a lower birth rate associated with it is, therefore, not sudden, but spread over a long period. Moreover, an acceleration, not a slowing down of the population growth, is to be expected in the near future in many Afro-Asian countries.

This applies first of all to Africa, where a considerable growth of the population can be anticipated as a consequence of a lowering, due to improved medical and hygiene services, of the still very high death rate, especially among babies and children. An increased birth rate will be promoted by generally improving the health of the population, particularly by eradicating diseases resulting in total or partial sterility in women.

The birth rate also rises as nomad peoples become settled. An instance of this is the Sudan, where the government has undertaken to settle the nomad tribes in the newly irrigated Gezira area. Research has provided evidence that the birth rate in the settled agricultural areas is 80 per cent higher than in the nomad cattle-rearing areas. It does not therefore appear justified to expect that the present high population growth in Africa and Asia will be substantially lowered in the next twenty to thirty years.

This rapid and accelerating growth of the population seriously complicates the already difficult economic and social problems facing young national states. Reasoning abstractly, growing manpower resources should favour social and economic development, for people are society's basic production force. But the concrete reality in the Afro-Asian countries is such that this favourable factor changes into its antithesis.

In the conditions of a backward agrarian economy inherited from colonialism with conservative forms of land tenure and cultivation, primitive agricultural technology and above all lack of the capital and qualified labour indispensable for radically reorganizing the economy, there is a "redundance" of manpower.

To begin with, the accelerated growth of the population leads to an irrational increase in its density in the main economic areas. This seems at first sight not to be so great a problem, since the density of the population in most of the liberated countries is as a rule much smaller than, say, in the European states. Africa, for instance, is one of the most sparsely populated continents, with nine inhabitants to the square kilometre in 1963 as compared with Europe's 89. Vast expanses of the equatorial forests and the south Sahara plateaus are entirely uninhabited and still await economic development. Many areas in Asia also are suitable for development.

But migration to such unpopulated regions involves huge preliminary capital outlays to put to use the deserts and semi-deserts, drain the swamps and clear the impenetrable forests or carry out anti-epidemic and sanitation work, particularly to get rid of the malaria mosquito and the tse-tse fly in Africa. For this, the overwhelming majority of the liberated countries, to say nothing of individual farms, still lack the necessary means. Besides the economic and geographical obstacles to development of uninhabited territories there are also political, national, religions and other hindrances.

That is why the expanding population does not migrate to thinly popu-

lated areas, but concentrates in the comparatively smaller, already settled localities, mainly in such areas as the valleys of rivers and
lakes and the coastal plains.

All attempts made by individual governments to achieve a more even
spreadout of the population have failed to produce any substantial
results. The Indonesian Government, for example, has always attached
great importance to this task. It succeeded from 1950 to 1958 in transferring annually up to 30 thousand inhabitants from Java to other parts
of the country, but this obviously could not have a great effect on
Java's annual average population increase of 700,000 - 800,000.

At the same time, migration from rural areas to the towns is increasing
in many African and Asian countries. This results in unhealty urban-
isation. Overcrowded areas without the requisite economic basis spring
up in the towns. Housing, industrial and transport development in such
towns as a rule seriously lag behind the population increase, and this
leads to more and more slums and a continued growth of the declassed
section of the population.

Accelerated population growth hinders food supply. By 1963, according
to FAO estimates, about one half of the world population were suffering
from chronic undernourishment. Calculations have shown that to elimate
undernourishment in the newly-liberated countries by 1975 and to improve
the nutritive qualities of their food, those countries' food production
must be raised by 4 per cent every year. But the actual increase from
1960 to 1965 was only 2.5 per cent. The result is that in many regions
population growth is outstripping agricultural production. Thus, in
Asia, foodstuff production rose in 1961-1962 by 40 per cent as compared
with the pre-war period, but, calculated per capita, it was only 93
per cent of the pre-war figure owing to population increase.

Whereas before the war the countries of Asia, Africa and Latin America,
according to data supplied by the American Society of Agronomy were,
on the whole, exporters of food, supplying annually some 11 million
tons of various cereals to developed countries, during the post-war
years of 1948-1952, they were already importing an annual average of
4 million tons of food, in 1957-1959 13 million tons, and in 1964 25
million tons. According to available estimates, the developing countries'
annual import needs will be at least 47 million tons of grain by 1980.

The factors of overpopulation facing us are those which the Malthusians
called manifestations of the "universal abstract law of nature," but
in reality they are the results of the economic backwardness rising
from completely concrete, historically transient socio-economic conditions, and first and foremost the preservation in the Afro-Asian
countries of widely developed survivals of feudal and primitive social
relations. These backward, anachronistic social relations, which have
persisted owing to the oppression of the colonial regimes, fetter the
production forces of those countries, hinder technical progress and
maintain agriculture in a state of stagnation and primitive routine.
It is in such conditions that the population increase begins to outstrip
the production of means of subsistence, and for that reason the solution
of the food problem in the liberated countries is possible only if the
primitive and feudal survivals are climinated through the abolition of
colonialism and neo-colonialism and radical socio-economic transfor-

mations, in the first place sweeping agrarian reforms.

But here again, the problem of capital is uppermost: without a definite minimum of capital investment it is impossible radically to reorganise the economy, to modernize agricultural technology, and so on. At the same time, the rapid population growth demands that the major part of the national income be used not for production, but to import food, to satisfy material and cultural requirements. The rapid growth of the population makes necessary increasingly high expenditures merely to maintain the former living standard, not to speak of raising it. There is growing demand for articles of primary necessity, for schools, educational equipment and teachers, hospitals, medicines, doctors and so forth. As a result, many countries postpone the liquidation of illiteracy among the adult population and the introduction of universal schooling for children. This is not so noticeable as long as the population leads a primitive way of life, but it becomes increasingly perceptible as national awareness develops and the material and cultural demands of the population grow.

Another economic problem resulting from specific population situation in the Afro-Asian countries is that owing to the high birth rate, the proportion of children under the age of fifteen to the total population is about 50 per cent higher than in the industrial states. Hence there are more dependants per worker, and this leads to especially great economic difficulties in conditions of low labour productivity. The economic burden resulting from the considerable proportion of dependants among the population is accentuated by the acute employment problem in the Afro-Asian countries: the number of adolescents on the labour market increases, as a rule, at a greater rate than the number of working places.

The acute shortage of capital and food, increasing with the growth of the population, seriously hinders the strengthening of national independence in the liberated countries. Forced to turn to the imperialist states for credits, grain and other agricultural products, to meet the immediate needs of the population, these countries thereby throw open the door to foreign capital. This leads in a greater or lesser degree to their losing freedom of action in foreign politics. Besides, imperialist "aid" generally tends to consolidate the reactionary forces within the recipient country.

In the young national states which have chosen the non-capitalist path of development, the reactionary forces try to make use of the economic difficulties, especially food shortages, to discredit the ideas of Socialism and to fan dissatisfaction among the people. These counter-revolutionary schemes have more chance to succeed in countries where leaders of the national-liberation revolution underestimate the complexity of the economic tasks, and population problems in particular. There have been some who sincerely hoped that the liquidation of the colonial regime would by itself ensure national economic upsurge and prosperity.

These over-optimistic expectations have been mercilessly chastised by reality. Indonesia, for instance, has achieved no substantial improvement of the economy and the living standard of the people for the whole twenty years the country has been independent. This could not fail to rouse disenchantment among the people and doubtlessly provided the back-

ground for the domestic policy crisis which broke out in the autumn of
1965.

Such circumstances should apparently be taken into account in analysing
home policy events in Ghana and a number of other liberated countries.

The problems rising from rapid population growth are naturally only one
aspect of the general economic problems in the liberated countries. As
has already been noted, they are rooted in the soil of backward social
structure inherited from colonialism and cannot be eliminated without
a radical change of that structure.

There can be no doubt that the serious food shortages and other economic
difficulties which India is now suffering from are due primarily to incomplete fulfilment of the basic tasks of the national-liberation revolution, which is anti-imperialistic and anti-feudal in content. The
implementation of the agrarian reform, on which the development of the
production forces in agriculture depends entirely, has been delayed for
many years. Big national capital is ruling the roost, and foreign
companies are again strengthening their positions.

That is why India's democratic forces are mainly demanding radical steps
to complete that reform and extend the state sector in the economy, in
particular, to nationalize a number of industries, the banks, and the
grain trade, as well as to limit and subsequently to eliminate monopoly
capital's economic might.

Nevertheless, it would be wrong to suppose that even the most rapid and
consistent fulfilment of these demands would immediately solve India's
difficulties caused by her rapid population growth. Because of the
"population explosion" from which the newly liberated countries are now
suffering, radical social and economic transformations are the chief
and indispensable requisites for solving the population problems, but
they will not necessarily solve those problems immediately.

This is well seen in the case of the U.A.R., one of the few liberated
countries where the tasks of the national-liberation revolution have, on
the whole, been completed. An agrarian reform has been carried out, the
land being confiscated from estate-owners without compensation. The
assets of big and medium national capitalists, as well as the property
of foreign companies, including the Suez Canal, have also been nationalized. Up to date, as much as 90 per cent of the basic means of production, including factories and plants, transport, banks and insurance
companies, building and foreign-trade companies, have been taken over
by the state. Compensation to capitalists for the nationalized enterprises is to be paid not earlier than in fifteen years. Progressive
income tax has been introduced.

The resolute measures taken by the Government to eliminate the domination
of foreign capital and limit the incomes of the exploiter classes have
permitted a considerable increase in state investments in the national
economy. The Suez Canal alone, for the eight years (1956-1964) since
its nationalization, has brought the state a revenue of 400 million
Egyptian pounds, as compared with one million pounds a year which the
Anglo-French administration used to pay Egypt.

Successful economic development has resulted in the share of industry, transport and construction in the national income rising from 25 per cent in 1952 to 38 per cent in 1965, while the national income as a whole has increased by 120 per cent during the same time.

However, as a result of the considerable population growth, the national income per capita has risen only by 60 per cent. This population increase, which amounted to 800 thousand in 1965, is especially adverse to agriculture because of the limited arable land available (2.4 per cent of the total area of the country), which is concentrated mainly in the Nile valley and delta. There, the density of the rural population in some places exceeds 1,000 per sq. km. The rapid increase in the number of inhabitants hampers the solution of the land problem. Even equal redistribution of the landed estates among the peasants cannot help. Suffice it to note that from 1927 to 1960 the average size of the plot cultivated per capita of the population decreased from 0.15 to 0.09 hectares.

The U.A.R. Government is now taking effective measures for a sharp expansion of agricultural lands. With all-out help from Soviet Union a giant hydrotechnical complex is being built at Aswan, which will allow the irrigation of virgin soil areas of the Libyan desert and will increase the area under cultivation by more than 800 thousand hectares in ten years. But if the present rate of population growth is maintained, the number of inhabitants in the U.A.R. will crease in ten years by approximately eight million and the cultivated area by only one third, so that only 0.1 hectare per capita will be under cultivation.

Apparently the U.A.R. will not be able to forego food imports for the next 10-15 years. Owing to the agrarian reform and gradual improvement of agricultural technology, the gross agricultural product will increase by an annual average of four per cent. Yet the food shortage will not decrease, since home demand is also influenced by improved living conditions. It is estimated that over the ten years from 1952 to 1962, the real income of the population rose by as much as 35 per cent, but per capita food consumption increased from 2,315 calories daily to no more than 2,590.

The U.A.R. industry is developing more rapidly than agriculture. Its annual output, not taking into account the production of the food, printing and certain other industries, has increased on the average 10.5 per cent. But even that rate of increase, high as it is in comparison with the rate in other liberated countries, was insufficient to solve the employment problem. Nearly the whole excess working population settled in the already overcrowded rural areas, so that notwithstanding the industrialization in the U.A.R., the proportion of the rural population is increasing instead of decreasing.

The U.A.R. Government has passed a law on free schooling and intends to introduce a universal education system. But given the high birth rate and the consequent greater number of children reaching school age, this is no easy task. To fulfil it, the Ministry of Education increased budget assignments for education over the ten years from 1952 to 1962 more than three-fold, from 33 million Egyptian pounds to 102 million, thus allowing the number of children receiving schooling to be doubled. But all the same, 38 per cent of school age children from 6 to 12 years of age remained unprovided for.

All this has led the U.A.R. Government to devote special attention to
population problems. At the end of 1953, a National Population Commis-
sion was formed under the chairmanship of the Minister of Social Affairs
and with the participation of the Ministers of Agriculture, Education
and Health, the Deputy Minister of Finance and experts in economics,
population, sociology, statistics and gynaecology. The first birth
control clinics began to open in the country under the auspices of this
committee in 1955, and their number rose to 38 by 1964.

The National Charter, proclaimed by President Nasser in May 1962 as
the revolutionary programme for the development of Egyptian society,
noted the great difficulties raised in the way of a national production
upsurge by population problems and justified the necessity for a family
planning policy to make the problem less acute. At the same time, the
Charter emphasised that irrespective of the results of birth control
measures, the country must set to work as soon as possible to develop
production so that the rate of increase of the national income would
outstrip the rate of population growth and ensure the people a higher
living standard.

In a speech on the Charter, President Nasser said: "The population increase constitutes the most dangerous obstacle that faces the Egyptian
people in their drive towards raising the standars of production in
their country in an effective and efficient way." He also stated that
"attempts at family planning with the aim of facing the problem of increasing population deserve the most sincere efforts, supported by
modern scientific methods."

An increasing number of governments of young national states are now
coming to similar conclusions and hope to diminish by means of a birth
control policy, the obstacles to eliminating their economic backwardness, that painful legacy of their colonial past. Besides the U.A.R.,
several other countries including India, Pakistan and Tunisia have
proclaimed such a policy. A large number of countries, including
Ceylon, Malaysia, Thailand, Indonesia, Turkey, and Nigeria are carrying
out, with government help, limited birth control measures, frequently
as yet experimental.

In 1964, answering a question of the U.N. General-Secretary on the
interaction between economic development and population changes, the
Indian Government stated: "...In common with other underdeveloped
countries, the level of national income and per capita income in India
are very low, and over decades the Indian economy was almost stagnant,
developing at a rate barely exceeding the growth of population. Over
the last decade, however, India's net national income has advanced at
an average rate of 4 per cent per annum--the increase in aggregate
national income being about 42 per cent...As population has been increasing during the last decade at about 2 per cent per annum, the increase in per capita income over this period has been only 17 per cent.
This low rate of economic development would have to be substantially
stepped up and special efforts made to reduce the rate at which the population is increasing if the level of living of the bulk of the country's
population has to be significantly raised."

In order to retard population growth, the Indian Government set about
implementing a National Family Planning Programme as early as 1950,
ahead of the governments of any other liberated countries. This programme envisaged a reduction in the birth rate from 39 per thousand
inhabitants in 1961 to 25 in 1973, for which purpose it foresaw the
relevant research work, training of the necessary medical staffs, wide
use of lectures, cinema, radio, press and other forms of propaganda to
acquaint the population with family planning methods, and establishment
of a system of special clinics to give the required medical assistance.

Government expenditures to finance this programme have been mounting.
In the third five-year period they totalled approximately half a rupee
per head of the population. The number of birth control clinics reached
12,000 in 1966, so that there is an average of one clinic for 40,000
inhabitants. Proceeding from its population policy, the Indian Government, among other measures, prohibited by law the marriage of girls under
16 years of age, exempted from taxation those companies which subsidised
the Family Planning Programme and decreased import duties on contraceptives.

The Pakistan Government undertook measures for a National Family Planning
Programme in 1960 by allotting approximately 8 per cent of the Ministry
of Health's annual budget for the purpose. There have been set up in
the country short courses for medical staffs and centres for study and
propaganda of methods in family planning; a National Research Institute
of Family Planning has been established and a special Government Commis-
sioner has been appointed to be responsible for carrying out the programme. The third five-year economic development plan, which began
in 1965, outlined a further extension of birth control measures.

A population policy is thus becoming an increasingly notable feature in
the social life of the young national states. In principle this testi-
fies to a more mature approach to problems of economic development. The
overwhelming majority of newly liberated states are planning their economic development, but this cannot be achieved unless population factors
are taken into account and efforts are made to influence them so as to
ensure a better combination of population growth and economic progress.

But for this influence to be effective, it is of great importance that
the place of demographic measures in the general system of state construction should be correctly determined. For example, it would be
senseless to expect propaganda of family planning methods to be effective within the traditional stagnant social society, untouched by new
ideas, bereft of prospects, insensible to real change in life and consequently unconscious of the need to change habits in the field of
family relations. Only in the course of a cultural revolution, relying
on economic reforms and not supplanting them, can a population programme
be effective.

In state construction in some liberated countries there is, it is true,
another approach to the solution of population problems. Birth control
measures are considered the chief means of overcoming difficulties, and
economic and social transformations are given only a secondary, subor-
dinate role. This approach coincides with the Malthusian assertion that
the peculiarities of social development are determined first and foremost by population laws, and not by the nature of the relations of

production, as is the case in reality. Such an assertion implies the
conclusion that the economic and cultural backwardness of the African
and Asian peoples bears a "natural", extra-historical and extra-class
character. It is therefore an obstacle to correct determination of the
ways for rapidly overcoming this backwardness. That is why a population
programme which proceeds from Malthusian recommendations is necessarily
doomed to failure and is capable only of worsening the economic situation of the liberated countries.

And, on the other hand, birth control measures can reduce the acuteness
of population problems and favour economic development if they are based
on profound socio-economic transformations and conform to the objective
social processes which arise in the course of these transformations.

READING 25

The following reading is, according to Professor Dennis L. Meadows himself, the best introduction to The Limits to Growth (1972), a book that created a considerable stir and sometimes highly emotional reactions. This study was sponsored by the Club of Rome, founded in 1968 by Dr. Aurelio Peccei. This club is an informal organization of scientists, humanists, educators, and managers who feel that traditional institutions and policies are no longer able to cope with today's complicated problems. The association aims at a better understanding of the functioning of global systems and the recognition and promotion of new, imaginative policies and strategies.

In 1970 the Club of Rome invited Professor Jay Forrester of the Massachusetts Institute of Technology to explain his systems dynamics method. Subsequently Forrester set up a computerized simulation model of the world. Such models reproduce or simulate processes and, given certain assumptions, calculate the simultaneous operation of all the separate elements in a social system over a period of time.

A group of scientists under the leadership of Professor D.L. Meadows was then organized. Their task was to develop, refine, and amend Forrester's global model and demonstrate what futures might stem from past trends if the same trends were to continue into the time to come. The resulting Limits suggested that sustained growth of population and production leads to infinite quantities which do not fit into a finite world. If we are to preserve the life-supporting thin envelope of air, soil, and water around the surface of our planet, very substantial changes must occur in man's activities and behavior. In the long run exponential growth produces terrible stresses, and if demographic and industrial growth are not voluntarily brought to a halt in the near future, catastrophic problems will descend upon humanity.[25]

Professor Meadows (born 1941) is presently associated with the Thayer School of Engineering at Dartmouth College. Professor Donella H. Meadows, (born 1942) also teaches at Dartmouth.

---

[25]Source: D.H. and D.L. Meadows, "A summary of Limits to Growth - its Critics and its Challenge," discussion presented at Yale University, September 1972, published in: Committee on Merchant Marine and Fisheries, Growth and its Implications for the Future, Part I, Washington: 1973, pp. 308-327.

A SUMMARY OF <u>LIMITS TO GROWTH</u>
—ITS CRITICS AND ITS CHALLENGE
Donella H. Meadows, Dennis L. Meadows

INTRODUCTION

Over the past two years we have worked with a group of scientists and students to understand the long-term causes and consequences of growth in the globe's population and material output. From our research we have been led to conclude that current growth rates cannot be sustained even for the lifetime of the children being born today. If society maintains its current reliance on growth to solve short-term problems, we believe that population and material production will grow past sustainable limits, that the carrying capacity of the earth will be eroded, and that there will then be an uncontrolled decline in population and economic activity. However, this outcome does not appear inevitable. Mankind could instead begin to assess realistically the limits to material growth. Society's goals and institutions could be altered to reduce growth now and to move ultimately towards an orderly accommodation with the finite constraints of the globe. If these changes were made, it would probably be possible to sustain the world's population more or less indefinitely and to provide for all its basic needs.

Our view of growth and its consequences were developed through the construction of World3, a mathematical model of the physical, biological, psychological, geological and other causes underlying growth. Many objections have been raised to our approach and results. In this presentation we would like to describe the history of our work, to summarize the basic foundations of our thesis, and to respond to the most common criticisms of our conclusions.

HISTORICAL SUMMARY

With the publication of <u>World Dynamics</u> [1] Professor Jay W. Forrester challenged the world's scientists and decision makers to extend their time horizons and to examine in holistic fashion the long-term causes and consequences of growth in the world's population and material output. To contribute to analysis and understanding of global problems Forrester proposed a formal model of the interactions among population, capital, and several factors that influence their growth: food, resources, and pollution. Recognizing that his model was not perfect or complete, Forrester emphasized that no perfect or complete model exists, and that the models on which decisions are now based are not even explicit enough to be discussed and improved:

> In spite of the tentative nature of the world model described here, various conclusions are drawn from it. Man acts at all times on the models he has available. Mental images are models. We are now using those mental models as a basis for action.

It is hoped that those who believe they already have
some different model that is more valid will present
it in the same explicit detail, so that its assumptions
and consequences can be examined and compared. To re-
ject this model because of its shortcomings without
offering concrete and tangible alternatives would be
equivalent to asking that time be stopped.

(World Dynamics, p. ix)

In order to facilitate the development of improved long-term global
models, our group has since prepared three additional documents on the
dynamic implications of physical growth in the global system. In
World Dynamics, Professor Forrester described the basic objectives of
the world modeling effort initiated by the Club of Rome and presented
the structure of a preliminary model called World2. This model was
subsequently expanded by our team and related more thoroughly to empirical data. The revised model was called World3. (Henceforth, when
we are discussing a point that applies to both World2 and World3, we
will speak simply of the World models.)

In Limits to Growth, we described several attributes of growth in population and material output; attributes that give the world system a
tendency toward unstable behavior.[2] We proposed material equilibrium
as a sustainable alternative to the goal of perpetual growth that is
the implicit basis of most contemporary policies.

Thirteen short papers that discuss the history and the implications of
our project and that describe the detailed simulation submodels underlying the World models were published in the technical literature.
They have now been collected into a third book, Toward Global Equilibrium: Collected Papers.[3]

Our technical report, The Dynamics of Growth in a Finite World, is the
fourth and final report on our work for the Club of Rome.[4] This technical report presents the assumptions, equations, and data underlying
World3 and analyzes the model's behavior under alternative assumptions.

FOUNDATIONS OF THE LIMITS TO GROWTH

The Limits to Growth (henceforth referred to as Limits) deals with
fundamental properties of the world system such as exponential growth,
finite limits, and feedback delays. These properties are the real
basis of our concern about physical growth, and they can be understood
and discussed independently of the precise numerical assumptions of
any model. In fact it was to call attention to these dynamic properties, rather than the model equations, that we presented them to a non-
technical audience in a publication separate from the technical model
description. We shall summarize here the five main points from Limits
and discuss critical responses to them.

1. Exponential growth is an inherent property of population and
industrial capital but not of technology. Population and material
capital grow exponentially by the very nature of the reproductive and
investment processes. This is not an arbitrary assumption, it is a
fact derived from empirical evidence and knowledge of underlying causes.

New people can only be produced by other people, and machines and factories are needed to generate other machines and factories. Whenever the change in a quantity depends on the quantity itself, the change tends to be exponential in form. The numerical exponent, or the rate of growth, varies both in the real world and in the World models. The growth process is, nevertheless, inherently exponential.

It may be true that human knowledge is also inherently exponential; knowledge can aid in the accumulation of more knowledge. However, it does not follow that any given technological application of that knowledge is inherently exponential. To bring a new technical discovery into widespread use requires social recognition of the existence of a problem. It may also require that new institutions be established, often at the expense of the old, and that investment be diverted from some other possible use into physical capital that embodies the new techniques. Social perception and consensus, institutional change, and the diversion of capital .to new needs are not inherently exponential.

Discovery of oil is not in the long run made easier by the fact that certain fields of oil have already been discovered. The next increment of pollution abatement is not directly facilitated by the increment that went before. One doubling of land yield does not enhance the possibilities for the next doubling. Any suggestion that these "exponential" technologies are inevitable is based on a profound misunderstanding of the inherent cause of exponential growth. The suggestion also implies a rather sweeping disregard for the social basis of technological change, the second law of thermodynamics and the law of diminishing returns.

2. There are physical limits to population and capital growth. The World models are built upon the Malthusian assumption that the earth is finite, and that some change in current exponential growth processes will thus be necessary to accomodate man's physical presence and activities to the earth's limits. The purpose of the models is to investigate what kinds of changes might and should occur. We chose to investigate a Malthusian view of a limited world because our own impressions and much empirical data suggest that the world is finite in several important ways. It seems to us not only more realistic, but more socially responsible and more useful to investigate the ways in which society might adjust itself to earthly limitations, rather than to assume away all such limitations.

The World models express the idea of the earth's limits through four explicit assumptions: there is a finite stock of exploitable nonrenewable resources, there is a finite capacity for the environment to absorb pollutants, there is a finite amount of arable land, and there is a finite yield of food obtainable from each hectare of arable land. No one has exact information about where these limits are. In fact it is probably impossible to express any one of these limits by a single number since they all vary with time. We know that to a certain extent they are expandable by technology. We also know that they can be reduced by misuse.

By attempting to represent the world's limits and the growth of the physical system toward them we did not expect to gain any more precise

information about the location or values of the limits themselves. We
did try to achieve two other purposes. First, we sought a framework in
which many growth processes and limits could be considered together, to
illustrate that solutions proposed for any one problem related to growth
are meaningless without considering the system as a whole. The traditional approach of specialists in any one area, for example, resource
economics, food production, or environmental deterioration, amply illustrates how easily any single resource, food, pollution, or population
problem can be mentally "solved" by assuming that sufficient capital,
energy, labor, land, material and time can be allocated to that one
problem. Because they are holistic, the World models force one to explore the possibility that several of these problems may have to be
solved simultaneously. We are interested in that possibility because
our perception of exponential growth indicates to us that these problems
will not come slowly, one at a time.

Our second concern was to represent not only the forces that can <u>increase</u>
the earth's carrying capacity for human activity but also the forces that
can <u>reduce</u> it. From our Malthusian point of view, Western man is entirely
too prone to rejoice in his newly-irrigated land, underwater oil-drilling
rigs, Green Revolutions, and catalytic converters and to ignore the
eroded, salinized, or strip-mined land, the dumps of wasted resources,
the depleted ore bodies, the simplified ecosystems, and the deprivation
of other humans in other cultures that he leaves in the wake of his
"progress". The World models contain assumptions of possibilities for
considerable future progress, but they also take into account mankind's
fallibility. They assume that the limits can be pushed downward, as
well as upward, by man's activities.

There are, of course, other limits we have not included in the World
models. The most obvious omissions are the limits to the sustainable
rate of use of renewable resources - fresh water, timber, fish, and
game for example. We also recognized the importance of social limits,
but omitted them from specific analysis. We stated in <u>Limits</u> (pp. 45-
46) that social limitations (unjust distribution, waste, wars) would
only decrease the possibilities for growth allowed by physical limits.

3. <u>There are long delays in the feedback processes that control the rate</u>
<u>of physical growth in the world system</u>. Delays are the main source of
instability in the global system. When rapid growth is coupled with a
long delay between cause and effect, the growth may proceed far beyond
sustainable limits before the effects that can stop it come into play.
We have not assumed that mankind is unresponsive to the changing situation around him. We have simple assumed that social institutions
respond only to situations about which they have information, that the
information they act on is often incomplete and late, and that the
social response is not immédiate but is itself delayed. The response
delay can be caused by political, physical, or biological processes.
It is increased by the time required to invent/construct/test/perfect
new technologies. Many response delays are beyond control, such as the
delays inherent in the population age structure or in the propagation
of persistent materials through the environment.

The combination of three major assumptions causes the "overshoot mode"
of the models: the assumption of feedback delays, the assumption of
limits to the earth's carrying capacity, and the assumption that the

human value system will promote population and material growth until
counteracted by very strong forces. When, in the "equilibrium" mode,
we assume a change in man's value system in favor of stability and
against sustained population and capital growth, the overshoot no
longer occurs. The overshoot could also be eliminated, or minimized
by assuming that the society can avoid the implications of delays by
conducting accurate long-term planning. Of course our purpose in
publishing Limits was to encourage both the value-change and the long-
term planning processes.

4. There are two possible social responses to the limits to growth;
weaken growth forces or remove the symptoms of impending limits. The
common response of modern social systems to the pressure caused by
limitation of any resource is to remove the pressure so that growth
can continue. Highways are jammed; build more highways. Copper reserves are depleted; import copper. Electric power is insufficient;
develop nuclear power plants. People are hungry; buy fertilizer.

It is only very recently and very weakly that an alternative set of
solutions has been seriously proposed; reduce the use of automobiles,
use less electric power, extend the useful lifetime of material goods,
have fewer children. This second set of responses recognizes that the
problem to be solved is not scarcity of a specific resource; highways,
copper, power or food. These scarcities are symptoms, or signals, of
the underlying problem; population and material growth against a finite
resource base. The first set of responses serve to remove temporarily
the adverse symptoms of growth. If they are not accompanied by responses of the second type, that weaken the social values causing growth,
further growth will eventually cause different resource scarcities.
These scarcities will call for additional technological solutions to
remove the signals of impending resource limits. The real danger of
responses of the first type, responses that ease the symptoms of the
problem is that they are often used to discourage responses of the
second type, those that control growth itself. The more successfully
the signals of resource scarcity are masked and denied, the more likely
it is that the necessary social value change will come too late.

As we stated in Limits, we have no desire to stop the development of
technology. Combined with the necessary value changes that will control
physical growth, carefully selected new technologies can create magnificent possibilities for human society. We are, however, concerned that
technological successes have almost invariably been used to enhance,
rather than reduce, the strengths of the positive population and capital
feedback loops that drive the global system. We do not oppose technology.
We do oppose the present trend of technological "progress" that is not
only poorly guided by social wisdom or restraint, but is used as an
excuse not to develop that wisdom or restraint.

5. The equilibrium state may be a desirable option, wherever the limits
to growth may be. It is not necessary to agree with the World models
or to believe in the imminence of any physical limits to growth to become intrigued by the nature and potential of an equilibrium state.
An equilibrium state is a society that has stabilized its population
at a desired level and that supplies its material needs with a minimum
throughput of nonrenewable, pollution-creating resources. Limits ends
with a rather Utopian description of such a state. We sincerely believe

that some form of deliberate material and population equilibrium is attainable, not immediately, but within a generation or two. We also believe that the exercise of understanding and planning how such a state might work is both exciting and useful in that it might provide the realistic, sustainable, long-term goal that is now lacking in nearly every part of world society. It seems impossible to us that material growth can be successfully controlled unless there is some well-defined goal towards which it may be directed. There is no way of deliberately changing the composition of growth or its distribution unless there is a clear vision of what growth is for. The specifics of the goal will change and develop as more is learned about the world. We feel that it is only important to have such a goal and to keep it consistent with present knowledge.

The idea of a physically non-growing society is so foreign to some people that they have invested the idea with some strange mental models of their own. They have suggested that an economy at material equilibrium must be stagnant intellectually or technologically; that it must be rigid and dictatorial; that it must preserve the present maldistribution of resources or income. We have already suggested in Limits that we would expect just the reverse. We would hope that more imaginative respondents will accept the challenge of thinking through the economics and sociology of a physically stabilized state.[5] We suspect that the exercise would be more than theoretical; that it would illuminate some of the current economic and sociological problems of a growing state as well.

We have not suggested in Limits or elsewhere that the equilibrium state should be attained immediately, or that physical growth should be brought to a sudden halt. On the contrary we have pointed out long delays in the social system and the necessarily gradual nature of demographic change, and we have suggested that an orderly shift to equilibrium from present rates of growth may take as long as 100 years. Thus although the first steps toward equilibrium should be small ones, they should be taken soon. A good beginning might be a common recognition that physical growth cannot be forever substituted for the social resolution of difficult choices.

In summary, we believe the basic points of our modeling effort, as described in Limits, merit consideration even though none of them can be supported by rigorous proof. No social model can be rigorously proved true. Together these points constitute a holistic hypothese about the world system that is generally consistent with real-world observations. We do not believe that the same can be said for the mental models on which important decisions with long-term implications are currently based.

PRICE, TECHNOLOGY, AND VALUES

Let us turn now to the three mechanisms that many critics of Limits believe will allow mankind to sustain and control material growth without any changes in the current system - price, technology, and social value change. All three are actually included in the World models, but in implicit and oversimplified form. Of course all three are important, complex, dynamic subsystems in themselves. We will describe here, very briefly, how more complete representations of these subsystems might be constructed. However, none of the added details would alter the basic conclusions of our work.

Economic price is a function of two socially determined variables---the current value society places on a certain good or service and the apparent cost of supplying that good or service. Economists postulate that the long-term stabilizing role of price in a growing system is to signal resource scarcity. They point out that price changes guide social values and the economic system so that the declining supply of a scarce resource is utilized more efficiently.

When increasing scarcity causes the price of some material to rise, numerous social responses may be triggered. There may be a more intensive search for natural deposits of that material, or increased recycling of discarded products containing it. Food shortages leading to rising food prices may stimulate farmers to adopt more efficient methods of production, governments to irrigate more land or people to eat less food. These dynamic effects of the price mechanism will indeed influence the way in which a growing system approaches its physical limits.

World3 contains several causal relationships between the real supply of some economic quantity (such as food, nonrenewable resources, industrial capital, service capital) and the response of the economic system to scarcity of that supply (develop more agricultural land, allocate more capital to resource production, increase investment rates). These relationships are most realistically represented with price as an intermediate variable:

decrease in supply---------rise in price-----social response

In World3 we have simplified the real dynamics of the price mechanism by eliminating explicit reference to price, the intermediate variable: The representation of the causal chain has been shortened to:

decrease in supply------------social response

The ultimate regulating effect of the price system is thus included, but price does not explicitly appear in the model.

The only purpose of eclipsing the price mechanism in this way is to increase the model's simplicity and understandability. Omission of price is equivalent to assuming that the signals provided by the price system are available to social decision points with a delay that is insignificant on a 200-year time scale. To check the validity of this omission, several of our submodels explicitly included price and its effects on technological advance and resource availability. The general long-term behavior of these submodels was similar to that of the World model's resource sectors.

To the extent that prices do not immediately reflect actual resource costs in the real world, the price system will be a source of additional instability in the world system. Instability will also be increased if cost information is transmitted immediately but to institutions that can adjust their production or consumption patterns only after a long delay. In either case, the delay between decreased availability and social response will reduce the stability of the economic system as it adjusts itself to any limit. Thus by assuming in World3 that the price

system works instantaneously we have omitted a source of system instability. To the extent that prices are actually delayed signals of scarcity,
our model will underestimate the tendency of real economic systems to
overshoot physical limits.

We view technology, like price, as a social phenomenon - it is the
application of man's general knowledge about the world to the solution
of a specific, perceived human problem. If we were to make a complete
dynamic model of the development of a given technology, we would include
the following:

> -a level of accumulating general knowledge, with the rate of
> accumulation dependent on the resources devoted to basic re-
> search.
> -a widespread perception of some human problem.
> -an allocation of physical resources, human effort, and time to
> search for a technical solution to the problem, with a realiza-
> tion that the solution may not be found if the level of know-
> ledge is not yet great enough.
> -a delay to allow social acceptance and implementation of the
> new technology, the length of the delay dependent on the
> magnitude of the required departure from the present way of
> doing things.
> -a representation of the total impact of the technology on
> the system, including social, energy, and environmental costs.

This model of technological advance might be contrasted with the one
advanced in separate papers by Boyd, Cerlemans, and the Sussex group.[6,7,8]
Each assumed that technology is inherently exponential and that the appropriate technical capabilities are instantaneously available whenever
needed. They have supposed that technological advance costs nothing,
requires no capital investment, has no harmful side effects, and encounters no resistance from institutions already present. Not sur-
prisingly, when their representations of technology were inserted in
World2, the model grew far beyond the original point of collapse. We
would suggest that their theories of technological advance are so completely foreign to anything available in the real world, that their
revisions of World2 provide no useful information whatsoever about the
real implications of physical growth in a finite world.

Nearly every causal relationship in the World models could conceivably
be changed by some sort of new technology. In the past various technologies have, directly or indirectly, improved birth control effect-
iveness, increased land productivity, and increased the average generation of persistent pollution per unit of industrial output. The advance of technology has created more costly and destructive weapons, increased life expectancy through medical advance, and hastened the rate
of land erosion. It is by no means certain that technologies will
continue to do any of these things in the future, since the human values
and social institutions that govern technological development are always
subject to change.

In other words, we view technology as socially-determined, discontinuous,
infinitely varied, and delayed. It is nevertheless an important determinant of the functioning of the world system. How can such a concept
be included in a world model? Since so many causal relationships might

be altered by some conceivable technological change, we had to consider
building technological change into each relationship as we formulated
it. We did this by assigning possible technologies to three categories;
those that are already feasible and institutionalized, those that are
feasible but not institutionalized, and those that are not yet feasible.

Some causal relationships have historically been altered by technology
and continue to be altered regularly today. These are in areas where
there is social agreement about the desirability of change, and where
resources and institutions to bring about that change are already in-
tegral parts of the system. Examples are medical technology to improve
health, industrial technology to raise production efficiency, agricultural
technology to increase land yields, birth control technology to plan
family size, and mining technology to discover and exploit lower-grade
nonrenewable resources. A significant fraction of the world's people
have adopted the value system that will continue to promote these technologies as long as their costs can be afforded. They are effectively
built into the world socio-economic system. Therefore, they are also
built into the relationships of the World models, with the assumption
that they will continue to develop and spread through the world, without delay, as long as there is economic support for them.

There are other technologies that have not been so widely accepted that
they can be considered a functioning part of the world system. It is
not yet clear that all the nations of the world are willing to instit-
utionalize and pay for technologies such as pollution control, resource
recycling, capture of solar energy, preservation of soil fertility,
alternatives to the internal combustion engine, or increased durability
of manufactured goods. All of these technologies are feasible, and
there are signs of the social value changes necessary to incorporate
them into the world system. It is not possible to know when or even
whether they will be adopted on a worldwide scale. Therefore we have
not assumed them in the model relationships, but we have included many
of them as optional functions, which a model operator can "turn on" at
any specified time in the future. The model can be used to test the
possible impact of any or all of these technologies and the relative
advantages of adopting them sooner rather than later.

There is a third set of technologies that is not included in the model
at all. That is the set of discoveries we cannot possibly envision from
our perspective in time. Of course no model, mental or formal, can incorporate these unimaginable technologies as they will actually occur.
That is one reason why no model can accurately predict the future.
Any long-term model that is being used to aid the policy making process
must therefore be updated constantly to incorporate surprising discoveries
as they occur, and to assess how they may change the options of human
society.

It is possible, of course, to include in the model the assumption that
some unimaginable discovery will come along in time to solve every
human problem, including the limited resource base of the earth. Many
mental models seem to be based on that assumption. However, our bias as
both modelers and managers is to search for understanding and for better
policies based on the constraints of the system as it appears now, not
to rely on developments that may or may not come in the future.

We have already indicated that both technology and price are dynamic
elements directly dependent upon the values, needs, and choices characteristic of the human society. Of course values underlie many of the
other dynamic elements of interest in a model of physical growth. In
fact the whole socio-economic system might be thought of as a constant
interplay of human desires and goals within physical and biological
constraints. Therefore, although the World models are not intended to
be models of social value change, they must contain some assumption
about the dynamics of human values insofar as they influence and are
influenced by the processes of physical growth.

In the difficult task of modeling human values we have tried to include
only those most basic values that can be considered globally common.
These basic values begin with requirements for survival, such as food,
and go on to include a hierarchy of other desires; for longevity.
children, material goods, and social services such as education. Some
of these values are represented explicitly in the model as variables
that have an important influence on economic decisions. Examples from
World3 are desired completed family size, and preferences among food,
material goods, and services at different income levels. Others are
included implicitly, for example in the allocation of service output
to health services or in the quantity of nonrenewable resources used
per capita.

All of the values included in World3 are assumed to be responsive to
the actual physical and economic condition of the system; they are all
involved in feedback loops. The patterns of dynamic value change included in the model, however, are limited to the patterns of change
historically observed in individual countries over the last hundred
years or so. During that time the major force behind value change in
the world system has been the process of industrialization, a process
that is still underway in most of the nations of the world. Therefore
the values that both shape and respond to the development of the model
system follow the historic pattern of industrialization. As industrialization increases in our model(measured, say, by the level of industrial
capital per capita) the aggregate social demand in our model shifts in
emphasis from food to material goods and finally to services. Other
changes occur in the model in the preferences for children, education,
and health care, and in the distribution of various goods and services
throughout the industrializing population.

We have not built into World3 any global shifts in values other than
those that might be expected to take place as the world becomes more
industrialized. Again, the model cannot predict value changes, but
it can serve as a test device to show the results of any given assumption
about the future evolution of values, Human values, like human technologies, may evolve in the future in directions we cannot possibly foresee at this moment in history. Therefore we have also included, in
several model relationships, test switches that can be used to activate
postulated value changes at any date specified by the operator.
(Examples of such changeable values are desired family size, fraction of
output consumed, and the relative desires for food and services. All
of these are changed to produce the model's "equilibrium" runs.) We
have used these switches extensively. As we demonstrated in <u>Limits</u>,
an appropriate set of value changes can bring the model system into a
stable and desirable equilibrium state. That set of value changes is

not one that has occurred historically as a result of industrialization
in any country. We believe that such value changes are possible to
achieve in the future, but only by a concerted and conscious effort.
The shift in values that normally accompanies industrialization, the
one we might expect to take place if the world continues "business as
usual", is the very value shift that leads to the overshoot and decline
behavior mode.

THE MODELER AND HIS ENVIRONMENT

It has been suggested that the World models arose only because of the
sudden widespread concern about the environment in modern western
societies. Of course computed models, like any product of man's intellect,
must be evaluated as part of the cultural context within which they are
constructed. This statement is also true for the mental models of the
critics of Limits and for the models that guide current public policy.

Every model of a social system must omit some details of the real world.
Simplification is the essence of model building. A model is constructed
to improve understanding of the nature and implications of complex relationships in the real world. If the model were identical to the real
world in all respects, it would be as difficult as the real world to
understand.

It is a very fundamental principle indeed that knowledge is always
gained by the orderly loss of information, that is by condensing and
abstracting and indexing the great buzzing confusion of information
that comes from the world around us into a form which we can appreciate
and comprehend.[9]

Thus even if we had comprehensive and accurate information on all
important aspects of the real world, our models would be simplifications
of reality.

Human judgment is inextricably involved in the choice of the issues
addressed by a model and in the identification of those "unimportant"
details that may be eliminated without detracting significantly from
the explanatory power of the model. Every model is thus inevitably
influenced by prevailing social values and goals. In short, there is
no model useful for understanding all issues and no "scientific" or
"objective" way to construct a perfect model.

The greatest advantage of formal, or written, models over mental models
is that their constituent assumptions are precise and explicit and
thus subject to the scrutiny of critics. This is no guarantee against
error or against the effects of unwarranted social biases, but it
makes the discovery of errors and biases more likely. Most critics of
Limits have not defined the bias that underles their own approach, nor
have they presented assumptions explicit enough to be judged by their
audience.

The accusation that the World models have been unduly influenced by the
prevailing environmental concern seems to imply that the models are
addressing random, unimportant, or spurious issues. The latest wave of
environmentalism may indeed turn out to be a fad, merely the product of
rising expectation, or boredom, or alarmist journalists, or all of
these. However, there is an alternate possiblity. The current concern

with the environment may be a response to a correct perception of a
changed external reality. It may be a result of the first glimmerings
of human understanding about total systems and the first perception
of a real worldwide negative impact of man's activities on the ecosystem.
If so, the World models may represent a small manifestation of a healthy
social reaction to an environmental change; a reaction that will lead
to new values, technologies, and economic prices that attempt to adapt
socioeconomic systems to the newly-perceived constraints. In that case
the critics, the technological optimists, the foot-draggers who claim
that there are no constraints and no reasons to change values from the
present pro-growth set, represent exactly the social and institutional
delays that tend to destabilize the system and send it shooting past
its ultimately sustainable limits.

GROWTH AND INCOME DISTRIBUTION

Some critics have rejected the no-physical-growth argument as irrelevant
to the "really important" problems of the composition and distribution
of growth. As we have already indicated, we find it impossible to view
the rate of physical growth, its composition and its distribution as
independent or mutually exclusive problems. Human societies will not
achieve a more equitable distribution of wealth until they better understand the processes of growth. Historically at least, growth of population and of capital has been correlated with the concentration of wealth
and with rising gaps between the absolute incomes of the rich and the
poor. We believe that there are at least two basic reasons for these
trends. First, physical growth inevitably worsens the resource/popu-
lation balance. When there are fewer available resources per person,
there are also fewer real social options to resolve conflicts of interest. Second, by relying on the false promise of growth, social institutions are able to delay facing the very important and difficult
tasks of making social tradeoffs and defining social goals. Until these
tasks are squarely faced there will be no real redistribution of income.

The no-growth argument is an appeal for readjusting the composition and
distribution of economic output. The pro-growth argument is an attempt
to postpone this readjustment; to confer it on future generations.
Simultaneously this approach ensures that those generations will have
fewer resources and thus fewer real choices to make. Our sociopolitical
concerns are actually quite similar to those who argue that redistribution must come first. We differ only in our perception of how to deal
with those concerns. Our own choice was to begin by questioning what
we view as the basic cause of the growing gap between the rich and the
poor - unexamined, uncontrolled physical growth.

THE CONCEPT OF MAN

This brings us to the final point that we regard as basic to all discussions among ecologists, "environmentalists", Malthusians, economists,
industrialists, pessimists, and optimists. The pro- and anti-growth
factions are organized around two very different concepts of man.

One concept of man, the one held by advocates of indefinite growth, is
that Homo sapiens is a very special creature whose unique brain gives
him not only the capability but the right to exploit for his own short-
term purposes all other creatures and all resources the world has to

offer. This is an age-old concept of man, one firmly rooted in Judeo-
Christian tradition and newly strengthened by stunning technical achieve-
ments in the last few centuries.

Not only ingenuity but, increasingly, understanding; not luck but
systematic investigation, are turning the tables on nature, making
her subservient to man.[10]

According to this belief man is essentially omnipotent, he can develop at
no cost a technology or a social change to overcome any obstacle, and
such developments will occur instantly upon the perception of the obstacle. Underlying this view is also the belief that mankind's social,
economic, political, and technical institutions operate flexibly and
without error, and the best response to any apparent problem is to
encourage these institutions to do more of whatever they have done in the
past.

The opposite concept of man is also an ancient one, but it is more
closely related to the Eastern religions than to the Western ones. It
assumes that man is one species with all other species embedded in the
intricate web of natural processes that sustains and constrains all
forms of life. It acknowledges that man is one of the more successful
species, in terms of competitiveness, but that his very success is
leading him to destroy and simplify the natural sustaining web, about
which he understands very little. Subscribers to this view feel that
human institutions are ponderous and short-sighted, adaptive only after
very long delays, and likely to attack complex issues with simplistic and
self-centered solutions. They would also point out that much of human
technology and "progress" has been attained only at the expense of natural
beauty, human dignity, and social integrity, and that those who have
suffered the greatest loss of these amenities have also had the least
benefit from the economic "progress". People who share this concept of
man, as we do, would also question strongly whether technology and
material growth, which seem to have caused many problems, should be
looked to as the sources of solution of these same problems in the
future. Technological optimists invariably label this view of the
fallibility of man as "pessimistic"; Malthusians would simply call it
"humble".

We see no objective way of resolving these very different views of man
and his role in the world. It seems to be possible for either side to
look at the same world and find support for its view. Technological
optimists see only rising life expectancies, more comfortable lives,
the advance of human knowledge, and improved wheat strains. Malthusians
see only rising population, destruction of the land, extinct species,
urban deterioration, and increasing gaps between the rich and the poor.
They would say that Malthus was correct both in his own time and today
in his observation that: ... the pressure arising from the difficulty
of procuring subsistence is not to be considered as a remote one which
will be felt only when the earth refuses to produce any more, but as
one which actually exists at present over the greatest part of the
globe.[11]

THE CHALLENGE

One glaring problem confronts mankind, if it should choose to conceive

of man as a humble part of the biosphere.   There is essentially no body
of knowledge from which to design the new institutions, and values
consistent with that concept of man.   Two hundred years of growth has
left biases and blind spots throughout the physical and social sciences.
There is today no economic theory of a technological-based society in
which there are essentially zero interest rates, no net accumulation to
society's productive capital, and in which the principal concern is
equality rather than growth.   There is no equilibrium sociology which
is concerned with the social aspects of a stable population, whose age
composition is skewed toward the elderly.   There is no equilibrium
political science in which we might look for clues to the ways democratic
choice could be exercised when short-term material gain is ruled out as
the basis for political success.   There is no equilibrium technology
that places high emphasis on the recycling of all matter, on the use
of the sun's pollution-free energy, and on the minimization of both
matter and energy flows.   There is no psychology for the steady state
which might provide man with a new self-image and with feasible aspira-
tions in a system where material output is constant and in balance
with the globe's finite limits.

Each of our traditional disciplines could respond to the challenge of
working out the details of a viable and attractive equilibrium society.
The effort would pose many difficult technical and conceptual problems,
whose solutions would be intellectually satisfying and of enormous
social value.   After all, we are not merely talking of a distant and
unattainable Utopian state.   Physical growth of population and capital
will stop on this finite planet.   The only uncertainties lie in when
it will stop and how - by deliberate social choice and under careful
human management, or by the harsh backlash of disturbed and depleted
natural environment.

We may all find that the study of a steady-state society may be the
best possible preparation for the real future - a future that we are
shaping already, with every social and individual decision we make.
We will almost certainly discover as we become better acquainted with
the possibilities for an equilibrium society that we would prefer the
end of physical growth to occur under our own management and sooner,
rather than later.   Those of us who have already spent several years
adjusting to the idea of a no-material-growth society find without
exception that we agree with John Stuart Mill, who contemplated the
limits to growth more than one-hundred years ago:
I cannot, therefore, regard the stationary state of capital and wealth
with the unaffected aversion so generally manifested towards it by
political economists of the old school.   I am inclined to believe
that it would be, on the whole, a very considerable improvement on our
present condition.   I confess I am not charmed with the idea of life
held out by those who think that the normal state of human beings is
that of struggling to get on; that the trampling, crushing, elbowing,
and treading on each other's heels, which form the existing type of
social life, are the most desirable lot of humankind...It is scarcely
necessary to remark that a stationary condition of capital and population implies no scope as ever for all kinds of mental culture, and
moral and social progress; as much room for improving the Art of Living
and much more likelihood of its being improved.[12]

REFERENCES

1. Forrester, J.W., World Dynamics, Wright-Allen Press, Cambridge, Mass., 1971.
2. Meadows, D.H., et. al., The Limits to Growth, Universe Books New York, New York, 1972.
3. Meadows, D.L. and D.H. Meadows (Eds.), Toward Global Equilibrium: Collected Papers, Wright-Allen Press, Cambridge, Mass., 1973.
4. Meadows, D.L., et. al., The Dynamics of Growth in a Finite World, Wright-Allen Press, Cambridge, Mass., forthcoming Spring 1973.
5. Several have already started, such as Kenneth Boulding, Ezra Mishan, Herman E. Daly, Nicholas Georgescu-Roegen.
6. Boyd, R., "World Dynamics: A Note" Science, Vol. 177, Aug. 11, 1972.
7. Oerlemans, T.W., et. al., "World Dynamics: Social Feedback may give Hope for the Future", Nature, Vol. 238, August 4, 1972.
8. Freeman, C., et. al., "Looking Toward the Future, A Critique of Limits to Growth", Futures, February 1973.
9. Boulding, K.E., Economics as a Science, McGraw-Hill, New York, 1971.
10. Barnett, H.J. and C. Morse, Scarcity and Growth, Johns Hopkins Press.
11. Malthus, T.R., A Summary View of the Principle of Population, 1830.
12. Mill, J.S., Principles of Political Economy, 1848.

READING 26

Since its publication, The Limits to Growth has provoked many reactions.
A publication that questions conventional wisdom and uses a relatively
new tool such as a world simulation model is likely to be subject to
some hostile criticism and abuse. In fact a number of commentaries
have been polemic and shallow. On the other hand it forced many people
to reconsider their positions. This and the fact that a new--often
very constructive--kind of discourse has followed the publication of
the Limits report must be considered a big plus.

The major areas of criticism of the MIT report are: (a) the high level
of aggregation of the model; (b) the assumption of a positive correlation
between income and family size which neglects the demographic transition
model; (c) the disregard of the price system as an adjustment mechanism
(if, for instance, raw material becomes scarce, its price will rise, evoking
economy, substitution, and recycling); (d) the assumption that technological innovation and discovery, as well as their application, will proceed at a relatively slow pace; and (e) the assumption that the environment can absorb only four times the present annual level of pollutants
emitted.

Among the many comments made on The Limits to Growth, Professor J.E.
Meade's paper (The 1972 Galton Lecture) stands out because of its
clarity and objectivity. Most of that paper is presented in the following reading.[26] Professor Meade (b. 1907) is well known for his work in
the economics of international trade and economic growth. He has taught
at such distinguished institutions as the London School of Economics.
Since 1957 he has been a Fellow at Christ's College, Cambridge University,
England.

---

[26]Source: J.E. Meade, "Economic Policy and the Threat of Doom,"
Resources and Population, eds. B. Benjamin, P.R. Cox, J. Peel (New
York: Academic Press, 1973), pp. 128-144.

ECONOMIC POLICY AND THE THREAT OF DOOM

James E. Meade

There are some basic truths which Professors Forrester and Meadows emphasize through their work.

First, there must be an end sooner or later to exponential growth of population and output, and the limit to such growth may come upon us unexpectedly unless we are careful. The facts about the present world demographic situation which will be familiar to all of you are sufficient to illustrate the point. At present growth rates the world population doubles itself about every 30 years. If it were 3,500 million in 1970 it would be 7,000 million in 2000, 14,000 million in 2030, 28,000 million in 2060, and so on. Whatever the upper limit may be--and there obviously is some upper limit--we may hit it very suddenly. Indeed a mere 30 years before the final catastrophe we might be comforting ourselves with the thought that the world was after all only half full.

Second, the ultimate limit to growth may become effective either because of the exhaustion of non-maintainable natural resources, or because of pressure upon the limited supply of maintainable natural resources, or because of the choking effects of excessive environmental pollution.

It is good that these basic points should be forcibly emphasized. But it is not necessary to construct a complex dynamic model for their demonstration. Clearly scarcities of natural resources and the choking effects of an ever-increasing reservoir of pollution would set ultimate limits-to-growth. An elaborate and sophisticated dynamic model is needed not to tell us this, but to tell us how soon and how suddenly the limits will be reached, which limit will operate first, how quick and severe will be the effects of reaching a limit, how effective a given change in policy will be in mitigating these effects, and so on. It is to answer questions of this kind that there is point in trying to construct models of dynamic interrelationships of the Forrester-Meadows kind.

What will happen with any set of dynamic causal interrelationships depends in a very important way not only upon the extent to which one variable (e.g. the standard of living) affects other variables (e.g. fertility and mortality), but also upon the speed with which the various influences operate. Indeed, one very real cause for concern about the present situation is the recent changes in the relative reaction speeds in different sectors of human activity. Many changes, and in particular technological changes, have speeded up very greatly. Disease and mortality have been reduced at unprecedented rates. New synthetic chemical and other materials, as well as new technological processes, have been introduced at previously unimagined rates. As a result world population and world industrial production are growing at speeds hitherto quite unknown.

But while some variables are changing in this way at much greater speeds
than before, other reactions are just as slow as ever and in some cases
have become more sluggish than before. Many of the new man-made chem-
icals and materials are slower to decompose than earlier natural sub-
stances and thus their effects (which in any case are novel and only
partially understood) may be persistent and reach into the distant
future.

To take another example, demographic reactions cannot be speeded up.
It still takes a baby fifteen years or so of dependency before it starts
to support itself, twenty years or so before it breeds, sixty years or
so before it becomes an elderly dependant, and perhaps seventy years
before it dies. Indeed, with the raising of school-leaving ages and
with medical advances which keep people alive and active to greater
ages than before, these demographic time-lags have in some respects
been lengthened rather than shortened by present-day technological and
social changes. Their importance may be illustrated in the following
way. The continuation of high levels of fertility combined with relatively recent rapid reductions in the rates of child mortality have
meant that there is an exceptionally high proportion of young children
in many populations which are now growing rapidly. In these conditions
population growth would continue for many years even if the fertility
of women of child-bearing age were to be reduced instantaneously and
without any delay whatsoever to levels which would merely replace
the parents. For many years, as the present exceptionally high number
of young girls grew up to motherhood, the total number of births would
go on rising in spite of this immediate dramatic decline in the fertility of each individual woman. Such a population might well grow for
another two or three generations and attain a size one-third greater
than it was when the dramatic fall in fertility occurred.

To take one more example, political delays between the observation of
a change and legislative and administrative reaction to it remain as
long as ever; and indeed the increasing insistence on democratic consensus in government may have lengthened the time needed to make acceptable a political decision which has obvious present disadvantages but
whose future advantages are not at all obvious to the inexpert man in
the street.

It is not therefore a sufficient answer to the prophets of Doom to say
that their cry of Wolf has been equally relevant since the beginning of
time. It has, of course, always been true that exponential growth
cannot continue indefinitely. But what is unique about the present
situation is the unprecedentedly rapid rate of population growth and
of technological innovation (which represent exceptionally rapid approaches to the finite limiting ceilings) in a situation in which the
results of population growth and of technological change are at least
as prolonged and as persistent as ever and in which the ultimate policy
reactions to danger signals are at least as slow as ever. Such time
relationships do, of course, increase the possibilities of catastrophic
overshooting of safe limits; and dynamic feedback models are in principle
the proper instruments for assessing the importance of the relationship
between different time lags.

One must therefore sympathize with attempts to think in terms of a dynamic model of these interrelationships; but an economist can only con-

template with an amazed awe the assurance with which Professors
Forrester and Meadows provide answers to our anxious questions.

The real world is a hideously complicated system and it is inevitable
that any dynamic model should be highly simplified. To be useful it
must, on the one hand, be sufficiently simplified to be manageable by
modern techniques of analysis and computation; but, on the other hand,
it must not omit any of the structural relationships which may have a
fundamental effect on the outcome, and the form and quantitative importance of the relationships which are included must be reasonably accurately estimated. Furthermore, the future course of certain outside,
exogenous influences must be reasonably well predicted--a hazardous
undertaking since it involves predicting the future effects of scientific
and technological inventions without any precise foreknowledge of the
inventions themselves; for if the inventions were already well understood, they would already have been made. These are very far-reaching
requirements.

Economists--or rather that special breed called econometricians, in
whose arts I am myself, alas, completely incompetent--have now much
experience in coping with problems of this kind in searching for answers
to much more limited questions. What is it which determines the demand
for new motor cars? What is it which causes money wage rates to rise
rapidly? What is it which governs businessmen's decisions to invest
in new plant and machinery? And so on. But often, after the most detailed empirical enquiries, different hypotheses as to the structure
of the causal relationships and as to the quantitative importance of any
given factor in any assumed relationship provide conflicting results
between which it is found difficult to choose even with the aid of the
most refined statistical techniques. But the structure of the relationships and the numerical value of the parameters in a dynamic system can
make a huge difference to the behaviour of the whole system; with one
set of hypotheses the system may explode into a catastrophic breakdown
and with another it may reach a stable equilibrium with or without moderate fluctuations on the way. But Professors Forrester and Meadows
give results for an immensely complicated economic--social--demographic
system of dynamic interrelationships for the whole world, having selected
one assumed set of interrelationships and having used for each of those
relationships estimates of the quantitative force of the various factors
which in many cases are inevitably based on very limited empirical data.

For these reasons the conclusions drawn by Professors Forrester and
Meadows are unquestionably surrounded with every kind of uncertainty.
One must therefore, ask what is the moral for present policy decisions
if the future results of present policies are still extremely uncertain.

This question can be put in a very sharp form by considering one of the
conclusions reached by Professor Forrester (1971) in his World Dynamics.
He very rightly emphasizes the fact that the ultimate effect of any
given set of present policies depends upon dynamic interrelationships
of the kind which I have expounded. Which influences work most quickly?
To what extent are the evil effects of a given influence hidden at first
and then operative with a sumulative, explosive effect? and so on.
Professor Forrester concludes from his model that in order to prevent
a worse ultimate disaster we should seriously consider the adoption of
some very tough-line present policies. I quote from his book:

Instead of automatically attempting to cope with population
growth national and international efforts to relieve the
pressures of excess growth must be re-examined. Many such
humanitarian impulses seem to be making matters worse in the
long run. Rising pressures are necessary to hasten the day
when population is stabilised. Pressures can be increased
by reducing food production, reducing health services, and
reducing industrialisation. Such reductions seem to have
only slight effect on the quality of life in the long run.
The principal effect will be in squeezing down and stopping
runaway growth.

In other words we might be well advised to forget about family planning,
to discourage the green revolution in agriculture and the economic
development of undeveloped countries and to let poverty and undernourishment play their role in restraining economic growth in the long-
run interests of human welfare.

Professor Meadows dissociates himself from these startling recommendations for which Professor Forrester alone is responsible, but this
paradoxical conclusion of Professor Forrester is not necessarily non-
sensical. It could well be the correct prescription. But it depends
upon a number of assumptions built into Professor Forrester's dynamic
model. It assumes that while a successful birth control campaign may
temporarily reduce population growth and thereby raise living standards,
it is not capable of preventing that rise in living standars itself from
causing a subsequent renewal of population explosion. It assumes that
economic development will be of a given polluting character and that
technology will not be capable of introducing sufficiently non-polluting
methods with sufficient speed. It assumes that the effect of pollution
is not a gradual effect, but stores up a cumulative reservoir of evil,
as it were, until there is a sudden explosive catastrophe. If these
assumptions are correct, then we ought perhaps to adopt tough-lone
present policies in order to avert ultimate, total Doom. One should
perhaps be prepared deliberately to starve one person today to avert
the starvation of ten people tomorrow.

But what if the outcome is uncertain? Should one starve one person today
to avert a 99 per cent probability of the starvation of ten persons
tomorrow? Perhaps, Yes; but should one do so to avert a 1 per cent
probability of the starvation of ten persons tomorrow? Pretty certainly, No.

Much work has been done in recent years, notably by economists, on the
pure theory of decision-making in conditions of uncertainty. In order
to make a precise calculation as to whether a given unpleasant decision
today is or is not worthwhile in view of its future potential benefits,
one would in theory have to have answers to the following five sets of
questions:

1. What are the different possible future outcomes of today's decision?
2. What probability should one assign to each of these possible outcomes?
3. What is the valuation--or, in economists' jargon, the utility--
   which future citizens will attach to each of these outcomes?

4. At what rate, if any, should we today discount the utilities of
    future generations?
5. What valuation or disutility to us, the present generation, is to
    be attributed to the unpleasant policy decision which we are con-
    templating?

One could then calculate whether or not the disutility to the present
generation of today's unpleasant policy was greater or less than the
discounted value of the weighted average of the utilities to be attached
to each of the possible future outcomes, each outcome being weighted
by the probability of its occurrence.

The models of Professors Forrester and Meadows are intrinsically incapable of such treatment. They are deterministic and not stochastic
in form, although in fact they are steeped in uncertainty. I am not
claiming that one could in any case make precise calculations of the
kind which I have just outlined about the present uncertain threats of
Doom; but I would claim that an appreciation of the principles of
decision-making in conditions of uncertainty is helpful as a framework
of ideas to inform one's hunches. My own hunch would be that the
disutility of Doom to future generations would be so great that, even if
we give it a low probability and even if we discount future utilities at a
high rate (which I personally do not), we would be wise to be very
prudent indeed in our present actions. But we should not, I think, be
prepared to carry prudence to the extent of abandoning our efforts to
control present births and our efforts to raise agricultural outputs
and the production of other essential products in the impoverished
underdeveloped countries, though we should be prepared to carry
prudence to the extent of a considerable shift of emphasis in the rich
developed countries away from the use of resources for rapid growth in
their material outputs towards the devotion of resources to the control
of pollution, to the aid of the poor, to the promotion of technologies
suitable for both developed and underdeveloped economies which save
irreplaceable resources and avoid pollution, and to measures for the
limitation of fertility.

We may conclude that the failure to deal with uncertainties is a
serious weakness of the Forrester-Meadows type of model. I turn now to
a second serious weakness, namely its gross aggregation of many distinct
variables. The model in my Figure 3 makes no distinction between events
in different countries. It assumes only one output, making no distinction between different goods and services. It assumes only two
uses of this single product, namely for personal consumption and for
capital investment, allowing nothing for governmental uses for defence,
space travel, supersonic aircraft, education, medicine, etc. It assumes
only one form of pollution, making no distinctions between the pollution
of air, water, or land or pollution by biodegradable wastes, by non-
degradable wastes, by radio-active wastes, and so on.

This criticism is broadly true also of the models of Professors Forrester
and Meadows, though they do both distinguish between agricultural and
industrial production and Professor Meadows adds a third type, namely
service industries. The introduction of this third distinction is also
an important improvement. Services use up much less irreplaceable
materials and cause much less pollution than does industrial production;
and wealthy countries tend to spend a higher proportion of their in-

comes on services, thus providing a feature which mitigates somewhat
the dangers of economic growth.

But all the models make no distinction between different countries,
between different pollutants, or between different non-maintainable
resources; and they make very little distinction between different
products or different uses of products. This lack of disaggregation
causes the models to exaggerate the threat of Doom in two important
respects.

First, in so aggregated a model catastrophes are concentrated in their
timing. Let me take the threat of a pollution crisis as an example.
Let us accept the assumption that the evils of pollution often turn up
unexpectedly with little forewarning when a reservoir of pollution
rather suddenly reaches a critical level. In an aggregated model this
must happen at the same time for every part of the world for every
pollutant. Ex hypothesi remedial action is taken too late, and the
result is, of course, catastrophic. But in fact atmospheric pollution
in London rises unobserved to a crisis level in which smog kills a
number of people; and belated action is taken to prevent that happening
again; then the mercury danger reaches a critical level in a particular
Japanese river; there is a local catastrophe; action is taken to deal
with that; and so on. I have no desire to belittle these things or to
deny that we should take these problems much more seriously than we
have in the past. Nor, what is much more important, do I wish to deny
that there may be some much more far-reaching, global dangers which
are creeping up on us, such as atmospheric changes which will turn
the world into an ice-box or into a fiery furnace. Natural scientists
should be given every opportunity and encouragement to speed up their
efforts to decide which, if any, of such evils is threatened by which
of our present activities. All that I am arguing is that what in the
real world might well take the form of a continuing series of local
pollution disasters or of shortages of particular non-maintainable
resources for which substitutes have not yet been found or of localized
population control by a particular famine in a particular phase of
development in a particular region are necessarily bound in an aggregated
model to show up as a single collapse of the whole world system in a
crisis of pollution, raw material exhaustion, or famine.

Second, an aggregated model cannot allow for substitutes between one
thing and another, and some lines of economic activity use much more
non-maintainable resources or produce much more pollution than do
others. You may feel that I am making too much of a consideration of
only secondary importance when I stress this lack of distinction in
the models between different lines of production and different uses of
products. Granted that there are some differences in the polluting
effects and resource requirements of different lines of production and
granted that economic growth may cause a shift in the relative importance of these different processes, yet, are not the shifts likely to
cancel out to a large extent--some polluting processes gaining ground
relatively and other polluting processes losing ground relatively?
And, in any case, is not the net effect of relative shifts of economic
structures of various industrial and other processes just as likely to
be negative as it is to be positive on the balance sheets of pollution
and resource requirements? In view of this, is it not perfectly
legitimate to start with models which neglect such shifts?

An economist's immediate reaction is to point out that these models make no allowance for the operation of the price mechanism in causing one economic activity to be substituted for another. This point helps to explain why it is that economists are often less pessimistic than natural scientists in their attitude towards these problems. A large part of an economist's training revolves round the idea of a price mechanism in which that which is scarce goes up in price relatively to that which is plentiful with what in his jargon he calls "substitution effects" both on the supply side and on the demand side. Producers will turn to the production of that which is profitable because its price has gone up away from the production of that which is unprofitable because its price has fallen, while consumers or other users will turn from the consumption or use of that which has become expensive to the consumption or use of that which has fallen in price.

In so far as a mechanism of this kind is at work it means that the changes of economic structure that are brought about in the process of economic growth will not be neutral in their effects on demand for scarce resources. They will be heavily biased in favour of activities which avoid the use of scarce resources and rely on the use of more plentiful resources. How far this process will help to put off the evil day depends, of course, upon the possibilities of substitution throughout the economic system; and it is here that economists are apt to be on the optimistic side. When a raw material becomes scarce and its price goes up, it becomes profitable to work ores with a lower mineral content, to spend money on exploration of new sources, to use scrap and recycling processes more extensively, to substitute another raw material, to turn to the production of alternative final products which do not contain this particular material, and -- above all--to direct Research and Development expenditure towards finding new ways of promoting these various methods of substitution. Indeed this process of substitution permeates the whole economic system. Family budgets are sensitive to relative prices; in India where labour is cheap and capital goods expensive clothes are washed by human beings but in the United States where the reverse is the case this is done by washing machines. Agriculture is intensive in the Netherlands where land is scarce and expensive and is extensive on the prairies of Canada where it is plentiful and cheap. Business enterprises succeed by finding a new process which, at current costs of the various inputs, is cheaper and therefore more profitable. Moreover--and this is of quite fundamental importance --commercial research and development is expressly geared to find new processes which economize in scarce and expensive inputs and rely on cheaper and more plentiful inputs; and technology, as we all know, can be a very powerful factor in modern society.

Some of you are probably losing your patience at this point. Is it any use fiddling with the price mechanism while the nuclear reactors burn? Has what I have just said got any relevance at all to the great problems of environmental pollution which constitute the major threat of Doom? It is in fact precisely here that we need a major revolution in economic policy to make the price mechanism work. Environmental pollution is a case of what economists call "external diseconomies". When you drive out onto the streets of London you pay neither for the damage done by the poisonous fumes from your exhaust nor for the cost of the extra delays to other travellers due to the extra congestion which you cause. When you take your seat to fly your supersonic

aeroplane over my house, you are not charged for the noise you make.
When you treat your farmland with artificial fertilizer, you do not pay
for the damage done to my neighbouring fresh water supply. When in
your upstream factory you pour your effluent into the river, you do
not pay for the damage to my downstream trout fishing. When you draw
water for that extra unnecessary bath, you are not charged extra on your
rates--unless you live in Malvern where domestic water supplies are
metered and so charged and where the inhabitants seem to live a happy
and clean life with an exceptionally low consumption of water per head.
When you put out that extra dustbin of waste for municipal disposal,
you are not charged extra on your rates. If you were you might not
merely insist on your suppliers reducing the unnecessary packaging of
the products which come into your house, but you might also collect
your glass bottles and offer to pay their users to come to collect them
for recycled use.

I have, I fear, descended to rather homely and flippant examples. But
the principle is the same for the most important and threatening examples of environmental pollution. We need politically to demand an
extensive series of cost-benefit analyses of various economic activities
and the imposition of taxes or levies of one kind or another at appropriate
rates which correspond to the external diseconomies of these various
activities. The price mechanism with its consequential process of
substitution of what is cheap for what is costly could then play its
part in the avoidance of environmental pollution just as it can in the
economizing of scarce natural resources. Business enterprise will be
induced to avoid polluting processes. Technologists will be induced to
steer their research and development into the discovery of new non-
polluting methods of production.

This is a vast subject fraught with difficulties with which I cannot
possibly cope at all adequately in a short section of a single lecture.
I can merely enumerate one or two of the main points.

First and foremost there are the problems of deciding what are the
probable ultimate results of different forms of economic activity.
These are matters primarily for the natural scientist and the technolo-
gist. Will the global effects on the atmosphere turn the world into an
ice-box or a fiery furnace? And what are the probabilities of these
outcomes?

Second, there is the problem of evaluating the social nuisance caused
by a given degree of pollution of a given kind. To make use of the
classical example of a factory belching smoke, how does one measure
in £s d-- or rather pounds and newpence -- the cost of a given output
of smoke when some people in the neighbourhood don't mind it much and
others cannot abide it? Quite apart from the question how one adds
up these different individual preferences, how does one discover them
in the first place?

Third, a great deal of the damage done through environmental pollution
is future damage. The use of DDT may confer important immediate benefits without any immediate indirect disastrous consequences; but it
may be storing up great trouble for the next generation or the next
generation but one. Quite apart from the technical difficulty in determining what will be the actual effects on the future of this pollutant,

how does one evaluate that damage? How does one weigh the interests of future generations against the interests of the present generation?

Fourth in most cases, if not in all, it is not a question of eliminating all pollution, but of keeping pollution down to its optimal level. I illustrate once more from the economist's favourite example, namely the smoking factory chimney. It may be prohibitively costly to eliminate all smoke, but not too costly to reduce significantly the output of smoke. To prohibit all smoke would leave the community without the smoke, but also perhaps without the product of the factory. To charge for the smoke the nuisance cost of the smoke might leave the community with some smoke nuisance, but also with the product of the factory. The latter situation might well be preferred. This is the basic reason for choosing, where possible, a policy of charging a levy or tax on the polluter which covers the social cost of the nuisance which he causes and then leaving him to decide how much pollution he will cause.

Fifth, in some cases -- though these are much rarer than many administrators and technologists believe -- it may be appropriate to act by a regulation rather than by a tax or charge on pollution. If the social damage is sufficiently grave, it may be wise to prohibit the activity entirely. I, for one, do not advocate discouraging murder by taxing it. But where it is possible to define and police a noxious activity for the purpose of regulating its amount, it is possible also to define and police it for the purpose of taxing it; and normally a tax on a noxious activity will be economically a much more efficient method of control than a direct regulation. Faced with a tax per unit of pollutant, those who find it cheap to reduce the pollution will reduce it more than those who find it expensive to do so; and thus a given reduction in the total pollution can be obtained at a lower cost than if each polluter was forced by regulation to restrict his pollution by the same amount. Moreover, with a tax on pollution each polluter can employ the cheapest known method and, above all, will have every incentive to search for new and cheaper methods of pollution-abatement, whereas a direct regulation may well tie the polluter down to one particular method of abatement.

Sixth, in this use of fiscal incentives to avoid pollution, it is of great importance to tax that which is most noxious rather than to subsidize that which is less noxious. We all realize now that motor transport in large cities is causing intolerable congestion, noise, danger to life and limb, and atmospheric pollution. We all realize that private transport causes much more trouble per passenger-mile than does public transport. Both cause these troubles, but private transport causes more trouble than does public transport. The proper conclusion is to tax both forms of transport but to encourage public relatively to private transport by taxing private transport much more heavily than public transport. The wrong conclusion is to leave the taxation of private transport where it is, but to subsidise public transport in order to attract passengers from the private to the public sector.

Such a mistaken policy has an additional obvious disadvantage. We already need heavy tax revenue to finance desirable public expenditures, and I shall argue later that the new economic philosophy which we must evolve to meet the threat of Doom will make additional public expenditures necessary for such purposes as the redistribution of income in

favour of the poorer sections of the community. The sensible thing for
us to do now is to go round the whole economy taxing those activities
which are noxious according to the degree of the social costs which
they impose rather than starting to subsidise those competing activities
which are somewhat less noxious. We can thereby help to kill two birds
with one stone: we could discourage anti-social activities and at the
same time raise revenue for the relief of poverty and for those other
desirable public activities which we shall need to promote.

I have confined the points raised in this lecture to the use of taxes or
other regulations to discourage economic activities which pollute the
environment. In principle the same types of tax or regulation could be
used to discourage economic processes which use up exhaustible materials;
but I leave undiscussed in this lecture the question whether it is necessary in this case to supplement the influence of the market price
mechanism which will in any case raise the cost of scarce materials.
There is not time in one lecture to deal with every question.

To summarize, it is a mistake to rely on models of future world events
which assume a constant flow of pollution or a constant absorption of
exhaustible materials per unit of output produced. Economic systems
in the past have shown great flexibility. If we were to make the production of pollutants and the use of exhaustible materials really costly
to those concerned, we might see dramatic changes. Indeed, there have
already been some marked improvements in the cleansing of local atmos-
pheres and waterways in those cases where the first steps of governmental action have been taken.   There is no a priori reason for denying
that if appropriate governmental action is taken to impose the social
costs on those who cause the damage, there could be dramatic changes
also in the more important and more threatening cases of the threat of
Doom through pollution or through the exhaustion of resources.

Such is the first fundamental reorientation which we need in our economic policies, namely to set the stage by fiscal measures or by governmental regulation which will give a commercial incentive to free enterprise to select a structure of economic activities which avoids environmental pollution and the excessive use of exhaustible resources.
But given the structural pattern of the economy, pollution and the
exhaustion of natural resources will also be affected by the absolute
level of total economic activity; and this means that there must be
restraint over both the rate of growth of population and, at least in
the developed countries, over the rate of growth of consumption per
head.

This last consideration points to the need for a second fundamental
change of emphasis in economic policies in the rich developed countries.
Much modern competitive business seeks new profitable openings for
business by commercial advertising which aims at generating new wants
or at making consumers desire to discard an old model of a product in
order to acquire a new model of what is basically the same product.
Thus the desire for higher levels of consumption of unnecessary gadgets
and of new models to replace existing equipment is stimulated at the
expense of taking out the blessings of increased productivity in the
form of increased leisure. I have for long disliked the moral atmosphere of restless discontent which this creates. The discouragement
of commercial advertisement by means of heavy tax on such advertisement

and the return to broadcasting systems which are not basically the
organs for the stimulation of new wants by advertisement could be
helpful moves in the right direction. Moreover, some steps could be
taken to give incentives to producers to produce more durable products
rather than objects expressly designed to need rapid replacement. For
example, if cars were taxed much more heavily in the first years than
in the later years of their life, consumers would demand cars which
were durable and did not need rapid replacement. In general, if a
heavy tax is laid on the purchase of a piece of equipment and if this
discouragement to purchase is offset by a reduction in the rate of interest at which the funds needed to finance the purchase can be borrowed,
there will be an incentive to go for durability in the equipment. Less
frequent replacement will mean a lower tax bill, and at the same time
the value of the equipment's yield in the more distant future will be
discounted at a relatively low rate.

The need to set some restraints on the levels of total production suggests
yet a third basic change of emphasis in our economic policies. If we
wish to improve the lot of the poorest sections of humanity, then either
we must rely on rapid and far-reaching growth of output per head or we
must rely on the redistribution of income from the rich to the poor.
In recent years both for the relief of domestic poverty and for the
closing of the hideous gap between standards of living of the rich,
developed countries and of the poor, under-developed countries the
emphasis has been on economic growth. The extension of social services
for the relief of poverty at home has, we have been told by our politicians, been impeded by the slow rate of growth of total output, it being
assumed that any relief of poverty must come out of increased total
production so that all classes may gain simultaneously. The raising of
standards in the under-developed countries must, we have all assumed,
come basically out of the growth of total world output, so that standards
in the developed countries can be raised simultaneously with those in
the under-developed countries.

I have no intention of asserting that we should avoid further economic
growth. Indeed a rise in output per head, hopefully of a less noxious
form than in recent years, is an essential ingredient in the relief of
world poverty. A glance at the arithmetic of national incomes is sufficient to show that it cannot possibly be achieved simply by a redistribution of income from rich to poor countries. But I am asserting
that we would be wise to shift the emphasis significantly from a mere
boosting of growth to a serious reliance on a more equal distribution of
what we do produce, although we must face the fact that this inevitably
multiplies possibilities of conflict of interest between different
classes in society.

But as soon as we emphasize redistribution we are faced with a very
difficult dilemma. Anyone who studies the financial arithmetic of
poverty in this country -- and I have recently undertaken a fairly intensive study of that subject -- is driven inevitably to the conclusion
that if anything effective and manageable is to be done more help must
be given to the large than to the small family. However one may do
this, whether by higher family allowances or by more indirect and
disguised means, it necessarily involves subsidising the production of
children. If we aim at shifting our philosophy from a mad scramble for
ever higher levels of production and consumption of goods, however
unnecessary they may be, to a more humane and compassionate society

in which basic needs are assured, if necessary at the expense of inessen-
tial luxuries, we come up against the thought that our children, who by
the way never asked to be born, are also human beings with basic needs
and that the more there are of them in a family the greater the total
needs of that family if every member is to be given a proper start in
life.

The same basic dilemma shows itself in a somewhat different form when we
consider the closing of the gap between the rich and the poor countries.
It is the poor countries with the highest rates of population growth
which will be in the greatest need of foreign aid and technical assistance in order to undertake those projects of capital development,
(building new schools, new hospitals, new houses, new machines, new
tools and so on), which are necessary simply in order to prevent a decline in the amount of capital equipment per head of the population.
However disguised, does not this amount to the international subsidisa-
tion of those countries which are producing the most children?

Restraint on consumption per head is a means of restraining total demands
on scarce resources which necessarily involves restraints on standards
of living. On the contrary, restraint of population growth is a means
of restraining total demands without any fall in standards of living.
Population control may for this reason be put high on the order of
priority for action to meet the threat of Doom, though it raises a
basic ethical question which I cannot discuss today. At what level is it
legitimate to maintain standards for the born by denying existence at
current standards to those whose births are prevented? It would appear
to me that, however one might answer this basic ethical question, the
population explosion is now such that restraints on fertility should
constitute our first priority as a means for restraining the growth
of total demands on scarce resources of land, materials, and environment.

In many of the poorer underdeveloped countries the rate of population
growth is exceptionally high; and their need for restraint is, therefore,
exceptionally obvious. But there is need for restraint also of the less
rapidly growing richer populations; and it should not be forgotten that
one more American citizen because of his high level of consumption puts
an immensely greater strain on world resources than does one more
Indian peasant.

But while the control of population might make the most desirable contribution to the control of the total demand on resources, it presents
in one way the most difficulty in its achievement. The price mechanism
together with a proper, extensive system of pollution taxes by imposing
appropriate pecuniary penalties can be used to restrain scarcities of
material and environmental goods; these instruments provide powerful
negative feedbacks in the total dynamic system. As the demands on
material and environmental resources become excessive, so prices and
charges rise to discourage demand and encourage supply. But with population, alas, it seems that we must introduce a vicious positive
feedback. We wish to discourage large families; but on distributional
grounds the larger the family the more we must subsidise it.

There is only one possible way out of this dilemma and that is to
devise population policies which restrain population growth by means
other than pecuniary penalties on the production of children. The first

thing obviously is to enable everyone to avoid having more children than
they want. Sterilization and abortion on demand, the development of
family planning advice and services in all maternity hospitals, the
complete incorporation of universal and free family planning into the
National Health Service, the provision of extensive domiciliary family
planning services, school education which inculcates that sexual intercourse should never take place without contraception unless a child is
positively planned, governmental promotion of research into contraceptive methods -- these are the first types of action to which we must
devote resources to match any help which we give to large families.
Whether or not we shall in the end be driven to consider more authori-
tarian methods is a question which need not be raised until we have fully
explored the effects of a fully developed attempt at voluntary family
planning.

I have, I fear, subjected you to a rapid and superficial survey of a
large number of economic issues; and yet there is one vast section of my
subject matter which I have hardly mentioned, namely the international
implications of these problems. Before I sit down, I would like briefly
to indicate one or two of the most important issues in this field.

First and foremost, there is the distinction between the rich and the
poor nations. The less developed countries fear that the concern of the
richer countries with the quality of the environment -- a luxury which
the rich can well afford -- will for various reasons impede economic
growth in the less developed countries -- a necessity which the poor
cannot do without. Past experience has shown that a recession of economic activity in the United States and other developed countries has hit
the under-developed countries by reducing the demand for their exports
and by reducing the amount of capital funds available in the rich countries for investment in the poorer countries. Might not a planned restraint on the growth of real income in the rich countries have similar
effects in reducing their demand for imports, their foreign aid, and
the capital funds available for the development of the poorer countries,
and indeed, in leading in general to an attitude unfavourable to industrialization and growth in the poorer countries?

This fear must be exorcized. The stimulation of output per head in the
poor countries is an absolute necessity for dealing with poverty in
those countries. Such economic development is not incompatible with
increased emphasis on population control, pollution control, and the
recycling of materials. These things must not be confounded with
policies to keep down the standards of living in the poorer countries.

A second set of major international problems arises from the fact that
many of the problems which I have discussed cut across national frontiers.
The supersonic aircraft of country A pollutes the atmosphere for country
B. The whalers of country C reduce the catch for the whalers of country
D. Country E may pollute a river, lake, or sea on which country F is
also situated. Many of the controls which I have discussed will need
international agreement and organization.

And finally there is the problem of international disarmament. It is
not merely that nuclear, chemical, and biological weapons of war would,
if used, represent the ultimate pollution of the environment. There is
a much more mundane day-to-day consideration. The production of armaments

itself constitutes an appreciable proportion of industrial output in the developed countries; and it is concentrated in sectors of the economy which make heavy demands on material and environmental resources. Moreover, there is a very heavy concentration in the richer countries of governmental research and development on weapons of war which, if turned to such topics as the control of the environment, might transform the outlook. Disarmament could make a major contribution to our problem.

The development of the will and the institutions for international action in these three fields is essential for the successful moulding of any set of effective economic policies to meet the threat of Doom.

READING 27

Lester Brown (born 1934), is presently a Senior Fellow at the Overseas
Development Council in Washington D.C. He has authored a large number
of books and articles and he is one of the more "involved" North American
agricultural economists. His emphasis tends to be interdisciplinary.

The following paper which was prepared for the World Population Conference in Bucharest discusses the race between food and population - a
problem which intrigued Botero and Malthus in the 17th and 19th century
and many scientists such as East thereafter.[27] The latter, however,
only considered the population effect.

Brown clearly establishes that there are two forces responsible for expanding food demand i.e. population growth and rising incomes. For
the world as a whole the population is rising by 2% per year whereas
the annual growth in effective demand due to expanding incomes has been
estimated at about 1.5%.

With regard to the supply side one could argue that all the good farm-
lands have already been taken into cultivation (about 3.5 billion acres).
Whatever is left is high-cost, low fertility land now used for other
purposes such as grazing and forestry. Increases in yields per acre
are possible but as Lester Brown notes such attempts may result in
erosion, soil depletion and we might add environmental destruction
through the increased use of commercial fertilizers and pesticides.

As our world food reserves are at an all-time low, future increases
in food prices seem inevitable. In most less affluent countries people
typically spend two-thirds of their income on food. In many of them
higher food prices inevitably entail more malnutrition or hunger.

---

[27]Source: L.R. Brown, "World Population and Food Supplies: Looking
Ahead", United Nations, World Population Conference, Conference Background Paper (E) Conf. 60/CBP/19, March 22, 1974,
pp. 3-19.

WORLD POPULATION AND FOOD SUPPLIES: LOOKING AHEAD
Lester R. Brown

INTRODUCTION

1. The international scarcity of major agricultural commodities in 1973 reflected important long-term trends as well as the more temporary phenomenon of lack of rainfall in the Soviet Union and parts of Asia and Africa. It appears that an extended period is beginning in which global grain reserves, which provide a crucial measure of safety when crop failures occur, will generally remain on the low side, and in which little, if any, excess cropland will be held idle in the United States. Food prices are likely to remain considerably higher than they were during the last decade, placing a special burden on the world's poor. Meanwhile, the world has become overwhelmingly dependent on one continent - North America - for exportable food supplies. From a global perspective the world is likely to be in a vulnerable situation on the food front in the years ahead. Strong international policy responses are called for in an area so basic to human welfare.

I. POPULATION AND AFFLUENCE

2. During the 1960s, the world food problem was perceived as a food/population problem centred on the developing countries, a race between food and people. At the end of each year, observers anxiously compared rates of increase in food production with those of population growth to see if any progress was being made. Throughout most of the decade it was nip and tuck. During the 1970s, rapid global population growth has continued to generate demand for more food, but, in addition, rising affluence is emerging as a major new claimant on the world's food resources. Thus there are now two important sources of growth in world demand for food.

3. Worldwide, population growth is still the dominant source of expanding demand for food. With world population expanding at nearly 2 per cent per year, merely maintaining current per capita consumption levels will require a doubling of food production in little more than a generation.

4. Throughout the poor countries, population growth accounts for most of the year-to-year growth in the demand for food. At best, only very limited progress is being made in raising per capita consumption. In the more affluent countries, on the other hand, rising incomes account for most of the growth in the demand for food.

5. The effect of rising affluence on the world demand for food is perhaps best understood by examining its effect on requirements for cereals, which dominate the world food economy. In the poor countries, the annual availability of grain per person averages only about 400

pounds per year. Nearly all of this small amount, roughly a pound a
day, must be consumed directly to meet minimum energy needs. Little can
be spared for conversion into animal protein.

6. In the United States and Canada, per capita grain utilization is
currently approaching one ton per year. Of this total, only about 150
pounds are consumed directly in the form of bread, pastries and break-
fast cereals. The remainder is consumed indirectly in the form of
meat, milk, and eggs. The agricultural resources - land, water, fertilizer - required to support an average North American are nearly five
times those of the average Indian, Nigerian or Colombian.

7, In the northern tier of industrial countries stretching from the
United Kingdom and Europe through the Soviet Union to Japan, dietary
habits more or less approximate those of the United States in 1940.
As incomes continue to rise in this group of countries (which contain
some 660 million people), a sizable share of the additional income is
being converted into demand for livestock products, particularly beef.
Many of these countries lack the capacity to satisfy the growth in
their demand for livestock products entirely from indigenous resources.
As a result they are importing increasing amounts of livestock products
or of feed grains and soybeans with which to expand their livestock
production.

II. SCARCE RESOURCES: LAND, WATER AND ENERGY

8. As the world demand for food climbs, constraints on efforts to
further expand food production become increasingly apparent. The means
of expanding food supplies from conventional agriculture fall into two
categories: either increasing the amount of land under cultivation,
or raising yields on existing cropland through intensified use of water,
energy and fertilizers. We face problems in the needed expansion of
each of these resources.

9. From the beginning of agriculture until about 1950, expanding the
cultivated area was the major means of increasing the world's food
supply. Since 1950, however, raising output on the existing cultivated
area has accounted for most of the increase. Intensification of
cultivation has increased steadily since 1950; during the early 1970s
it has accounted for an estimated four-fifths of the annual growth in
world food output, far overshadowing expansion of the cultivated area.

10. The traditional approach to increasing production - expanding the
area under cultivation - has only limited scope for the future. Indeed
some parts of the world face a net reduction in agricultural land because of the growth in competing uses, such as recreation, transportation and industrial and residential development. Few countries have
well-defined land use policies that protect agricultural land from
other uses. In the United States, farmland has been used indiscrim-
inately for other purposes with little thought devoted to the possible
long-term consequences.

11. Some more densely populated countries, such as Japan and several
Western European countries, have been experiencing a reduction in the
land used for crop production for the past few decades. Other parts
of the world, including particularly the Indian subcontinent, the

Middle East, North Africa, the Caribbean, Central America and the Andean countries, are losing disturbingly large acreages of cropland each year because of severe soil erosion.

12. The availability of arable land is important, but perhaps even more important in the future will be the availability of water for agricultural purposes. In many regions of the world, fertile agricultural land is available if water can be found to make it produce. Yet most of the rivers that lend themselves to damming and to irrigation have already been developed. The expansion of world irrigated area is likely to fall into the familiar S-shaped curve as we run out of easy opportunities to construct new irrigation reservoirs. Future efforts to expand fresh water supplies for agricultural purposes will increasingly focus on such techniques as the diversion of rivers (as in the Soviet Union), the manipulation of rainfall patterns to increase the share of rain falling over moisture-deficient agricultural areas and, depending on the cost of energy, the desalting of sea water.

13. The intensification of agricultural production on the existing cultivated area in many developing countries requires a several-fold increase in energy supplies. With world energy prices rising rapidly, the costs of intensifying food production will rise commensurately and the needed increases in energy use will become increasingly expensive. In countries already engaged in high energy agriculture, such as the United States, Japan and those in Western Europe, high energy prices and the possibility of fuel rationing may reduce future food production prospects below what they would otherwise be.

14. In addition to arable land, fresh water and energy, fertilizer is also now in short supply, and the outlook is for higher prices. It is impossible to separate the future availability of fertilizer from the scarcity of energy. In part this is because the manufacture of nitrogen fertilizer, the most widely used chemical fertilizer, commonly utilizes natural gas or naphtha as a raw material and in part because the manufacturing process consumes large amounts of energy. Fertilizer requirements over the remaining years of this century will soar to phenomenal levels.

15. One of the key questions concerning future gains in agricultural production is whether the more advanced countries can sustain the trend of rising per acre yields of cereals. In some countries, the rate of increase in per acre yields for some crops is beginning to slow down and the capital investments required for each additional increase may now start to climb sharply. In agriculturally advanced countries such as Japan and some in Europe, the cost of further raising yield per acre for some crops is rising. For example, raising rice yields in Japan from the current 5,000 pounds per acre to 6,000 pounds could be very costly. Raising yields of corn in the United States from 90 to 100 bushels per acre requires a much larger quantity of nitrogen than was needed to raise yields from 50 to 60 bushels. Higher fertilizer prices will, in this context, further reduce the potential for continuing yield increases.

III. CONSTRAINTS ON PROTEIN PRODUCTION

16. At a time when rising affluence is beginning to manifest itself in

the form of rapidly growing demand for high quality protein, we suddenly find ourselves in difficulty in our efforts to rapidly expand supplies of three major protein sources - beef, soybeans and fish. Two major constraints are operative in the case of beef. Agricultural scientists have not been able to devise any commercially satisfactory means of getting more than one calf per cow per year. For every animal that goes into the beef production process, one adult animal must be fed and otherwise maintained for a full year. There does not appear to be any prospect of an imminent breakthrough on this front.

17. The other constraint on beef production is good grassland. The grazing capacity of much of the world's pastureland is now almost fully utilized. This is true, for example, in much of the Great Plains area of the United States, in sub-Sahara Africa and in parts of Australia. There are opportunities for using improved grasses and for improved range management, but these are limited and slow to be realized.

18. A second potentially serious constraint on efforts to expand supplies of high-quality protein in the inability of scientists to achieve a breakthrough in per acre yields of soybeans. Soybeans are consumed directly as food by people throughout densely populated East Asia and they are an important high-quality protein ingredient in livestock and poultry feeds throughout much of the world. The economic importance of soybeans in the world food economy is indicated by the fact that they have become the leading export product of the United States - surpassing export sales of wheat, corn, and such high-technology items as electronic computers and jet aircraft.

19. In the United States, which now produces two thirds of the world's soybean crop and supplies more than four-fifths of all soybeans entering the world market, soybean yields per acre have increased by about 1 per cent per year since 1950; corn yields, on the other hand, have increased by nearly 4 per cent per year. One reason why soybean yield have not climbed very rapidly is that the soybean, being a legume with a built-in nitrogen supply, is not very responsive to nitrogen fertilizer.

20. More soybeans are produced essentially by planting more land to soybeans. Close to 85 per cent of the dramatic four-fold increase in the United States soybean crop since 1950 has come from expanding the area devoted to it. As long as there was ample idle cropland available, this did not pose a problem, but with this cropland reserve rapidly disappearing and with one in every six acres of American cropland already planted to soybeans by 1973, serious supply problems could emerge.

21. The oceans are a third major source of protein. From 1950 to 1970 the world fish catch expanded rapidly, going from 21 million to 70 million tons. This phenomenal growth in the catch of nearly 5 per cent annually, which far exceeded the annual rate of world population growth, greatly increased the average supply of marine protein per person. This is shown in table 1.

22. In 1969, the long period of sustained growth in the world fish catch was interrupted by a slight decline of a few hundred thousand tons. In 1970 the catch resumed its upward trend, but the sharp re-

bound was shortlived. Since then it has declined for three consecutive
years, falling some 8 million tons. With population continuing to grow,
the per capita availability of fish declined 16 per cent during this
three-year span, triggering dramatic price rises. As stocks of some
key commercial species are depleted, the amount of time and money ex-
pended to bring in the shrinking catch continue to rise every year.
Many marine biologists now feel that the global catch of table-grade
fish is at or near the maximum sustainable level. A large number of
the 30 or so leading species of commercial-grade fish currently may be
over-fished, that is, stocks will not sustain even the current level of
catch. If the world fish catch stabilizes or declines, then that share
of the growing global demand for protein until recently filled by growth
in the fish catch, must now either be filled by land-based protein supplies or it must be choked off by further price rises. The importance
of evolving a co-operative international approach to the management of
oceanic fisheries is underlined.

Table 1. World fish catch: total and per capita

Year	Total catch (million metric tons)	Per capita (kilograms)
1950	21	8
1951	24	10
1952	25	10
1953	25	10
1954	28	10
1955	29	11
1956	30	11
1957	32	11
1958	33	12
1959	36	13
1960	40	14
1961	43	14
1962	46	15
1963	48	15
1964	52	16
1965	52	16
1966	57	17
1967	60	18
1968	63	18
1969	63	18
1970	70	19
1971	69	19
1972 (prel.)	64	17
1973 (prel.)	62	16

23. Unfortunately, there is no prospect whatsoever that fish farming could offset more than a small fraction of the decline in the oceanic fish catch for the foreseeable future. Substantial expansion in the global fish supply from fish farming await further advances in technology and extensive capital investment in fish farming facilities.

24. Although there are substantial opportunities for expanding the world food supply, it now seems likely that the supply of food, particularly protein, will lag behind growth in demand for some time to come, resulting in significantly higher prices during the decade ahead than prevailed during the 1960s. It may be that the world protein market will be transformed from a buyer's market to a seller's market, much as the world energy market has been transformed over the past few years.

IV. ECOLOGICAL UNDERMINING OF THE WORLD FOOD ECONOMY

25. The increasing demand for food is putting more pressure on the food producing ecosystem in many parts of the world than it can withstand. One dramatic example is the anchovy fishery off the western coast of Latin America. During the early 1970s this vast fishery accounted for one-fifth of the global fish catch. During late 1972 and throughout much of 1973 the anchovies seemingly disappeared from the traditional offshore fishing areas. This did not cause a great deal of alarm since a slight shift in the Humboldt current and the change in temperature of a few degrees had caused the anchovies to move away at least temporarily before.

26. There is now growing evidence that the very heavy offtake from the anchovy fishery ranging from 10 to 12 million tons in the late 1960s and early 1970s may have exceeded the capacity of the fishery to regenerate itself. Over-fishing may have seriously damaged the anchovy fishery. If so, it may take years before it can recover to its full productive capacity, assuming it is given the opportunity to do so.

27. A second example of ecological overstress, which is diminishing the earth's food producing capacity, is now all too evident in the Sahel, just south of the Sahara in Africa. For many months in 1973 the news media reported the situation in sub-Sahara Africa as being the product of drought. The problem was described in terms of the need for a temporary food relief effort. The need was to get perhaps 600,000 tons of grain into a half dozen seriously affected countries over the next several months. This was indeed a problem. The need was real.

28. However, there is a much more basic problem in the Sahel. Over the past 35 years, human and livestock populations along the sub-Saharan fringe have increased rapidly, in some areas nearly doubling during this period. As the human and livestock populations multiply, they put more pressure on the ecosystem than it can withstand. The result is over-grazing, deforestation and over-all denudation of the land.

29. As a result of this denudation and deforestation, the Sahara desert has begun to move southward at an accelerated rate all along the 3,500 mile southern fringe, stretching from Senegal to northern Ethiopia. An "in house" study undertaken by the United States Agency for International

Development, in August 1972 indicated the desert is moving southward
at up to 30 miles per year, depending on where it is measured.

30. As the desert moves southward, human and livestock populations
retreat before it. The result is ever-greater pressure on the fringe
area. This in turn contributes to the denudation and deforestation,
setting in process a self-reinforcing cycle.

31 Coping with this situation requires far more than a temporary food
relief effort. The world must recognize that a continuing food relief
effort for this region will be required for the foreseeable future.
But this treats only the symptoms of ecological overstress. There is
also now a need to attempt to arrest and reverse the southward movement
of the desert. This will require an extensive infusion of technical
expertise in desert reclamation and land management from outside the
region. It will require economic resources from outside the region,
until some of the desert land can be reclaimed.

32. There is now a pressing need to address and alleviate the causes of
ecological stress in the region which facilitates the southward movement of the Sahara. Failure to do so means the Sahara may engulf much
of central Africa in a matter of years destroying a significant slice
of the continent's food producing capacity. It will require among other
things a concerted co-operative effort by the tier of countries most
immediately affected, by the next tier of countries southward which is,
or will shortly be affected, and by a large number of external donors
who must supply much of the resources. Above all it calls for the
launching of efforts to slow and stabilize population growth in the
region.

33. The need to arrest the southward movement of the desert presents
the international community with one of its severest challenges. It
will require a co-operative international effort comparable with that
which was used to launch the Green Revolution in the late 1960s. If
this co-operative effort is not forthcoming, we much accept the fact
that a growing share of Africa's food producing capability will be
totally destroyed. This is occurring at a time when population in the
African continent is still expanding in an unimpeded fashion.

34. Ecological over-stress is also very much in evidence in the Indian
subcontinent. Over the past 15 years as human and livestock populations
have increased, the subcontinent has been progressively deforested.
One does not need much training in soil and water management to be
greatly alarmed at the long-term consequences of this progressive and
accelerating deforestation. This is most serious in the Himalayas and
the surrounding foothills, for this is where nearly all the major river
systems of the Indian subcontinent - the Indus, the Ganges and the
Bramaputra - originate.

35. One could have predicted several years ago with great confidence
the long-term dangers inherent in deforestation, particularly of the
Himalayas and the surrounding foothills. It should not have come as
any surprise that during the late summer of 1973 reports came of the
worst flood in Pakistan's history, a flood so severe that it destroyed
a large share of the spring wheat crop which was in storage on farms as
well as a sizable share of the crops standing in the fields. Entire

communities were washed away.

36. Since the deforestation is continuing, one can now say with considerable confidence that the incidence and severity of flooding in Pakistan,
India and Bangladesh will be much greater in the future than it is at
present. In effect, deforestation in the subcontinent, particularly in
Nepal where the major rivers originate, may be undermining the food
producing capability of the subcontinent on which nearly 750 million
people now depend.

37. The pressures of continuously growing demand for food are beginning
to undermine the food producing ecosystems in many parts of the world.
The examples above are only a few of the many which could be cited.
The time has come to systematically inventory these ecological stresses
at the global level. Two generalizations can be made concerning agricultural stresses on the ecosystem. First, the situation is certain
to worsen in the years immediately ahead and, secondly, future world
food production prospects will be affected.

V. THE GREEN REVOLUTION: OPPORTUNITY LOST?

38. Efforts to modernize agriculture in the less affluent countries
in the 1950s and early 1960s were consistently frustrated. When farmers
in these countries attempted to use varieties of corn developed in Iowa,
they often failed to produce any corn at all. Japanese rice varieties
were not suited either to local cultural practices or to consumer tastes
in India. When fertilizer was applied intensively to local cereal varieties, the yield response was limited and occasionally even negative.

39. It was against this backdrop of frustration that the high-yielding
dwarf wheats were developed by the Rockefeller Foundation team in Mexico.
Three unique characteristics of these wheats endeared them to farmers
in many countries - their fertilizer responsiveness, lack of photoperiod
sensitivity (sensitivity to day length) and early maturity.

40. When farmers applied more than 40 pounds of nitrogen fertilizer
per acre to traditional varieties having tall, thin straw, the wheat
often lodged or fell over, causing severe crop losses. By contrast,
yields of the short, stiffstrawed dwarf varieties of Mexican wheat
would continue to rise with nitrogen applications up to 120 pounds per
acre. Given the necessary fertilizer and water and the appropriate
management, farmers could easily double the yields of indigenous varieties.

41. Beyond this, the reduced sensitivity of dwarf varieties to day
length permitted them to be moved around the world over a wide range of
latitudes, stretching from Mexico, which lies partly in the tropics, to
Turkey in the temperate zone. Because the biological clocks of the new
wheats were much less sensitive than those of the traditional ones,
planting dates were much more flexible.

42. Another advantageous characteristic of the new wheats was their
early maturity. They were ready for harvest within 120 days after
planting; the traditional varieties took 150 days or more. This trait,
combined with reduced sensitivity to day length, created broad new opportunities for multiple cropping wherever water supplies were sufficient.

43. Within a few years after the spectacular breakthrough with wheat in
Mexico, the Ford Foundation joined the Rockefeller Foundation to establish the International Rice Research Institute (IRRI) in the Philippines.
Its purpose was to attempt to breed a fertilizer-responsive, early-
maturing rice capable of wide adaption - in effect, a counterpart of
the high-yielding wheats. With the wheat experience to draw upon,
agricultural scientists at IRRI struck pay dirt quickly. With in few
years they released the first of the high-yielding dwarf rices, a variety known as IR-8.

44. The great advantage of the new seeds was that they permitted developing countries to quickly utilize agricultural research that had taken
decades to complete in Japan, the United States and elsewhere. In
those areas of the developing countries where there were requisite
supplies of water and fertilizer and price incentives were offered,
the spread of the high-yielding varieties of wheat and rice was rapid.
Farmers assumed to be bound by tradition were quick to adopt the new
seeds when it was obviously profitable for them to do so.

45. Early in 1968, the term "Green Revolution" was coined to describe
the introduction and rapid spread of the high-yielding wheats and
rices. In 1965 land planted with these new varieties in Asia totalled
about 200 acres, largely trial and demonstration plots. Thereafter
the acreage spread swiftly as follows:

Year	Acres
1965	200
1966	41,000
1967	4,047,000
1968	16,660,000
1969	31,319,000
1970	43,914,000
1971	50,549,000

46. Acreage figures for Mexico are not included in the series above
since the new wheat had largely displaced traditional varieties before
the Green Revolution became an international phenomenon in the mid-
1960s. Among the principal Asian countries to benefit from using the
new seeds are India, Pakistan, the Philippines and Turkey, and more
recently Indonesia, Malaysia and Sri Lanka.

47. During the late 1960s the Philippines was able to achieve self-
sufficiency in rice, ending a half-century of dependence on imported
rice. Unfortunately, this situation was not sustained because of a
number of factors, including civil unrest, the susceptibility of the
new rices to disease and governmental failure in some cases to continue
the essential support of the rice programme.

48. Pakistan greatly increased its wheat production, emerging as a
new exporter of grain in recent years. In India, where advances in
the new varieties were concentrated largely in wheat, progress has
been encouraging. During the seven-year span from 1965 to 1972, India
expanded its wheat production from 11 million tons to 27 million tons,
an increase in a major crop unmatched by any other country in history.

49. One result of this dramatic advance in wheat production in India
was the accumulation of unprecedented cereal reserves and the attainment of cereal self-sufficiency in 1972. This eliminated, at least temporarily, the need for imports into a country that only a few years before had been the principal recipient of American food aid. Economic
self-sufficiency in cereals - when farmers produce as much as consumers
can afford at prevailing prices - is not to be confused with nutritional
self-sufficiency, however, which requires much higher levels of productivity and purchasing power.

50. During late 1971 and in 1972, India was able to use nearly 2 million tons from its own food reserves, initially to feed nearly 10 million Bengali refugees during the civil war in Pakistan, and later as
food aid for Bangladesh. A poor monsoon in 1972 temporarily forced
India back into the world market as an importer of grain, but on a
much smaller scale - 4 million tons - than the massive import of nearly
10 million tons that followed the 1965 monsoon failure.

51. This is not to suggest that the Green Revolution has solved the
world's food problems, either on a short- or long-term basis. The
drought of 1973 clearly demonstrated that Indian agriculture is still
at the mercy of the vagaries of weather. A second monsoon failure or
a shortage of fertilizer would seriously disrupt the pattern of progress
that has characterized Indian agriculture over the past five years.

52. The Green Revolution can be properly assessed only when it is
considered what things would have been like in its absence. The grim
scenario that this question calls forth lends some of the needed perspective. Increases in cereal production made possible by the new seeds
did arrest the deteriorating trend in per capita food production in the
developing countries. The massive famine anticipated by many has been
avoided. Although there have been some spectacular localized successes
in raising cereal output, relatively little progress has been made in
raising the per capita production of cereals among the less affluent
countries as a whole over the past several years.

53. The Green Revolution does not represent a solution to the food
problem; rather, it is a means of buying time, perhaps an additional
15 or 20 years during which the brakes can be applied to population
growth. Close to a decade has now passed since the launching of the
Green Revolution, but success stories in national family planning programmes in the less affluant nations are all too few. Among the population giants of Asia, the People's Republic of China appears to be
substantially reducing its birth rates, but reductions in Bangladesh,
India, Indonesia and Pakistan are minimal.

VI. DEPLETED GLOBAL RESERVES

54. The period since the Second World War has been characterized by
excess capacity in world agriculture, much of it concentrated in the
United States. In many ways the world was fortunate to have, in effect,
two major food reserves during this period. One was in the form of grain
reserves in the principal exporting countries and the other in the form
of reserve cropland, virtually all of which was land idled under farm
programmes in the United States.

55. Grain reserves, including substantial quantities of both food grains and feedgrains, are most commonly measured in terms of carryover stocks - the amount in storage at the time the new crop begins to come in. World carryover stocks are concentrated in a few of the principal exporting countries - namely Argentina, Australia, Canada and the United States.

56. Since 1960, world grain reserves have fluctuated from a high of 155 million metric tons to a low of about 100 million metric tons. When these reserves drop to 100 million tons, severe shortages and strong upward price presures develop. Although 100 million tons appears to be an enormous quantity of grain, it represents a mere 8 per cent of annual world grain consumption, or less than one month's needs - an uncomfortably small working reserve and a perilously thin buffer against the vagaries of weather or plant diseases. As world consumption expands by some 2.5 per cent annually, so should the size of working reserves, but over the past two decades reserves have dwindled while consumption has continued to climb.

57. The second major source of stability in the world food economy throughout much of the post-war period has been the reserve of idle American cropland. Roughly 50 million acres have been idle under farm programmes for the past dozen years or so. Though not as quickly available as the grain reserves, much of this acreage can be brought back into production within 12 to 18 months once the decision is made to do so.

58. In recent years, the need to draw down grain reserves and to utilize the reserve of idle cropland has occurred with increasing frequency. This first happened during the food crisis years of 1966 and 1967 when world grain reserves were reduced to a dangerously low level and the United States brought back into production a small portion of the 50 million idle acres. It happened again in 1971, as a result of the corn blight in the United States. In 1973, in response to growing food scarcities, world grain reserves once more declined and the United States again resorted to cultivating its idle cropland, but to a much greater degree than on either of the two previous occasions. Government decisions in early 1973 permitted much of the idle cropland to be brought back into production. In 1974, there will be no Government payments to keep cropland idle.

59. Reserve stocks fell to close to 100 million tons in 1973 and are not expected to be rebuilt in 1974. World grain reserves have now fallen to their lowest level in two decades, though the world's population has increased by half in the interim.

60. By combining global reserve stocks with the potential grain production of idle cropland, a good indication may be obtained of the actual total reserve capability in the world food economy in any given year. Taking this total as a percentage of total world grain consumption then provides a rough quantitative indicator of global food security for the year. As the following table demonstrates, the world is now in a situation of extreme vulnerability. In 1973 and 1974 world reserve capabilities in relation to consumption needs have fallen far below any previous level in the post-war era.

Table 2.   Index of world food security

Year	Reserve stocks of grain	Grain equivalent of idle American cropland	Total Reserves	Reserves as share of annual grain consumption (per cent)	Reserves as days of consumption.
		million metric tons			
1961	154	68	222	26	94
1962	131	81	212	24	88
1963	125	70	195	21	77
1964	128	70	198	21	77
1965	113	71	184	19	69
1966	99	79	178	18	66
1967	100	51	151	15	55
1968	116	61	177	17	62
1969	136	73	209	19	69
1970	146	71	127	19	69
1971	120	41	161	14	51
1972	131	78	209	18	66
1973	103	20	123	10	37
1974 (proj.)	89	0	89	7	27

61. From the end of the Second World War until quite recently, world
prices for the principal temperate zone farm commodities, such as wheat,
feedgrains and soybeans, have been remarkably stable. In part, this is
because throughout much of this period world prices have rested on the
commodity support level in the United States. Since world food reserves
may become chronically low and the idle crop acreage in the United
States may decline sharply or even disappear entirely in the years ahead,
there is the prospect of very volatile world prices for the important
food commodities.

VII. THE NORTH AMERICAN BREADBASKET

62. The extent of global vulnerability is particularly underlined by
examining the degree of global dependence on North America for exportable
food supplies. Over the past generation the United States has
achieved a unique position as a supplier of food to the rest of the
world. Before the Second World War both Latin America, especially
Argentina, and North America (Canada and the United States) were major
exporters of grain. During the late 1930s net grain exports from Latin
America were substantially above those of North America. Since then,

however, the combination of the population explosion and the slowness
of most Latin American Governments to reform and modernize agriculture
have eliminated the net export surplus. With few exceptions, Latin
American countries are now food importers.

63. As the following table illustrates, over the past three decades
North America, particularly the United States which accounts for three
fourths of the continent's grain exports, has emerged as the world's
breadbasket. Exports of Australia, the only other net exporter of
importance, are only a fraction of North America's. The United States
not only is the world's major exporter of wheat and feedgrains, it is
also now the world's leading exporter of rice. North America today
controls a larger share of the world's exportable surplus of grains
than the Middle East does of oil.

64. Exportable supplies of the crucial soybean are even more concentrated than those of grains. Although as late as the 1930s China supplied nearly all the soybeans entering world markets, continuing population growth during the ensuing decades has gradually absorbed the
exportable surplus. As of 1973 China is importing small quantities
from the United States. The position of principal

Table 3. The changing pattern of world grain trade

Region	1934-38	1948-52	1960	1966	1973 (prel.) (fiscal year)
		MILLION METRIC TONS (plus = net exports; minus = net imports)			
North America	+5	+23	+39	+59	+88
Latin America	+9	+1	0	+5	-4
Western Europe	-24	-22	-25	-27	-21
Eastern Europe and U.S.S.R.	+5	--	0	-4	-27
Africa	+1	0	-2	-7	-4
Asia	+2	-6	-17	-34	-39
Austrial and New Zealand	+3	+3	+6	+8	+7

supplier has been taken over by the United States, which provided over
90 per cent of world soybean exports in the 1960s and early 1970s. With
world demand for high-quality protein surging upward, Brazil - virtually
the only other nation capable of producing soybeans on a sizable scale
in the foreseeable future - has rapidly boosted its soybean production
and exports. However, the United States is likely to continue supplying
three fourths or more of the world's soybean exports for many years to
come.

65. At a time when dependence of the rest of the world on North American
food exports is increasing so dramatically, there is also a growing
awareness that this extreme dependence leaves the world in a very dangerous position in the event of adverse crop years in North America. Both
Canada and the United States are affected by the same climatic cycles.

66.   Considerable evidence has now been accumulated indicating that
North America has been subject to recurrent clusters of drought years
roughly every 20 years. The cyclical drought phenomenon has now been
established as far back as the 1860s when data were first collected on
rainfall. The most recent drought, occurring in the early 1950s, was
rather modest. The preceding one occurring in the early 1930s was
particularly severe, giving rise to the dust bowl era in the United
States.

67.   If the United States experiences another stretch of drought years,
quite possibly during the current decade, its impact on production will
not likely be as great as during the 1930s due to improved soil management and water conservation practices. But even a modest decline in
production, given the rapid growth in global demand and extreme world
dependence on North America's exportable margin of food, would create a
very dangerous situation. It would send shock waves throughout the world
triggering intense competition for available food supplies.

VIII. REDEFINING FAMINE

68.   High food prices and shortages are an inconvenience for the more
affluent societies and individuals, but the less affluent nations, and
the poor within nations, are in an especially dangerous predicament.
When global reserve stocks are low, the capacity of the international
community to respond to emergencies such as droughts or crop failure
with food aid is greatly diminished. At the same time, high prices may
keep needed food out of the reach of poor nations and individuals.

69.   When one spends about 80 per cent of one's income on food, as does
a sizable segment of mankind, a doubling in the price of wheat or rice
cannot possibly be offset by increased expenditures. It can only drive
a subsistence diet below the subsistence or survival level.

70.   One reason it is possible for the world's affluent to ignore such
tragedies is the changes which have occurred in the way that famine
manifests itself. In earlier historical periods, famine was largely a
geographic phenomenon. Whole nations or regions, whether Ireland or
West Bengal, experienced dramatically high rates of starvation and death.
Today the advancements in national and global distribution and transportation systems have insured that famine is generally more evenly
spread among the world's poor rather than concentrated in specific lo-
cales. (The current tragedy in sub-Saharan Africa is an obvious exception.) The modern version of famine does not often permit dramatic
photographs, such as those of the morning ritual of collecting bodies
in Calcutta during the Bengal famine of 1943, but it is no less real
in the human toll it exacts.

IX. A GLOBAL RESERVE SYSTEM

71.   The global food outlook calls for serious consideration of the
creation of an internationally managed food reserve system. Just as
the American dollar can no longer serve as the foundation of the international monetary system, so American agriculture may no longer have
sufficient excess capacity to ensure reasonable stability in the world
food economy over a multi-year period.

72. World food reserves can be built up in times of relative abundance
out of production surplus to immediate needs, and drawn down in times
of acute scarcity. This would help to hold down price increases to the
consumer during times of scarcity and to hold up prices to the producers
during the inevitable periods of production in excess of immediate world
demand. In effect, the cushion and stability that surplus American
agricultural capacity have provided for a generation would be provided
at least partially by a world food reserve system. A system of global
food reserves would provide a measure of price stability in the world
food economy that would be in the self-interest of all nations. The
world community, of course, also has a basic humanitarian interest in
ensuring that famine does not occur in the densely populated low-income
countries following a poor crop year - an assurance the affluent nations
may be less able to provide in the future if the current system of
autonomous, nationally oriented food planning is allowed to continue
without modification.

73. In 1973, one Director-General of the Food and Agriculture Organization of the United Nations (FAO), Mr. A. H. Boerma, proposed a new system
of internationally co-ordinated national food reserve policies. Under
the FAO plan all nations - both exporters and importers - would hold
agreed minimum levels of food stocks. Governments would consult regularly to review the food situation, evaluate the adequacy of existing
stocks and recommend necessary actions. The FAO plan received preliminary international approval at the FAO conference in Rome in November
1973. 1/ If it is to be implemented effectively, the nations of the
world must provide strong political and economic support in the coming
year.

74. In the past, the United States has provided the world with safe
reserve levels largely as a side benefit of its domestic farm income
programme. In the seller's market for food-stuffs which emerged in
1973, these reserves - both large grain stocks and idle cropland - were
reduced substantially. Under such conditions, it would be highly un-
realistic to expect the United States to bear the considerable expense
of building grain reserves large enough to ensure world security. The
FAO plan has the positive impact of spreading responsibility for reserve
maintenance among both the exporting and importing nations of the world.

75. Under the FAO or any other world food reserve plan, special measures
will be necessary to assist less affluent nations in establishing storage facilities and building up needed reserves. A new source of con-
cessional assistance, perhaps in the form of an earmarked expansion of
the World Bank's soft loan programme, or a special fund within the FAO,
will be necessary.

76. Prudence suggests that every effort be made to keep total world
grain reserves of, at a minimum, 15 per cent of annual consumption.
Historically, strong upward price pressures have developed when reserves
have fallen below that level. At the present time, this would imply a
need for about 180 million metric tons of grain held in reserves.

1/ Report of the Conference of the Food and Agricultural Organization
of the United Nations, Seventeenth Session, paras. 116-132.

X. MODIFYING DIETS AMONG THE AFFLUENT

77.   A variety of economic and moral forces may compel those in countries
like the United States to reduce the demands they place on world food
resources.   This can most readily be accomplished through the substitution of vegetable-based protein for animal protein.   Such a shift has
already occurred in the substitution of vegetable oils for animal fats;
in 1940 the average American was consuming 17 pounds of butter and two
pounds of margarine, but by 1971 consumption averaged 11 pounds of
margarine and five pounds of butter.   Lard has almost been pushed off
supermarket shelves by vegetable shortenings and a dominant share of
whipped toppings and coffee whiteners marketing in the United States are
now of non-dairy origin.

78.   Technology for the substitution of vegetable for animal proteins
has made considerable progress, mainly in the area of soya-based meat
substitutes.   Food technologists can now compress soya fibres into meat
form and, with appropriate flavouring and colouring, come up with nut-
ritious substitutes for beef, pork and poultry.   Soya protein "extenders",
augmenting meat proteins in ground meats, are already in wide institutional use in the United States, and began appearing in supermarkets for
general use in 1973.   There are now good economic, ecological and nutritional reasons for reducing the average consumption of animal products
in the United States.   This fact should be reflected in governmental
research budgets and in nutritional education programmes.

XI. THE AGRONOMIC POTENTIAL OF THE LESS AFFLUENT COUNTRIES

79.   One of the most immediate means of expanding the food supply is to
return the idle cropland in the United States to production, a process
already in motion.   Over the longer run, however, the greatest opportunities lie in the developing countries, where the world's greatest
reservoir of unexploited food potential is located.

80.   In those countries having the appropriate economic incentives,
fertilizer water and other required agricultural inputs and supporting
institutions, the introduction of new wheat and rice varieties has increased production substantially.   However, the recent jump in per acre
yields in many developing countries appears dramatic largely because
their yields traditionally have been so low relative to the potential.
Today rice yields per acre in India and Nigeria still average only one
third those of Japan; corn yields in Brazil and Thailand are less than
one third those of the United States.   Large increased in food supply
are possible in these countries at far less cost than in agriculturally
advanced nations if farmers are given the necessary economic incentives
and have access to the requisite inputs.

81.   When global food scarcity exists and the capacity of the international community to respond to food emergencies has diminished, a more
convincing case than ever exists for strengthened international support
of agricultural development in such populous food-short countries as
Bangladesh, India, Indonesia, and Nigeria.   An almost equally convincing
case can be made that in doing so, particular attention should be placed
on effectively involving small farmers in the production effort.   These
is evidence that small farmers, when they have effective access to

agricultural inputs as well as health and education services, engage in labour-intensive agriculture and generally average considerably higher yields per acre than do large farmers.

82. Concentrating efforts on expanding food production in the less affluent countries could reduce upward pressure on world food prices, create additional employment in countries where continuously rising unemployment poses a serious threat to political stability, raise income, improve nutrition for the poorest portion of humanity and, by improving social conditions, help create a climate in which birth rates will fall more rapidly.

READING 28

Many economically advanced countries now experience declining fertility
levels, and zero population growth has been achieved in West Germany,
East Germany, and Luxembourg. Another group of countries including the
United Kingdom and the United States could achieve equilibrium between
birth and death rates within decades if fertility levels keep falling.

A lively debate is developing about the effects of a nongrowing population. The following paper, written by the well known economist J.J.
Spengler (born 1903), is one of the first attempts to explore the implications for mature economies where population has ceased to expand.
Spengler gives an account of some of the benefits of a stationary population as dictated by economic, ecological, and social considerations.
He also discusses a number of disadvantages and suggests some measures
to help minimize them.[28]

Professor Joseph J. Spengler was for many years professor of economics
at Duke University and is now associated with the Carolina Population
Center. One of his earliest works, entitled France Faces Depopulation,
appeared in 1938. His most productive period in the field of population
economics, however, began after 1945. Many of his articules, papers,
and books are first-rate sources of information for the population
economist. The following paper was presented at the annual meeting of
the Population Association of America in April 1971.

---

[28]Source: J.J. Spengler, "Economic Growth in a Stationary Population"
(unpublished paper presented at the Annual Meeting of the Population
Association of America, April 23, 1971) pp. 1-17.

ECONOMIC GROWTH IN A STATIONARY POPULATION
Joseph J. Spengler

I can best deal with my assigned topic by approaching it from three
points of view, the impact of a declining rate of population growth
upon the growth of aggregate and average output, economic advantages
associated with a zero rate of population growth, and economically
oriented domestic and international problems accentuated by the absence
of population growth.

I. IMPACT OF A DECLINING RATE OF POPULATION GROWTH

Let us define $\underline{Y}'$, the rate of Growth of Net National Product, or National
Income, $\underline{Y}$, roughly as follows:
$$\underline{Y}' = \underline{P}' + \underline{a}'$$
where $\underline{P}'$ denotes the rate of growth of population $\underline{P}$, a fixed fraction
$\underline{f}$ of which is in the labor force $\underline{L}$, and $\underline{a}'$, the rate of growth of output per capita $\underline{a}$ (= $\underline{f}$ times the rate of growth of output per member of
the labor force). Then abstracting from increasing returns, the pro-
bability of which is zero or close to zero in the United States (particularly if one allows for all costs of population growth), $\underline{Y}'$ will approximate $\underline{a}'$ if $\underline{P}'$ descends to zero. The decline of $\underline{P}'$ to zero may,
however, given ceteris paribus, together with slow change in age compo-
sition, increase $\underline{a}'$.

Whether this will happen depends upon the degree to which shrinkage of
widening investment is replaced by deepening investment. Suppose $\underline{P}'$
declines from one per cent to zero per cent. Then the aggregate of
inputs $\underline{C}$ invested in this one-per-cent-per-year rate of population growth
becomes available for investment in "capital" per head (i.e., $\underline{C}/\underline{P}$) at the
current rate of return $\underline{r}$ on new investment. Should all of $\underline{C}$ be so invested, $\underline{a}$ will be increased by $(\underline{r}\underline{C})/\underline{P}$. Thus, if, under the condition
given, $\underline{C}$ approximates $.05\underline{Y}$, and $\underline{r}$ approximates 0.1, $\underline{Y}$ increased by
$.005\underline{Y}$, and $\underline{a}$ by 0.5 percentage point above its initial level $\underline{1}$ (say 2
per cent per year), that is, from $\underline{1}$ to $\underline{1} + [(\underline{r}\underline{C})/\underline{P}] = 2.5$ per cent. Of
course, should a portion of the released inputs $\underline{C}$ be devoted to leisure
instead of to production, $\underline{a}'$ will increase by less than one-half a percentage point. We may say in general that in an advanced economy, a
decline of one percentage point in the rate of population growth will
result in a decline of something like 3/4 to 1/2 percentage point in the
rate of growth of aggregate income or output. In an underdeveloped
economy, however, as Coale and Hoover showed, a decline in the rate of
population growth may tend to increase the rate of growth of aggregate
output.

Should we include non-physical investment in $\underline{C}$, it may approximate $0.1\underline{Y}$,
with the result that $\underline{r}\,\underline{C}/\underline{P} = 0.01$, and $\underline{1}+1 = 3.0$ per cent; then the one
percentage point decline in $\underline{P}$ does not lead to a decline in $\underline{Y}'$.

While the advent of a stationary population does not end aggregate economic growth, it makes the ending of aggregate economic growth somewhat easier. Growth ends either because the rate of growth $\underline{S}'$ of Aggregate Supply $\underline{S}$ declines to zero, or because the rate of increase $\underline{D}'$ in Aggregate Demand $\underline{D}$ descends to zero. We shall assume that $\underline{S}'$ remains positive, though it could in the end descend to zero given inability on the part of man and his societal apparatus to overcome the finiteness of the physical environment upon which he is dependent, either in the world as a whole or in a more or less isolated part of the world.

Turning now to the behavior of $\underline{D}$ let us write

$$\underline{D}' = \underline{P}' + \underline{e}\ \underline{y}'$$

where $\underline{D}'$, $\underline{P}'$ and $\underline{y}'$ denote, respectively, the rates of growth of Aggregate Demand, Population $\underline{P}$ and average income $\underline{y}$. (Here $\underline{y}'$ corresponds to $\underline{a}'$ in the second paragraph preceding.) With $\underline{P}'$ reduced to zero, $\underline{D}'$ depends upon $\underline{y}'$ and $\underline{e}$ which denotes income elasticity of demand. Given that $\underline{y}'$ corresponds to $\underline{a}'$ which, by supposition, remains positive, $\underline{e}$ becomes the strategic variable. While the value of $\underline{e}$ for categories of commodities or services may exceed 1.0, it cannot exceed 1.0 when $\underline{D}'$ denotes the rate of growth of Aggregate Demand inclusive of all goods and services. Because leisure is a positive good and consumption imposes costs in terms both of time and of physiological burden, $\underline{e}$ tends to decline as $\underline{y}$ increases, though not so rapidly, as a rule.

Eventually, however, even in a non-sybaritic society, $\underline{e}$ can descend to zero. This outcome is conditioned mainly ceteris paribus by the rate of increase in variety of products, the depression of time and physiological costs of consumption, and the level and rate of increase of $\underline{y}$ (which corresponds to average output $\underline{a}$). The decline in the value of $\underline{e}$ is conditioned also by what happens to man's tastes or preferences and by the extent to which he resists the efforts of producers to generate purposeful obsolescence of the goods and services men purchase. It is conditioned finally by the degree to which men develop a taste for collective goods, public and otherwise, and a capacity to supply them.

II. ADVANTAGES

We may list the economic advantages of a zero rate of population growth under six heads.

(1) Potential output per head will be higher in a stationary than in a growing population. I have already indicated one source, namely, greater investment per capita. To this source two others must be added: the fraction of the population of working age will be higher, and there will be less capital required to countervail the pressure of population upon components of man's natural environment which are depletable or non-augmentable.

(2) Trade-cycle tendencies will be reduced insofar as these are associated with irregularities in private and public expenditures upon durable wealth or capital. For the relative importance of expenditure upon all forms of physical capital will decline, since less demand will be generated for structures and equipment of the sort highly correlated with growth of population and with internal migration consequent upon this

growth.

(3) The family milieu, so important (as James Coleman has shown) for the development of the potential of children and hence of their future productive capacity, should improve. For the advent of a zero rate of population growth should be accompanied by a decrease in the fraction of all births that are unwanted -- probably somewhere between 13 and 18 per cent. As a result fewer births should take place under circumstances denying the child affection and care as well as freedom from poverty, the risk of which increases with the number of dependents under 18 per family.

(4) Given a stationary population and elimination of the need to counterbalance population growth, the multiplication of pollution and environmental degradation by population growth and concentration (as distinguished from the parallel effects of increase in average consumption) is at an end. This outcome is important because measures and devices designed to reduce the impact of pollution and environmental degradation are costly. In general, growth of population usually worsens the trade-off between pollution and environmental degradation, on the one hand, and countervaillants on the other. Illustrative are the pollution and other costs associated with increasing the flow of energy, currently viewed as the open sesame to Lucullan abundance.

(5) It is possible that the advent of a stationary population will make man more sensible of that part of welfare which is not nicely measurable in terms of money as well as of the costs and negative externalities associated with the growth and maldistribution of population. Men would become less disposed to listen to the siren call of Madison Avenue Lorelei enticing them to sacrifice time, health, and money for transitory luxury.

(6) Since population concentration, often accompanies by maldistribution in space, is a concomitant of population growth, the slowing down of this growth will make possible improvement in the spatial distribution of the population. Interstate differences in population density, when corrected for differences in resource structure (e.g., water supply), indicate our population to be quite maldistributed and destined to become more so should the anticipated increment -- 75-100 million inhabitants and 30-40 million jobs -- be distributed at all like our present 208 million.

While this increment will settle in cities and nearby rural areas, the location of these cities need not be dominated by stochastic processes and continuation of our anarchic system of national transportation. Man no longer is bound to the soil and mineral deposits. Moreover, while he is not free to locate at will, the locational options available to him can be increased by miniaturizing plants of optimum size. Most men, being Job Takers, must, however, settle where Job Makers provide employment.

Since about one job in four is provided by 750-850 business firms managed by perhaps 10,000 Strategic Decision Makers, locational freedom is very great, particularly given supplementary assistance at the hands of the state and private undertakers and in the form of infra-structure and residential facilities. These Strategic Decision Makers should be

able, over the next 50 or more years, to establish self-sustaining bases
for 400-500 or more new cities. The new cities could accomodate both the
prospective increase in the nation's urban population and the increasing
number who are fleeing the disadvantages, including high vulnerability
to thermonuclear extinction, associated with a number of today's metro-
politan and megalopolitan concentrations.

III. PROBLEMS

A variety of problems will emerge with, or be intensified by, the advent
of a stationary population. Let me dismiss as unimportant a concern of
the 1930's, namely, that ex ante savings, given full employment, would
exceed ex ante offsets to savings, with the result that underemployment
would persist. This inference rested on the assumption that substitute
investment outlets would not be found for those eliminated by decline
in the rate of population growth. Demand for investment may long exceed
its supply and, should it fail to do so, a variety of offsets in the
form of collective goods, public and otherwise, can be provided by the
state.

Even should the optimistic assessment prove realistic, other problems
will have to be faced. How serious they prove will turn, even as does
balance between savings and investment, on how flexible the American
economy remains, on how free it is kept of dominance, as today, by
oligopolists and trade-union czars, and on the degree to which the
apparatus of state is devoted to the maintenance of economic stability
rather than to the fomenting of inflation and economic instability as
in the past 25 years.

(1) The relative number of older persons will increase. For example,
in a male stationary population, with a life expectancy of around 74
years, about 16 per cent of the population would be 65 or more years
old. As a result three types of corrective action may prove necessary.
(a) Steps to prevent the concentration of too much power of decision in
the hands of those 65 and over may be required, steps already taken in
France. At issue here is not so much the correlation, if such there be,
of efficiency and creativeness with being under 50 or 60, as the fact
that man's planning time-horizon tends to shrink as he ages. (b) With
so large a fraction of the population pensioners -- about 11 per cent of
the males if most retired at 70, and over 17 per cent of the females --
steps will have to be taken to prevent their being defrauded by a fin-
ancially irresponsible federal government which has eroded over 27 per
cent of the purchasing power of the dollar since the arrival in Washington in 1960 of the New Frontiersmen, armed with New Economics and
Old Politics. Pensioners are entitled, in addition, to security against
inflation, to something like a one-per-cent-per-year increase in their
pensions, if they are to share in income growth attributable to public
investment in education, science, and their application. (c) The right
of older persons to employment, now often denied them by trade-union,
corporation, and governmental bureaucrats, needs to be guaranteed, both
to help them cope with inflation and to guard the health of older persons insofar as it is dependent upon being employed.

(2) A second problem is associated with promotion in terms of advance
in income and occupational status. Given a life expectancy of about
42.5 years at age 20, by age 50 only about 77 of each 100 persons aged

20 would still remain alive, and some of these would have withdrawn
from the labor force. Death and morbidity would thus have created
openings for ambitious youngsters, much as wars and sickly seasons do
for a military establishment. However, given a life expectancy of 55
or better at age 20, then at age 50, of each 100 who had reached aged
20, about 96 would still be alive; and opportunities for advancement
would thus remain relatively closed. It will become necessary, therefore, to reduce the current degree of correlation between remuneration
and age, a correlation not borne out by the relation between age and
productivity.

(3) Slowing down of the rate of population growth may intensify the
task of maintaining inter-industrial, inter-occupational, inter-regional
balance, particularly in a world in which control of access to employment is too dominated by trade-union czars, heads of license-issuing
professional associations, and their bureaucratic and legislative fellow-
travelers. When a population is growing, a portion of the annual increment to the labor force tends to flow into relatively expanding
activities. But when a population is stationary, preservation of balance
depends upon movement by those who are migration-prone, and by those who,
being in relatively unattractive or declining occupations, stand to
benefit from occupational change. Information is sufficient or may be
made sufficient to make easy the maintenance of something like optimum
occupational balance even with a labor force that changes little or not
at all in size. Such interoccupational mobility is not adequately
realizable, however, when output is subject to control by monopolies
and oligopolies, or when access to employment is controlled by national
trade-unions and professional organizations, usually with the aid of
our "modern" bureaucratic state. Under the best of circumstances,
having to attract already employed workers instead of workers newly
entering the labor force will exercise upward pressure against the wage
level.

(4) The problem just described will be intensified by increase in the
relative amount of discretionary time and income at the disposal of individuals as average income rises and the work-week or work-year is
shortened. It may also be intensified by increase in the share of our
Leviathan state in the nation's annual expenditure, since a state's
pattern of expenditure, subject as it is to political whim, can vary
significantly and thus function anticybernetically. For the reasons
described, volatility may characterize demands for particular categories
of goods. The economy can be kept adjusted to shifts in demand resulting from this volatility, only insofar as it is flexible, inputs are
mobile, and current governmental, trade-union, and other practices
subversive of flexibility and mobility are eliminated. For no longer
will new increments to the labor force facilitate the shifts indicated.
Of the impact of this volatility we currently have evidence in the
distortions produced in our industrial structure by inflation, about
three-fifths war-connected, and by the inflexible aerospace industry,
beneficiary of potlatch and war, and now apparently in search of what
amounts to W.P.A. status.

(5) The advent of a zero rate of population growth will accentuate the
tendency to inflation and financial instability in an economy whose
population is concentrated in space and disposed to spend an increasing
fraction of its national income upon services. In such an economy the

seemingly normal tendency of populations to increase the relative magnitude of their expenditure upon services is accentuated both by the more rapid rise of average income y and by the tendency (noted by Baumol) of the costs of congestion, pollution, and so on to rise "roughly as the square of the number of inhabitants." For not only does the income elasticity of demand for services exceed unity but also services are likely to constitute an important component of countervaillants to the tendency of congestion, pollution, and other negative externalities to rise with population concentration. At the same time the production of services amounts to an activity susceptible to only "sporadic increases in productivity" and its suppliers tend to experience increases in remuneration greatly in excess of increases in their productivity. For, as W.J. Baumol points out (<u>American Economic Review</u>, June, 1967, pp. 415ff.): "If productivity per man hour rises cumulatively in one sector relative to its rate of growth elsewhere in the economy, while wages rise commensurately in all areas, then relative costs in the nonprogressive sectors must inevitably <u>rise, and these costs will rise cumulatively and without limit</u>." The resulting inflation will fall most heavily upon older and retired persons, since relatively large fractions of their expenditures are upon services.

To the problems associated with these tendencies there is no easy solution. The collective burden resulting will be less heavy, however, if the nation's population is dispersed among a large number of cities as suggested earlier, with a resulting reduction in the tendency of federal aid to cities to perpetuate urban waste and inefficiency. Of course, only a change in monetary policy can reduce the increasing pressure to inflate costs and intensify inequity in distribution. Should the stock of money increase little more rapidly than the population, however, relative prices would fall commensurately with decreases in real unit costs and real incomes would rise mainly as a result of a corresponding increase in the purchasing power of the dollar. After all, workers in technologically progressive industries are themselves responsible in very small measure for increase in the productivity experienced in these industries. Yet, under the leadership of their greedy czars they attempt, usually without long-run success, to appropriate what others (scientists, technologists, etc.) have produced, largely with the aid both of public and private investment of all types of capital. Of course, were our economy fully competitive, neither labor nor its employers could long appropriate such surpluses as emerge with invention and innovation or with favorable conjunctures in the market. (6) One should include in a list of problems one which, in my opinion is merely a pseudo-problem, namely, that when a population is stationary, overestimations of future demand will no longer be corrected by population growth. This allegation overlooks the fact that demographic components of demand are highly predictable and that man's disposition to take risks is a linear function of his security against risk and uncertainty. The tendency to windfall profits or corresponding losses should not be significantly modified.

(7) I turn now to two more general types of adjustment which men will have to make in their ways of planning, in their expectations, and so on. The first is essentially objective in character. For nearly two centuries, even as Benjamin Franklin, Thomas Jefferson, and Abraham Lincoln foresaw, American businessmen have looked to growth of population even more than to growth of average income to expand markets for

their products, usually oblivious to the fact that the Stork who brings
customers also brings the hands and brain-power needed to meet the demands of these customers. American businessmen will therefore have to
adjust their views of the determinants of market expansion to new demographic conditions, an adjustment not difficult given the fact that the
rate of population growth will decline gradually, and the additional
fact that in some states (e.g., Florida, Colorado) these is growing
recognition of disadvantages associated with continuing population growth.

The second type of adjustment is essentially subjective in character.
A nation must accomodate its overall set of expectations to its rate of
population growth. In the present instance it must replace anticipation
of continuing population growth by acceptance of a zero rate of population growth. Such accomodation would not have been difficult in most
of the world before the eighteenth century, or even before the nineteenth
century; for then numbers were growing very slowly as was average income. In the United States, however, the annual rate of population
growth has always been relatively high, 2-3 per cent in the nineteenth
century and below one per cent in only one decade in the present century,
namely, in the 1930's, the Decade of the Great Depression, recovery
from which was facilitated by the coming of the second modern Peloponnesian War and completion of the dissipation of European hegemony and
the world political order which it had assured. Moreover, with the
exception of the 1930's, average income and output rose notably.

The emergence of a set of expectations resting upon continuous and accelerating growth is reflected in the life of Henry Adams. Writing in 1904
he observed that "fifty years ago, science took for granted that the
rate of acceleration could not last" and many assumed that J. S. Mill's
stationary state was at hand and would persist. But energy of all
sorts had been made subservient to man, setting in motion a rate of
progress that would enable every American who lived into the year 2000
"to control unlimited power." A "law of acceleration" was at work. A
new "social mind" was required. Perhaps by 1938 "for the first time
since man began his education among the carnivores, they would find a
world that sensitive and timid natures could regard without a shudder."
Adams could no more conceive of a possible return of the tempo of change
to its state a century earlier than he could anticipate 1939 and the
subsequent advent of a nuclear and thermonuclear age. With the slowing
down of population growth it will become necessary for men to conceive,
not of that of which Adams could not conceive, but of life in a world in
which the forces of change other than migration and adverse selection
are non-demographic in character.

Adjustment may prove easier, however, than I have suggested, given
multiplication of spokesmen for an increasingly popular "fin de siecle"
mood -- one that runs counter to the vision of endless horizons entertained by futurologists armed with little more than adeptness at applying
exponential curves. Thus Seidenberg anticipates posthistoric man living
in a changeless posthistoric society, and Stent foresees, somewhat in
the tradition of Aldous Huxley, a stasis-rudden society from which
Faustian Man has been largely displaced by beatniks and hippies deriving
support from a small number of technologists. Even Bentley Glass finds
"endless horizons no longer exist." Men are becoming increasingly aware
of the variety of limitational factors which constrain the growth as
well as the application of science, though perhaps not of the possibility

of selectively reducing man's size and increasing his capacity for idleness or boredom. It is up to the sociologists and social psychologists
to anticipate the alternative adjustment paths.

IV. STATIONARY IN A GROWING WORLD

Turning from the internal to the external impact of the advent of a
stationary population, two aspects may be noted. First, though the
rate of increase of the use of raw materials in the United States may
decline somewhat, the relief that might otherwise be had will be denied
by the growth of world consumption which may treble within the next
three decades and, by the year 2100 be 36-57 times what it is currently.
Indeed, given such increase, the economic security of the United States
as of Japan, both of which are highly dependent on foreign sources, may
be less than at present.

Second, the international political position of the United States may
be weakened, should its share of the world's population, about 6 per
cent in 1960, decline to 3-4 per cent by 2100. The probability of such
outcome is low, however, even given the smallness of the probability
that many underdeveloped countries will greatly abridge the economic
distance separating them from advanced countries. The military power
of each of the six largest underdeveloped countries, wherein live somewhat over half the world's population, is negligible or merely defensive
in character, in part because average income is so low. The security
of the developed countries, even should their populations become stationary, need not be endangered, therefore, unless (as in 1914 and 1939)
they should engage in what would amount to a modern Peloponnesian War
with one another, and in particular should the United States and the
Soviet Union prove so short-sighted. It is overwhelmingly to the advantage of all the advanced countries, and especially of the Soviet
Union and the United States, to remain at peace; the probable alternative would be their destruction and their investment by people of the
underdeveloped world that developed countries remain at peace and greatly
reduce mutually their excessive and wasteful military expenditures. For
the underdeveloped world is dependent, if it would progress, upon aid
from, as well as trade with, the developed world. Indeed, were the
developed countries to provide as aid one per cent of their GNP, it
would amount to about 5 per cent of the GNP of the underdeveloped world.

V. CONCLUSION

Since each dimension of the multidimensional population problem is
functionally related to one or more socio-economic variables, population
policy as well as analysis cannot be developed apart from the societal
structure within which the population under analysis nests. Turning to
policy as such, major emphasis needs to be placed upon peace in the
international sphere and flexibility in the domestic sphere. These is
need to deinstitutionalize inflexibilities in the economy and undergird
flexibility, factor mobility, effective and cost-minimizing competition,
and stability of the standard monetary unit. There is need also to guard
against the accumulation of unfavorable genes in the human gene pool,
"the primary resource of mankind today and tomorrow," since this pool
now is increasingly fed by those whose survival into reproductive age has
been made possible for the first time by modern medicine. For, in the
absence of further development in the field of genetic application, and

in light of the possibility of less rigorous selection in a stationary society, dysgenic selection could increase societal burdens. In sum, solution of the population problem is contingent largely upon solution of the multiplicity of problems that plague our malfunctioning and essentially Hobbesian economy.

INDEX

About the Editor

Johannes Overbeek is a specialist in the economics of population change and population policy. He has taught at the University of British Columbia, the University of Hawaii, and the University of Guelph. He is currently teaching and doing research in Iran at Pahlavi University. His articles have been published in such journals as *Economic Development and Cultural Change,* and his previous works include *History of Population Theories* and *The Population Challenge,* published by Greenwood Press in 1976.